A COMPLETE GUIDE TO BASIC
WOODWORKING

Skills and Projects Every Woodworker Needs

Creative Publishing
international

CHANHASSEN, MINNESOTA
www.creativepub.com

CREDITS

Creative Publishing international

© Copyright 2005
Creative Publishing international, Inc.
18705 Lake Drive East
Chanhassen, Minnesota 55317
1-800-328-3895
www.creativepub.com

Printed in China
10 9 8 7 6 5 4 3 2 1

President/CEO: Ken Fund
Vice President/Publisher: Linda Ball
Vice President/Retail Sales & Marketing: Kevin Haas

Executive Editor: Bryan Trandem
Creative Director: Tim Himsel
Managing Editor: Michelle Skudlarek
Editorial Director: Jerri Farris

Authors: Chris Marshall and Philip Schmidt
Project Designer: John Drigot
Editors: Andrew Karre, Karen Ruth
Copy Editor: Linnéa Christensen
Art Director: Jon Simpson
Technical Photo Editor: Randy Austin
Illustrators: David Schelitzche,
   Jon Simpson, Earl Slack
Photo Researcher: Julie Caruso
Photographer: Tate Carlson
Scene Shop Carpenter: Randy Austin
Production Manager: Helga Thielen

A COMPLETE GUIDE TO BASIC WOODWORKING

Library of Congress
Cataloging-in-Publication Data
A complete guide to basic woodworking : skills & projects
every woodworker needs / [editors, Chris Marshall,
Phil Schmidt].
     p. cm. -- (Weekend woodworker)
   Includes bibliographical references and index.
   ISBN 1-58923-179-1 (pbk. : alk. paper)
1. Woodwork--Amateurs' manuals. I. Marshall, Chris,
1967- II. Schmidt, Philip. III. Creative Publishing
international. IV. Series.
   TT185.C66 2005
   684'.08--dc22

                                   2004027147

CONTENTS

INTRODUCTION

Convenience is a welcome friend these days, whether it's in the form of an all-in-one shopping mall, an online bank, or a handsfree cell phone. The less time we spend searching for what we need or standing in lines, the more time we "buy back" for the really important things—family, friends, and leisure activity. Having what we need in one place just seems to make sense.

Any woodworker knows that shop time is cherished time. Woodworking is a way to get away from the hustle and bustle for a while and make time slow down. Even a few hours here and there spent turning boards into projects is a great way to reduce stress and explore your creative side. Life seems a little simpler when you're clamping up a drawer or brushing varnish on a new table. And few things are more satisfying than giving projects to those you love.

Our goal in creating *A Complete Guide to Basic Woodworking* was to compile a wealth of woodworking information in one source to save you time and effort. Think of it as your all-in-one guide to learning the craft. Whether you need a refresher course on making box joints, a few tips on which drill to buy, or a fresh design for a table project, you'll find answers here. We've packed these 300 pages with virtually everything you'll need to get a shop set up, make wise tool choices, and use them efficiently and safely. You'll learn how to buy lumber, design new projects, assemble them in sensible ways, and finish them, too. We've even included 15 great projects with step-by-step directions and a full set of measured drawings, just to cover all the bases.

No matter what your shop needs may be, keep this convenient reference book right where you can thumb through it. Whatever your skill level, we hope this book will take the hassle out of finding the woodworking knowledge you want so you can spend even more time actually woodworking.

Chapter 1
SETTING UP SHOP

Whether you're planning to just tinker on an occasional project or to pursue your craft more ambitiously, woodworking is one of those hobbies that demands space. You're going to need a certain amount of room to store tools, lumber, and projects at various stages of completion. It's also a messy and often noisy pastime. Sawing, sanding, planing, and drilling create plenty of debris and airborne dust, and adhesives and finishes can be smelly—not to mention toxic. A workshop provides a place with some degree of isolation from the rest of the household. The less invasive your hobby is to the rest of the household, the more others will enjoy living with a woodworker.

This chapter will help you identify the likely spaces in your home that could become workshops. We'll review what your needs for lighting, electricity, climate, and dust control will be, then suggest a plan for arranging your machines and supplies so you can work safely and efficiently.

Choosing a shop space

Whether you rent or own your home, and regardless of the region in which you live, there's bound to be space for a workshop—if you think creatively. Even a small area can become an effective shop if you plan the space carefully and stay organized. The usual shop locations include basements and garage stalls, so we'll focus on these options here.

Basement shops. If you live in a northern region with cold winters, a basement shop offers the luxury of climate control. Nothing will chill you to the bone as quickly as handling metal tools in the dead of January in an unheated workshop. Your furnace will keep workshop conditions pleasant all winter, and a below-grade basement shop will stay comfortably cool during summer's worst heat. If your home was built within the past 30 to 40 years, it probably has a ceiling that's high enough to keep you from bumping your head on suspended ductwork or plumbing. Ceilings should be at least 7 feet high in a shop, and the higher the better for maneuvering long boards or sheets of plywood.

With ample overhead lighting and sufficiently high ceilings, basements can offer pleasant spaces for woodworking.

A garage can easily be converted to a workshop. The garage doors provide instant ventilation, and they allow machinery, lumber, and finished projects to be moved in and out of the shop conveniently.

Despite the pleasant climate and convenient location, basement shops can have drawbacks. If your basement stairwell is narrow or steep, it can be difficult and even dangerous to carry heavy building materials and large tools up and down the stairs. Finding enough room to cut long lumber or wide sheet materials can also be challenging.

If the laundry room is in the basement, you probably won't want sawdust mixing with freshly laundered clothes. Fine dust and fumes from wood finishes shouldn't mingle with the pilot lights on furnaces, water heaters, and gas clothes dryers, either. In high concentrations, dust or fumes can combust. Some adhesives and finishes produce fumes that are heavier than air, so they'll be trapped in a basement shop unless you have fans and windows to circulate the air.

There are plenty of ways to help minimize these sorts of problems. Install a few windows with screens in your workspace to improve fresh air exchange. Attach a dust collector to larger machines and hook up a shop vac to smaller power tools to trap dust and debris close to the source. Use an ambient air cleaner with replaceable filters to capture finer dust particles. You might even consider separating your shop from the rest of the basement with a wall and door, which will help control both dust and noise.

Dampness is another relatively common basement problem. High humidity leads to corrosion on metal tools, and lumber can mold or warp if it gets wet. Keep work areas dry by running a dehumidifier during humid months.

Garage shops. In more temperate climates, garages often make better shops than basements. Living spaces stay cleaner when a woodshop is in the garage rather than the basement. Ventilating the shop is as easy as opening the garage door or rolling machinery outside for doing dusty work. Garages usually have high finished ceilings or open trusses, so you can maneuver larger building materials and make taller projects without overhead restrictions. Having a shop on ground level also saves your back from potential straining when you need to move machinery, supplies, and projects in and out of the workshop.

If you'd rather not dedicate your entire garage to a workshop, you can still keep one or more stalls available for parking a car, bicycles, or lawn tractor by simply mounting your tools and workbench on wheels. Wheels make it possible for one person to easily move even the largest machinery.

One problem with most garages is they don't have enough electrical outlets. Those that are present are often fed with an inadequate electrical supply. Many garages, even on new homes, are wired with a single circuit. Some garages on older homes have no electricity at all, especially if they are detached from the house. When a garage only serves as parking and storage space, a single electric circuit is sufficient for servicing a garage door opener, an overhead light, and maybe a few light-duty outlets. But once your garage becomes a workshop, you're going to need more electricity to power tools with larger motors, such as table saws and planers (see page 10).

With ample cross-ventilation, a garage shop is pleasant to work in during spring and fall months, especially if you work in the cool of the day. Winters and summers are a different story, depending on where you live. Garage walls typically aren't insulated, so your workshop can become nearly intolerable to work in on bitterly cold days or during hot, humid summers. Uninsulated spaces will be difficult to heat or cool efficiently. Wood glues and finishes won't cure properly below 55°, so you'll have to move gluing and finishing tasks indoors or save them until spring.

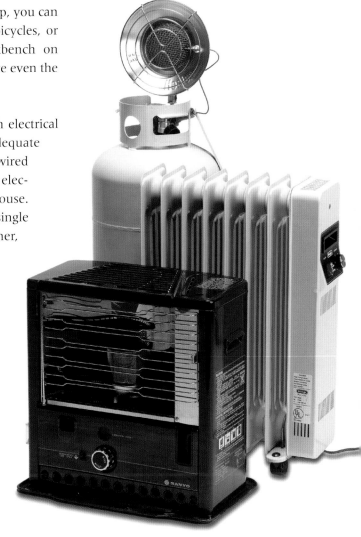

A couple of heating options can make winter woodworking more tolerable and even pleasant. Electric heaters designed for heating a room simply won't generate enough heat to warm an entire garage. Kerosene or propane-fueled heaters, especially those with built-in blowers, will do the job more efficiently. Either choice is safe to use in a garage, provided you open a window or door or raise your garage door a few inches to exhaust carbon monoxide. You'll also need to turn off the heater when routing or sawing for long periods of time so the heater flame doesn't ignite the dust.

Don't let winter leave your unheated shop in the cold. Propane, kerosene, or electric heaters all are options for making workspaces more tolerable.

Cooling a garage shop during the summer can be equally challenging. Cross-ventilation will help draw breezes through the shop, especially if you use a fan to help move the air.

Unfinished garage walls make it easy to store supplies, lumber, and tools. Mount shelving, workbenches, lumber racks, and pegboard directly to the wall studs. You can even store lumber and other odds and ends overhead if the roof trusses are accessible.

Preparing the workspace

Getting your shop up and running is one thing, but refining it to suit your specific working style will take years. Most woodworkers enjoy the process of creating and re-creating a workshop as their tool collections and skills grow. For our purposes, we'll discuss the basics of turning a space into a workshop. Of course you'll need to adapt this general advice to fit your context, budget, and personal preferences. Depending on your space limitations and expectations, the job may be as easy as clearing out some clutter and putting up a workbench.

Lighting & electrical requirements. It's probably impossible to have too much light in a workshop. Try to have enough light so you won't be forced to work in the shadows. Ideally, workshops should be lit with a combination of overhead and task lighting. Overhead lights illuminate the general workspace, while task lighting directs focused light on the workbench and other machines where you need it most.

Ordinary ceiling-mounted incandescent lightbulbs provide reasonable amounts of light in the immediate area under the fixture, but the light drops off quickly as you move away, creating shadows. If you prefer the "warm" light produced by lightbulbs, or if your workspace is already outfitted with bulb fixtures, use the highest wattage bulbs they can handle. If you're adding new fixtures, plan for one fixture to illuminate about 16 square feet of floor space. Be sure to install fixtures with protective covers over the bulbs if the shop ceiling is low.

Fluorescent tubes provide more diffuse, even lighting than incandescent lightbulbs. The tubes operate on a fraction of the energy used by incandescent lightbulbs, yet they produce about five times as much light and last about ten times as long.

Fluorescent fixtures come in several sizes and qualities. On the low end, you can buy 4-foot "shop lights" for less than $10 each. However, these budget-priced fixtures have low-quality ballasts that often make an annoying buzzing sound when the lights are on. In colder temperatures, the ballasts warm up slowly and make the bulbs flicker or light dimly. For about two or three times the price of economy fixtures, you can buy better quality 4-foot lights with "industrial" ballasts that start quickly in cold weather. The ballasts operate quietly and outlive their cheaper cousins.

You can illuminate your shop with fluorescent or incandescent light, but the best solution is to use both. Supply general lighting with fluorescents and use incandescents for more direct task lighting where it's needed.

For larger workspaces, consider installing 8-foot fluorescent lighting. Each fixture will cost around $50, which is usually still more economical than buying two premium 4-foot lights. Long fluorescent fixtures are made for commercial applications, so you'll be assured of good-quality ballasts designed for cold-weather use. Long fixtures also make for easier installation. You'll only need to hang and wire half as many lights.

Make the most of natural light if your workspace has windows. Sunlight produces wonderful workshop lighting. A few windows, a skylight, or simply opening garage and service doors can largely replace artificial lighting during the daytime. Natural light makes even small shops more pleasant to work in while providing some radiant heat. Install skylights so they face north or east if you live in a hot climate. You'll get the benefit of indirect sunlight brightening your space without all the extra heat. For cooler climates, position skylights southward to capture more direct sunlight.

Along with ample lighting, you'll need sufficient electricity in your shop. At a minimum, workshops require two circuits. One 15-amp circuit should be dedicated to shop lighting. Otherwise, you could be left in the dark if you trip a circuit breaker while using a machine. The other circuit supplies power for electrical outlets. Read the labels on your tools to identify how many amps they draw at peak loads, then use a circuit rated 20 to 30 percent over this number. For smaller corded power tools, a 15-amp circuit is usually sufficient. Full-size table saws, planers, jointers, and dust collectors should draw power from a 20-amp circuit. Large tools that produce 2 hp or more are generally wired for 220-volt operation, which requires at least a 30-amp circuit.

If you're installing new shop light fixtures, fluorescent tube lights are the best value. Or replace incandescent bulbs with screw-in fluorescents if incandescent fixtures are already in place.

Check your home's main electric service panel to see how many circuit slots are still open. If you don't have room to add two or more new circuits for the shop, a licensed electrician can install a smaller panel of additional circuit breakers, called a subpanel. Subpanels are also useful when your shop is located in the garage far from the main service panel. Having a subpanel in the shop allows you to switch circuits on and off conveniently without having to walk all the way to the main panel.

CAUTION: Adding new circuits to the main service panel may exceed its amperage capacity, even if there are slots available for more circuits. An electrician can determine whether adding more circuits or a subpanel will be safe for your current main panel.

Another economical way to expand the number of outlets in your shop is to use power strips. Position your workbench close to an outlet and mount the power strip right on your bench. You'll be able to plug in a number of power tools or battery chargers at once, provided all these tools and devices aren't used simultaneously. Choose power strips with built-in overload protection for safety.

Use heavy-gauge extension cords in the shortest usable lengths to power your tools. This cord will be adequate for tools drawing 15 amps or less, provided it's not overly long.

You'll probably also have to use extension cords to deliver power where it's needed or move machines around the shop in order to plug them in. Extension

Tool motor labels will specify how much amperage the machines draw at maximum load. On the motor label here, the amperage draw is 16.4 amps when the motor is wired for 115-volt service. It draws 8.2 amps when wired for 230 volts. Be sure your shop circuits exceed this limit to keep them from tripping.

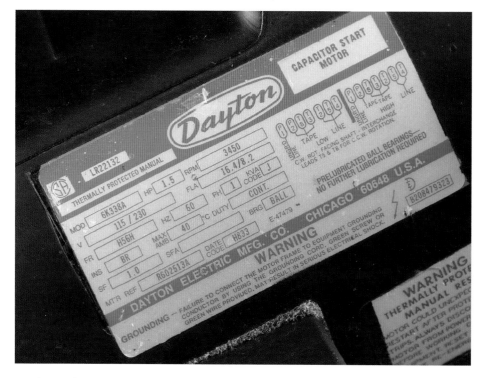

Clear the air and keep your shop cleaner with one or more dust-collection devices. Dedicated dust collectors, ambient air cleaners, and shop vacs are all options.

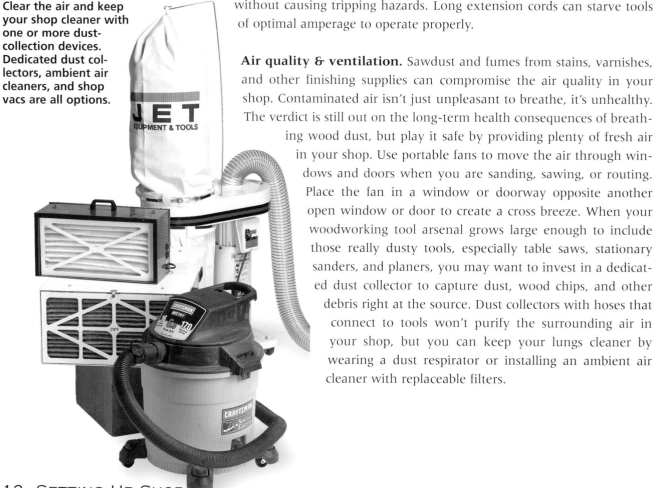

cords can be used safely to power most tools provided the cord's amperage rating is greater than the tool's peak amperage draw. In other words, if the tool draws 12 amps under maximum load, use an extension cord rated for 15 or more amps. Keep the length of the extension cords as short as possible without causing tripping hazards. Long extension cords can starve tools of optimal amperage to operate properly.

Air quality & ventilation. Sawdust and fumes from stains, varnishes, and other finishing supplies can compromise the air quality in your shop. Contaminated air isn't just unpleasant to breathe, it's unhealthy. The verdict is still out on the long-term health consequences of breathing wood dust, but play it safe by providing plenty of fresh air in your shop. Use portable fans to move the air through windows and doors when you are sanding, sawing, or routing. Place the fan in a window or doorway opposite another open window or door to create a cross breeze. When your woodworking tool arsenal grows large enough to include those really dusty tools, especially table saws, stationary sanders, and planers, you may want to invest in a dedicated dust collector to capture dust, wood chips, and other debris right at the source. Dust collectors with hoses that connect to tools won't purify the surrounding air in your shop, but you can keep your lungs cleaner by wearing a dust respirator or installing an ambient air cleaner with replaceable filters.

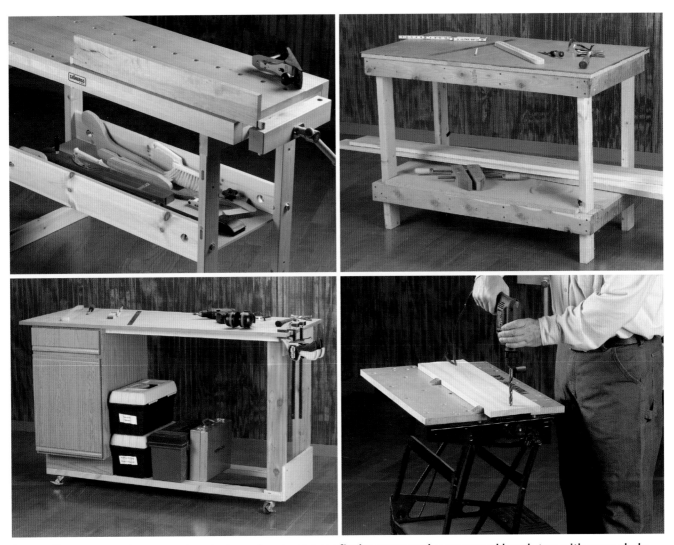

Depending on your storage and project needs, you can outfit the space under your workbench top with open shelving, closed cabinets, or a combination of both. If floorspace is in short supply, buy a collapsible workbench and fold it up for storage.

Workbenches. Workbenches are fundamental shop fixtures that help you work at a comfortable height. They hold project parts securely while you work on them and keep tools and supplies within easy reach. Woodworking supply catalogs and home centers sell workbenches, but you can probably build a bench of equal or better quality yourself for less than what you'll pay for a ready-made bench. Project books often include plans for workbenches, and woodworking magazines publish workbench stories nearly every year.

Benches fall into three broad categories: traditional cabinetmaker's benches, utility workbenches, and collapsible/portable styles. Traditional benches are those with thick hardwood tops and sturdy wooden leg bases. They're freestanding, so you can position them wherever you need to and work around all four sides. Bench dimensions are typically 2 feet wide and 4 to 6 feet long. The top worksurface tends to be a laminated blank of hard maple, beech, or other hardwood. The extra thickness helps absorb vibrations produced by heavy pounding, and the added weight keeps the bench stationary. Benchtops are often outfitted with a series of holes along one long edge or at the end. Wood or metal pegs, called bench dogs, fit into these holes and work in conjunction with a vise on the bench to hold long boards or large workpieces. If you buy a traditional bench, expect to pay more than $500 for a good one.

Utility workbenches are easy to build and a good value for woodworking and general home-improvement tasks. These benches may resemble cabinetmaker styles with a heavy top and a skeletal base, or they can be as simple as a sheet of plywood on top of a closed cabinet or two. A utility workbench can be freestanding, or you can fasten it to wall studs. Your bench will be more useful with a vise, but you can often forego the vise and use C-clamps or other short clamps to secure your work to the benchtop. Or buy a clamp-on bench vise.

If you're organizing your shop on a tight budget, you can build a sturdy workbench using framing lumber and plywood for less than $100. Double-up 2 × 4s to make the legs, and design the bench with a sturdy framework of 2 × 4s under the top to keep it flat. Make the top with two layers of ¾-inch plywood, or use heavier medium-density fiberboard (commonly called MDF). Size the bench so you can work comfortably while standing and still reach across the top from one side. For average-size people, 30 to 40 inches is a good working height. Keep the bench width to 3 feet or less and the length not more than about 7 feet.

Ready-made portable workbenches are economical and versatile alternatives to larger, permanent benches. They make great companions to your full-size workbench, but they probably won't meet all your bench needs. Most styles have a worksurface that opens and closes like a clamp. The metal base folds up for convenient storage. Portable workbenches make stable outfeed tables for supporting workpieces as they leave your table saw or planer. Their wide stance keeps them from tipping over or shifting like other lightweight roller stands do.

Sawhorses make handy supplemental worksurfaces for cutting or assembly tasks. Plastic or metal sawhorses are lightweight and collapsible, or make your own inexpensive sawhorses from scrap wood.

Ample storage is an important component of a workshop. This shop features drawers and shelves as well as pegboard for storing and organizing tools and materials.

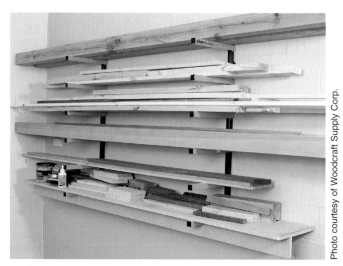

Wall-mounted lumber storage racks keep lumber off the floor and out of your way. Racks ensure the lumber stays flat and dry until you're ready to use it.

Clamp a large piece of plywood in the top vise of a portable workbench to create a broader surface for project assembly, staging parts, or doing light machine work. Simply fasten a cleat to the underside of the plywood and tighten the benchtop clamp onto this cleat.

Sawhorses serve as portable workbenches, too. Whether you buy or build yours, have a pair in the shop to provide extra worksurfaces for assembly or for small power tool use. Metal or plastic styles are lightweight, sturdy, and inexpensive.

Material storage. Organizing the sundries and tools in your shop will require several types of storage. Narrow shelving works well for storing spare lumber, bins of fasteners, containers of finishing materials, and smaller power tools. Drawers, provided they aren't too deep or large, work well for organizing loose articles that don't stand on their own, stack well, or fit into uniformly sized containers. Locking drawers keep sharp blades and bits out of children's hands and store smaller, valuable shop tools securely. Mechanic's multidrawer tool carts are particularly useful shop fixtures, because they offer a bank of sturdy drawers in various depths as well as a bit of flat workspace on top—all on wheels.

You'll also need a container for collecting smaller pieces of scrap lumber or for tossing cutoffs as you make them. A spare trash can works reasonably well for this purpose. Resist the urge to save every scrap. Keep your scrap bin small and cull it from time to time.

Plywood and other large sheet materials are best stored flat on their faces, but it's tough to do this in a small shop. To help keep plywood flat, store it on edge against a wall and strap it to the wall framing. Or build a narrow plywood storage cart that holds the sheets at a slight angle so gravity helps keep them flat and stacked neatly.

Pegboard is a thrifty way to hang hand tools near the workbench. Fasten furring strips or other scrap material to the back of the pegboard to form a shallow framework, then screw the pegboard to wall studs. Buy hooks made to stay in their holes to keep them from falling out as you hang and remove tools.

Shop layout. Arranging tools, materials, and fixtures in your shop will depend on the shape of the space you have; where doors, windows, stairwells, and outlets are located; and the size and mobility of the machinery you own. Here are some general guidelines to start with when laying out your shop: Locate shelves or racks for storing lumber or sheet goods close to entry doors and stairwells. This way, you'll carry them the shortest distance into the shop. If you own a power miter saw, situate it close to these raw materials so you can size them down before moving them to other places in the shop.

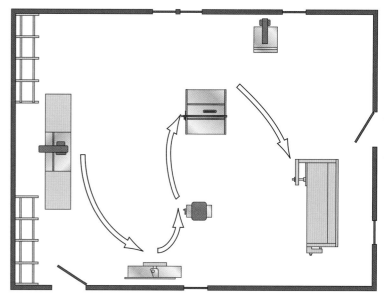

A well-organized shop has a logical order of machinery, with the table saw placed in the center and the lumber stored conveniently near the door. Set up machines in such a way that you minimize carrying heavy lumber.

Heavy machinery doesn't have to be stationary, thanks to an abundance of rolling base options. They make woodworking possible even in garages that double as parking spaces.

It's likely that you'll use a table saw for making some of the first cuts on lumber and sheet goods after they enter the shop. Table saws require 4 to 8 feet of clear space all around so there's room to work without hitting walls or other obstructions. Place the saw near the center of the shop. Keep the thickness planer and jointer near the table saw so you can move easily from jointer to planer to table saw for sizing and surfacing stock efficiently.

Arrange other machines and shop fixtures where they are convenient for you. Have a bin near the miter saw for collecting short scraps. Place a stationary sander near a window to draw out the airborne dust. Router tables and band saws can be stored anywhere, provided they are on wheels. A drill press should stand against a wall where it's less likely to tip over. Keep measuring and marking tools, hand tools, containers of fasteners, and glue close to the workbench.

You'll need flat worksurfaces for general assembly and finishing tasks as well as for staging parts for machining. If space allows, put a worktable in your shop in addition to the workbench. Choose a table that's small enough to move around so you can use it as an ancillary bench surface wherever it's needed.

Your arsenal of safety gear should include both hearing and eye protection. Buy comfortable styles so you'll wear them willingly whenever you're using machinery.

Safety overview

Shop accidents happen in an instant, especially with power tools. The results can be irreversible and even life-threatening. Your first line of defense against mishaps is really simple: Think before doing. Respect the capabilities and dangers of your tools and know how to use them safely. Plan your work so you can get help lifting or moving heavy objects. Keep your tools in good repair and your bits and blades clean and sharp. Remove guards and other safety devices only when absolutely necessary. Keep the workspace clean and the floor clear of debris so you can avoid stepping over scraps and piles of shavings.

Personal safety gear will help you avoid accidents and work comfortably. Virtually every task that requires a tool creates some degree of danger for your eyes. Buy safety glasses or goggles that fit your face properly and have an anti-fog coating. They should protect your eyes from both the front and sides. Keep them clean and protected against scratches when not in use.

Power tool use can be equally damaging to your ears. Safety gear manufacturers offer a variety of different ear protection devices to suit personal preference. You'll find ear muffs that cover your ears and earplugs that fit inside. Some plugs are disposable and made of soft foam that you compress and insert in your ear canals. Once inside, the foam expands for a tight seal. Other earplug styles are reusable and outfitted on bands or cords for wearing around your neck. You'll even find combination head gear with safety glasses mounted on ear muffs. Whatever style of hearing protection you choose, be sure it has a noise reduction rating (NRR) of at least 25 decibels, which is a safe standard for general power tool use.

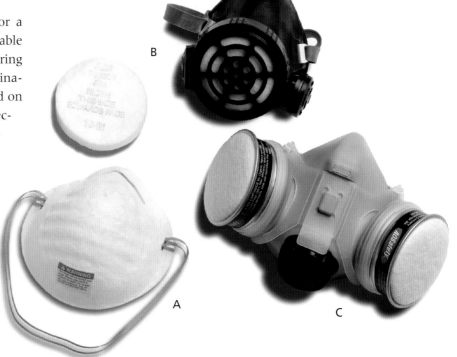

Research now suggests that wood dust can be a carcinogen as well as an irritant. When you are using dust-producing machinery, especially saws, routers, and sanders, wear a respirator. Respirators approved for wood dusts are different than inexpensive, hospital-style masks, although they look similar to one another. Usually, dust respirators will have two head straps rather than one, and the packaging will clearly identify

Wood dust is irritating to breathe and probably harmful to your health over the long haul. Wear a disposable respirator (A) or one with replaceable filters (B) to protect your lungs. When you work with solvents and finishes, wear a canister solvent respirator (C).

the product as a respirator and not a dust mask. Dust masks actually offer little protection from fine wood dust. If you are working with solvent- or oil-based strippers, cleaners, or finishes, a dust respirator will not filter out the mists and fumes produced by these materials. Wear a respirator outfitted with replaceable canister filters, and change the filters as soon as you can smell solvents through the mask.

As for other apparel, roll up long shirt sleeves to keep them clear of machinery and messes. Wear comfortable shoes with rubber soles if you'll be standing for long periods of time. Athletic shoes are a great choice for woodworking wear. Dress warmly if you work in an unheated shop, but avoid wearing gloves when using power tools. Gloves can get caught on blades or bits and pull your hands into harm's way. Some woodworkers wear aprons while they work to keep clothes cleaner. If you do, be sure to empty the pockets of loose articles and tie the apron strings.

If you work alone in the shop, plan your woodworking sessions when someone else is home and can check on you from time to time or lend a hand if necessary. To avoid accidents and mistakes, stop working if you are feeling tired, frustrated, or rushed. It should go without saying that it's never safe to operate woodworking machinery when you're under the influence of alcohol or other drugs that impair your judgment.

Keep a first-aid kit, fire extinguisher, and phone in a convenient location near the shop exit.

Chapter 2
OVERVIEW OF POWER TOOLS

Before the advent of electricity and for a good while after that, woodworking was done with nonmotorized hand tools—and a lot of sweat. You can still work wood this way if you wish. Learning to use and master hand tools like jack planes, rip saws, spokeshaves, and drilling braces is an admirable pursuit, and woodworkers with these talents make beautiful furniture. However, woodworking with power tools offers you several advantages. For one, the guides, fences, variable-speed controls, and ergonomics designed into these machines will give you a leg up on precision right from the start. Power tools will also allow you to tackle work that was formerly time-consuming and labor intensive much more quickly and easily. And although hand tool purists might argue this final point, power tools are enjoyable to own and use.

This chapter will provide an overview of the handheld and stationary power tools available to you. Tools are grouped into portable and stationary categories, with a suggested buying guide at the beginning of each section. Read this material before you buy and in conjunction with other tool reviews published in woodworking magazines. This information will help you make informed decisions about selecting the tools that will make your woodworking pleasurable and safe. Then ask other woodworkers you know about which tool brands and models they prefer, and try these tools for yourself. In the end, buy machines that feel comfortable to you, offer solid performance, and fit your budget. If you shop carefully, you'll be rewarded with years or even a lifetime of reliable service from your machines.

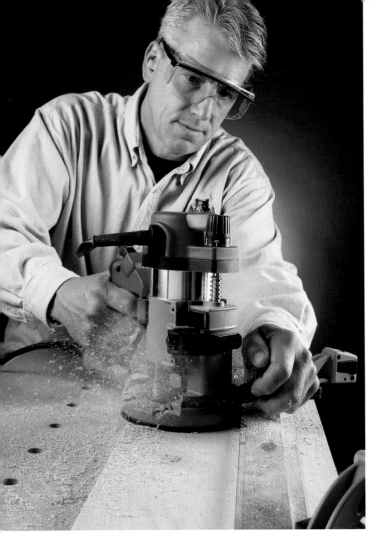

Every woodworker needs a collection of high-quality portable power tools. A good router is well worth its price.

Portable power tools

No hobbyist shop is complete without a selection of portable power tools. In fact, if you are just beginning to equip your shop with tools, a few good-quality portables will allow you to build a variety of woodworking projects while you save for larger, stationary machines. Depending on your woodworking interests and the quality of portable power tools you buy, you may never need to move up to stationary tools.

Most midpriced portable tools offer ample power and a range of beneficial standard features. Tool reviews in woodworking magazines can direct you to these machines, but the qualitative differences between midpriced tools is diminishing as manufacturers continue to refine their tools. It's still worthwhile to read those tool reviews, but be sure to try different models of the same tool yourself to see what you prefer. Buy from reputable tool manufacturers, and the portable tools you invest in now may still be in your shop a decade or two from now.

Jig saws

Among portable power tools, no saw makes a wider range of cuts than a jig saw. Jig saws use narrow, straight blades and drive them in sewing-machine fashion to cut wood. The narrow blade width allows these tools to excel at making curved cuts (see page 104), but they can also be guided along a straightedge for making reasonably accurate rip and crosscuts (see pages 90 and 95). You can also make bevel cuts with a jig saw by pivoting the base.

Since the blade moves in a reciprocating motion rather than spinning as it cuts, jig saws are among the safest power tools to use. Unlike table saws or miter saws, there's no danger of kickback when using a jig saw. Jig saws are generally quieter to operate than other power tools, and better models have vibration-dampening counterbalancing mechanisms to make them more pleasant to handle. Their mild manners and ease of use will quickly build your confidence and accuracy when using these versatile machines.

PORTABLE TOOLS TO BUY

Here's a suggestion for how to prioritize buying your tools. If your budget is limited, the first five tools on this list form the essential collection.

Portable tools to buy
1. Jig saw
2. Corded or cordless drill
3. Router
4. Circular saw
5. Miter saw
6. Random-orbit or pad sander
7. Biscuit joiner

Types of jig saws. Jig saws are made with two different gripping configurations. Saws with top-mounted handles are more common, usually with a trigger and a speed control dial mounted in the handle. The other handle style, called a barrel grip, originated in Europe. Instead of a separate handle above the motor, the motor housing serves as the grip. Barrel-grip jig saws will have the trigger mounted either underneath the motor or on the side of the barrel. The handle style you choose really depends on personal preference.

At one time, jig saw blades typically mounted to the blade plunger shaft by tightening a setscrew in a small collet. It was relatively easy to strip the screw, and blade changes always involved a screwdriver. Today, many jig saws come with Allen bolts rather than screws for tightening the blade in the plunger, and the Allen wrench usually stows right on the saw. Professional-grade saws often have tool-free blade locking mechanisms. On these saws, a spring-loaded lever or twist knob releases the blade.

Jig saws are made in two handle styles: top-mounted (top) and barrel-grip (bottom). Both offer comfortable and controlled use of the tool, so personal preference really dictates which handle style to buy.

Features to consider. Jig saws have a number of important features worth shopping for. Most saws have variable-speed control. You can adjust the cutting speed either by squeezing the trigger further or turning a speed control dial. Variable speed is definitely a feature worth having on your saw. You'll want to use slower speeds for cutting metals or splinter-prone woods like oak.

Aside from speed control, you can also adjust the orbital action on most jig saws. Saws with adjustable orbit controls generally have four or five settings.

Jig saw innovations make blade changes easier than ever. On this saw, sliding a lever releases the blade without the need for additional tools.

Spring-loaded rollers and side guides support the blade from behind on this saw and help keep the blade tracking properly in the cut.

One setting will lock the blade in a straight in-line motion, which produces the cleanest cuts but the slowest feed rates. Switching to other orbital settings changes the blade stroke from up-and-down to one in which the blade also moves forward as it comes up and backward as it moves down. The orbital action allows the blade to cut more aggressively but with more splintering along the cut edge.

Since jig saw blades are supported on only one end, blades will wander somewhat in the cut. The amount of wandering increases when using longer blades, cutting thick or harder materials, and during curve cutting. To counteract this tendency, good-quality jig saws will have a spring-loaded roller supporting the blade from behind. If you plan to use your jig saw for making finish-quality cuts, be sure to buy a saw with some form of blade support.

Most jig saws also have provisions for dust control. Some do this by blowing sawdust away from the cutting path. Other models have a dust port that connects to a shop vacuum. Jig saws don't generate the same amount of debris that circular saws or routers do, but even some dust control is helpful.

Finally, look for a jig saw with a base that's easy to swivel and lock for bevel-cutting. The larger and easier the tilt scale is to read, the more accurate your cutting angle will be. Many saw bases adjust with an Allen wrench, although a few saws have a handy flip-lever to make this a tool-free task.

Corded drills and cordless drill/drivers

A corded drill or battery-powered drill/driver will be an essential item in your woodworking tool arsenal. Either style of drill can accomplish a variety of woodworking functions, including general hole drilling, boring pilot holes for fasteners or dowels, and driving screws. Outside the woodshop, a drill can also be outfitted with sanding disks, wire wheels, buffing bonnets or paint stirrers for

The fundamental choice concerning drills is whether to choose a corded or cordless model. Each style will tackle a range of drilling and screwdriving tasks, although cordless drill/drivers have even more helpful features to offer.

tackling other metal-finishing and home-improvement projects. Some heavy-duty drills have a percussion feature that produces a hammering action for drilling through concrete and masonry, but these kinds of hammer drills are unnecessary for woodworking.

In the last couple decades, improvements in rechargeable-battery technology have revolutionized the cordless-drill/driver market—so much so that the virtues of corded drills almost aren't discussed in woodworking books and magazines anymore. However, midsize corded drills are nearly as useful for woodworking as cordless drill/drivers, and they are often less expensive. While some might argue that the power cord gets in the way or limits versatility, a corded drill offers ample and constant power. It weighs about the same as a battery-powered drill/driver or just slightly more, so the tool isn't tiring to use regularly.

Pistol-grip drill/drivers (left) were first-generation cordless drills, with a battery that fit inside the handle. You can still buy them, but in limited lower voltages. The more common style today is the T-handle drill/driver (right), with a battery that attaches below the handle grip.

Features to consider in corded drills. Corded drills are categorized by the maximum bit-shank diameter the chuck can handle. Years ago, drills were sold in three chuck capacities: ¼-, ⅜- or ½-inch. Today, ⅜- and ½-inch chuck drills are the norm. Drills with ¼-inch chucks will limit your bit choices and generally have undersized motors, so avoid buying one for general woodworking.

Corded drills come with two styles of chucks: those requiring a geared key to tighten the bit and those that can be adjusted without a key. Keyed chucks aren't difficult to use and offer great holding power. Be sure to attach the chuck key to the drill cord so it doesn't get misplaced—you can't change bits without it. Keyless chucks are options on a few corded drills. They tighten by twisting one or two sleeves on the chuck by hand.

For general woodworking, a ⅜-inch corded drill should provide all the power and capacity you'll need. It will accept bit shanks up to ⅜-inch, but the actual cutting size of the bit can be considerably larger. Corded drills with ½-inch chucks usually have the percussive feature and are larger and heavier tools. Be sure the corded drill you buy has a variable-speed motor and a reversing feature for backing out bits and screws.

Features to consider in cordless drill/drivers. Cordless drill/drivers are made in a variety of battery voltages ranging from 9.6 volts up to 24 volts. As voltage increases, so does the amount of torque the drill/driver produces. So, a 24-volt drill will be able to spin larger drill bits or drive bigger screws than a 9.6-volt drill. In addition to this measure of peak voltage, drill/driver batteries are also categorized by amp hours, which range from one to three hours. More amp hours means the battery will run for a longer time between charges.

Battery technology and charger costs, as well as the higher demand for cordless drills, means you'll pay more for a battery-powered drill than you will for a comparable corded drill. But the principal advantage to the battery is that you can use the tool anywhere you build your projects—even in a power outage or without an electric outlet close by. All good cordless drill/drivers come with a pair of batteries, so provided you are diligent about recharging a battery as soon as it needs it, you'll rarely be left with two dead batteries. Most battery chargers refresh a dead battery in about an hour, and some with rapid-charge circuitry can do it in as little as 15 minutes.

Cordless drills are sold with ⅜- or ½-inch-capacity chucks. Either size is a good choice for woodworking—the size of the drill doesn't increase with the larger chuck size. Most cordless drills have keyless chucks with single- or double-sleeve designs. Those with a single sleeve have an internal brake that locks the motor shaft in place so you can tighten or loosen the chuck with one hand. If you're considering a cordless drill/driver with a double-sleeve chuck, make sure the sleeves are comfortable to grip and large enough for two-handed use.

Buy a drill/driver with variable-speed control. Squeezing the trigger should allow you to control the speed from a dead stop up to full power. Most battery-powered drills will have a two-speed transmission, typically controlled by a hi/low switch on top of the drill. Use the low transmission speed for spinning large bits or driving long fasteners where torque is more important than speed. Switch to the higher speed for drilling with smaller bits where torque is less important than speed.

One great feature shared by all cordless drill/drivers is an adjustable clutch. Drills will have as few as 4 or up to 20 or more clutch settings. The clutch allows

One significant advantage of cordless drills is the ability to adjust a clutch mechanism. This way, you can limit the drill's driving torque so the clutch disengages the chuck before it overdrives or breaks fasteners. The clutch can also be locked in a drilling mode to take advantage of the tool's full torque.

you to set the drill either for drilling holes at maximum torque or limiting the torque incrementally. At lower clutch settings, the chuck will disengage when the torque reaches a peak to avoid overdriving fasteners. Experiment with different torque settings when you're working with softwoods or hardwoods as well as different screw lengths and compositions. There's bound to be a clutch setting that will drive the fastener just far enough for the task.

Cordless drill/drivers come in two handle styles: pistol grip or T-handle. The pistol-grip style resembles corded drills with the handle behind the motor. The configuration offers more driving pressure behind the bit. It's a less common style than T-handle drill/drivers, where the handle is positioned beneath the motor. Choose the handle style most comfortable for you. Grips with rubber overmolds are particularly comfortable and offer optimal control of the tool.

Among the many practical functions of a drill, you can use it in tandem with a jig to bore pocket holes for making quick and easy joinery.

The big question you'll need to answer when choosing a cordless drill/driver is what size battery to buy. Most experts agree that drills ranging from 9.6 volts to 14.4 volts offer ample torque for woodworking tasks without the extra weight that comes with the heavier batteries on higher voltage drills. For all-around use, a 12- or 14.4-volt drill is probably the ideal choice.

Routers

Among workshop tools, the router is the undisputed king of versatility. With a router, you can cut, shape edges, build joints, create decorative inlays, and even drill holes. More research and development goes into router innovations each year than virtually any other woodworking tool. And for all these various capabilities, routers don't cost a fortune. A good-quality router is worth every cent you pay.

The plunge router (left) and fixed-base router (right) are the two main types of routers for general workshop use. A trim router (center) is smaller and used primarily for trimming plastic laminate.

The two main types of routers for general workshop use are fixed-base and plunge. A third type, called a trim router, is a much smaller tool primarily used to trim plastic laminate.

Fixed-base routers are the standard-issue tools of the router family. They have a motor that's adjusted up or down on its base and is fixed in place for the routing operation. Standard fixed-base models range in power from 1½ to 2¼ horsepower and are suitable for most

handheld and table routing jobs. Large fixed-base tools, with 3 horsepower or more, are called heavy-duty, or production, routers and are used for heavy work with large bits. They also make excellent table routers.

Plunge routers have a special base that allows the motor to travel up and down while under power. This feature lets you plunge the spinning router bit down into the workpiece, move the tool sideways for a horizontal cut, then retract the bit from the wood at the end of the cut. Plunge routers can do everything standard fixed-base routers can do but are especially useful for inside cuts, such as mortises.

Trim routers, also called laminate trimmers, have small motors (1 horsepower or less) and are easy to grasp and control with one hand. They are convenient and effective for trimming countertop laminate and for light edging work on wood and other materials. Like regular-size routers, trim routers make clean, accurate cuts, but their size limits them to small bits and shallow, light-duty work.

If they end up logging a lot of hours on the router table or get into heavy production work, most woodworkers look to a second, heavy-duty router with more horsepower. On the other end of the power scale, a trim router is a handy second tool for jobs that don't require much muscle.

Choosing a router. Good routers are not inexpensive, but they are a good value. The majority of quality models fall into a midlevel price range, and any of them will likely be as much tool as you'll ever need. So, aside from price and features, the big decision you have to make is which type of router to buy. For general workshop routing the question is (or used to be) whether to go with a fixed-base or plunge router. Both can tackle most handheld routing tasks, and both can be used in a router table. For those who can't decide, several major manufacturers now offer router kits that come with a motor and interchangeable fixed and plunge bases. Most people buy a midsize handheld router for general use.

Many manufacturers now make router kits that consist of a motor and both plunge (left) and fixed (right) bases.

Fixed-base routers are perfectly simple. From a user's standpoint, they have two main parts: the motor unit and the base. One distinct advantage of a fixed-base tool is that the motor slips or twists completely free of the base to facilitate bit changes or switching to a different type of base. The router is set up for action by securing the bit in the collet, which is fixed to the motor's shaft. The motor is inserted into the base, and the bit depth is adjusted by raising or lowering the motor position within the base; then it is locked in place using the base's clamping system.

Compared to plunge routers, the key drawback of the fixed-base tool is that the bit remains at one depth setting for each operation and cannot truly be plunged into the work as with a plunge router. "Plunging" with a fixed-base router involves setting one edge of the base on the workpiece so the bit spins freely, then slowly tipping the router to the horizontal while the spinning bit cuts into the wood at an angle. This is dangerous and difficult to do without ruining the cut.

Plunge routers have been around since the 1950s but have only recently taken the limelight from fixed-base routers. Plunge routers have motors that travel up and down on spring-loaded posts or tubes, allowing precise, vertical plunging action of the bit to a preset depth. Bit depth is controlled by a depth stop that is set and locked in place before starting the router. At the end of the plunge stroke, the depth stop contacts the turret stop on the router's base. For multistage excavations, the turret stop can be rotated one step at a time to increase the bit depth incrementally with successive cuts.

For some router operations, like cutting hinge mortises, a plunge router offers more convenience than a fixed-base router.

Other design features include the plunge locking mechanism, which automatically locks the motor in place on the posts; flipping the lock lever is the last step before starting the cut. An up-stop feature limits the upward travel of the motor so it stops at its original position. This can also be used to adjust bit depth when the router is in a router table. Many plunge routers have a spindle lock—a button that's depressed to hold the motor spindle in place while you loosen the collet with one wrench. Because some plunge motors can't be removed from their bases, as fixed-base motors can, this feature simplifies bit changing.

Bit changing for table routing is easy with a fixed-base router because the motor can be removed from the base.

Plunge routers can accomplish any task that a fixed-base tool can, but not always with the same ease and stability. The higher motor and handles and the relatively small (on many models), lightweight base of the plunge tool makes it more prone to tipping when the base isn't fully supported. Where plunge routers excel is making mortises and any other inside cuts that can't be accessed from the workpiece edge. Depending on the type of work you do, that can amount to a lot of cuts for which the plunge router is better suited.

Features to consider in routers. Midsize routers carry a power rating between 1½ and 2¼ horsepower. However, because horsepower ratings aren't precisely standard, amperage is a better indicator of true power. Look for a router in the 10- to 12-amp range.

Router accessories include (clockwise from left to right) template guides, dovetail jigs, clear sub-bases, and various edge guides.

The hex-nut-shaped bit holder on the end of the motor spindle of a router is called the collet. Router bits are made in ¼- and ½-inch shank sizes. All good routers include both ¼- and ½-inch collets as standard equipment, to accept either bit shank size. Don't even consider a midsize tool that accepts only one shank-size bit, as this will limit your bit choices considerably.

Once a feature common only among production routers, electronic variable speed (EVS) now comes standard on many midsize tools. This feature allows you to set the router's top speed at five or six different levels for specific routing situations. Electronic circuitry automatically maintains the motor speed through varying workloads and also helps absorb the shock of a sudden change in material (knots, etc.), giving you more control. Soft start brings the motor up to speed gradually and eliminates the kick you get when starting a standard router.

Router accessories. Routers not only have more bit options than any other power tool, they also have more accessories. Some, like extra collets and template adapters, come as standard equipment with new routers; others are optional products supplied by router manufacturers or aftermarket tool companies.

Subbases come in several shapes and sizes for both plunge and fixed-base routers. Common styles include clear bases for improved visibility, bases with large or small center holes to accommodate different bit diameters, and a stepped (underscribe) base for cutting seamed edges in plastic laminate. Offset subbases have a teardrop shape and a handle on the base to provide increased support and improved control of the router for edge work.

Edge guides connect directly to the router with steel rods fed through mounts in the router base. The guide's fence rides along the edge of the workpiece to make a variety of controlled cuts, including dadoes, grooves, and rabbets. Some edge guides also make circular and elliptical cuts (with additional accessories).

Commercial templates and jigs typically are high-grade metal fixtures manufactured to precise tolerances. Hinge-mortising templates, squaring guides, straightedges, and, most commonly, dovetail jigs are available to help you make exact, repeatable cuts indefinitely without wearing out the jig. These sorts of jigs greatly increase the range of uses you'll get from your router.

Circular saws

If you're just getting started in woodworking but already have some carpentry or remodeling projects under your belt, you're probably familiar with circular saws. These workaday saws have a circular blade mounted to the saw's motor spindle and an adjustable base that wraps around the blade. The base pivots up and down to change the blade's depth of cut. It also tilts either left or right depending on the saw to set the blade at an angle to the work.

Portability and ease of use make circular saws ideal for framing or carpentry tasks, but they're generally not as accurate as table saws or miter saws for woodworking. However, when a good-quality circular saw is fitted with a sharp, carbide-tipped blade and guided against a straightedge, it can make precise rip or crosscuts on par with a table saw or miter saw. You'll really appreciate having one when you need to cut up full-size sheets of plywood or other long or wide lumber. It's much easier to guide the small saw over a large sheet or board than trying to lift and steer the wood through a stationary saw. (For more on cutting sheet materials with a circular saw, see page 94.)

Circular saws are ideal for making quick crosscuts to size down lumber or for cutting up large sheet materials into manageable pieces. When guided against a straightedge, these tools can produce remarkably accurate and clean results.

Types & features to consider. Most circular saws are still corded tools, but more cordless circular saws are being added to the market all the time. Corded saws have motors that range in size from 4 to 15 amps, and battery-powered saws come in 14.4- to 24-volt models. From a practical standpoint, what's more important than power ratings is blade diameter. The larger the blade, the greater the cutting capacity. Circular saws that take blades in the 3- to 6-inch-diameter range are often called "trim saws." They're lightweight and perfect for cutting sheet goods or ¾-inch lumber, but cutting capacity is limited to about 1⁵⁄₁₆ inch. If you want a circular saw that will be suitable for a

The foot on a circular saw can be tilted off 90° for making bevel cuts. A protractor-style gauge helps set the exact blade angle.

wider range of woodworking or home improvement applications, buy one that takes 6-inch or larger blades. This way you can cut through 2× dimensional lumber in a single pass. Circular saws with 7¼-inch blades are the typical size, and all saw blade manufacturers make blades to fit this size tool.

As far as features go, buy a saw with a sturdy foot made of cast aluminum or magnesium. Stamped steel bases are common on consumer-grade saws, and they bend easily if you drop the tool. The saw should feel well balanced in your hand. Some saws come with rubber over-molds on the handles for added control and comfort. Make sure the saw's trigger handle fits your palm well, especially if you plan to use the tool frequently. The other, front-mounted handle should be equally comfortable and well proportioned for two-handed operation.

As far as other controls are concerned, the bevel-tilt and blade-depth controls should be easy to see and operate. The lower blade guard should be equipped with a large lever for retracting the guard and a stiff return spring to keep the blade covered whenever possible. Some saws come with sawdust collection bags, dust ports, or vacuum adaptors so you can keep debris to a minimum.

Most circular saws have blades mounted to the right of the motor, which means you'll have to lean over the tool in order to see where the blade is actually cutting. Some manufacturers now offer models with either left- or right-mounted blades. If you're right-handed, try a saw with a left-mounted blade. You'll probably appreciate the easier visibility.

You'll need to become accustomed to how your saw's blade index marker relates to the actual blade position. Most saws have a narrow slot along the front edge of the saw base to help locate the blade's cutting path. Some saws come with an adjustable cursor or laser guide instead of the slot for aligning the blade. Whichever saw you buy, practice will improve your cutting accuracy.

Circular saws also come in corded and cordless options. Most cordless circular saws have smaller blades than their corded cousins and are useful for lighter-duty trimming tasks or for cutting up sheet materials.

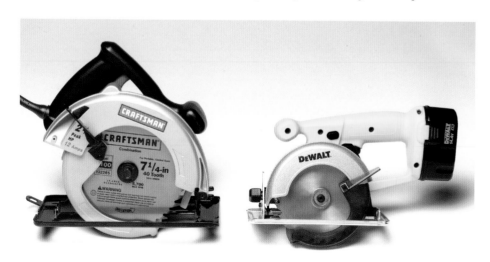

Miter saws

Miter saws once were predominantly contractor tools, but they're now commonplace woodworking machines for hobbyists. Miter saws excel at both crosscutting and making angle or bevel cuts. Essentially, a miter saw is a circular saw attached by an arm to a swiveling saw table. The motor and blade assembly pivots down into a slot in the table to make the cut. The base is outfitted with a protractor-style scale so the swiveling table can be set to precise angles, relative to the blade. The scale also has a number of preset stops, called detents, to help lock the table accurately at common angles like 0°, 15°, 22.5°, and 45°. A fence supports the workpiece on both sides of the blade.

Miter saw styles. Miter saws are sold in standard, compound, and sliding styles. Standard miter saws, sometimes called power miter boxes, swivel left and right for mitering, but the blade cannot be tilted out of square to the table for bevel cutting. These are first-generation miter saws, and they are the least expensive options. If you plan to use a miter saw now and then but not regularly, a standard miter saw may be a good fit for you.

For all-around woodworking, a compound miter saw offers more features and versatility than a standard miter saw. This style allows you to swivel the blade left and right while also tilting it off of 90° for making bevel cuts. When the blade is both tipped and swiveled, the resulting cut creates a compound angle from which the tool gets its name. Older models of compound miter saws tip in only one direction, but newer machines commonly tip both left and right.

Sliding miter saws are a cross between a compound miter saw and a radial arm saw. The motor head is mounted on a rail or pair of rails forming a sliding carriage that moves forward and backward. The blade still pivots up and down for cutting, but the added front-to-back motion allows a sliding miter saw to

Standard miter saws (center) are the least expensive miter saw style. They're not as versatile as compound miter saws (left) or sliding compound miter saws (right).

RADIAL ARM SAWS

Radial arm saws function similarly to sliding compound miter saws, with the saw motor mounted on a sliding overhead carriage. Instead of pushing the carriage forward through the workpiece, however, you pull the saw carriage back to make the cut. Radial arm saws are typically used for making crosscuts, angle cuts, and even for making joinery with a dado blade. Most have a swiveling motorhead that can be turned for making rip cuts, although ripping with a radial arm saw is a more dangerous operation than ripping with a table saw or circular saw.

The popularity of radial arm saws has dropped sharply in the past two decades or so, despite the fact that these saws were once mainstays in both professional and school woodshops. Radial arm saws have passed out of woodworking fashion for a couple reasons. First, these saws have a reputation for being more dangerous to operate than other saws. Whether this is caused by the tool's design or operator error is debatable. In any case, the cutting action of a radial arm saw can cause the blade to climb up over the workpiece and back toward the operator, particularly when the blade is fed too quickly through the wood. Use extreme caution when cutting with a radial arm saw, just as you should with any other saw. Aside from this issue of cutting safety, radial arm saws have been eclipsed by miter saws, which are more portable, equally accurate, and less expensive.

crosscut wider workpieces than a compound miter saw with the same blade size. The blade on a sliding miter saw can be tipped off of 90° for making compound angle cuts, just like a compound miter saw.

Miter saws are sized by blade diameter, and the common sizes are 8¼, 10, and 12 inch. Before you buy a miter saw, consider how much crosscutting capacity you'll need. From time to time, you may crosscut lumber thicker than ordinary 2× stock, but generally you'll work with ¾-inch-thick material more often than oversized stock. Choose a saw that allows you to cut through 2× material with the widest cutting width you can afford. A good all-around saw for general woodworking is a 12-inch compound miter saw. It will crosscut ¾-inch lumber up to about 8¼ inches wide, a standard 2 × 6 or a 4 × 4 in a single pass. Sliding compound miter saws with 10-inch blades will crosscut wider lumber (up to 12 inches), but they cost more than 12-inch compound miter saws. A 12-inch sliding compound miter saw offers the largest cutting capacity, both in terms of thickness and width, but it will cost nearly twice as much as a 12-inch compound miter saw.

For more on using a miter saw, refer to the crosscutting and miter-cutting sections in Chapter 5.

Helpful features to consider. The popularity of miter saws among both tradespeople and woodworkers means that new innovations are being developed by saw manufacturers all the time. A few models now come with rechargeable batteries instead of a power cord, but corded saws are still more practical for shop use. Saws that come with side support wings or pull-out extensions make it easier to cut long workpieces.

All miter saws have dust bags to help collect sawdust during cutting. Depending on the saw, the port for connecting the dust bag may also fit the nozzle of a shop vacuum. Dust-collection efficiency improves dramatically when the saw is connected to a vacuum.

The latest trend in miter saws is laser guides that project a beam onto the workpiece for lining up the cut. Lasers are beneficial for lining up cuts on contoured molding where the blade can't

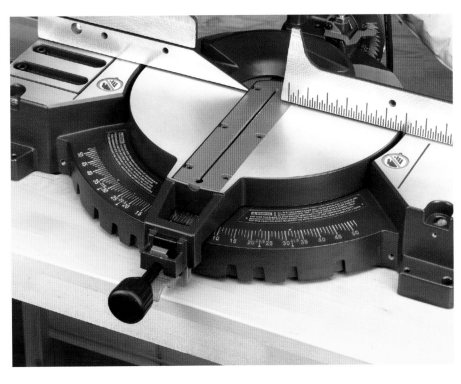

touch the cutting line directly. However, it isn't difficult to align the blade without a laser, so don't base your buying decision heavily on the laser feature. If you buy a saw with a laser, make sure the laser is adjustable so you can set it up to mark the precise location of the blade on the workpiece. Not all lasers are adjustable, and the manufacturer's settings aren't always accurate.

When shopping for a miter saw, swivel the saw table and make sure the detents lock positively. Move the table to a non-detent angle and tighten the locking knob to make sure the saw locks firmly in these positions, too. Buy a saw that offers bright, easy-to-read miter and bevel-tilt scales and convenient adjustment features. You'll need to adjust the blade angle initially and from time to time afterward. Most saws these days have horizontal handles, which tend to be more comfortable than vertical or pistol-grip handles.

A miter saw table swivels left and right so you can set up angle cuts using the protractor scale in front of the tool. Most saws have preset detents around this scale for locking the saw accurately to several common angles.

Saws that come with hold-down clamps, flip-up stops for cutting crown molding, and front-mounted controls for setting miter and bevel angles are particularly convenient for woodworkers. Over the long term, you'll also appreciate a miter saw with externally-accessible motor brushes so you can perform your own motor maintenance when that time comes.

Miter saws with hold-down clamps make it easier to support long workpieces safely without added fuss.

Portable sanders

Few woodworkers enjoy the time and effort it takes to sand a project by hand, so a number of motorized sanders can help you speed the task along. As far as portable sanders go, there are four principal types: belt sanders, orbital finish sanders, random-orbit sanders, and detail sanders. You won't need all of them necessarily,

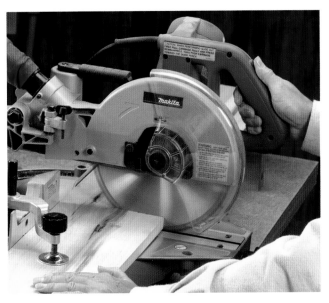

There are four principal styles of portable sanders (clockwise from the top left): belt sanders, orbital finish sanders, detail sanders, and random-orbit sanders.

but it will help to know a bit about each one to choose those machines most beneficial to your work.

Belt sanders. Belt sanders drive a continuous sanding belt for fast, aggressive stock removal as well as for rough part-shaping tasks. These machines are sized according to the width and loop length of the sandpaper belts that fit them. The belts are 3 or 4 inches wide and 18, 21, or 24 inches long. For general woodworking, a 3 × 18 or 3 × 21 belt sander is about the right size. Larger machines are heavier to lift and more expensive, but they're worth considering if you plan to sand lots of large panels for tabletops or cabinetry projects.

Belt sanders have a drive roller in the rear and an idler roller in front that maintains spring tension on the sanding belt. Some belt sanders have a third roller as well. A tracking knob allows you to adjust the position of the belt on the rollers. Belt sanders generate considerable dust, so all the quality models come with a dust-collection bag. For even cleaner sanding, some belt sanders can also be connected to a shop vacuum, which is a subtle but helpful feature to look for.

When choosing a belt sander, buy one with comfortable handles and that feels evenly weighted. Variable speed is beneficial so you can start the machine slowly and increase the belt speed as you go. Try the belt-changing feature before you buy, to see how easy it will be to switch belts. The process of changing a belt should take no more than a few minutes. Some manufacturers offer frames that hold the sander in place like a stationary machine so you can sand small parts freehand. It's a good accessory to buy if you don't plan to invest in a combination sander (see page 51).

It takes some practice to get comfortable using a belt sander. The main goal is to keep the machine from tipping to one side as you sand, which will leave gouges and scratches that are hard to remove. Set the machine on the workpiece and then start the belt slowly to keep the tool from jerking out of your hands. Once sanding is underway, keep the machine moving in a sweeping motion at all times to sand evenly. It isn't necessary to bear down on the machine. You'll find that sanding happens rapidly, especially with coarse-grit belts, so let the machine do the work for you. As a general guideline, start with the finest grit belt that will do the work. For

You'll need to replace the sanding belt on a belt sander when it wears out or in instances when you need to change belt grits. Choose a sander that makes this routine task easy.

sanding rough surfaces, a 60- or 80-grit belt is a good grit to start with, then switch to 100- or 120-grit belts. If the wood has already been planed before you sand it, or if the wood is soft, start sanding with a 100- or 120-grit belt instead. Do your final sanding with a random-orbit or finish sander. Belt sanders aren't intended to be finish-sanding machines.

Orbital finish sanders. Orbital finish sanders have been around since electric sanders were invented. The sanding pad moves in a tight, vibrating circular motion. You can distinguish these machines from other portable sanders because they take square or rectangular pieces of sandpaper instead of belts or disks. Orbital sanders are sized by the section of a 9 × 12-inch sheet of sandpaper that fits them. Sander sizes include ¼-, ⅓-, or ½-sheet models. The sandpaper fits over a dense felt or rubber pad, and a pair of clamps on each end of the pad hold the paper in place.

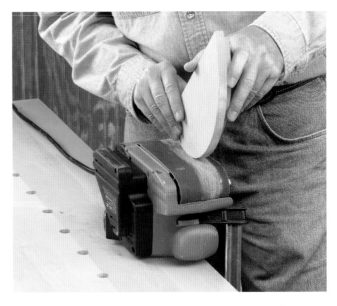

In addition to sanding flat surfaces and panels, belt sanders can also be inverted and held in place in a sanding frame or with a clamp to shape contoured or smaller workpieces.

Of the three sander sizes, the ¼-sheet sander is the best value. It will sand broad surfaces but also fit into tighter spaces than the other two sizes. Buy a sander with a grip that fits your hands well and with easy-to-use pad clamps. Some finish sanders come with dust collection canisters, but the performance is usually mediocre.

Orbital sanders are simple to use, even when you're just learning to sand. Basically, turn the machine on and apply it to the wood, then gently glide the sander over the work and keep it moving. Use the four-step sequence for sanding shown on page 177. There's no need to apply more pressure against the wood than the weight of the sander, or you'll leave scratches. If the sander doesn't seem to be working efficiently, switch to a coarser grit to remove deeper scratches, or try a clean piece of sandpaper.

Orbital finish sanders aren't as common as random-orbit sanders these days, but they can still produce good results for a small investment. With a little practice you'll quickly master these mild-mannered machines.

Random-orbit sanders can make quick work of a variety of smoothing tasks where belt sanders might be cumbersome or awkward.

Random-orbit sanders. If you buy only one sander for general smoothing tasks, make it a random-orbit sander. The pads on these machines are round rather than square. The pad spins as well as moves in an orbital pattern, which produces more rapid smoothing than orbital finish sanders and leaves fewer scratches. Better models have variable-speed control so you can adjust the speed to suit the job. As with other sanders, the key to using a random-orbit sander is to keep it moving over the worksurface. Even though the dual motion of the pad helps to minimize scratches, it will still leave tiny pigtail swirls if you bear down too hard or skip grits when you sand.

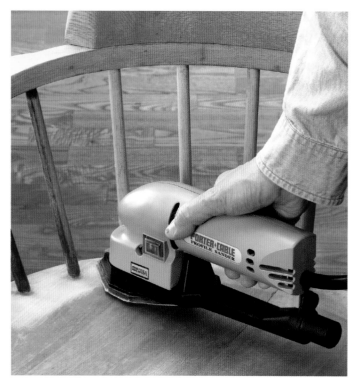

For best results, work through successively finer grits and remove the final tiny swirl scratches by hand.

Most consumer-grade random-orbit sanders have a palm-grip handle, and these are fine for general woodworking and finishing. Sanders are sized by the diameter of the pad, which ranges from 4 to 6 inches. Buy the size that suits your budget. Larger pads will help speed things along on larger surfaces, but a small sander will squeeze into tighter spaces.

You'll have to choose between sanders that take adhesive-backed or hook-and-loop sanding disks. The hook-and-loop style is more convenient. It's simple to switch between disks during sanding with hook-and-loop style, and the disks are reusable until the abrasive wears out. Adhesive-backed disks can't be reused, and you'll occasionally have to clean residual adhesive off the sanding pad.

When you need to sand into tight spaces or contours, or if disassembly isn't an option, as in refinishing projects, a detail sander may just be the perfect tool for the job.

Random-orbit sanding disks have five or eight holes in them, which aid in dust collection. The motor draws dust through these holes and into a collection canister. The number of holes doesn't really make a noticeable difference in efficiency, but you'll need to buy replacement disks with a hole pattern that matches your machine.

Some random-orbit sanders have a pad-brake feature that slows the pad down when you first apply it to the work to minimize scratches. It's a helpful feature to have. If your sander doesn't come with a pad brake, set the sander on the worksurface before turning it on to avoid scuffing the workpiece.

Detail sanders. Detail sanders are designed to reach into tight corners and narrow crevices as well as the contours of shaped moldings. These machines are the newcomers in the portable sanding market. They feature an orbital action, like finish sanders, and some have variable-speed control. Entry-level machines usually have a single triangular-shaped pad. Better models come with interchangeable foam pads in various contoured shapes for smoothing curves and corners.

These sanders can serve a helpful function, especially if you refinish furniture and need to sand without disassembling the project. But for woodworking, the easy way to sand details without a detail sander is to do your sanding before assembling the parts when all the surfaces are accessible.

Biscuit joiners

Here's a portable-tool category that has risen sharply in popularity among woodworkers over the past decade. Biscuit joiners use a circular blade to cut slots into two pieces of wood that will be joined together. Both workpieces

Biscuit joiners are becoming increasingly affordable—and thus more popular with hobbyist woodworkers.

receive a crescent-shaped slot cut, which you make by plunging the blade into the wood. Football-shaped "biscuits" of compressed birch or beech wood fit into the slots along with glue to assemble the joint. The biscuit swells up when it absorbs water from the glue to add more strength. Biscuit joiners are particularly useful for gluing up large panels from multiple boards. They're also ideal for making quick joints in cabinetry, face frames, and picture frames.

All biscuit joiners function similarly. A fence in front of the tool registers the blade's position relative to the thickness of the wood you're cutting. It also pivots on a protractor scale so you can install biscuits into beveled joints. The fence should be easy to adjust, lock firmly to its settings, and have markings that are large and legible. Look for small metal pins, rubber nibs, or an abraded surface where the tool presses against the wood to hold it in place for cutting. You don't want the tool to shift once you've got it aligned.

Biscuit joiners are designed to cut slots for three common biscuit sizes: #0, #10, and #20. Biscuits range in length from 1¾ to 2¼ inches, depending on the size. A dial on the tool lets you switch between these three sizes. It changes the blade's cutting depth so it cuts a longer or shorter slot. Some manufacturers also make biscuit joiners that cut slots for biscuits as small as ⅝ inch. These tiny sizes are practical mainly if you use biscuits to make mitered picture frames with small corner joints.

Helpful features to consider. Biscuit joiners generate a surprising amount of shavings and dust, so buy a machine that has a large, zippered collection bag. Some models can also be fitted with an oversized dust port for connecting to a shop vac.

Biscuits are sold in three common sizes and one micro size (above) for assembling joints with various part widths and thicknesses. A circular blade in the tool (below) plunges forward to cut a half-biscuit shaped slot in each part.

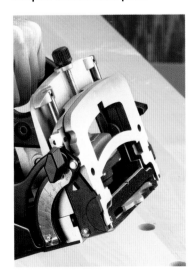

Stationary tools provide power, accuracy, and stability. The table saw is king among stationary machines.

Stationary power tools

Along with your portable power tools, you'll probably eventually own a few floor-standing or benchtop stationary tools. The design and function of these machines will improve your woodworking in various ways. For one, most stationary tools are outfitted with larger motors that are designed for rigorous or even constant use. Tables, bases, and important frame components are made of cast iron or heavy-gauge steel, which helps to damp vibration and create a sturdy platform to work from. The guides and fences on tools such as table saws, band saws, and drill presses will enable you to do more precise work than you can accomplish with portable power tools. Some functions of stationary tools, like resawing, simply can't be done with portable tools.

Table saws

Just as routers offer a degree of versatility unmatched by other portable power tools, table saws deserve similar accolades among stationary power tools. A table saw will allow you to make both rip and crosscuts, cut miter and bevel angles, and mill scores of different woodworking joints for your projects. About the only cutting functions you can't accomplish with a table saw saw are curves.

Table saws can be grouped into five general styles. From smallest and least expensive to largest, the various types of saws are benchtop saws, contractor's saws, cabinet saws, and an emerging mix of hybrids and multipurpose machines. For a tool that performs a fairly straightforward number of tasks, it's remarkable how many different models and varieties of table saws exist, in a range of prices and levels of quality. Choosing the right saw takes some honest assessment on your part. Your decision should be influenced by several factors, and key among these is saw performance. Think about the range of cutting tasks you typically do now and the kinds of advanced operations you might like to explore in the future. If remodeling jobs and light-duty woodworking are your fare, a lower-priced table saw might be a good fit. Budget-priced machines from any reputable manufacturer are powerful enough to rip and crosscut ¾-inch-thick lumber, especially softwoods such as pine and cedar. These machines are reasonably accurate. Since slicing up plywood and 2 × 4s for rough construction is less exacting work than making box joints and tenons for furniture, there's no sense in paying top dollar for accuracy that you don't need.

STATIONARY TOOLS TO BUY

Most woodworkers will agree that the table saw is the most versatile stationary power tool to own, which puts it at the top of the list of stationary tools to buy. Here are some other stationary machines you may eventually like to own:

1. Table saw or band saw
2. Jointer and planer
3. Drill press
4. Disk, spindle, or panel sander
5. Scroll saw

If your workshop needs to travel with you from time to time, a benchtop table saw may be the answer. Lightweight components and small proportions make it easy to lift into and out of a trunk or truck bed.

On the other hand, if you plan to pursue woodworking as a serious hobby or an eventual vocation, buy a table saw that will grow with you. Furniture building and cabinetry demand more versatility and accuracy from a table saw than making simple rips and crosscuts for remodeling or basic woodworking. Cutting through thick hardwood and spinning dado blade sets or molding heads also requires a saw motor with plenty of muscle. To cut precise furniture joints, you need a saw that holds its tuning, runs smoothly, and allows workpieces to be guided accurately against the rip fence and miter gauge.

To help choose the saw that's right for you, here's an overview of the five table saw styles from which to choose:

Benchtop saws feature scaled-down and lighter-duty versions of the features found on full-size tools.

Benchtop saws. If you're an occasional woodworker or looking for a table saw to tackle light- to medium-duty cutting tasks, a benchtop saw might be the perfect machine. These saws could also be the right choice if your "workshop" amounts to what you can carry in a truck bed or fit underneath a workbench. You can tuck a benchtop saw into the same space as a full-size microwave.

All benchtop saws these days have aluminum tabletops, and most have integrated extension wings. Table dimensions vary, but typically they are about 20 inches deep and 26 inches to 36 inches wide— about a foot shorter in both dimensions than larger saws. Benchtop saws have lighter-duty internal components made of pressed steel or cast alloy instead of iron. Blades mount directly onto the end of the motor's armature shaft, which is threaded to receive an arbor nut. In a sense, this direct-drive configuration makes benchtop saws function like inverted circular saws. The handwheels raise and lower or tilt the motor, just like the shoe on a circular saw. The bases on these saws are usually sheet metal or heavy plastic.

Lightweight components and smaller table dimensions make benchtop saws attractive to contractors who need their saws to be portable. In fact, most benchtop saws weigh just 50 to 75 pounds, so they're easy for most people to lift and carry without help. Motors on these saws are the universal type, just like routers, corded drills, and other handheld power tools. Universal motors take up less space than the larger, heavier induction motors that come with bigger saws, so they fit neatly into small saw bases. These powerplants develop short bursts of respectable horsepower—up to 2 horsepower in some cases—and draw around 15 amps at the plug.

Collapsible saw bases set benchtop saws to a comfortable working height on the job site. This saw is also equipped with table extensions to provide a larger surface area for cutting sheet materials and long stock.

Photo courtesy of DeWALT

A contractor's saw fitted with a rolling base offers power and stability but also a measure of mobility that's helpful for garage shops.

Features to consider in benchtop saws. As far as cutting capacities go, nearly all benchtop saws accept standard 10-inch-diameter saw blades and offer a 3-inch depth of cut at 90°. Buy a saw with a ⅝-inch diameter arbor. Some benchtops have ½-inch-diameter arbors, which limits your range of blade options to mostly what you can find for use in portable circular saws. Choose a benchtop saw with an arbor that's at least 1¼ inches long so it can accept dado blades as well as standard saw blades. Dado blades greatly increase a saw's versatility.

Not long ago, most benchtop saws came with low-quality rip fences that were difficult to align and adjust. Miter gauges were outfitted with flimsy, undersized heads and crude protractor scales. Now most benchtop saws come with precision rip fences and improved miter gauges. Other attractive features on pricier saws include rack-and-pinion table extensions that extend the tabletop for wider ripping, left-tilting arbors, and provisions for improved dust collection. Not all benchtop saws have better components, so beware of budget-priced saws, especially those sold by lesser-known tool manufacturers.

Contractor's saws. The next step up in capacity and size is the contractor's saw. Developed during the housing boom of the 1950s, these saws were a portable alternative to the heavier cast-iron saws of the time. Carpenters could transport a contractor's saw weighing 200 to 300 pounds from job site to job site much more easily than table saws designed for stationary use.

Contractor's saws offer the best combination of features, performance, and quality for the average woodworker. For starters, the saw tables are about the same size as cabinet saws—about 27 inches deep by 40 inches wide. These dimensions provide ample surface area for carrying out most ripping and cross-cutting tasks. Some saws come with side extension tables that increase the maximum ripping width from 24 inches to more than 50 inches. The extra room comes in handy for supporting and cutting full-size sheets of plywood. Tables are cast iron with steel or iron extension wings. Some iron wings are webbed, but the preferred style is solid. Most contractor's saws come with first-rate rip fences that are easy to keep aligned and require little or no routine tuning. Miter gauges on these saws tend to be much larger and heavier than those on benchtop saws for better workpiece support and improved accuracy.

Unlike either benchtop or cabinet saws, which have motors mounted beneath the table, contractor's saw motors hang behind the saw on a hinged plate. One long drive belt extends from the motor to the arbor pulley, and it's kept tensioned by the weight of the motor. Motors are induction style rather than universal, and they range from 1½ to 2 horsepower. Most are the TEFC (totally enclosed, fan cooled) variety, which requires no lubrication or periodic cleaning. These larger motors deliver ample power to drive standard 10-inch saw blades through all types of wood up to around 3⅛ inches thick. They're also well suited for spinning heavier dado blade sets and molding heads. Induction motors are typically wired for regular 115-volt outlets, but they can be rewired fairly easily to 230-volt service, which cuts their amperage draw in half. Motors run cooler and ultimately longer when wired to the higher voltage.

Contractor's saws have induction motors that hang behind the machine. They're quieter to operate than the universal motors on benchtop table saws.

Contractor's saws have open bases and legs that place the saw table height at around 34 inches. The open base style and legs help shed some pounds off the machine, but these saws are far too heavy to be called portable. You'll need help to tote one up and down a flight of stairs or lift it into a truck bed. A rolling base makes these saws easy to move into position for cutting and then out of the way for storage.

A new, middle-of-the-road contractor's saw can be had for around $500, which is significantly cheaper than buying a cabinet saw and only a bit more expensive than most benchtop models. There are a host of aftermarket accessories available for contractor's saws, including microadjust rip fences, guards and splitters, precision miter gauges, and tenoning jigs, which make these workhorses even more accurate and versatile. Most contractor's saws have arbors that tilt the blade to the right, but some new models now feature left-tilting

A cabinet saw offers unmatched power and precision, making it the usual choice for professionals.

mechanisms. All this said, contractor's saws are a great value for your tool dollars. If you are more than an occasional woodworker but don't have aspirations beyond a hobby, buy a contractor's saw.

Cabinet saws. Cabinet saws have been the preferred table saws of professional woodworkers for more than a century. While contractor's saws provide solid performance for a fair price, they can't match the precision, reliability, and power offered by these flagships of the table saw family. Cabinet saws get their name because the bases are fully enclosed. The undercarriage and motor are accessible through a door in the cabinet or a hinged or removable motor cover. Closed bases provide a rigid platform for the machine and help capture the sawdust. All cabinet saws come with a port or opening on the cabinet for connecting to a dust-collection system. Enclosing the motor also helps the saw run more quietly.

A door or hinged cover on a cabinet saw provides access to the motor and undercarriage for routine cleaning and maintenance tasks.

Sheer heft is probably the single biggest attribute that sets cabinet saws apart from the rest. Table and extension wings are always made of cast iron, and so are the important inner components that hold the blade in position and allow it to tilt and move up and down.

Cabinet saws are equipped with large, heavy-duty induction motors. Motor sizes range from 2 to 7 horsepower, and they are capable of producing substantial amounts of torque. Two or three drive belts deliver this power to the blade arbor. The shorter cabinet saw belts provide more efficient power transfer than the long contractor saw belts. Stout undercarriage parts prevent the motor and belts from literally twisting the arbor cradle out of alignment, which would skew the blade's orbit.

Cabinet saws come in both right- and left-tilt styles, depending on your preference. You can buy saws that accept 12-, 14- or 16-inch blades, but 10-inch-capacity machines are still the standard woodworking choice. Most of these machines are wired for 230-volt electric service. You can outfit a cabinet saw with a rolling base to make it somewhat portable, but moving 500 or more pounds of table saw around the shop is a chore you won't want to do often.

Owning a cabinet saw is a tantalizing thought, especially if you're a woodworker who demands precision and long tool life. A cabinet saw will likely be the last saw you'll ever need to buy, and it may even pass down a generation or two. However, adding one to your shop will set you back at least $800, and twice this amount or more for a professional-grade machine.

Hybrid table saws are the new kids on the block, blending the lighter weight of contractor's saws with the stouter undercarriages of cabinet saws. Larger motors, improved dust collection, and more standard features are other factors that put these new saws a step ahead of many contractor's saws.

Photo courtesy of DeWALT

Hybrid saws & multipurpose machines. A new category of hybrid table saws is now emerging to bridge the gap between cabinet and contractor's saws. Essentially, these hybrids look like a cabinet saw from the outside but share some aspects of both cabinet and contractor's saws inside. They also sport a more affordable price tag. The motor and undercarriage are concealed inside a partial or full cabinet, and the rip fence, miter gauge, and table casting are more robust than you'll find on the average contractor's saw. Inside the base, the motor and cradle configurations loosely resemble a contractor's saw. Motors hang from a pair of steel tubes or from a modified iron cradle and trunnion assembly that bolts to the table. The induction motors on these machines fall in the 1¾ to 2 horsepower range, so they're a bit larger than many contractor's saw motors but smaller than a cabinet saw's motor.

Aside from conventional-looking table saws, there are also numerous multipurpose machines that combine several stationary tools into one compact package. These tools have a single heavy-duty induction motor that drives all the different tool functions. Usually the motor slides on a pair of tubes to engage the various drive mechanisms of separate tools. You'll get a table saw, lathe, and drill press as standard equipment. The tool can also function as a jointer and band saw, but these features must be purchased separately.

Single-motor multipurpose machines convert from one woodworking function to another, but many of the tools that fit these machines must be purchased as add-ons. A table saw, drill press, lathe, and horizontal borer are standard equipment.

Photos courtesy of Shopsmith Inc.

Band saws are excellent tools for making a wide variety of cuts. And unlike rotating-blade tools, band saws do not kick back.

Band saws

Compared with table saws, band saws are underrated machines. They are nearly as versatile, generally quieter, and much safer to operate. A band saw can make rip cuts, crosscuts, and angle cuts, but it excels at curve-cutting. Some woodworkers use their band saws for resawing, a technique that involves slicing thin sheets of veneer from the face of a board. A band saw can even be set up to cut dovetail joints.

Band saws are so named because instead of using a circular-shaped blade, they have a thin, flexible band-style blade that spins around two large flywheels. All the cutting forces are directed toward the band saw table as the blade passes through it, which eliminates the kickback hazards of circular-bladed tools like table saws. Band saws cut a thin kerf, which makes them cleaner to use than other saw styles and allows you to save more wood and produce less sawdust.

Common band saw features. On most band saws, the table pivots for making angled cuts while the blade angle remains the same. A protractor-style scale beneath the table establishes the table angle. Many band saws come with rip fences, just like table saws, and the band saw table has a miter gauge slot to assist in crosscutting or cutting angles.

As the blade spins, guides above and below the saw table keep the blade tracking properly on the flywheels. Both sets of guides can be adjusted to suit blades of different widths, and the upper guides also move up and down along with a solid blade guard to minimize blade exposure during cutting. The typical blade-guide configuration has three parts: a bearing behind the blade that keeps it from drifting backward and two blocks or bearings on each side to minimize flexing. The upper flywheel is spring-loaded to maintain tension on the blade. A hand wheel or knob adjusts tension on the upper wheel. Both flywheels and most of the blade are enclosed behind doors to help contain the dust.

Band saws that are made for frequent or heavy-duty use will have frames made of cast iron or welded steel. Some benchtop band saws have cast-aluminum frames, but iron or steel frames offer better rigidity and dampen more vibration.

Choosing a band saw. Band saws are manufactured in both benchtop and floor-standing models in a variety of sizes. To pick the right one for you, you'll have to consider each of the following factors.

Benchtop band saws offer reasonable cutting height and throat clearance at an affordable price, but they don't have the stout frames and springs necessary for heavy-duty operations like resawing or cutting thick lumber. You'll need a full-size floor-standing band saw for these operations.

Regarding sizing, band saws are categorized by the diameter of their flywheels. Benchtop band saws have the smallest flywheels, which range from 8 to 12 inches. Band saws with larger flywheels are all floor-standing machines, with wheel sizes range from 14 to 24 inches or more. The larger the wheels, the greater the distance between the blade and rear housing of the tool. This distance is called throat depth. Large throat depths are an asset, because the saw can cut wider workpieces or deeper curves before the housing gets in the way.

Another factor of saw sizing is the distance between the table and the upper blade guide when the guide is raised to its highest point. This measurement determines the maximum workpiece thickness the saw can handle as well as the widest wood it can resaw. Floor-standing band saws will provide at least 6 inches of clearance here, and as much as 15 inches, depending on the machine.

For years, the band saw of choice among woodworkers has been the 14-inch size with a cast-iron frame and table. These machines offer a good pairing of resaw and throat capacity at a reasonable price. Most 14-inch saws come with ¾- to 1½-horsepower motors that offer enough power for general cutting. The popularity of this saw makes it easy to find a wide range of blades that don't cost a fortune. You can also upgrade a 14-inch saw

One advantage to buying a 14-inch floor-standing band saw is that you'll have a wide range of blade widths and tooth configurations to choose from. Since this is the most common woodworking band saw, blades are reasonably priced and easy to find.

with precision blade guides, rolling bases, quick-release blade tensioners, and even kits that extend the length of the column for resawing wider boards.

Benchtop band saws are light-duty tools. Some are made in a three-wheel, triangulated design that provides greater throat capacity than a two-wheel saw, but the blades tend to break more quickly. Unless you're certain that you'll only need a band saw occasionally, it's better to buy a full-size band saw instead of a benchtop model.

Regardless of which machine you buy, band saws all have a set of upper and lower blade guides to ensure that the blade will track straight and true. These guides will need adjustment every time you change blade sizes.

Jointers

If you plan to glue up large wood panels for your projects, a jointer is a must-have tool. It's also invaluable for flattening board faces to true them up before thickness planing (see page 83 for more on this technique). Essentially, a jointer works like a giant inverted hand plane. The machine has a cylindrical head that holds from two to four replaceable knives. Once the planer head is spinning, sliding boards over the jointer tables slices a thin layer of wood from board faces or edges. The infeed and outfeed tables on a jointer are both adjustable, with the infeed table kept slightly lower than the outfeed table. The difference in table height establishes the thickness of shavings that are removed from the wood. Jointers have a fence for supporting workpieces squarely, or you can tip the fence for jointing beveled edges, if necessary. These machines operate at a single speed that ranges from 4,000 to 6,000 rpm, depending on the model and motor size. When properly tuned and outfitted with sharp knives, a jointer produces perfectly flat, smooth board faces or edges that are ready for glue up.

Jointers are sized by the length of their knives. The knives on full-size jointers range from 5 to 12 inches long. As the length of the knives increases, so do the lengths of the infeed and outfeed tables, the motor capacity, and the jointer's overall proportion. A few manufacturers also make benchtop jointers with shorter knives and tables. Jointers in the 12-inch size are really outside the realm of hobbyist woodworking and cost several thousand dollars. Most hobbyist woodworkers buy 6- or 8-inch jointers, which fall in the middle of the jointer spectrum.

Jointers can make quick work of flattening out-of-flat board faces and edges.

Choosing a jointer. Buying a benchtop jointer may seem tempting from a cost standpoint, but the combined table length will be less than 3 feet. This is too short to provide enough support for making larger project parts or flattening longer boards. The knife length on a benchtop machine will be about 3 inches, which also limits your ability to flatten board faces wider than 3 inches. The better investment is to buy a floor-standing 6-inch jointer. Any model you choose will come with a leg stand or enclosed steel base with dust collection. You'll get around 4 feet of combined table length, cast-iron construction, and a continuous-duty motor. The next step up—8-inch

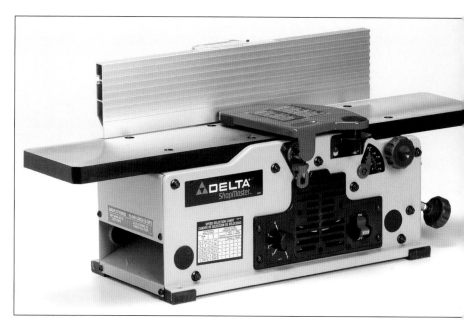

jointers—offers even longer tables with a bed that's wide enough to handle most boards you'll commonly buy, but these machines are often double the price of 6-inch jointers.

Benchtop jointers are more economical than full-size jointers, but they offer shorter and narrower tables as well as smaller motors.

Whichever jointer you buy, make sure the fence and tables are easy to adjust. The tables will have either hand wheels or levers for moving them up and down. Wheels tend to offer more precise depth control. Investigate how to change the knives on a jointer before you buy it. Installing and setting jointer knives can be difficult, usually requiring a specialized knife-setting jig. Some machines make knife replacement easier than others. It's also a good idea to check the table and fence surfaces for flatness with a good straightedge before you buy or as soon as you set up the machine. Generally warping isn't an issue with good-quality cast-iron machinery, but occasionally the metal will distort during manufacturing. Return a jointer that has a warped fence or tables.

All jointers feature a revolving cutterhead with two to four knives that do the work. These knives must be kept razor sharp and perfectly aligned for a jointer to produce flat edges and faces on workpieces.

Generally, you'll keep the fence on a jointer set square to the bed for flattening workpieces. When necessary, the fence can also be tilted and locked to other angles on full-size jointers and some benchtop machines.

Thickness planers are the perfect companions for joiners—and they're now quite affordable.

Thickness planers have the cutterhead mounted above the workpiece rather than in the bed. Two to four knives mount in the cutterhead to do the work. A pair of drive rollers on either side of the cutterhead pull workpieces through.

Thickness planers

In the last 20 years or so, thickness planers have evolved from giant machines found only in factories, trade schools, and professional furniture shops into benchtop models that you can lift onto a workbench and plug into an ordinary wall outlet. Portable thickness planers are perfect companions for jointers. You really should have one of each for flattening boards and modifying lumber thickness.

Thickness planers consist of a motor carriage that drives a pair of rubber feed rollers on either side of a spinning cutterhead. The rollers push and pull the lumber past the planer knives, which sheer off the high and low areas creating a flat board face. The cutter assembly raises and lowers over a fixed table on two or four threaded posts. Usually, you must crank the motor carriage up and down to set the depth of cut, which reads on a scale in front of the machine. A few new planers have power-assisted depth adjustment features that eliminate hand cranking.

Planers are similar to jointers in the way they are sized; the knife length classifies the machine size. Typical home-shop planers have 12- to 13½-inch knives. Larger 15- to 20-inch planers certainly exist, buy they're more than you'll need for a home woodshop. Portable planers will have two- or three-knife cutterheads. The knives are typically disposable and sharpened on both edges so you can flip them and use the second edge before replacement is necessary. Most planers have a pair of infeed and outfeed tables to support wood as it enters and leaves the machine as well as a dust hood that connects the machine to a dust collector hose. Leg stands come with some planers, or you can set them on a cabinet, bench, or a workstand you make yourself.

Choosing a thickness planer. Here are the features to look for in a thickness planer: Buy a planer with knives that are easy to access and replace. In general, disposable planer knives are easy to change and require no finicky depth adjustment, like jointers do. Four-post planers are preferable to machines with two posts, because the additional posts anchor the motor carriage on all four ends of the machine.

Some new planers have two-speed transmissions—a fast speed for planing lumber to rough thickness and a slow speed for creating glass-smooth final surfaces. The two-speed feature is worth the extra investment. Most planers have a motor carriage lock that helps to minimize sniping. "Snipe" refers to the tendency of planers to take a deeper "bite" near the ends of a board—a bite that you'll need to cut off or sand away. You'll usually have to engage a lever to activate the snipe lock, but some models are now engineered with posts that lock the carriage at any height setting automatically.

Make sure the planer you buy either comes with a dust port or bag for removing or collecting the shavings. Planers are the messiest machines in the shop and create a mountain of shavings in a matter of minutes. The shavings can also get trapped under the outfeed roller and leave tiny dents in the finished surface of the wood unless they are drawn out of the machine. If you don't buy a dust collector when you add a planer to your shop, it will probably be one of your next major tool investments down the road. Or buy a planer with a built-in impellor that blows the chips into a dust bag.

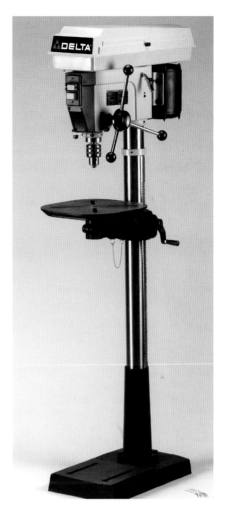

Floor-standing (above) and bench-top (below) drill presses perform drilling operations that are difficult or impossible with a hand drill.

Drill presses

Drilling straight holes or drilling at a consistent angle into a workpiece with a portable drill is harder than it seems. A drill press takes all the frustration out of the process. By rotating the drill press table and clamping your project parts to it, you can lock the drilling angle precisely. What's equally helpful is that the drill press quill—the column that holds the chuck and moves up and down—can be set to stop the drill bit at a given hole depth. The machine controls all the drilling variables, including speed settings. A drill press also allows you to drill oversize holes with bits that would be unmanageable or unsafe to use in a portable drill. You can even use a drill press for making mortises (see pages 50 and 163) or drum sanding with the right attachments. Neither of these tasks is practical with a hand drill.

Choosing a drill press. Drill presses are sized by the distance between the center of the chuck and the vertical column that forms the tool's spine. Manufacturers double this span, so a drill press with an 8-inch span between the chuck and column will be sold as a 16-inch model. This measurement is called the throat capacity. A tool with a 16-inch throat capacity will drill anywhere in a 16-inch-wide workpiece without the column interfering.

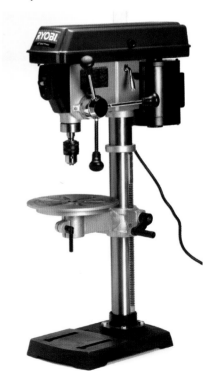

Drill presses are made in both benchtop and floor-standing models. Benchtop machines generally have smaller throat capacities and a shorter maximum vertical distance between the table and the chuck when the table is lowered as far as it will go. Benchtop drill presses have a shorter quill travel, too—the distance you can plunge the chuck downward. However, these smaller capacities are only limitations if you build large projects or use your

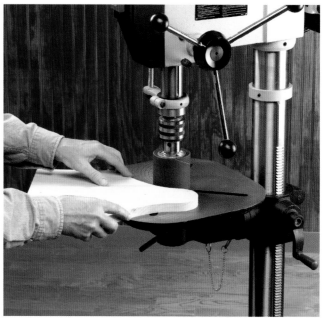

In addition to boring straight holes (above), drill presses can also sand (right) and cut mortises for joinery (below) with the proper sanding drums and mortising attachments. Any floor-standing machine can accomplish all three operations.

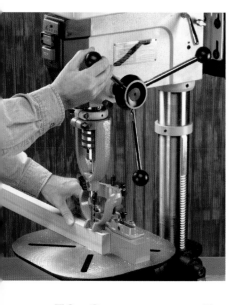

drill press with accessories like mortisers that aren't made for the benchtop versions. Most benchtop drill presses are still built for heavy-duty use, take up minimal storage space on a bench, and cost about half of what you'll pay for a full-size machine.

Benchtop drill presses range in size from 8 to 12 inches, but a few manufacturers make 14-, 15-, and 16-inch machines, as well. Floor-standing drill presses are sized from 13 to 20 inches. A full-size drill press will accept bits with shanks as large as ⅝ or even ¾ inch in diameter, but these bits are uncommon to hobbyists. Even benchtop models can accept bits with ½-inch shanks, which really are as large as you'll ever need for woodworking.

Most drill presses have variable-speed control, an important feature for using a full range of bits or for working in a variety of materials including wood, metal, and plastic. A pair of pulley clusters on top of the tool sets the number of speed options. To change speeds, you loosen and slide the motor forward and move a rubber drive belt between the different pulley sizes on each cluster. A few drill presses have a centrifugal clutch instead of pulleys to change speeds at the turn of a dial, but these models are more expensive than the pulley variety.

When shopping for either a benchtop or floor-standing drill press, look for a machine with a table that's easy to swivel off of square. It should also move up and down the column easily. The best table-raising mechanisms are geared cranks that raise and lower the table on a rack-and-pinion mechanism.

Make sure the drill press you buy has a depth-stop system so you can drill stopped holes easily. Depth stops are either engineered into the handle that moves the quill or as a threaded rod with stop nuts. Either style works well. For intricate work, you'll also appreciate having a light on your drill press. Many floor-standing machines have built-in lights, or buy a magnetic lamp and attach it to your machine for better visibility.

Benchtop disk sanders are ideal for sanding flat or convex edges on workpieces.

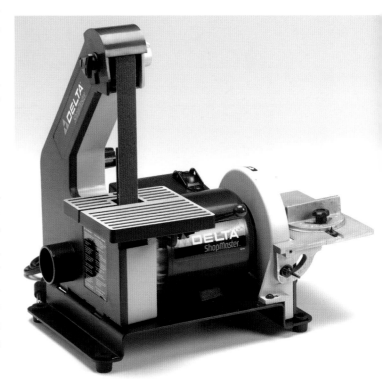

Oscillating spindle sanders can sand inside cutouts as well as both convex and concave edges.

Stationary sanders

While it's possible to clamp a portable belt sander to a workbench or sanding frame and use it in a stationary way, its range of function won't match that of sanders built for stationary use. They consist of three principal varieties: disk sanders, oscillating spindle sanders, and combination sanders.

Disk sanders. Disk sanders are fairly compact machines that can be set on a benchtop or a leg stand. The motor spins a 12-inch-diameter metal platen in one direction. You mount adhesive-backed sanding disks to the platen, which are available in several grits up to 120-grit. A cast-iron table in front of the platen provides workpiece support. It can be tilted and locked for bevel-sanding. A miter slot on the table enables you to sand square corners and refine miter angles. You can use a disk sander for creating flat or convex surfaces, but it won't sand internal or concave curves. Most models are relatively inexpensive compared to other stationary tools. All these machines will come with a dust port for connecting to a shop vacuum or dedicated dust collector. Some have a dust canister designed for capturing even the finest dust particles.

Oscillating spindle sanders. Oscillating spindle sanders work like a drum sander attachment on a drill press with the added advantage that the spindle also moves up and

Combination sanders package a belt and disk sander into one machine. A few newer models also add an oscillating spindle sander to increase versatility.

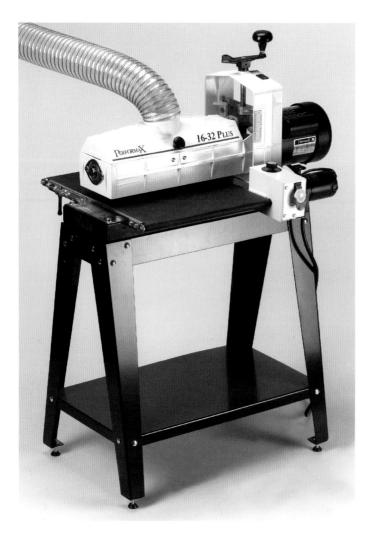

Panel sanders aren't for most hobbyist budgets, but they make quick and accurate work of sanding large panels flat.

Oscillating spindle sanders come with several rubber drums of different diameters that accept pre-formed sanding tubes in various grits.

down. The dual action helps to minimize scratches and speed up the sanding process. Typically, you mount rubber drums in different diameters onto a metal rod, which forms the spindle. Sandpaper sleeves fit over the drums and are held in place by tightening a nut on the shaft, which compresses the drum. A large worktable surrounds the spindle. On benchtop machines, the table usually is fixed in place, perpendicular to the spindle. Spindle sanders should also be equipped with a set of throatplates that fit around the range of different drum sizes.

Spindle sanders are ideal for sanding both convex and concave curves. You may not need a spindle sander often, but sooner or later you'll be glad to have one in your shop. Benchtop versions are moderately priced, compared with other stationary tools.

Combination sanders. These machines usually combine two sanders in one—a 4- to 6-inch-wide belt sander and a 6- or 12-inch disk sander. One motor drives both the disk and belt, usually at a fixed speed for each sanding option. The belt sander works like a portable belt sander. A pair of rollers— one driven by the motor and the other spring-loaded—maintains tension on the sanding belt. The belt assembly pivots from horizontal to vertical to provide greater versatility, and often the machine will have a small adjustable worktable or stop bar for use with the sanding belt. Belts come in a full range of grits and are easy to replace by flipping a tension lever. A few combination sanders also now include a spindle sander to create a complete system in one tool.

Panel sanders. One other sander style not commonly found in hobbyist shops is the panel sander. This machine has a drum-shaped sanding platen mounted above a feed belt that draws workpieces through the machine. Panel sanders are designed to sand wide glued-up panels for tabletops, doors, and whenever other large solid-wood panels are required. While a panel sander is a handy machine to own, you'd probably need to build large projects on a regular basis to justify the $500-and-up price tag of these tools. Otherwise, a thickness planer and a couple portable sanders make good substitutes for a panel sander. Or you might consider taking a large panel to a millwork company, lumberyard, or cabinet shop and have it sanded there for a nominal fee.

Scroll saws

No other stationary or portable power saw can beat a scroll saw for making intricate and tiny cuts. Scroll saws are also the perfect tools for making internal cutouts, where the starter cut can't happen from the edge or end of the board. Unlike band saws, scroll saws use short, straight blades more in keeping with a jig saw, only the width and thickness of the blades are much finer, and blades are held under tension on both ends. The saw uses a deep-throated, U-shaped arm to drive the blade in a reciprocating motion. A clamp on each end of the arm locks the blade in place. Blade changing is generally quick and easy—a real benefit of scroll saws. All it takes to begin an internal cutout is a starter hole drilled through a workpiece. Feed the blade through the hole, clamp the blade in the saw, and you're ready to begin cutting.

Scroll saws excel at making intricate curved cuts as well as internal cutouts.

The major differences among scroll saws are the maximum depth of cut and the design of the arm. Scroll saws range in size from 16 to 20 inches or more. The number refers to the distance from the blade to the back housing that covers the arm assembly. For hobbyist use, a 16-inch saw should provide ample capacity.

Choosing a scroll saw. When shopping for a scroll saw, it's a good idea to spend some time comparing the subtle features. Choose a saw with easy-to-access blade clamps that adjust without extra tools. Make sure the blade tensioning mechanism is also easy to adjust. Scroll saw blades tend to break relatively easily and wear out faster than the blades on other woodworking tools. The faster and easier it is to change blades, the better.

When you buy your saw, buy a variety pack of blades at the same time. Scroll saw blades come in a wide range of tooth configurations and tooth counts. It's surprising how differently these blades cut, so you'll want to have a good selection on hand to match the material and cutting task. You'll see that blades are made either with or without a cross pin on both ends. Many scroll saws will handle both types of blades, but the pin style is faster and easier to install.

Most scroll saws these days have variable-speed motors, which is beneficial for fine cutting. You'll discover that the specific blade and motor speed you choose will need to vary, depending on whether you're cutting metal, plastic, or wood. Motor sizing varies, but don't let it influence your choice significantly. Scroll saws are intended for delicate work where horsepower isn't a major concern.

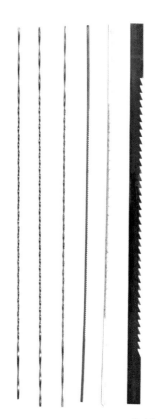

Scroll saw blades are available in various tooth counts, configurations, and sizes for cutting a wide range of materials, including wood, sheet materials, soft metal, and plastic.

Chapter 3
CHOOSING LUMBER AND SHEET GOODS

For many woodworkers, the experience of buying lumber is just as exciting as unpacking a long-awaited tool. There's something gratifying about driving to the lumberyard with list in hand, then rummaging through the stacks for the best boards. The fragrance of freshly sawn wood, the whine of a saw somewhere in the background, and aisles upon aisles of woodworking supplies really bolster the creative spirit. Once you've got that fresh stack of lumber home, waiting until you have time to commit it to a project can be a challenge.

In the midst of all the excitement, it's important to choose lumber thoughtfully. First, become familiar with the species of lumber available at your local home center or lumberyard. Most lumber retailers will stock at least a half-dozen different species, and the options can vary from region to region. Some lumber types will be appropriate for your project, while others will not. Better lumberyards will offer several grades of the same species, sometimes in limited sizes and with varying degrees of surfacing already done at the mill. You won't find a list of the best uses on the lumber rack tag, so it's up to you or a helpful store employee to know which wood to select.

Picking what's best for your application will also depend on the tools you have to use, the limits of your budget, and even your skill level, to some degree.

This chapter will help you sort through these types of real-world issues. You'll also learn about various sources of lumber beyond the local home center, in case you can't find what you need there. Once you find a source, you'll need to know how to decipher the lumber industry's grading and sizing systems, which are covered here. And finally, it's important to know how to store lumber wisely until you need to use it.

This chapter will also cover the many sheet-good options available to you. Sometimes plywood or other composite wood products are a better or more economical choice than wood for a project. There are lots of options here, too. Learn more about them in these pages.

Hardwoods vs. softwoods

Lumber can be grouped into two broad categories—hardwoods and softwoods—based on a botanical distinction. Hardwoods are those species that come from deciduous, or leaf-bearing, trees that produce fruits, flowers, or nuts. Common North American hardwood lumber includes oak, maple, cherry, ash, walnut, beech, birch, and poplar. There are many less common Western hardwoods as well, including butternut, mesquite, pear, holly, and sycamore. Other countries log innumerable hardwood species, too. Some of these exotics include teak, cocobolo, mahogany, ebony, rosewood, purpleheart, and bubinga. You can find them through mail-order houses or specialty lumberyards. Most are expensive and may be available only in limited sizes.

Softwoods come from conifers—the large family of cone-bearing trees that have needles rather than leaves. Pines and firs of many sorts, redwood, cypress, and cedar are typical North American softwoods made into board lumber. Because these species are well suited for construction purposes, all lumber used for framing and rough construction comes from softwood trees. They're sufficiently strong for structural applications, yet still are easy to work with common hand or power tools. Another advantage is that conifers grow rapidly and develop straighter trunks and branches than deciduous trees. More softwood trees can be planted per acre than hardwood trees, so they produce a higher lumber yield in less time.

It's a common misconception that hardwoods are called hardwoods because the wood is hard, while softwoods are soft. It's true that many hardwoods are more difficult to machine than softwoods, but the distinction actually has nothing to do with hardness or workability. Southern yellow pine, for instance, is a heavy, dense softwood used for stair treads and large framing lumber. It machines and accepts fasteners like hardwood. Walnut and poplar are common hardwoods, but they can be routed and sawn as easily as cedar or redwood. Even pricing isn't a good indicator of hardwoods or softwoods. More softwood is manufactured into building materials than furniture-grade lumber, but what does become lumber can be quite expensive. For example, clear sugar pine lumber is just as costly as premium cherry or white oak. Actually, the basic economics of supply and demand have more to do with lumber pricing than the particular species of wood or even its grade designation.

Lumber can be divided into two botanical categories: softwoods and hardwoods. Softwood lumber comes from coniferous, or cone-bearing, trees. Hardwood lumber comes from broad-leafed trees that produce fruits, flowers, or nuts.

Choosing what wood to use

Hardwoods generally end up as indoor furniture, cabinetry, turnings, and trimwork because the wood grain and figure are highly desirable. Softwoods tend to become outdoor furniture, children's projects, and other sorts of utility or painted projects. However, these are merely guidelines. So, what species should you choose for a particular project? The answer isn't cut and dried, and usually you'll have many options. To help pare down your choices, here are some questions to ask yourself:

Is this an indoor or outdoor project? If you're building outdoor furniture or other yard and garden projects, the most durable outdoor woods include Western red cedar, redwood, cypress, and white oak. These woods contain natural oils or tannins that resist rot and help repel insects. Boatbuilding woods such as teak and mahogany are excellent choices as well, but they are much more expensive than the common weather-resistant species. If you're building an outdoor project that won't come in contact with food or skin, consider using pressure-treated lumber. It takes paint well once the infused chemicals dry, and the wood tends to be warranted for decades against rotting.

Will the project be painted or receive a clear finish? For painted projects, choose lumber that has a smooth texture without a heavy grain pattern. Ideally, the lumber should sand and finish so smoothly that the grain entirely disappears. Good paint-grade hardwoods include poplar, birch, and aspen. These also tend to be less expensive than hardwoods with more attractive grain patterns. Softwoods generally produce a blotchy, uneven grain pattern when they're finished with stain, but they make excellent, economical painted woods. Pines, firs, and other "white woods" are good candidates for paint finishes. Another option for painted projects is to build them from sheet material such as medium-density fiberboard (see page 69) instead of solid wood.

If you plan to finish your project with stain and a transparent topcoat, the best wood choices are those that accept stain evenly without blotching. Oak, ash, and mahogany are good all-around candidates for stain, but cherry, maple, and pine sometimes absorb stain unevenly.

What thicknesses and proportions of lumber does your project require? Virtually all the board lumber you'll find at a home center or general-purpose lumberyard will be milled to ¾ inch thick. There may be a small display of "craft" lumbers in ¼- and ½-inch thicknesses made of oak or poplar as well as laminated blanks in a few sizes up to 3 inches thick. Lengths will be limited to about 3 feet. If you need thin lumber in larger sizes, some specialty yards will plane down thicker stock for you for a nominal planing fee. Or find another woodworker with a surface planer to plane down your wood. For lumber thicker than ¾ inch, shop at a lumberyard that specializes in furniture lumbers, or glue several ¾-inch-thick pieces together and plane down the lamination to the desired thickness.

Which project parts show? It's always been a common practice in furniture building to reserve the most attractive wood for the parts that show: drawer faces, aprons, tabletops, doors, legs, and so forth. If your project includes parts that won't show or are usually concealed, consider buying less expensive wood and using it here. Poplar and pine are often integrated into projects made from more expensive hardwoods to serve as "secondary" woods for drawer sides and bottoms, internal framework, and back panels. It's a good way to save money without compromising function or durability.

What does the budget dictate? Lumber is expensive, particularly if you buy it completely surfaced. Sometimes sticker shock will push you over the edge and make your choice of lumber obvious. When tallying up the amount of lumber you'll need, factor in another 20% to 30% more wood. The overage invariably gets used in the end. If the price is out of reach, consider using a more economical lumber and staining it to match the color of a costlier wood.

How do tools and your skills impact wood choice? Some woods are easier to work with than others. Resist the urge to buy exotics, or even hardwoods, for those first few projects. As lovely as they are, exotics are expensive, and many are tougher than nails to cut, drill, and fasten together. Some present special gluing and finishing hassles too. Same story goes for domestic hardwoods such as oak, maple, ash, and beech. While it's certainly possible to work these woods with a portable drill and circular saw, the tasks are much easier with a drill press and table saw. Softwoods such as pine or cedar are more forgiving choices in the beginning, and they produce attractive projects more economically.

ASH

Origin: Southeastern United States
Properties: Straight-grained with coarse texture. Shock-resistant. Moderately heavy and hard.
Workability/Finishing: Takes fasteners, glue, and finishes well. Excellent for steam-bending and turning.
Uses: Tool handles, baseball bats, general furniture construction, veneer.
Price: Inexpensive

ASPEN

Origin: United States and Canada
Properties: Tight-grained and moderately hard.
Workability/Finishing: Takes routed profiles, fasteners, glues, and painted finishes well. Stained finishes produce blotchy, uneven appearance.
Uses: Good secondary wood for furniture construction.
Price: Inexpensive

BIRCH (YELLOW)

Origin: Northeastern United States
Properties: Straight-grained with even texture. Dense and heavy.
Workability/Finishing: Easily worked with both hand and power tools. Good for turning and steam-bending. Takes glue and clear finishes well.
Uses: General furniture construction, veneer, shop jigs.
Price: Inexpensive to moderate

CHERRY

Origin: Eastern and Southern United States
Properties: Even to figured grain pattern and moderately hard. Warpage common during drying. Good steam-bending properties.
Workability/Finishing: Excellent working characteristics with hand or power tools. Takes finishes well.
Uses: General furniture construction, turning, veneer.
Price: Moderate

HICKORY
Origin: Southern United States, Mexico, and Central America
Properties: Hard and dense with varied grain pattern. Excellent shock resistance.
Workability/Finishing: Will dull steel blades and bits quickly. Machine with carbide cutters.
Uses: Tool handles, sporting equipment, veneer, furniture construction.
Price: Moderate where regionally plentiful

MAPLE (HARD)
Origin: Northeastern United States and Canada
Properties: Dense, with straight, curly, or wavy grain patterns and good figure.
Workability/Finishing: Can dull steel blades and bits. Predrill before installing screws or nails. Uneven grain pattern can produce blotching with stain finishes.
Uses: Flooring, butcher block and cutting boards, general furniture construction, veneer.
Price: Moderate to expensive, depending on figure

POPLAR
Origin: Northern Canada and Alaska
Properties: Moderately hard with fine grain pattern and varied color.
Workability/Finishing: Works easily with steel blades and bits. Takes paint finishes well, but stains will produce blotching.
Uses: Good secondary wood for furniture construction, toys, shop jigs, pallets, and crates.
Price: Inexpensive

RED OAK
Origin: Eastern United States and Canada
Properties: Varied density and grain pattern, from straight to slight figure. Large open pore structure on end grain.
Workability/Finishing: Works easily with sharp steel or carbide blades and bits. Takes fasteners, glue, and stain finishes well. Coarse texture can lead to splintering.
Uses: General furniture construction, veneer, flooring.
Price: Moderate

WALNUT

Origin: Eastern United States and Canada, Central and South America
Properties: Moderately soft and dense with varied grain pattern and color.
Workability/Finishing: Works easily with hand and power tools. Good for turning. Exceptional for clear finishes.
Uses: General furniture construction, gun stocks, musical instruments, carving and turning, veneer.
Price: Moderate to expensive

WHITE OAK
Origin: Central and Eastern United States
Properties: Moderately heavy and hard with varied grain pattern and texture. Striking medullary rays when quarter-sawn. Naturally weather- and rot-resistant.
Workability/Finishing: Works easily with sharp steel or carbide blades and bits. Good for stain finishes.
Uses: General interior or exterior furniture construction.
Price: Moderate to expensive

WESTERN SOFTWOODS

AROMATIC CEDAR

Origin: Eastern United States and Canada
Properties: Soft with variable grain pattern and texture. Emits distinct aroma that deters moths.
Workability/Finishing: Works easily with hand or power tools. Takes glues and clear finishes well, but fasteners should be coated or stainless to prevent corrosion.
Uses: Closet and chest linings, veneer, turning, paneling.
Price: Inexpensive

CEDAR (WESTERN RED)

Origin: Pacific Northwest into Canada
Properties: Soft, straight-grained with coarse texture. Lightweight. Naturally weather- and insect-resistant.
Workability/Finishing: Similar working properties to aromatic cedar. Can be stained, primed and painted, or left unfinished and allowed to weather to a silvery gray.
Uses: Exterior furniture, arbors, decks, fences.
Price: Inexpensive

CYPRESS

Origin: Southern United States
Properties: Soft, straight-grained, and lightweight. Naturally weather- and insect-resistant.
Workability/Finishing: Works easily with hand and power tools. Accepts glue, fasteners, paints, and stains well.
Uses: Exterior furniture, boatbuilding, trimwork, beams.
Price: Inexpensive where regionally plentiful

REDWOOD (SEQUOIA)

Origin: Western United States into Pacific Northwest
Properties: Soft, even-grained with varied coloration. Naturally weather- and insect-resistant.
Workability/Finishing: Works easily with hand and power tools. Accepts glue, fasteners, stains, and paints well.
Uses: Exterior furniture, structures, siding, decks, fences.
Price: Expensive

WHITE PINE (WESTERN)

Origin: Western United States and Canada
Properties: Soft with straight-grained, uniform texture.
Workability/Finishing: Works easily with hand and power tools. Accepts glue, fasteners, and paints well.
Uses: General furniture construction, millwork, veneer.
Price: Moderate

EXOTICS SAMPLER

MAHOGANY (AMERICAN)

Origin: Central and South America
Properties: Medium density with straight, interlocked, or irregular grain pattern that produces striking figure. Naturally weather-resistant.
Workability/Finishing: Ideal for hand-tool work as well as machining. Accepts fasteners, glue, and finishes well.
Uses: General furniture construction, carving, boatbuilding, turning, veneer.
Price: Moderate to expensive

PADAUK (AFRICAN)

Origin: West Africa
Properties: Straight to interlocked grain. Texture varies from moderate to coarse. Naturally weather-resistant.
Workability/Finishing: Easily worked with sharp steel or carbide blades and bits. Excellent carving and turning wood.
Uses: Furniture construction, carving, turning, veneer.
Price: Moderate to expensive

ROSEWOOD (INDIAN)

Origin: Southern India
Properties: Even texture, dense and heavy. Decorative grain pattern.
Workability/Finishing: Dulls steel blades and hand tools quickly, so carbide cutters are recommended. Difficult to join with fasteners.
Uses: Inlay, turnings, carving, musical instruments, boatbuilding, veneer.
Price: Expensive

TEAK

Origin: Central America, Southeast Asia
Properties: Hard, dense, heavy, and evenly textured. High oil content makes teak naturally weather-resistant. Wood dust can be a respiratory irritant.
Workability/Finishing: Hardness makes teak difficult to machine. Use carbide blades and bits. Accepts glue and stain well, but predrill before installing fasteners.
Uses: Interior and exterior furniture, boatbuilding.
Price: Expensive

ZEBRAWOOD

Origin: West Africa
Properties: Hard, interlocked grain pattern with light-and-dark variegated grain pattern.
Workability/Finishing: Will dull steel bits and blades, so carbide cutters are recommended.
Uses: Turning, inlay, decorative veneer, furniture.
Price: Expensive

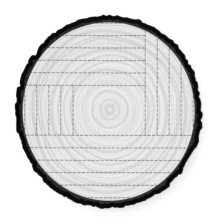

Plainsawn

End grain

Plainsawn lumber is what you'll typically find at the lumberyard or home center. Look for a sweeping elliptical grain pattern on the face and concentric arches on the board ends.

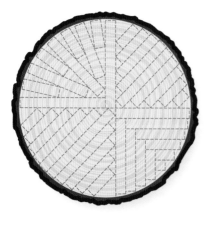

Quartersawn

End grain

Depending on the species, quartersawn lumber will show straight grain or medullary rays and flecks on the face and end grain that is perpendicular or nearly so to the face.

How lumber is cut and sized

Lumber mills use several methods for cutting logs into boards and drying the water-logged "green" wood into useable lumber. Once the lumber dries, it's trimmed and surfaced again to final dimensions, then carefully sorted and graded according to federally regulated standards before it's ready for shipment and sale. While you don't need a degree in forestry to be a woodworker, you'll buy more wisely if you have a general working knowledge of how boards are cut, seasoned, and sized.

From logs to boards. Logs are cut into boards in three ways, based on the species of tree as well as the quality and size of the logs. Sometimes a log will be cut to take advantage of the lumber's attractive grain and figure, but more often it's cut to maximize yield. The typical cutting method used to mill what you'll find at the home center is called *plainsawing*. Here, the mill slices boards from a log until defects emerge, then the log is rotated one quarter-turn to saw from an adjacent face. Plainsawn lumber is easy to spot: the face grain shows a sweeping cathedral pattern of light and dark grain. The growth rings on the ends of boards resemble concentric arches stretching widthwise.

When picking through plainsawn lumber, choose boards with the flattest end-grain growth rings. These boards were cut closer to the perimeter of the tree, and they'll be less likely to cup when the humidity rises. Avoid boards with rings that radiate from a central point; these come from the center pith area of the log, and they'll be more prone to warping. Select board faces that show regular arches of light and dark grain rather than elliptical patterns. Boards with ellipsoid face grain may be hard to plane and will tend to bow.

Quartersawing is a second log-milling method. Here, the process involves splitting the log in half, then into four wedges. The wedges are ripped into boards so the growth rings are nearly perpendicular to the board faces. Quartersawn lumber will have tight, straight face grain rather than a cathedral grain pattern. Inspect the end grain and you'll see the growth rings look like straight, perpendicular lines. If the rings run at an angle to the face but aren't concentric or perpendicular, the board is actually *riftsawn* and not truly quartersawn.

When certain species such as oak and sycamore are quartersawn, the cut exposes striking translucent medullary rays and flecks that are highly prized and unmistakable. In other species such as Douglas fir, the growth rings will show through on the face grain as regular, parallel lines. Quartersawing produces fewer boards per log than plainsawing, and the process is time-consuming, so the lumber costs more. However, the lumber expands and contracts less than plainsawn boards, and the perpendicular growth ring orientation minimizes warpage. You'll rarely find quartersawn lumber at a general-purpose lumberyard or home center, but it's commonly sold through specialty lumberyards.

A third milling method, called *through-and-through* sawing (or *flatsawing*), involves slicing through the log in successive passes without rotating it. Any defects present in the log end up in the boards because the log isn't turned to avoid them. This method maximizes the log's yield, but it produces a mixed bag of lumber cuts and qualities. Boards sawn through the center pith area will actually have a quartersawn region on either side of the pith.

If price were no object, most experts will argue that quartersawn lumber is the best value from the standpoint of durability and stability. However, since many wood types aren't available in quartersawn cuts, you'll have to settle for plainsawn or flatsawn lumber. Either of these cuts will make attractive, sturdy furniture if the lumber is properly dried first and if you take wood movement into account when designing your projects.

Lumber sizing & grading. Walk the aisles of your home center or discount lumberyard and you'll find pine, cedar, and other softwood boards sold by "nominal" (or named) dimensions rather than actual dimensions. Hardwood boards sold to the general public are often milled nominally as well. Stretch a tape measure across these boards and you'll find that the nominal board size listed on the rack may say 1 × 4, but the thickness and width are actually ¾ inch by 3½ inches. The nominal dimensions indicate the size of the board when it was initially cut from the log, prior to drying, surfacing, and final trimming. Boards sized nominally up to 1 × 6 will be ¾ inch thick and ½ inch narrower than the named width. Boards wider than a nominal 6 inches will be ¾ inch narrower than their nominal width. In the nominal system of lumber sizing, the only actual dimension is length. You'll buy boards by the lineal foot, in lengths starting at 4 feet and going up to 10 or 12 feet. Nominal sizing is a bit confusing and not really helpful to the end user, but it doesn't take long to get used to the system.

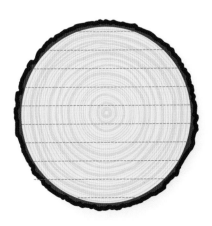

Flatsawn

End grain

Flatsawn lumber may contain the center pith area of the tree, but boards also may resemble plainsawn or quartersawn lumber, depending on where in the log they are cut from. Sometimes, a board that contains the center pith of a large tree will actually have quartersawn areas on either side of the pith.

Retail lumber outlets sometimes sell premium softwood and hardwood boards that aren't sized by quite the same nominal standards. The thickness will still be ¾ inch, but the width will match the actual dimension of the board. A 1 × 4 will be a full 4 inches wide. More common woods such as oak and pine won't be sold this way unless they are "select" cuts with no visual defects. Here's where you may also find a small sampling of less common lumber varieties including cherry, maple, walnut, or mahogany. Premium lumber is surfaced smooth on both faces and edges, and it may even be shrink-wrapped to help minimize warping. It will also be the most expensive lumber available.

When you shop for hardwood lumber at a specialty yard, you won't find it sized nominally. Lumber thickness is sized according to a quartering system. Boards that are 1 inch thick are sized as 4/4, called "four quarter," and it means the thickness is equal to four quarter inches. Generally, 4/4 is the thinnest

NOMINAL VS. FINISHED LUMBER SIZES

Nominal	Finished
1 × 2	¾ × 1½
1 × 3	¾ × 2½
1 × 4	¾ × 3½
1 × 6	¾ × 5½
1 × 8	¾ × 7¼
1 × 10	¾ × 9¼
1 × 12	¾ × 11¼
2 × 2	1½ × 1½
2 × 3	1½ × 2½
2 × 4	1½ × 3½
2 × 6	1½ × 5½
2 × 8	1½ × 7¼
2 × 10	1½ × 9¼
2 × 12	1½ × 11¼

Quartering System for Lumber Thickness (Rough Dimensions)

Quartered size	Measured thickness
3/4	¾ inch
4/4	1 inch
5/4	1¼ inch
6/4	1½ inch
8/4	2 inch
10/4	2½ inch
12/4	3 inch

cut, and thicknesses go up from there. Five, six, eight, ten, and even twelve-quarter thicknesses are common for many hardwoods. These sizes translate into 1¼-, 1½-, 2-, 2½-, and 3-inch rough thicknesses.

Specialty hardwoods are sold in random widths and lengths rather than standardized dimensions. Since the sizing varies, you buy this lumber by volume, not by length and width. The unit of measurement is the "board foot," which equals a board unit measuring 1 inch thick, 12 inches wide, and 12 inches long—a volume of 144 cubic inches. Of course each board will have different dimensions, so the proportions you'll get per board foot will vary. Every specialty hardwood board you buy will be priced according to board feet, regardless of thickness, width, or length.

The easiest way to calculate the price of a board is to measure thickness, width, and length in inches, multiply these numbers together, then divide the total by 144 to determine the number of board feet. The lumberyard will post a board-foot price for every quartered thickness of each species. Multiply your number of board feet by the board-foot price to arrive at the board's overall price, not including applicable sales tax.

Both softwoods and hardwoods are graded according to federal standards to assure consistent quality within the lumber commodities industry. Softwoods are categorized with various grade names that include B Select and Better, C Select, D Select, Superior Finish, Prime Finish, No. 1 Common, and No. 2 Common. The grade is often stamped right on the board or specified on a label stapled to the end. These grades indicate how many natural blemishes a board may have, as well as the size of the defects. From highest to lowest grade, B Select is the clearest grade and No. 2 Common will have the most blemishes. You'll rarely be able to pick and choose from among these grades if you shop at retail lumber outlets. They'll likely stock a select grade and a common grade only.

"Board feet" is a product of multiplying the length (A) times the thickness (B) times the width (C). When each of these measurements are made in inches, divide the answer by 144 to determine the number of board feet.

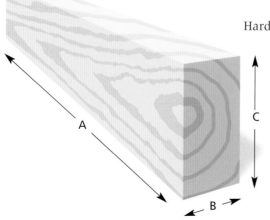

Hardwoods are graded by different standards than softwoods. Boards are evaluated in terms of the percentage of defect-free lumber they contain. From highest to lowest percentages of clear lumber, the grades include Firsts and Seconds, Select, and numbers 1, 2A, 2B, 3A, and 3B Common. Lumber graded as Firsts and Seconds (FAS) or Select must be 83⅓ percent clear, while No. 3B Common need only be 25 percent clear. Not even specialty yards will stock all these grades, but you'll find FAS or Select and at least one common grade of each species sold there.

Surfacing options. Softwood lumber is usually planed smooth on all surfaces when you buy it. So is the hardwood you'll find at discount lumberyards and home centers. If you buy lumber directly from the sawmill or a specialty yard, all the final surfacing might not be done. This is particularly true for hardwoods. What you'll find instead may be lumber with no finished surfaces, called "rough-sawn;" boards with two surfaced faces but rough edges, called "Surfaced Two Sides," or "S2S"; and lumber with the edges and faces planed smooth, called "Surfaced Four Sides," or "S4S." The more surfacing the mill does for you, the higher the board-foot cost will be. If you have access to a surface planer and join-ter, roughsawn lumber offers great value, but you won't know how the finished lumber will look until you remove the rough surfaces. Some yards will allow you to take a few shavings off roughsawn lumber with a hand plane to help evaluate the underlying grain pattern or fig-ure. Ask before you try this. For yards that don't allow a sneak peak, you'll have to take your chances on what you get.

Three common surfacing options are shown here. The board on top is "S4S," which means both faces and edges are planed flat. The middle board is "S2S," with only the faces planed and not the edges. The bottom board is simply roughsawn with no additional planing. Generally, the more surfacing that's done for you, the more it will cost at the yard.

Typical lumber defects

Lumber is hygroscopic, which means it absorbs and releases moisture like a sponge. Even after boards are dried, they'll still swell and shrink to some degree as the relative humidity of their surroundings changes. Boards "move" mostly across their width but also through their thickness to a lesser degree. They move very little lengthwise. Some amount of wood movement is unavoidable, and you'll need to account for it when you build your projects.

Lumber will expand or contract until the internal moisture content reaches equilibrium with the environment. Often, the process happens unevenly, which is part of the reason why lumber warps. Distortion is also a product of how the tree grew, what stresses were present inside the log, and how the boards were cut and dried. Lumber mills try to correct initial warping by plan-ing lumber before they sell it, but that generally isn't the end of the story. Boards prone to warping will continue to do so at the lumberyard, in your shop, and unfortunately even in your finished projects from time to time.

The four common types of distortion are bow, crook, cup, and twist (also called wind). You can easily check for these distortions by sighting down the face and edges of lumber. Bowing means the faces of a board curve lengthwise. A crooked board is flat across both faces but the edges curve. Cupping occurs when board faces curl but the edges are still flat. Boards with twist will have one or both ends curling so the faces aren't flat. Your eyes will detect even

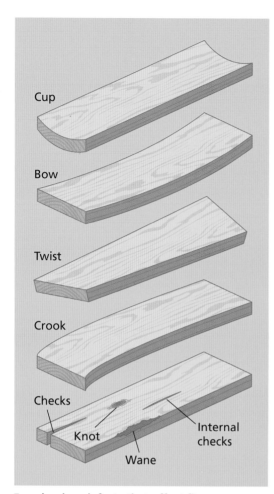

Four lumber defects that affect flatness include cup, bow, twist, and crook. Even boards that are flat along edges and faces may still contain other natural defects like knots, splits, checks, or waney edges.

It's easy to spot cup, bow, or twist in a piece of lumber by holding it near one end and sighting along its length.

subtle deviations from flat surfaces. It's common to find several of these defects in a single board. Often, you'll be able to salvage boards with minor warping by cutting off the warped areas or splitting the board into flatter, smaller sections.

Aside from warp, lumber may have other natural defects that you'll need to deal with. Knots are common, but they're really only problematic if they're loose. Loose knots can get pulled free by a spinning bit or blade and become projectiles. Pockets of soft pitch and resin can foul blades, but they're mainly a problem when it comes to finishing. Paints and varnishes won't stick to soft wood pitch. Cut away pitch pockets to avoid problems. Sometimes you'll run across boards that have green, bluish, or grey discoloration or streaking called *spalling*. It's a sign of fungal growth. Once the board dries, the spalling process will stop, but the discoloration remains. Woodworkers often like to incorporate spalling into their work as a design element rather than remove it.

Checks are cracks that start at the ends of boards. Checking is a natural part of the drying process. They're easy to deal with by simply cutting away the defect a few inches in from the end of the crack. Sometimes you'll run across a board with cracks contained entirely inside the board, not starting from the end. It's best to avoid using these pieces. Inboard cracks can sometimes be attributed to a defect called case hardening, and they're the result of rapid, uneven kiln-drying. The cracks show where the board literally pulled itself apart trying to reach a moisture equilibrium with the atmosphere inside the kiln. The cracks you see on the surface are one thing, but there may be more hiding inside the board that you won't find until you machine it further. Be leery of a lumber supplier's kiln-drying practices if you find a case-hardened board—where there's one case-hardened board, there are bound to be more.

Sources for buying lumber

Your local home center or lumberyard will be a convenient source for lumber, but there are other options as well. Here are a few to consider:

Sawmills. If you live in a wooded state, there's likely to be a sawmill somewhere near those forests, and many of these smaller businesses gladly sell lumber to the general public. Check your local Yellow Pages under sawmills for possible sources. You'll probably pay less money buying locally, and you'll have the satisfaction of knowing you are using lumber from locally grown trees. Be aware that these sawmills probably won't kiln-dry their lumber, so you'll need to check it for moisture content and possibly store it for some time before it's usable. You may also need to do all the surface planing and jointing work yourself—the wood likely will be roughsawn if it comes from a small mill. Some adventurous woodworkers even buy portable, trailer-mounted sawmills and saw their own lumber from trees they fell themselves.

Specialty lumberyards. Some lumberyards specialize in furniture lumber, usually hardwoods of many sorts. If you need an unusual size or species for your project, these are the places to call. Large specialty yards buy roughsawn stock in volume and either sell it this way or do some degree of surfacing. Some yards sell to the general public, so you can buy any quantity of lumber down to a single board. Other yards target their business to cabinet shops and professional woodworkers, so there may be a minimum board foot requirement for purchasing there. In these cases, talk with other woodworkers you know and pool your resources to buy larger quantities of lumber together, then split the cost.

Woodworking stores. There are several national chains of woodworking stores with outlets in most large cities. These stores carry a variety of hardwood lumber species including many hard-to-find exotics. You'll also find reference books, tools, and unique hardware. The sales staff can provide helpful advice about what wood might work best for your project. Generally, the lumber you'll find at these stores will be premium grade FAS, and though there may be many species to choose from, the prices tend to be higher than buying from larger lumberyards.

If you live in an area where trees are harvested for lumber, you may want to try buying boards directly from a sawmill.

Catalogs/mail-order sources. Large lumber suppliers often run ads in woodworking magazines and offer catalogs of their lumber inventories. Most now have web sites. If you're looking for an unusual species or cut, or if you plan to order lumber in volume, mail-order sources can offer good value. Reputable lumber companies will offer satisfaction guarantees on what you buy since generally you'll be buying lumber sight-unseen. Ask about return policies in case you receive defective or unsatisfactory wood. Be sure to inquire about moisture content and lumber grade as well. You should know the specific sizes of lumber you need and be prepared to make alterations if the lumber supplier doesn't offer the dimensions you're after. Don't forget to ask about shipping costs—you're paying for it.

Online auctions. In our Internet-driven world, you have the option to bid on lumber using online auction houses such as eBay. Internet lumber sources are all over the board. You may be bidding on lumber from small mills, lumberyards, or even the results of a fallen backyard tree. Anyone can sell lumber this way, not just reputable dealers. However, most sellers auctioning their lumber do this sort of thing regularly.

Lumber quality will be difficult to evaluate, and you'll take more risks buying by auction than from a dedicated mail-order source or a store or yard close to you. Before bidding, e-mail or call the seller and ask the same questions you'd direct to a mail-order lumberyard. Inquire about moisture content, lumber grade, and any guarantee that may apply to your purchase. Remember also that shipping isn't generally included in the final winning bid—that's extra. Ask the seller to estimate your shipping costs as well as any other charges that may apply, such as crating or wrapping your wood. Most sellers will be happy to disclose the details, because it reduces their risk of buyers failing to pay once the auction ends. Lumber auctions pose the same benefits and risks to you as any other Internet auction. You may snatch the wood for a song, or it may end up costing you as much as buying it retail. Don't bid more than you are willing to pay, and protect yourself against unexpected surprises by asking lots of questions before becoming the winning bidder.

Storing lumber

Dry lumber isn't difficult to store, provided you keep it in a dry place with a reasonable amount of fresh air exchange. If your shop is in the basement, run a dehumidifier during summer months. For particularly damp basements, you may want to wrap dry lumber in 4- or 6-mil polyethylene to protect it from the surrounding damp air. Try to keep the relative humidity around 40 percent wherever you store your lumber, if possible.

If you store lumber in the basement, run a dehumidifier during humid summer months and check the relative humidity near the lumber with a hygrometer. Separating boards in a stack with scraps of lumber called stickers is also a good practice. Stickers promote air circulation around each board.

It's tough to control humidity levels in garages, sheds, and other outbuilding shops, particularly if the shop doubles as a place to park cars and the garage door gets opened and closed every day. One preventive measure you can take is to separate the boards in a stack with stickers to improve air circulation. Keep lumber off of dirt or concrete floors to prevent moisture from wicking up and saturating the wood. If your garage shop has a large accessible attic, store your lumber there. The air will be drier and warmer than near the floor.

You might buy air-dried lumber that's only partially seasoned. When there's more drying to do, store the lumber outside on a hard, flat surface with stickers in between. The goal here is to get as much air circulating around the boards as possible so they dry evenly and relatively quickly. Keep the bottom board off the ground with stickers, too. Put a cover over the top of the stack, but keep the sides open to promote air movement. A plastic tarp weighed down with cinder blocks makes a good top cover. Or use a piece of corrugated metal. If you have a carport or other open-sided building that offers shelter from the elements, stack your lumber there to dry and skip the top cover.

As soon as the moisture content drops below 14 percent, move boards inside where they are safe from the elements. The amount of time it takes to reach this level will depend on factors like the relative humidity in your area and the species of wood you are drying. Some will say that you should plan on drying lumber one year for every inch of board thickness, but this is just a general guideline. A better way to track the drying process is to check it periodically with a moisture meter (see the sidebar on this page for more information about moisture meters and their use).

Once in the shop, the best way to store long lumber is horizontally on shelves or in a stack elevated off the floor on blocks. If you store boards vertically, they can warp. Make sure your shelving is solidly built and supports the lumber every 16 inches or so lengthwise. This will also help prevent warping. Lumber shorter than four feet can be stored either horizontally or vertically, whichever is more convenient.

Allow new lumber to acclimate to your shop air for a few weeks before using it. This may seem like a long time to wait, but it gives the wood a chance to distort some as it reaches a level of moisture equilibrium with the air in your shop.

Sheet goods overview

Sheet goods are an economical alternative to board lumber for creating wide panels. Plywood, particleboard, and other sheet materials tend to stay flatter than solid wood, although they aren't impervious to some warping and swelling as the humidity rises or if they're stored improperly. Home centers and lumberyards stock a selection of plywoods and composite sheet materials, but specialized sheet good companies sell about as many customized materials as you can imagine. The possibilities are particularly wide for custom plywoods covered with virtually every wood veneer made.

Here's a sampling of the sheet good options available to you:

Plywood. Plywood is generally sold in 4 × 8-foot sheets in thicknesses ranging from ¼ inch up to ¾ inch. Your supplier may sell half or quarter sheets, as well. The core material is usually multiple thin layers of wood veneer sandwiched

MOISTURE METERS

You can determine the moisture content of lumber before you use it, and sometimes even before you buy it, using a moisture meter. Moisture meters typically have a pair of sharpened probes that you press into a piece of lumber to take a reading, but some meters use internal sensors instead of probes. Better meters will also come with a calibration chart for setting the meter to test different wood species. To take a reading, cut several inches off the end of a board, press the probes into the board, and read the meter. It will indicate the percentage of moisture inside.

Meters are relatively reliable and easy to use, but they're expensive. Unless you buy lots of air-dried lumber, they probably aren't worth the cost. However, if you're buying roughsawn lumber from a specialty yard or directly from a sawmill, ask to have the wood moisture content measured in your presence. The yard should be willing to disclose this information to you readily. Or they may have a moisture meter you can borrow to test the lumber yourself.

together so the grain pattern alternates from ply to ply. The alternating veneers give plywood its strength and dimensional stability. Plywood cores are also made of various grades of ground wood pulp or strips of solid wood. The plys may also have small voids.

Your local source for building materials will probably stock two families of plywood: construction plywood and higher-grade plywood suitable for cabinetry and general woodworking. Plywood made for construction purposes has rough layers of veneer made of various softwoods on the surfaces. The outer face veneer is graded alphabetically by quality. "B-C" plywood is a common sheet material used for sheathing and subfloors. The "B" face will have fewer imperfections than the "C" face, but both will have some irregularities. Reserve this kind of construction plywood for utility projects.

Better grades of plywood for woodworking and cabinetry are easy to spot: Look for smooth birch, oak, or maple face veneers on the sheets. One face of the veneer is rated A through D from highest to lowest quality, and the other face has a numeric rating from 1 through 4. Hardwood plywood will be much more expensive than construction-grade plywood, which should come as no surprise. The outer veneer is furniture quality and requires little sanding. If you need plywood with a face veneer that matches other solid wood in your project, you can order it covered with virtually any species of wood veneer, including cherry, walnut, mahogany, pine, and even exotics.

Another high-grade plywood product is Baltic birch. Made in northern Europe, Baltic birch is relatively easy to find in the U.S., particularly from lumberyards that stock specialty plywoods. Baltic birch has about twice the number of veneer layers as cabinet-grade plywood sheets, and there are no voids between the layers. The sheets are sized metrically with the overall proportions of a sheet being smaller than standard plywood. A full sheet is approximately 5 × 5 feet. Baltic birch is an ideal choice for drawer parts, cabinetry, or shop jigs and fixtures. The edges are so consistent that they make attractive accents.

Cabinet-grade plywoods come in a wide variety of surface veneer options. Your local home center probably stocks oak and birch, but you can special-order walnut, pine, cherry, mahogany, maple, and other veneers, as well.

Melamine & particleboard. Particleboard is the sheet material that looks like ground-up wood glued together. Melamine is a general term for particleboard covered with a colored facing of resin-impregnated paper. The coating creates a durable surface that's easy to keep clean. White melamine is most common, but you can also buy it in black, beige, or gray. It's sold in full 4 × 8-foot sheets and in narrower shelving with a bullnosed edge.

Both melamine and particleboard are made of coarsely ground wood pulp and adhesive resins pressed together under extreme heat and pressure. They're less expensive than plywood and somewhat more dimensionally stable, provided the sheets stay dry. Melamine and particleboard will swell and crumble in the presence of moisture. Melamine is a good fuss-free choice for box and cabinet interiors because you won't need to paint or finish it. Particleboard can be painted, but usually its rough surface texture shows through the paint. Use particleboard for shop fixtures, jigs, shelving, and other utility projects. Melamine and particleboard machine easily, but they don't hold nails, screws, or other fasteners as well as plywood. Cut or routed edges will be rough and filled with tiny voids.

Medium-density fiberboard. Commonly known by its acronym, MDF, medium-density fiberboard is essentially particleboard made with finely ground wood fibers. MDF is commonly sold in ½- and ¾-inch thicknesses, but other thicknesses are available by special order. It costs about the same as particleboard and less than melamine. You may even find MDO (medium-density overlay), which has a water-resistant paper facing.

The material consistency of MDF is much finer than particleboard. In fact, MDF hardly looks like wood at all. As a general-purpose building material, MDF is hard to beat. The fibers are pressed together under such extreme pressure that MDF machines and sands without voids or tearout. It holds fasteners reasonably well and is an excellent choice for painted projects. However, the machining process creates copious amounts of fine dust. Be sure to wear a respirator and keep the windows open when machining or sanding MDF.

Another disadvantage to this otherwise useful and versatile sheet material is weight. The density of MDF makes it extremely heavy. A single ¾-inch-thick sheet weighs nearly 100 pounds—about twice the heft of a sheet of ¾-inch plywood. If you need the smoothness offered by MDF but the part you're making isn't a critical structural member, use ½-inch material instead.

Hardboard. Hardboard, also known by the brand name Masonite, is essentially a darker, denser form of MDF with the same general characteristics. It is sold as full 4 × 8-foot sheets as well as smaller half and quarter sheets. This material is much thinner than MDF; you'll find it in ⅛- and ¼-inch thicknesses. Hardboard is an economical material for building drawer bottoms and the back panels of cabinets or painted bookcases. It makes durable, reusable patterns for template routing (see page 114) or as parts for other workshop jigs and fixtures.

Other commonly available sheet-good options include hardboard (top), medium-density fiberboard (center), and medium-density overlay (bottom), which has a tough, water-resistant paper facing. All three are good choices for painted panels, drawer bottoms, or shop jigs.

Chapter 4
PLANNING PROJECTS

The first step of any woodworking project involves planning. Simple projects may take just a bit of forethought before you're ready to build, but more complicated furniture usually takes much more noodling. Either way, some degree of planning is essential. Try to think of the "shop phase" of woodworking as an exercise in delayed gratification, preceded by time at the drawing board. If you're poised in front of a stack of lumber with saw in hand and no paper plans on the bench, good luck! Chances are, your best intentions will be met with some degree of frustration when you miscut a table leg, build a drawer that won't fit its opening, or realize at a late hour that you are two boards short.

Project planning has three basic stages: determining what you want to build, working out the details through drawings and prototypes, then calculating material and cutting lists from your drawings. This chapter will introduce you to each stage so you can plan your next project confidently and have a good time building it. After all, woodworking should be enjoyable, right? Planning first will keep you smiling later.

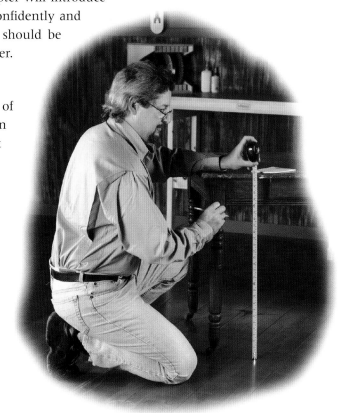

Deciding what to build
The motivation to build something has any number of sources. Maybe your family has outgrown the kitchen table and you want to replace it with something a bit out of the ordinary. You can design any table you want and customize it to suit your individual needs or tastes. Maybe you've had your eye on an Arts & Crafts sideboard at the local furniture gallery, but it's priced beyond your means. Building one yourself allows you, rather than the furniture retailer, to control the quality and cost. Perhaps you just want to try some new woodworking projects to expand your skill base.

Gathering ideas. Whatever your motivation may be for building something, chances are you've already thought about it enough to have some initial ideas about a design. The idea-gathering stage is important. It's the time to let your imagination go without committing to

Keep a file folder of clippings for those furniture styles and designs that appeal to you. Someday they may serve as the inspiration for a project you build.

any one notion. Feed your ideas with lots of concrete options so you can start to clarify a design. Furniture stores are good places to examine a variety of furniture styles up close. Pay attention to the furnishings you find in your friends' homes, as well as what's for sale through furniture catalogs. Leaf through woodworking magazines and project books. You'll find loads of published plans for every conceivable woodworking project in an assortment of styles. Hit some web sites of professional woodworkers to see galleries of their work, and download and print out examples that look interesting. Keep catalog or magazine clippings, advertisements, photocopies, and photographs of possible projects in a file folder so you can refer to them often.

In your ongoing search for ideas, you'll discover that furniture follows some classic style trends, and it always has. Certainly everything you make doesn't have to conform to an accepted style, but basic furniture design is the end result of centuries of trial and error. Study proportions of cabinetry, tables, chairs, and chests to get a sense for how furniture functions in harmony with the human body. You'll know a comfortable chair when you sit in one, even if you can't pinpoint why it feels so supportive. Seat size, leg height, and the tilt of the back rest are all factors that contribute to comfort. (Seat height and depth are around 15 to 18 inches; the seat width is a bit wider still. Arm leans are generally about 8 to 10 inches above the seat.) These proportions have been tested over time. Bookcases are generally not taller than you can reach, so books remain accessible without using a step stool. (They usually have a maximum height of 76 inches.) Drawers are deep enough to store a layer of items, but not deep enough to lose them. (Keep general-purpose drawers shallower than 6 inches.) Dining tables tend to be wide enough to accommodate place settings on either side as well as a few serving dishes. However, they shouldn't be so wide as to make it impossible to reach across easily. (Each place setting around a table should be about 24 to 30 inches wide.)

Evaluate your skills, budget & tools. Keep your skill level in mind as you study furniture. Furniture with relief carvings, delicate inlays, or parts that join at angles or curves will be more difficult to build than pieces with straight lines and minimal ornamentation. If you're just starting out, consider making projects in the Mission, Shaker, and country styles. These are good options for building sturdy furniture without needing advanced woodworking skills or a full arsenal of machinery. Try a new technique here or there within the furniture style that suits your skill level to keep every project interesting. Your roster of skills will grow bit by bit without jeopardizing the success of a whole project.

Building sensibly means working with some project budget in mind. When your pockets for a project aren't deep, the dollars will go farther by building with ¾-inch lumber rather than thick slabs of exotic hardwood. It's almost always true that the larger your project becomes physically, the more it costs. One way to help keep from blowing the budget on big projects is to substitute sheet goods for solid lumber. Sheet goods are generally less expensive, and you can steer clear of the wood movement issues you'll face when designing panels made of solid wood. Or consider using a less expensive secondary wood for drawer boxes, interior cabinet shelving, blocking, and for other project parts that don't show. Why use expensive quartersawn oak or fiddleback maple for the top of a cabinet if no one will ever see it?

Remember to include the cost of special hardware your project will need, such as slides, hinges, doorknobs, and drawer pulls. These items definitely add to the bottom line of what your project costs to build. In fact, depending on the project, hardware can even exceed the cost of the lumber. Don't forget to add those other project "extras" such as a new router bit, a package of sandpaper, or the cans of varnish and stain you'll need for finishing. It all contributes to the total cost of the project in the end.

Before embarking on a project, have a look around your workshop at the tools you own. Do you have all the equipment you'll need for cutting out your project parts, shaping the edges, assembling wood panels, or smoothing the part surfaces? If your project parts are small and curved, how will you safely cut the tiny curves? A scroll saw is the best tool for this task. Will you need one, or can you modify the design or accomplish the task another way? Think through the construction phase of the project and how you'll manage each machining step. Otherwise, you could end up midway through a project and stumped over how to proceed. If you can't accomplish the project without buying a new tool, will your budget support the expenditure?

Building from published plans or from scratch. Designing from scratch is a wonderful way to take full ownership of a project, but it's not always the wisest move for beginners. You'll need to evaluate whether the greater good is to make something totally new and unique or follow the plans of someone else. Your inspired design may work beautifully, but you're taking on the full brunt of determining size, shape, joinery, materials, and tooling methods for executing your idea. Published plans aren't always accurate (often they aren't!), but they're darn close. Accomplished magazine and book editors or seasoned woodworkers have worked out the design bugs for you in advance. You'll have the benefit of measured drawings, a material list, some helpful how-to photos, and a finished example of the project.

From ideas to sketches

To help firm up your project ideas and make them tangible, they need to be drawn out on paper. Drawings lay all the groundwork of your design and help you avoid pitfalls. Don't let the paper stage intimidate you. Starting is as easy as making crude sketches to give your ideas some substance and vision.

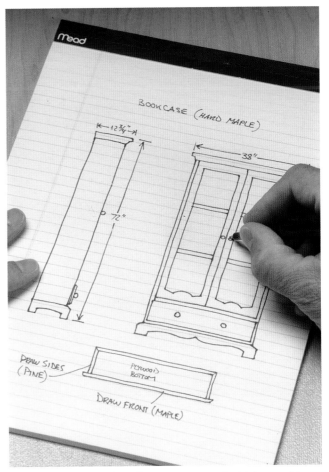

Collect your thoughts about a new project idea and try some design elements on for size by making a concept sketch. Make it freehand and without restrictions to see how your ideas gel.

Concept sketches. The first round of drawings, called concept sketches, should be almost as free-flowing as your ideas for a project. At this stage, you are still playing around with any number of possibilities. Try to doodle and sketch several different options for what you want to build, incorporating as many different features as you like. If it's a chest of drawers, make a half-dozen equal-sized rectangles to serve as the overall chest shape, and try a different drawer arrangement on each rectangle. If none of your drawer configurations will work, make the rectangle taller or shorter, or try turning it on its side, then play around with the drawer options again.

Sketch a couple views of your project while you're at it. You'll probably start with a front view, but draw a side view as well. A top view is helpful for objects like chairs that have more parts relating to one another than, for example, a table with a square top. Plot some rough dimensions for height, width, and depth on your drawings, and do the best you can to make thicker or thinner parts look that way on the sketch. There's really no need to draft these sketches with perfectly straight lines or exacting details. That happens later. Use lots of inexpensive paper and don't be afraid to erase or start over. When you happen on a feature you like in your sketch, trace it onto your next sketch so you can save time redrawing it. You might find it helpful to grab the colored pencils and shade a sketch in.

One way to spare your budget and still build an attractive, sturdy project is to use secondary woods like poplar and pine for those parts that don't show. On this drawer, the face is made of alder, but the box is made of pine. When it's closed, no one will see the secondary wood. Craftsman have built furniture this way for centuries.

Among the many design issues you'll face in each project is what hardware to choose for the project. Knobs, pulls, and handles add character to the project, while hinges, slides, and other mechanical components affect function.

Once you've got an overall form sketched out, think about the kinds of joinery you'll use to assemble the project, as well as other features that need closer attention. Will you build the drawers with rabbet joints or dovetails? How will the doors swing or a drawer slide open and close? What sort of edge shape would look attractive around a tabletop? Will the legs of your chair design have a graceful curve or a gradual taper on two sides? Now is a good time to think about these kinds of details. Make some additional freehand sketches to figure these issues out. Detail drawings of this sort help you simplify the complicated aspects of your project. Make these sketches as large as you need to get a realistic perspective on proportions.

The concept stage is an excellent time to think about some practical issues as well. First off, be mindful of both form and function. Will the style of your project blend in with other furniture in the room? If it's somewhat different than the rest, consider adding a few design details to bring it closer to the style of furniture it will live with, or build it from the same wood. Will the project fit the space you have in mind for it? Is there enough room for doors and drawers to open without blocking windows, doorways, or heat registers? Can you build the project in your shop and get it out the door or lift it without a crane once it's finished?

One way to bring your concept sketches to life in three dimensions is to create a miniature prototype.

There are also hardware and other lumber decisions to make. What hardware will you use for the project? The outer hardware can add distinctive flair, while hinges, catches, and slides impact how the wood parts fit together and move. This is particularly true for drawers and doors. Hardware need not limit your creativity, but it will affect how closely you can build what you sketch.

Think also about the lumber you'll need to buy for building your project. If, for instance, you are designing a table with 3-inch-square legs, how will you make the legs? Can you find solid wood in this size or will you have to glue individual boards together? Will glued-up legs be visually acceptable to you?

Making prototypes. Prototypes are essentially rough models of what you plan to build. Whether built to a small scale or full size, they provide a three-dimensional representation of your project. Make scale models with whatever odds and ends you have on hand. Scrap-bin wood, cardboard, or foam-core board all make good building materials to assemble into miniatures. Make the model a convenient size, maybe the same size as your sketches, to keep all the proportions consistent. Join the parts with tape, hot-melt glue, staples, or whatever is quick and easy. The point is to enhance your sketches, not create elaborate doll-size furniture.

Full-size prototypes will clearly indicate whether the proportions and features you have in mind will fit the human body or a physical space properly. A little time spent prototyping before you build can save you lots of money and frustration.

A full-size prototype need not be carefully detailed to provide the information you need, so keep it simple. Here, a prototype that helps you determine, say, the size of the tabletop and overall height may be all you need it to do. Place the prototype in your dining room. How does the size of the table work in the space? Will all your dining room chairs fit around it?

If you're building a chair, full-size prototyping is essential. A sketch won't tell you a thing about how a piece of furniture fits your body. Use scrap lumber and plywood connected with drywall screws to construct your prototype chair. Now sit on the prototype. How does it feel? Probably not great to start with. If not, start tweaking the prototype. Add more scraps to raise the seat height. Tilt the back a little more or less, and move armrests up or down to improve the ergonomic aspects of the chair. Work at the prototype until you find a pleasing fit, then keep the model to measure those important dimensions when you make your measured scale drawings.

Drafting scale drawings

When you're happy with your sketches and prototypes, it's time to draw the project accurately. It isn't difficult to make construction drawings that provide a reliable representation of what your finished project will look like. Line drawings of this sort are usually drawn to a smaller

DRAFTING SUPPLIES

YOU'LL NEED

An art supply store will stock all the drafting tools necessary to make scale drawings. Buy the following items and you'll have everything you'll need to get started:

- Mechanical pencil with fine, hard leads
- Soft gum eraser
- Architect's scale or ruler
- 45° × 45° drafting triangle
- 30° × 60° drafting triangle
- T-square
- Drawing board (around 2 × 3 feet) or portable drafting table with a sliding rule
- Vellum, graph, or other translucent drawing paper
- 4- and 8-inch compasses
- French curve

ARCHITECT'S SCALE

To make reduced-scale drawings, you'll need an architect's scale. Essentially, it's a three-sided ruler with 11 different scales. Architects use these scales to measure foot increments, but the scales work just as well for sizing down inches. Five of the six edges of the ruler are divided into two scales, one scale reading left to right and the other from right to left. Each scale plots a different fraction of an inch to represent whole foot or inch units. For instance, one edge has both a ¾ and ⅜ scale. The ¾ scale, reading left to right, plots fourteen ¾-inch units plus a 15th unit subdivided into twelve parts. With this scale, you could draft a woodworking drawing where each ¾-inch unit equals 1 full inch or 1 full foot. The ⅜ scale includes 28 units measuring ⅜ inch, and these read right to left. One edge of the ruler, labeled "16," is a full-size inch scale divided into ¹⁄₁₆-inch increments. The "3" and "1½" scales plot units larger than 1 inch. These are handy to enlarge small details.

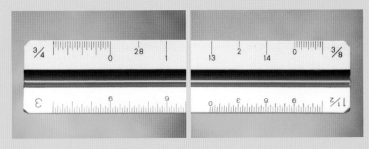

Once you've chosen a scale for your drawings, an architect's scale isn't difficult to use. Plot line lengths on your drawing using whole units on the scale, starting from the "0" mark. Then add any fractions of a foot or inch using the subdivided end unit of the scale. The only real trick is to keep from inadvertently flipping the ruler and measuring off the wrong scale.

scale than the actual project, and all the dimensions are true to that scale. Two-dimensional drawings, called *orthographics*, come first. Here's where you'll draft the elevation drawings, which include the front, side, and back views. Top and bottom views, called plan drawings, can also be helpful. Detail drawings round out the orthographic package. The measurements you determine in your plan and elevation drawings can then be used to create a three-dimensional drawing, called an *isometric*. When done carefully, you can use your collection of scale drawings to create accurate lists for buying lumber and cutting parts.

It's helpful to fit several views of your project onto each page of your drawings. The more information you can see at a glance, the easier it will be to keep the overall project in mind. More importantly, you can extend measurements from one drawing up or over on the page to help draw another view. The scale won't change between the elevation and plan views, so common measurements are transferable. Try to have the front, side, and top views on one page.

The first task is to choose a scale for your drawings. Larger scales make it easier to draw fine details, but the size of your project and paper will influence how big a scale you can use. To pick the scale, find the largest dimension of your project and measure this distance on your paper using several different edges of the architect's scale. Pick the largest scale that affords you enough extra space to draw a couple other views. For example, if your project's largest dimension is 4 feet, the ¾ scale will make this line 3 inches long. Since the other measurements of the project are shorter than 3 inches, you should be able to draw several plan and elevation views on two sheets of standard-sized paper taped together. With this scale, your proportion would be ¾ inch equals 1 foot, or ¾" = 1'.

Eventually your concept sketches and prototyping should culminate in making a set of scaled plan and elevation drawings. Careful measurements and accurate line drawings are essential here.

The usual convention for laying out elevation and plan drawings is to start with the front view roughly centered top to bottom on the paper and near the left edge. Top and bottom views are drawn directly above and below the front view. Side and back views are drawn to the right of the front view and in line with it. This way, all the relevant widths of the top and bottom views can be taken directly from the front view by drawing vertical guide lines up and down from it. The project's overall height and other vertical measurements can be transferred to the side and back views with guide lines drawn horizontally off the front view.

Draw the front view first, using your architect's scale for plotting distances and the T-square and triangles for making horizontal, perpendicular, and angular lines. Add elements from your concept sketches, such as leg shapes and the locations of knobs, pulls, or hinges. If your prototypes provided helpful information about proportions, be sure to include those dimensions here. These drawings should tell the whole story about your design, so take the time to make each view information-packed. Once the front view is complete, extend faint lines up and down from the front view to plot the overall width of the top and bottom views. Use the architect's scale to determine the depth of these plan views, then fill in the necessary details. Draw the side and back views next. Use the T-square to project as many common lines over from the front view as possible to mark part heights on the side and back views.

You'll need to determine what sorts of detail drawings to make for your project. Joints are good candidates for detail drawings, because they allow you to work out the best proportions for the parts. Consider making detail drawings for joints that attach legs to aprons or stretchers, door stiles and rails, drawer box corners, and so forth. It's also helpful to draw details showing how doors and hinges relate, and how to size a drawer to leave clearance for metal drawer slides. Any aspects of the project that are difficult to see in your plan and elevation views or are difficult to work through in your mind should get mapped out in detail drawings. If you need to determine how some aspect of your project will look on the inside, make a drawing showing part of the project cut away in cross-section to help clarify things. Imagine slicing a line down the center of your project or project part. Draw what you'd find if you were to do this.

Full-size detail drawings of joint parts help to ensure that you'll cut parts accurately the first time. The more intricate the joint, the more beneficial the detail drawing will be.

Draw the details or cross-sections right on the same pages as the plan and elevation drawings, if they'll fit. This way you'll keep the details close to the overall drawings of the project, so related information stays together. Draw the details at a larger scale than the rest of your drawings or even full size.

Once all your drawings are finished, you should feel confident about your design as well as how you'll build it. If some aspects still seem vague, you probably aren't finished drawing the necessary details.

After you've drawn the plan and elevation views, add leader lines alongside the drawings to show the necessary measurements. The drawings should include measurements for overall height, width, and depth. Make these stand alone so they are easy to find. Then draw more leader lines in from the overall dimension lines and divvy them up to show particular part dimensions. All the smaller dimensions you plot on these inner leader lines should add up to the overall dimensions. You'll develop a cutting list to accompany your drawings, which can provide dimensions that won't fit on the other drawings.

Creating an isometric drawing. Use the measurements created in the 2-D plan and elevation drawings to make a three-dimensional representation of the project. There are a couple options here, but the easiest 3-D drawing to make is called an *isometric*. Basically, an isometric drawing renders the project from a front corner so you can see the front, one side and the top from an angle. Usually, the vantage point is the front left corner. Isometrics are created primarily with vertical and 30° lines, drawn with the 30° × 60° triangle and the T-square. What's convenient about isometric drawings is that each line is at the same scale as the plan and elevation drawings. You'll take the measurements directly off those drawings and apply them to the isometric. Although the drawing will be dimensionally correct and to scale, it creates a skewed perception of depth because

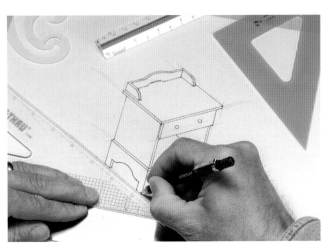

Isometric drawings, which are essentially combinations of vertical and 30° lines, transform your 2D drawings into 3D forms.

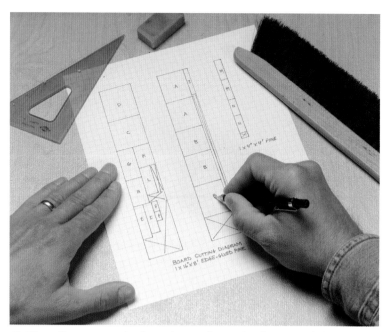

Cutting diagrams make it easier to determine how much board lumber and sheet goods you need to buy. Draw common board sizes to scale, then lay out and label every part.

the project doesn't get smaller as its depth increases. The background is as large as the foreground. However, even with the distortion, isometrics are easier to draw than perspective views, which show a more true representation of depth.

Let's use the typical left corner vantage point to draw an isometric. The actual left corner line is the left line of your front view drawing, drawn vertically and to the same length. Now draw the bottom edge of the project front by scribing a line at 30° up from horizontal and to the right of the left corner line. Make the bottom edge of the project's left side by drawing a 30° line up and to the left of the front corner line.

Extend height lines up from the ends of these angled lines to create the project's overall height. Draw four more 30° lines left and right to form the top of the project and, essentially, the box that will contain the full project. From here, use the measurements in your plan and elevation drawings to fill in the details inside the isometric box and flesh out the project. When parts are inset from the outer faces of the isometric box, use faint 30° or vertical lines drawn in from the box faces to locate these parts.

Drawing curves, circles, and parts with non-square angles requires more careful description than we'll explain here. These curved lines will appear skewed on the sides of an isometric drawing to mimic the way they look on the side of any object seen in three dimensions.

Another method of drawing an object in three dimensions is called *perspective*. This technique provides a more realistic impression of depth than an isometric view, but it's not as easy to draw. The measurements for "depth" lines cannot be taken directly off your plan and elevation drawings like they can for isometrics. Instead, the illusion of depth is created by using two vanishing points. These points, drawn on a horizontal line near the top of the drawing, represent two points on the horizon, behind the drawing. One vantage point is located near the right edge of the paper and the other is near the left edge. While the vertical lines of a perspective drawing are all drawn at 90° to the bottom edge of the paper, the horizontal lines of the drawing extend from the vertical lines to the vantage points. This technique makes the project appear progressively smaller from front to back, just like objects really do when we look at them at an angle from front to back.

Developing shopping and cutting lists

Once your plan, elevation, and detail drawings are complete, use them to create a shopping list that tallies up the lumber you'll need to buy and another list of every part in the project with its exact dimensions spelled out.

Itemizing a shopping list involves calculating the amount of lumber and sheet material that will be required for your project. The easiest way to do this is to make scale drawings of boards in their common lumberyard sizes to represent a virtual stack of lumber. If your project includes sheet goods, draw full and half sheets as well. Then draw each part of your project on these board and sheet-good models to map out a rough idea of how much material will be required. These become cutting diagrams. Try to sketch the parts with reasonable accuracy and to scale, or at least parcel each board into squares or rectangles that represent the overall size of the parts. Label each part with a name and a letter or number to account for it on your cutting diagrams. Work carefully to be sure every part finds a place on a cutting diagram. If you need more than one type or thickness of lumber, label the cutting diagrams to keep these particulars clear.

Cutting diagrams have their limitations. For one, they can't account for the natural defects you'll encounter on the boards you buy. Rarely will you be able to maximize every inch of the board you draft as a cutting diagram. Remember also that you'll lose a certain amount of material to the saw blade just cutting the parts out of a board. Sometimes you'll create a shopping list from cutting diagrams and find that the lumberyard won't have stock in the board sizes you've drawn. This is especially true for specialty yards that sell lumber in random lengths and thicknesses. It's frustrating, but it happens. In these situations, you may have to revamp your cutting diagrams right at the lumberyard to work with what's available on the rack. Whatever the case may be, you can always buy more lumber than you need and return what you don't use. Ask about the return policy before you buy.

Shopping lists should include more than just lumber and sheet goods. They are good records for logging other items you need for the project, like fasteners, hinges, slide hardware, and glass. Add glue, sandpaper, and finishing supplies to your list too, if you need these items. With luck and a carefully detailed shopping list, you should be able to buy everything you need in just one trip.

A cutting list provides a detailed inventory of all the wood and sheet good parts in the exact sizes that are required to build the project. Use your plan and elevation drawings to list each part, the quantity of that part, and its thickness, width, and length. The list should also identify the wood species or material type for each part. Label each cutting list part with name and letter or number from the shopping list, then go back and label your drawings to match the cutting list naming convention. Now the drawings and cutting list work together to provide all the necessary information you'll need to start building.

DRAFTING BY COMPUTER

A pencil and paper aren't the only means to create construction drawings, especially if you use a Windows-based PC. Any number of computer assisted drafting (CAD) programs are available for accomplishing the same task. CAD software allows you to draw in scale, change the scale as needed, and revise your drawings without erasing or starting over. Many have dimensioning tools so you can label your drawings with all the appropriate measurements. Some programs are quite sophisticated, allowing you to render both 2-D and 3-D views, color them with realistic wood tones, and even rotate them around as you like. Simpler software packages are inexpensive and usually limit you to making plan and elevation drawings. CAD software is available for Macintosh computers as well as PCs, but the programs tend to be more expensive and there are fewer options to choose from.

Chapter 5
BUILDING PROJECT PARTS

After you've drafted a set of measured drawings, itemized a cutting list, and bought the necessary lumber and sheet materials, the next step is part-making. For most woodworkers, here's where the real fun starts! Preparing parts begins with surfacing your lumber, followed by careful stock layout, based on the dimensions you've determined in the cutting list. After parts are measured and marked, you'll cut them to rough size, then refine the proportions with more cutting, drilling, and shaping operations. Learn more about these procedures here.

Surfacing lumber

If you buy lumber already surfaced on the faces and edges, this may be all the surfacing it needs before use. Inspect each board carefully for straightness before you buy it. Lumber that's kiln-dried and flat at the lumber yard or home center will often stay that way once you've got it stored in your shop, but there's always a chance it may warp, even in the best conditions. When that happens, you may be able to twist the wood flat again just by fastening it to your project or dividing it into smaller, flatter pieces. Eventually you'll encounter a situation where neither of these options will do, and you'll have to do some additional surfacing with a power planer and jointer. You could also do this work with hand planes, but jointers and planers smooth and flatten stock in a fraction of the time it takes to do the work by hand, and the learning curve is more forgiving.

The jointer flattens faces and edges, and it makes these surfaces square to one another. It isn't designed to make opposing faces or edges parallel. Planers keep surfaces parallel, provided one face or edge is already flat. Their primary purposes are smoothing and reducing stock thickness.

Here's how the surfacing process works: Let's assume you have a roughsawn board to surface smooth or a board with minor warp to flatten out. Start by jointing one face flat to create a reference surface. Joint the flatter

Start the surfacing process by flattening one face of a board on the jointer. Use push sticks or push pads to feed the stock over the jointer knives and to keep your hands clear.

For particularly rough or uneven lumber, you may need to make several passes to flatten the first face. Continue jointing until the face is clean and smooth. Then flatten the other face in a thickness planer and joint one edge.

face whenever possible; you'll save more wood this way by removing just enough of the surface to obtain a flat face. Set the jointer to a cutting depth of $\frac{1}{32}$ inch and adjust the fence so it's square to the jointer bed (the long, horizontal work surface). If your board is wider than 6 or 8 inches, which is the typical maximum cutting width of most home shop jointers, it will be too wide to joint easily. Rip the board so it's narrow enough to joint completely in each pass. (For more on making rip cuts, see page 90.)

Hold the board so its face is flat against the jointer bed. Use a push stick or push pad in each hand to keep your fingers and palms safely out of harm's way. Push the board smoothly along the jointer bed and over the spinning knives. Press down on the board evenly as you slide it, shifting more pressure to the jointed side of the board after it passes the knives and less pressure on the portion that still must pass over the knives. Examine the jointed face after the first full pass. If the knives missed some areas, make a few more passes until the entire face makes contact with the knives. Check the face for flatness both lengthwise and widthwise with a long straightedge.

This jointed face becomes a reference surface for smoothing and flattening the other face with the surface planer. Measure the board thickness and set the planer's cutterhead so it will trim the board about $\frac{1}{16}$ inch thinner than it presently is. Deeper passes produce rougher surfaces, dull the planer knives prematurely, and can even stall the motor. For hardwoods, you may need to take an even shallower pass than $\frac{1}{16}$ inch to keep from bogging down the motor. Lock the cutterhead in place if the planer has a locking control for reducing snipe. Feed the board into the machine with the reference face against the smooth planer bed to plane the other face. Drop the cutterhead down another $\frac{1}{16}$ inch if the board needs another pass to smooth the entire face. Now both faces are parallel.

Look closely at the planed face by holding the board up to a light. If the planer is tearing away bits of wood along with smoothing other areas, you're planing against the board's grain direction. Turn the board end for end and try again. This will often correct the tearout problem, but it may not if the board's grain pattern shifts from one direction to the other. When both feed directions produce tearout, try wetting the board with a damp rag to raise the grain, set the machine for shallower passes, and plane the faces again.

Continue the planing process to reduce the board to whatever thickness you need, but keep the thickness at least ¼ inch. Thinner stock becomes flexible, and it can shatter if the board ends get caught in the planer knives. Flip the board from one face to the other with each pass. This practice removes equal amounts of material from both faces, which can help prevent warping.

With both board faces planed smooth and parallel, run the board on edge over the jointer to flatten a reference edge. If the jointer fence is square to the bed, the reference edge will be square to both faces. Now the board can be ripped to any width you need. When ripping boards to width on the table saw, be sure to orient the reference edge against the saw's rip fence. This way, the saw will cut an edge parallel to the reference edge.

Resist the urge to plane all your lumber down to a finished thickness as soon as you get it home. A bit of light surfacing can be helpful for assessing the grain patterns and figure of the lumber you have on hand, but keep this surfacing to just a pass or two. Let the wood acclimate to your shop environment in its oversize form until you need to use it. Lumber will need to reach a moisture equilibrium with your shop, and it may distort some in the process as it takes its final shape. Better to allow warping to happen before you've surfaced the lumber to size so you can joint and plane away the distortion. You'll never go wrong starting a project with rough stock that's thicker than you need.

Snipe

Most power planers will take a slightly deeper bite from the ends of boards when the feed rollers grab or release the lumber as it passes through. This phenomenon is called snipe. Look for shallow dished-out areas usually extending about 2 inches into the board faces. Snipe is difficult to eliminate entirely, and it's not really a sign of a malfunctioning planer. Most manufacturers of portable planers these days outfit their machines with "anti-snipe" locks on the cutterhead to help minimize the problem. The easiest way to contend with snipe is to do your planing on stock about 4 to 6 inches longer than you need, then trim off the sniped portions after surfacing. If the snipe is minimal, just sand these areas to blend them in to the rest of the board face. Jointers are capable of producing snipe, too, but generally you can fix this by adjusting the jointer beds and cutterhead.

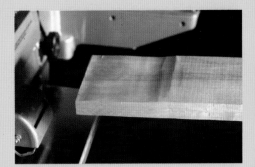

One way to lay out parts for a project is to mark the parts on the appropriate stock and then cut them all to size at once.

LAYOUT TOOLS

A few key tools will provide most of what you'll need for the usual layout tasks. Here are the ones to keep on hand:

- No. 2 pencils or carpenter's pencils
- White colored pencil (for dark woods)
- Tape measure (10 feet or longer)
- Combination square with 12-inch or longer blade
- Framing square
- Bevel gauge
- 3- or 4-foot straightedge
- Chalk line
- 8-inch compass
- Try square

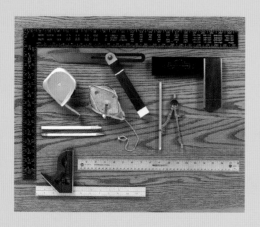

Layout

Laying out workpieces is the time to strategize the best arrangement of parts on each board so you can cut them out easily and minimize waste. Now is also when you select boards with the best figure and grain pattern for parts you'll want to highlight on your project, while leaving less desirable wood for pieces that won't show.

Three approaches to part layout. There are three schools of thought on how to lay out parts. Many woodworking project books and magazines advocate laying out all the parts at once and cutting them to size, one after the next. All the layout work happens at the beginning of a project. The main advantage to this method is efficiency. Marking all the parts to size, then cutting them out in one fell swoop takes care of part-making in a hurry. The downside to this method is it leaves you precious little margin for error. Once the boards are cut to size, you can't change your mind about the details or proportions of the project. You're committed to the design as is. If mistakes happen in the building process, you may have to remake some parts entirely rather than modify other part sizes to account for the mistake.

Another option is to lay out and cut parts in stages as you work through your project. Layout becomes a task that happens from the beginning of the construction process to nearly the end. For example, if you're building a table with a drawer, you might lay out and cut the legs, aprons, and other parts that form the table's base, then mill the joinery and assemble the base before moving on to the tabletop. After building the tabletop, more layout and cutting would produce the drawer components. The upside to this approach is that you can make changes as the building process unfolds. It's an especially forgiving method for working through those inevitable mistakes. If the tabletop looks too small or the drawer needs to be a bit wider than you planned in your construction drawings, you can change the proportions before laying out and cutting the parts.

A third layout technique, which is really a hybrid of the first two approaches, is to lay out and cut all the parts on your cutting list at the beginning, but make them a few inches longer and wider than necessary. This approach works well for large projects with long cutting lists that require lots of lumber. Sometimes it helps to size those stacks of boards down into smaller pieces immediately to get them off the floor and out of your way. Once the parts are cut to oversize proportions, you'll also know if you have enough material for all the parts you need. Occasionally, boards will warp after they are cut up. If the parts are larger than final size, you can correct for minor warpage at the rough size stage, then trim the parts to final size. The drawback to this approach is that cutting everything oversize produces more waste.

Whichever layout method you choose, the process of arranging parts on a board really depends on the types of parts you need to make and the sizes of lumber you have on hand. Here are some general guidelines to keep in mind as you work through the layout process:

• Spread out your boards and select the straightest or most attractive stock first. Start by marking the parts that need to be made from prime material. Usually these parts include drawer faces, panels for doors or tabletops, face frame rails and stiles, and any other pieces that should take advantage of interesting or matching grain pattern and figure.

• Don't feel obligated to work your way down the cutting list, laying out and cutting each part in order. Instead, try to keep the overall cutting list in mind, but arrange parts on boards in ways that use the lumber efficiently. If, for instance, you have a 27-inch-long part and a 30-inch-long part to make, look for a board around 5 feet to lay out both parts. A 6-foot board could work too, but you'd end up with 1 foot of lumber in the scrap bin unless you have some smaller parts to use it for. This might mean that Part A fits next to Part M on your board layout, which is fine.

Before laying out project parts, separate your lumber by quality. Reserve the prime material for parts that will show. Try to match grain patterns if you're making wide panels. Cut up less desirable lumber into smaller parts.

• As you measure and mark parts onto each board, label them according to the cutting list. Parts without labels are easy to confuse once you've cut them. Mark each part label on both a face and an edge or end. More than likely, you'll machine away at least one of these labels, but the other label usually stays intact. At some point, parts become unmistakable as you machine them to shape. Until that time comes, relabel parts as needed to keep things clear.

• Use a permanent marker or carpenter's pencil with a heavy lead to label the parts. These identifiers should be easy to read and tough to rub off. Masking tape also works, but cheap tape can be difficult to peel off once the adhesive sets on the wood.

• When cutting parts from long boards or heavy, unwieldy sheets of plywood, lay out the material in such a way that one or two cuts will size it down into more manageable workpieces. A quarter sheet of plywood is easier to lift onto a workbench or feed through a table saw than a full sheet.

Using a square. Squares are invaluable layout tools for drawing perpendicular lines. Hold the head of the square against a flat edge or end of a workpiece, and scribe along the blade to mark a square corner. Combination squares offer the added benefit of both 45° and 90° angles on the head for drawing either of these line angles. The blades of most squares are outfitted with rulers, so the tools double as measuring devices. The square's head forms a solid starting point for "zero distance" to plot line lengths. If you need to draw a line parallel to the edge of a workpiece, lock the blade of a combination square so the end matches the distance you want between the parallel line and the board edge. Hold a pencil against the end of the blade, and slide the pencil and square together along the board edge to draw the parallel line.

If you buy just one square for woodworking, make it a combination square. The head sets the rule for scribing either 90° or 45° angles, depending on how you set the square on a workpiece.

Try squares have heads that are permanently fixed to the blade. They can be used like combination squares for marking square corners, although the blades are generally shorter. All-metal try squares are handy for checking machine fences for square. They're often called engineering squares and calibrated to higher degree of accuracy than try squares with wooden heads.

Use a framing square for drawing larger square corners. Framing squares are generally less accurate than smaller try or combination squares, but they work fine for marking parts to rough size. The 4-foot T-style squares used for marking drywall are also useful here; they have a flat ledge along the T for holding the tool in position, and the blade is long enough to reach across the width of a full sheet of plywood. Be aware that these squares aren't engineered for high precision. Check yours by holding it against a known square corner to see if it creates a true 90°.

Bevel gauges can be adjusted to any angle using a protractor as a reference. They're also helpful tools for matching an unknown angle and transferring it precisely to another tool or workpiece.

Using a bevel gauge. Bevel gauges are really just squares with adjustable blades. A bevel gauge can be locked to any angle by tightening the nut at the base of the blade. Bevel gauges make wonderful duplicating devices in layout work. In cases where you don't know the measure of an angle but need to transfer it to another surface, a bevel gauge takes out the calculation work. Hold the head of the tool against one reference surface and adjust and lock the blade to match the angle you're transferring. If you need to create an angled line with a specific degree of measure, set the gauge with a protractor, then lock the bevel.

Using a tape measure. A tape measure is indispensable for rough layout work. To plot part lengths, hook the tape's clip over a reference edge, extend the tape, and mark the distance you need. Measuring off the end of a tape is accurate enough for general layout tasks, but once parts are cut to rough size, switch to a modified approach for taking fine measurements. Instead of measuring off the clip, use the 1-inch mark as your starting point. The moveable clip makes the first inch a less precise unit of measure than the others. When starting from the 1-inch mark, remember to subtract 1 inch from the overall measurement indicated on the tape to determine the actual distance—as is, you're offset by 1 inch.

It's also a good idea to stick with one tape measure for your whole project. Otherwise, the zero points referenced by the tape hook can vary somewhat from tape to tape, which could throw off your measurements.

Plotting long lines with a chalk line or straightedge. One way to mark long layout lines on large sheets

For better accuracy, measure beginning at the 1-inch mark on a tape measure, then subtract 1 inch from the measured distance.

of plywood or wide boards is to use a chalk line. Mark reference points on each end of the line you want to plot, then stretch the chalk line and hold it against the reference marks. Stretch the string taut from one end and hold it against both reference marks. Pull the string up, like drawing the string on a bow, and let it snap back. The string will leave a straight chalked line in its place on the workpiece.

You can also use a long metal straightedge or even a piece of straight scrap wood to draw long layout lines. Make a series of reference marks with a tape measure to mark the path of the layout line. Connect the marks with the straightedge and a pencil.

Drawing circles & curves. For circles with radii less than 8 inches, use a compass to scribe the shape. Spread the legs of the compass to the correct radius measurement and lock the setting. Push the sharpened tip into the workpiece to register the circle's centerpoint, and swing the compass pencil around the tip to draw the shape. For larger circles, mount a pair of trammel points onto a piece of scrap wood and draw the circle this way. The trammel points slide to any position along the scrap.

A pair of trammel points attached to a strip of wood enables you to draw circles of almost any size.

To make curved but noncircular shapes, you'll have to be a bit more resourceful. Art and drafting supply stores sell French curves, which provide a template of different curvatures for making smaller curves. You can also buy flexible curves from woodworking suppliers that are made of lead and bendable to any curved shape. Or use a piece of heavy-gauge wire bent to shape.

When you need to scribe a smooth arch, a long narrow strip of hardboard or a thin scrap of solid wood produces a smooth shape when flexed and held between a few nails tacked along the curve.

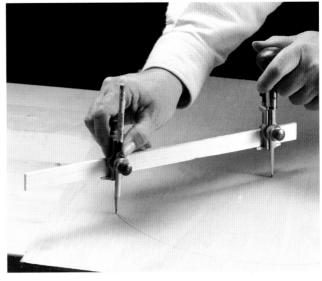

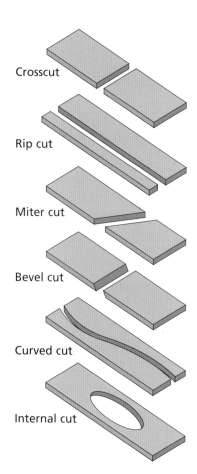

Crosscut

Rip cut

Miter cut

Bevel cut

Curved cut

Internal cut

Any cut you make will fall under one of the categories illustrated above or a combination of two.

Making basic cuts

Cutting out parts requires three basic types of cut: rip cuts, crosscuts, and curved cuts. Some cuts will be combinations of two sorts, like beveled rips or mitered crosscuts. Curved cuts can be edge curves or internal curves. Generally, stationary power tools produce cleaner cuts than handheld power tools, but you can do respectable work with a circular saw or jig saw with the right jig or accessory.

RIP CUTS

The common understanding of rip cutting, or ripping, is to cut parallel with the long grain pattern. This definition is more accurate for cutting solid wood than plywood, which doesn't have a consistent grain pattern running through its thickness. Either way, rip cuts commonly form the width of a workpiece.

Rip cutting with a table saw. Table saws are well-suited for rip cutting, and they're probably used for this purpose more than for making any other type of cut. A table saw has a long rip fence oriented parallel with the saw blade that stretches across the saw table. It can be positioned any distance from the blade on the table and locked for ripping purposes. Making rip cuts involves feeding workpieces through the blade and against the rip fence, pushing the wood with your hands or with push sticks when the material is narrow. The saw's broad table provides good support for workpieces, but generally you'll want to add more support behind the machine when cutting particularly long boards to catch the pieces and keep them from tipping off the table. A work table, roller stand, or even a tall saw horse is a good support option behind a table saw. The outfeed device should be about ¼ inch shorter than the saw's table to keep workpieces from catching on it.

Understanding kickback. One inherent danger of using a table saw for ripping is that boards can bind between the rip fence and the blade. Another danger is that the cutting channel created by the blade (called the kerf) can close up behind the blade. In either of these scenarios, if the blade teeth catch the wood, they will lift the workpiece off the table and fling it back in your direction forcefully and at great speed. This situation is called kickback, and it's the leading cause of table-saw-related accidents. The way to avoid kickback is to install the guard and splitter assembly that comes with your saw and use it every time you make rip cuts. Be sure that your saw's rip fence is parallel with the saw blade, and the blade is clean and sharp.

Making rip cuts with a table saw. First, adjust the rip fence so the distance between the fence and the closest face of the saw blade equals the workpiece width you want to cut. Lock the fence in place. With the saw unplugged, set the workpiece on the saw table and raise the blade so the teeth project above the wood all the way to the bottom of the gullets (the curved cutouts between the teeth). This height generally produces cleaner cuts than setting the blade lower in the work, and it's safer than exposing even more blade.

To make the cut, stand to the left of the workpiece. When cutting shorter lumber, touch your left foot to the front left corner of the saw base, if you are close

Start a rip cut by standing to the left of the workpiece, placing your left leg against the corner of the saw with your hip touching the front fence rail.

Feed the workpiece into the blade with your right hand while pressing the board against the fence with your left hand.

As you near the end of the cut, use a push stick to feed the board past the blade.

enough to reach it. This stance will help you maintain your balance during the cut. Start the saw and rest the workpiece on the saw table in front of the blade. Press the workpiece against the rip fence while slowly sliding it forward until it engages the blade teeth. Once the blade "kisses" the board, feed it into the blade with your right hand and hold the board against the rip fence with your left hand. Feed the workpiece as quickly and smoothly through the blade as you can without causing the motor to labor or stall. Maintain forward motion at all times. If the motor starts to bog down, slow your feed rate so the blade can build up speed again. When the back end of the board reaches the saw table, use a push stick in your right hand to feed the board the rest of the way past the blade. Hold a second push stick in your left hand to keep the work tight against the fence. Stop feeding with the left push stick when the end of the board approaches the blade. Once the board slices in two and the right portion is clear of the blade, shut off the saw and slide the wastepiece away from the blade with the left push stick.

When the board is cut through and the workpiece clears the blade, shut off the saw.

CAUTION: Never allow your hands to come within 6 inches of a spinning table saw blade for any reason. Use a push stick instead.

Ripping sheet materials with a table saw. You can rip full-size sheets of plywood or other composite material with a table saw using essentially the same ripping procedure as for solid lumber. The challenge is to maintain control of these unwieldy and sometimes heavy sheet materials while feeding them through the saw. Provide some means of sturdy workpiece support behind the saw to bear the weight. A work table or a pair of roller stands set just lower than the saw table height make good support devices. When ripping wide sheet goods, you may also want to position workpiece support alongside the saw. If the proportions or weight of your sheet material make the ripping process seem too daunting at the table saw, use a circular saw instead.

Use the push stick to slide the wastepiece away from the blade to complete the process.

Bevel-ripping. When you tilt the blade to an angle and make a rip cut, you're technically cutting a bevel, or bevel-ripping. Beveled edges are commonly used around the center panels of cabinet doors or as a means of easing sharp edges.

The process for ripping bevels on a table saw is largely the same as making standard rip cuts, but there are a few special considerations to keep in mind. For one, position the rip fence on the side of the blade opposite the direction it tilts. If your blade tilts right, the rip fence belongs on the left side of the table. This way, the waste piece that's cut free during bevel-ripping doesn't become trapped between the fence and table where the blade can catch it and throw it back your way. The waste also ends up resting on the table below the blade rather than on top where the teeth can catch and throw it.

When making beveled rip cuts, tilt the blade away from the rip fence so the wastepiece ends up below the blade.

To make a bevel with the workpiece lying flat on the saw table, tilt the blade and clamp the fence in place. It helps to draw an angled reference line on your workpiece to help line up the blade before you make the cut. Or you can start the saw and slide the workpiece forward until the blade teeth just "kiss" the workpiece at your reference mark. Turn off the saw and adjust the fence as needed to correct any misalignment. Feed the workpiece through the blade with your left hand if the fence is on the left or your right hand if the fence is positioned right of the blade. Use your other hand like a featherboard to hold the workpiece tight against the fence as you slide the wood along.

If you need to cut a bevel that's steeper than 45°, you'll have to stand the workpiece on edge instead of on its face. For boards wider than 8 inches, attach a tall auxiliary fence to the rip fence to help support the workpiece and keep it from teetering. Install a zero-clearance throat plate as well. The narrow blade slit on

CHOOSING A TABLE SAW BLADE

A good all-around blade to keep in your saw is one intended for "general purpose" or "combination" use. These blades usually have 40 or 50 carbide-tipped teeth configured to make smooth rip and cross-cuts in hardwoods, softwoods, and sheet goods. If you do a significant amount of ripping, consider buying a dedicated ripping blade. These blades usually have 18 to 36 large, flat-topped teeth designed for faster material feeding. Crosscutting blades have 60 to 80 or more teeth and make glass-smooth cross-grain cuts, but the high tooth count makes for slow ripping. Unless you do a lot of crosscutting, a specialized crosscut blade probably isn't worth the extra money. If you need to cut melamine, veneered plywood, plastic, or nonferrous metal, specialized blades are available for these purposes too.

a zero-clearance throat plate prevents the board from tipping down into the blade opening. When the bevel you're cutting removes most or all of the board's supportive lower edge, clamp a piece of scrap to the board so it rides along the top of the auxiliary fence (see photo, right). The scrap will act like a runner and help keep the workpiece from tipping down into the blade slot.

Bevel-ripping tends to generate more blade marks and swirls than standard ripping. To help minimize these problems, check the alignment of the blade and rip fence. Tune the saw if you discover any blade heel.

Ripping tapers. Tapers are rip cuts that follow the long grain but cut the edge of a board at an angle. You'll see tapers used most commonly on table and chair legs, and generally the legs are tapered on two adjacent edges. Tapers are an attractive way to slim down the proportions of furniture parts, and they're easy to cut on a table saw using a simple tapering jig. Do not attempt to cut tapers by holding a workpiece at an angle to the blade without anchoring it in a jig. There's no way to accurately make a freehand cut, and the wood will probably kick back in the process.

Tapering jigs sold in woodworking supply catalogs are relatively inexpensive and easy to use, or you can build your own. Manufactured tapering jigs are adjustable so you can use them for making a variety of tapers with different angles. They consist of two adjustable "arms" joined by a hinge on one end. One arm rides against the rip fence, and the other arm holds the workpiece at an angle to the blade. A stop on the end of this arm steadies the workpiece as you slide the jig and workpiece past the blade. An adjustable brace spanning both arms locks the arms in place.

To cut tapers with an adjustable jig, begin by marking the workpiece with layout lines showing the tapered edge. Then use a straightedge and pencil to draw a line across the front of the saw table that shows the exact path of the saw blade. Set the straightedge against the side of the blade closest to the rip fence to mark this line. Place the tapering jig against the rip fence and the workpiece in the jig. Adjust the arm that holds the workpiece until the line you made on the workpiece aligns with the blade reference line on the table. Using the reference line on the saw table, you'll know exactly where the blade will enter the workpiece. Lock the jig arms and rip fence to hold their positions.

Back up the jig to the front of the table so the workpiece clears the blade. To cut the taper, slide the jig and workpiece along the fence as you would a normal rip cut. To cut a matching taper on an adjacent edge, flip the workpiece in the jig so the first taper faces up, then cut the second taper. To taper all four faces, reset the jig for twice the first angle when you have to place a tapered edge against the adjustable arm.

For cutting steep bevels along the edge of a board, you may need to stand it up on the saw table. Make the cut with the workpiece against a tall auxiliary fence attached to the rip fence. Clamp a runner to the workpiece to ride on the auxiliary rip fence. This keeps the workpiece from falling into the throat plate blade slot.

Tapered cuts are easy to make with an inexpensive tapering jig. The jig holds workpieces safely at an angle to the blade.

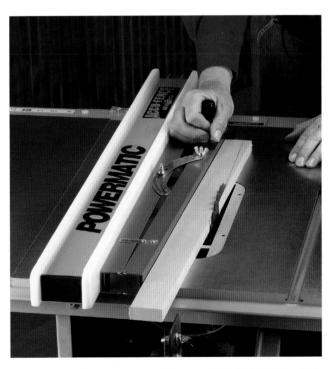

Rip cutting with a circular saw. A circular saw outfitted with a general-purpose carbide-tipped blade makes a fine ripping tool for less exacting applications. Circular saws tend to produce more splintering around the cut edges than table saws, but they can be safer than table saws for rough-cutting large workpieces. Circular saws should only be used for ripping when workpieces are wider than the saw base. Otherwise, the saw will be tippy and difficult to control.

Circular saws pose the same kickback hazard as table saws if the blade gets pinched while cutting. Avoid kickback by following a couple easy preventive measures. First, keep your circular saw blade clean by removing pitch and other deposits with spray-on blade cleaner. Dirty blades bind more easily than clean blades. Set the blade depth so the teeth project ¼ to ½ inch below the workpiece. Provide plenty of support beneath your workpiece to keep it from sagging and binding the blade,

One method of making accurate rip cuts with a circular saw is to guide the saw base against a straightedge clamped in place.

which can lead to kickback. If the saw kerf begins to close up behind the tool— a common problem when cutting solid wood—insert a wedge in the kerf to spread it open again before proceeding with the cut.

For ripping situations where accuracy isn't critical, you can guide a circular saw freehand along a cutting line. In most woodworking situations, you'll want more control and precision than "eyeballing" your rip cuts. Clamp a straight piece of scrap lumber or a metal straightedge firmly to your workpiece to form a makeshift rip fence, and run the edge of the saw base against the straightedge. You'll need to offset the straightedge from your cutting line to account for the saw base width. Find the amount of offset by measuring from the edge of the base to the blade teeth.

Another option for making rip cuts close to the edge of a workpiece is to install a ripping guide on the saw base. Make the cut with the bearing surface of the guide riding along the workpiece edge.

Another way to make rip cuts with a circular saw is to use the adjustable ripping guide that comes with most saws. It resembles a T and fits on the saw like an outrigger. Clamp it to the front of the saw base so the bearing surface of the guide will ride against the edge of the workpiece. When using this guide, set up the cut so the wider side of the saw base rests on the portion of the workpiece that won't be cut free. Always try to keep the wider side of the base planted on a stable surface. When making the rip cut, keep the ripping guide pressed against the work edge as you push the saw forward and through the cut. This will keep the saw from wandering off the cutting line.

Rip cutting with jig saws & band saws. Jig saws and band saws are safer power tools for making rip cuts than table saws or circular saws. Because the blades cut in an inline rather than circular motion, they don't produce the rotational forces that lead to kickback. These blades also cut thinner kerfs, which reduce the amount of wasted wood. Both jig saws and band saws can make curved as well as straight cuts, unlike circular saws or table saws, which are limited to just straight cuts. However, jig saws and band saws make rip cuts more slowly than saws with circular blades.

Rip cutting with a jig saw is done by guiding the tool freehand or against a clamped straightedge, like a circular saw. Jig saw blades are quite narrow and only supported from above the cut, so they tend to flex and wander a bit when cutting thick material. For fast rip cuts, choose a wide blade with a low number of teeth per inch. The blade will have large teeth and gullets. Thicker blades will help reduce flexing, too.

Band saws cut more smoothly than jig saws. You'll also have improved control over the cut. A band saw blade is held under tension both above and below the cutting surface, so it tends to cut square, clean edges if properly adjusted. Band saws are also better choices than jig saws for ripping narrow stock; it's easier to feed a narrow workpiece through the blade than to work the other way around, moving the tool over the wood.

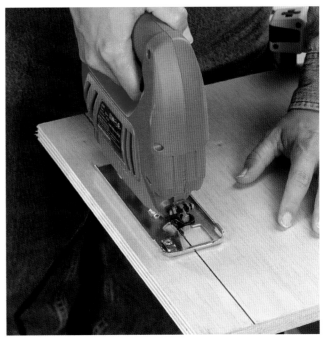

Jig saws make decent ripping tools, and they're easier to guide freehand along a cutting line than a circular saw. For greater accuracy, clamp a straightedge to the work and guide the saw against it.

For ripping, choose a wide skip-tooth band saw blade. It cuts more quickly and

CHOOSING A CIRCULAR SAW BLADE

Most ordinary circular saws accept 7¼-inch-diameter blades, and there are many to choose from. For general ripping, blades with fewer teeth cut more quickly but make rougher edges. "Combination" blades with between 16 and 24 teeth do a good job of ripping and crosscutting most woods. Choose a

blade outfitted with antikickback shoulders. These small humps behind the teeth limit the amount of material each tooth can remove.

Most circular saw blades now have thinner blade bodies than table saw blades, so they cut a narrower kerf and require less energy from the tool during cutting. Look for a "thin kerf" designation on the package. When cutting splintery materials such as plywood, or melamine and particleboard that are prone to chipping, switch to a blade intended for cutting plywood. These blades have scores of small teeth that take tiny bites of material. You'll have to feed the tool more slowly, but the smaller teeth produce virtually splinter-free edges.

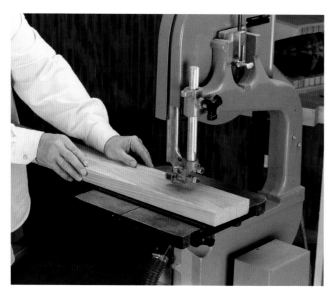

Band saws make both straight and curved rip cuts with equal ease. You can guide the cuts freehand or against a rip fence clamped in place.

cleanly than narrower blades with more teeth. Make the cut by feeding the work freehand through the blade and following your cutting line by eye. For more accuracy, you can also use a rip fence or straight piece of scrap clamped to the saw table and feed the work into the blade like you would for making rip cuts on a table saw. If the blade wanders off the cut when using a rip fence, you may need to adjust the fence so it's slightly skewed to the blade. This phenomenon is called blade drift, and it's a common problem with band saws.

CROSSCUTS

As the name suggests, crosscutting involves cutting solid wood across the grain. Rip cuts establish the width of a workpiece, and a pair of crosscuts set the length. The common definition of crosscutting implies that these cuts are square to the board edges, although angled cross-grain cuts—like miters—are technically crosscuts as well. Any tool capable of making rip cuts can be used for crosscutting, but the more accurate tools for this operation are the table saw, power miter saw, circular saw, and radial arm saw.

Crosscutting with a table saw. For crosscutting on a table saw, use a miter gauge. Miter gauges are standard equipment on every brand of table saw. They

CROSSCUT SLEDS

Many professional woodworkers use crosscut sleds instead of miter gauges for crosscutting. A crosscut sled is simply a sheet of plywood with a tall fence along either edge mounted to a couple runners that fit in both miter slots. A saw kerf divides the middle of the sled in two to provide a clear track for the blade. Plans for building crosscut sleds are available in many woodworking project books and appear as project stories in woodworking magazines from time to time.

Using the jig involves placing workpieces inside the sled and against the back fence, then sliding the sled across the table to make the cut. Crosscut sleds provide several advantages over miter gauges. By holding workpieces stationary and sliding the sled, you keep the wood from moving laterally during cutting, so cuts are much more precise. The sled fence provides a backing surface behind workpieces to help minimize splintering. Once the fence is set perpendicular to the saw blade, it never needs readjustment to make perfect square cuts.

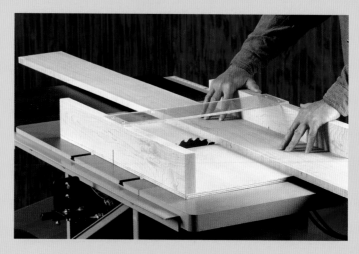

consist of a protractor-style head attached to a metal bar that slides in a pair of slots on either side of the saw blade. When set to 0°, the miter gauge forms a 90° angle relative to the blade.

The procedure for making a crosscut with a miter gauge is easy: Hold or clamp the workpiece against the miter gauge fence and slide both up to the blade with the saw turned off. Adjust the workpiece by sliding it along the miter fence until the layout line on the board edge is even with the blade teeth. Make sure the thickness of the blade falls on the waste side of your layout line.

With the workpiece and blade aligned, slide the miter gauge and workpiece away from the blade. Start the saw. Position your body behind the miter gauge so you are standing clear of the blade path. If the miter gauge is to the right of the blade, hold the workpiece with your right hand and grip the miter gauge handle with your left hand. Reverse the hand positions when the miter gauge is in the left miter slot. This way your arms aren't crossed over one another and both are clear of the blade.

Slide the miter gauge forward and gently feed the workpiece into the blade. As soon as the teeth engage the workpiece, move the gauge smoothly and rapidly past the blade so the teeth cut cleanly and without burning. When the workpiece cuts in two, a waste piece is left next to the blade. Continue to push the miter gauge forward and clear of the blade. Turn off the saw and remove the waste before proceeding with another crosscut. Or move it out of the blade area with a push stick.

Sometimes the piece you cut free is the workpiece you're actually making. In these cases, arrange your crosscuts so both ends of this workpiece will be square when you cut it to length. In other words, make one crosscut on the longer initial stock to square one end of your soon-to-be shorter workpiece, then crosscut the workpiece free and to length. Typically, it will take two crosscuts to make any final workpiece square on both ends. You'll make these cuts more safely by performing them on longer stock.

Align the blade carefully with the layout line before starting the saw and making the crosscut.

With the workpiece held firmly against the miter gauge, slide both past the blade to make the cut. Stand behind the miter gauge so your body is clear of the wastepiece.

Slide the wastepiece away from the blade with a push stick. If it is too small to reach easily, turn off the saw first. Do not remove short wastepieces by hand while the blade is spinning.

The fence on a miter gauge is often too small to support larger workpieces adequately. Add more bearing support by attaching a larger wood fence to the miter gauge with screws.

CAUTION: *It is never safe to make crosscuts using the rip fence instead of the miter gauge. The rip fence does not support workpieces from behind like miter gauges do. Workpieces crosscut against the rip fence tend to veer off the fence, bind the blade, and kick back. It is also not safe to hold workpieces against both the miter gauge and the rip fence during crosscutting. Although the rip fence would seem to make a handy stop for cutting workpieces to the same length, it actually can trap them between the blade and miter gauge, leading to kickback.*

Miter gauges are capable of making fairly precise crosscuts on workpieces up to a couple feet in length. However, several adjustments and simple improvements will boost their accuracy and performance significantly. First, hold the stock of a combination or try square against the fence of your miter gauge and adjust the miter head until the square's blade is flush against the miter bar. If your miter gauge has an adjustable flip-up stop for 0°, set it here after checking for square.

If the bar on your miter gauge fits loosely in the miter slots, tap a series of dimples along the edges of the bar with a nailset or metal punch. The resulting dimples will improve the fit.

Notice that the fence on your miter gauge is only about 6 or 8 inches long. As is, it is too short to provide adequate support behind longer workpieces. Remedy the problem by attaching a flat scrap of wood about 16 to 24 inches long and 3 or 4 inches wide to your miter fence with short screws. This forms an auxiliary wood fence. Then glue a strip of medium-grit sandpaper to the face. Position the auxiliary fence on the miter fence so the end near the blade stops just short of the blade guard. With this added bearing surface, you'll be able to crosscut longer workpieces, and the sandpaper will keep them from creeping away from the blade during cutting. Or build a crosscut sled to replace your standard miter gauge for making crosscuts (see the sidebar on page 96).

Another way to help your miter gauge cut more accurately is to minimize a sloppy fit in the miter slots. Set the gauge in a miter slot and try to jiggle it from side to side. If the bar moves in the slot, this extra play will result in rough crosscuts. To improve the fit, tap a series of dimples along the edges of the bar

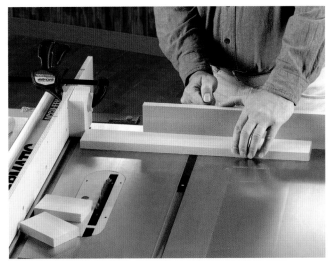

Use a stop block clamped to the rip fence to set up repetitive crosscuts. Set the block well forward of the blade so the workpiece will clear it before it reaches the blade.

Another option for making repetitive cross cuts is to clamp a stop block to an auxiliary fence on the miter gauge and use this as the indexing stop for establishing the length of the workpieces.

using a nailset and hammer. The dimples provide a bit of extra metal to fill the gap in the miter slot. File down the dimples slightly if the fit goes from being too loose to too tight. Ideally, the gauge should slide smoothly but without any noticeable side-to-side play. If you have a newer or aftermarket miter gauge on your saw, it may have expansion screws or adjustable disks along the miter bar to take up extra play.

Repetitive crosscutting. Most woodworking projects will have some parts with matching lengths. You could measure and cut each of these like-sized parts individually, but the process is time-consuming, and odds are the part lengths won't be exactly the same in the end.

A better method for cutting several parts to precise, matching lengths is to use a stop block. A stop block is simply a piece of scrap with smooth, square edges and ends that you clamp temporarily to an auxiliary miter gauge fence, a cross-cut sled, or the rip fence. Stop blocks create a fixed distance to the blade so you measure just once to cut as many same-length parts as you need.

When attaching a stop block to the auxiliary miter fence or the back fence of a crosscut sled, clamp the block on the same side of the blade as the work-piece you want to make. Position it so the distance between the block and the blade matches the workpiece length. Cut one end of the workpiece square, and butt this end against the stop block. If you need to make work-pieces longer than the auxiliary fence, you may have to install a longer aux-iliary fence.

You can also use the rip fence as a mounting surface for a stop block, provided you follow a few safety requirements. First, be sure to clamp the stop block to the fence ahead of the blade on the infeed side. Place the stop block far enough forward of the blade so the full width of the workpiece clears the stop block before it engages the blade. It's a good idea to make the stop block from stock

To set precise miter angles, use a bevel gauge locked to the angle you need. Hold the bevel gauge against both the saw blade and miter gauge. This yields a more accurate setting than using the protractor scale on the miter gauge.

Set up miter cuts so the workpiece leads the miter gauge into the blade. This way, you can clamp a stop block to the opposite end of the miter gauge's auxiliary fence to keep the workpiece from shifting when it's cut.

that's at least ¾ inch thick. With these provisions, the workpiece and the stop block are clear of one another so the workpiece can't jamb between the stop block and the blade, and cause a kickback. The stop block also creates an important relief space between the workpiece and rip fence. To index the cut, clamp the block to the fence, and mark your workpiece to length. Set the workpiece against the miter fence so the blade aligns with your cutting line. Slide the rip fence over until the stop block touches the end of the workpiece, and lock the fence. Make the cut by sliding the workpiece forward along the stop block, then off the block and into the blade.

Crosscutting miters. Crosscutting a standard miter involves pivoting the miter gauge head to an angle other than 0° and cutting the wood with the blade set square to the table. Miter gauges can be pivoted to cut angles up to 45°, which tends to be the most common angle for woodworking situations. Unless you are using a precision miter gauge with preset detents for locking exact angle settings, it's best not to trust the protractor markings on the miter gauge head. They're usually slightly inaccurate. Instead, set the head by using a drafting square or a bevel gauge locked to the cutting angle you need. To do this, place the square or bevel gauge against the saw blade and position the miter gauge in a miter slot next to the blade. Pivot the miter head until it makes even contact with the reference tool, and lock the miter-head setting. Cut a miter on test scrap to check the angle before cutting your actual workpiece.

Miter cuts must be performed carefully or your wood joints won't meet evenly when assembled. However, making miter cuts on a table saw has the potential to be even less precise than making square crosscuts. Pivoting the miter head actually decreases the amount of support the head provides to the workpiece. As you slide the wood forward and into the blade, it tends to creep along the miter fence. If the workpiece moves at all, accuracy is lost.

To improve your mitering accuracy, add an auxiliary fence to the miter gauge and apply a sandpaper face. The grit will give it better "grip" on workpieces. Make the fence long enough to support the workpiece right up to the blade and provide enough room to clamp a stop block in place on the opposite end. Set up the miter cut so the longer portion of the wood is what you're holding against the miter fence, regardless of whether it is actually the workpiece you want to make or the waste end.

Another way to better your odds is to orient the miter gauge and workpiece so the end you're cutting will lead the workpiece into the blade rather than trail behind it. This way you can clamp a stop block to the other end of the miter fence to support the back end of the workpiece and keep it from shifting. This arrangement is called a "closed" miter cut. An "open" miter cut occurs when the end you're cutting follows behind the rest of the workpiece and the stop block is clamped to the leading end of the fence instead of the trailing end. In this setup, the blade will tend to pull the workpiece along the fence and away from the stop block during the cut, ruining accuracy. Whether you're cutting an open or closed miter, it's a good idea to clamp the workpiece against the miter fence. This way, you can use both hands for pushing the miter gauge without also having to hold the workpiece steady.

When you need to cut several mitered workpieces to the same length, use a stop block just as you would for making repetitive square crosscuts. Be sure the stop block is sized wide enough so it can support the tip of a workpiece with an end already cut into a miter. Or cut the end of the stop block at an angle to capture the mitered end of the workpiece.

If you have a crosscut sled or sliding miter table, you can use these accessories instead of the miter gauge for cutting miters. With either device, workpieces won't creep during the cut because they are held off the saw table and stationary in the jig. Crosscut sleds usually won't come with an adjustable fence for mitering, but you can make angled cuts by clamping a piece of angled scrap inside the sled to hold your workpiece in the proper position.

Crosscutting bevels. Beveled crosscuts involve tilting the blade to an angle other than 90° with the miter gauge locked for a square cut. They're easier than miters to perform accurately since the miter gauge isn't pivoted to an angle. The most important issue to keep in mind for bevel cutting is which miter slot to use for the miter gauge. Choose the miter slot that's opposite the direction of the blade tilt. If your saw tilts right, use the left slot, and vice-versa for newer left-tilt saws. This way, the offcut will rest on the saw table as soon as it's cut free rather then end up on top of the tilted blade where it can catch on the blade teeth and kick back.

By swiveling the miter gauge as well as tilting the blade, a table saw will cut accurate compound miter cuts.

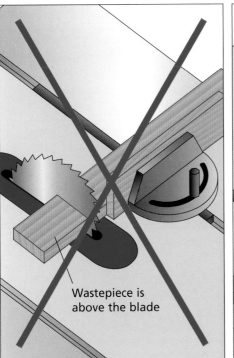

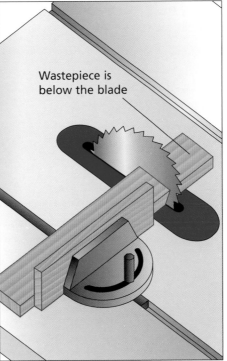

Wastepiece is below the blade

Wastepiece is above the blade

When cutting bevels, arrange the workpiece so the waste will end up below the blade and on the saw table, not above it. Otherwise, the blade teeth are more likely to catch the loose wastepiece and throw it off the saw.

When cranking the blade to a bevel angle, use a drafting square or a bevel gauge to find the precise degree of tilt. Your saw's bevel scale isn't a precision measuring device. On contractor's saws, the arbor assembly may even twist slightly when it's tilted, regardless of what the bevel pointer reads as the tilt angle. Verify the bevel setting by making a test cut on scrap, then perform the final cut on your workpiece just as you would a square crosscut.

In addition to miter and bevel cuts, you can also make compound miter cuts on a table saw by pivoting the miter gauge and tilting the saw blade. These cuts are common for installing crown moldings. A table saw will cut them accurately, provided you set the bevel and miter angles carefully. Test your setup on scrap and adjust accordingly before cutting your workpiece.

Crosscutting with a power miter saw. Of all the crosscutting machines, power miter saws are arguably the most accurate. With the appropriate cross-cutting blade, these handy saws are engineered to make glass-smooth crosscuts that need no further finishing work. Their primary limitation is width of cut. Large plunge-style miter saws offer a maximum crosscutting capacity of about 10 inches. Sliding miter saws can cut wider workpieces, but they're still limited by the travel length of the motor carriage.

Making crosscuts with either a plunge-style or sliding miter saw is a straight-forward operation. For a plunge saw, set the workpiece snug against the fence on the saw base so the cutting line is even with the blade. Check for alignment by pivoting the blade down against the workpiece with the saw turned off. Be sure to register the cut so the blade is on the waste side of the cutting line. If the workpiece is long enough to keep your hands outside the danger zone designated on the tool, you can hold the wood against the tool by hand. Use a push stick to hold shorter workpieces against the fence or use a hold-down clamp if your saw has one. Make the cut by turning on the saw and gently

Making a crosscut with a plunge-style miter saw involves holding the workpiece against the saw fence and pivoting the spinning blade down into it.

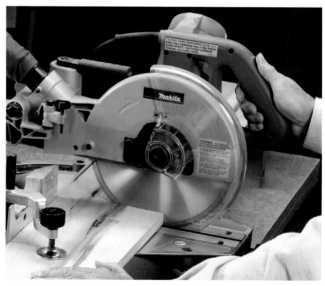

Crosscutting with a sliding miter saw is a little different. Here, you pull the saw carriage forward, lower the spinning blade into the workpiece, and push the carriage back through the wood.

pushing the blade down through the workpiece. Once the saw drops to its full cutting range, release the motor trigger and let the blade stop before raising the blade out of the workpiece.

The cutting procedure for a sliding miter saw is a bit different than for a plunge saw. Pull the motor carriage toward you and lower the blade onto the workpiece to check for blade alignment. Raise the blade all the way up and start the saw. Lower the blade down into the saw base kerf, and push the motor carriage away from you to make the cut. Wait until the blade stops before withdrawing it from the workpiece.

When using either saw type, it's a good idea to clamp or bolt the saw base securely to a work surface before cutting. This is especially true for sliding miter saws with narrow bases. The sliding motion can shift the machine's center of gravity and cause it to tip backward during a cut. If you're cutting particularly long workpieces, you may also need to provide additional support alongside the tool to keep the wood from tipping off the saw table after it's cut.

Crosscutting with a circular saw. For the occasional "quick and dirty" crosscut, a circular saw is a good choice. Use the same blade depth settings as for rip cuts. When accuracy isn't critical, simply guide the saw freehand to make the cut. Clamp a straightedge across the workpiece for cutting more accurately. Contractors often use a speed square with a flared base as a jobsite crosscutting fence. Hold the square against the workpiece so the flare fits over an edge. Position the saw base against the square, and adjust both until the saw blade lines up with the cutting line on the workpiece. Slide the saw along the square to make the cut.

To make bevel cuts with a circular saw, unlock the saw base and tilt the blade to the desired angle. Make the cut just as you would an ordinary crosscut.

Crosscutting with a radial arm saw. Radial arm saws work in reverse of sliding miter saws. The motor and blade ride along a carriage above the saw table, but with this machine, you pull the motor toward you during a cut rather than push it away. The blade maintains the same cutting depth throughout the cut instead of pivoting. Radial arm saws are especially useful for crosscutting long, heavy workpieces. They can also be outfitted with dado blades for cutting wide grooves for joinery.

To make a crosscut, slide the motor carriage away from you and position the workpiece against the saw's fence. Line up the cut with the motor off, then push the carriage back so the blade is clear of the fence and workpiece. Start the saw

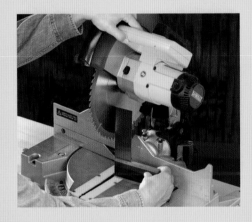

TUNING A MITER SAW

Before making crosscuts with a power miter saw, tune the blade so it is square to both the saw base and the fence. Use a square held against the blade body—not the teeth—to check both of these positions. All saws have adjustment screws for fine-tuning blade and fence alignment. The owner's manual will outline the tuning process. Once these adjustments are made, the saw should hold blade and fence settings permanently unless the tool is transported often or damaged in some way. Check the blade and fence settings occasionally just to be sure.

Guide a circular saw against the blade of a speed square to improve the tool's accuracy when making crosscuts.

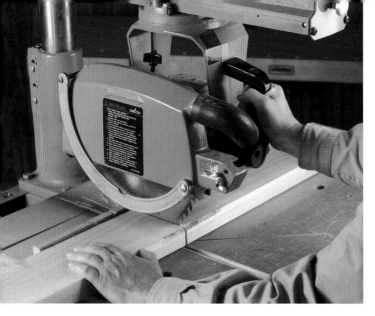

Radial arm saws function in the reverse of sliding miter saws for making crosscuts. Start the blade and pull it toward you and through the workpiece. Be sure to hold the workpiece firmly against the fence on the saw table.

RELIEF CUTS

When cutting tight curves with any of the three curve-cutting saws, even narrow saw blades sometimes bind in the cut. If the blade binds or twists severely, it will break. An easy way to avoid this problem is to make a series of relief cuts through the surrounding waste material and up to the curved cutting line you plan to follow for the final cut. This way, you can break up a tight curve into smaller sections of waste rather than forming one long cut.

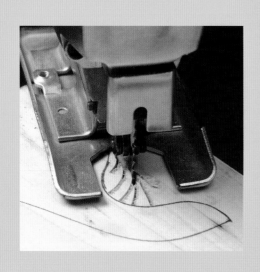

and slowly pull the motor carriage toward you until the blade cuts the workpiece in two. Release the trigger and allow the blade to stop before removing the workpiece sections and sliding the saw carriage back to the starting position. Use hand pressure or push sticks to hold workpieces against the fence.

CAUTION: Use extreme care when advancing the motor and blade through the cut. Feeding the blade too rapidly into a cut can cause the blade to climb up over the workpiece and propel itself with great force in your direction. Always keep a firm grip on the motor handle during the entire cut.

CURVED CUTS

Three machines excel at curve-cutting. In terms of lowest to highest precision, they are the jig saw, band saw, and scroll saw. Band saws can only make curve cuts that form outside edges of a shape because the blades are closed loops that can't be opened up to insert inside a workpiece. Jig saws and scroll saws can make internal cutouts as well as edge curves.

Cutting curves with a jig saw. The secret to cutting curves with a jig saw is to work slowly and not force the blade. Curve-cutting involves guiding the tool along a layout line or just outside of it using a moderate speed and the proper blade. Narrower blades allow the tool to cut tighter curves without binding and burning or breaking. Blades with larger teeth, especially those arranged in an aggressive offset pattern, cut curves more quickly than fine-tooth blades. Blades with 8 teeth per inch (tpi) are a good choice for general cutting and smoother edges. Use 10- to 14-tpi blades for the smoothest cutting. As tooth counts increase, cutting speed decreases.

Occasionally you'll need to remove the center of a workpiece without cutting from the edge inward. Jig saws make easy work of these sorts of internal cutout tasks. To start the cut, drill a hole inside the cutting area with a bit that has a larger diameter than the blade width. Use this starter hole to begin cutting out the waste.

Cutting curves with a band saw. Band saws provide more control for curve-cutting than jig saws, especially on smaller workpieces. The large saw table offers ample support, and the blade is held under tension so it resists flexing. You can also cut through much thicker stock with a band saw than a jig saw, and band saws can be outfitted with a larger range of blade widths and tooth counts to suit the task and material.

Blades between ⅛ and ⅜ inch wide are the best choices for curve cutting. Narrower blades will follow tighter curves. Tighter curves are easier to navigate with a band saw by making relief cuts first, just as you would with a jig saw (see sidebar, facing page). When the design of the workpiece doesn't allow for relief cuts, don't back the blade out of a long cut with the saw running. Instead, shut the saw off and then back the workpiece out carefully.

Cutting curves with a scroll saw. The basic procedure for using a scroll saw is the same as for band saws. Simply feed workpieces into the blade and move the workpiece right or left to follow the curve.

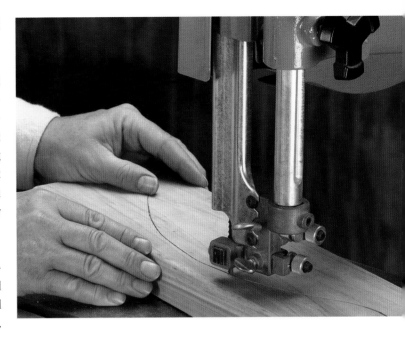

Scroll saw blades can be quickly removed and reinstalled for feeding into starter holes of internal cutouts. Be sure to orient the blade in its mounts so the teeth face downward toward the saw table. Install the blade and tighten the blade tension knob until there's no side-to-side play when you wiggle the blade by hand. It takes some experience with the tool to determine just how tight to tension the blade. Overtightening will break the blade or cause it to pull free from its mounts. Undertightening allows the blade to wander as it cuts, which causes it to cut roughly, and may cause it to break in a short time. If your saw has variable speed, experiment with different speed settings to find a speed that best suits the material you're cutting.

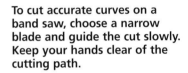

To cut accurate curves on a band saw, choose a narrow blade and guide the cut slowly. Keep your hands clear of the cutting path.

Whether you're cutting curves or straight lines with a band saw, position the upper blade guard and guides within ¼ inch of the top surface of the workpiece. This keeps the blade tracking properly in the blade guides, and it protects you from blade injuries.

Scroll saws are handy for cutting tight curves or making internal cutouts. The blades can be fed through a clearance hole inside a workpiece without starting the cut from an edge.

Drilling holes

Sometimes your workpieces will require holes of various sizes or you'll need to drill clearance holes for driving dowels, screws, or nails. Hole-drilling for woodworking can be done with a drill press, corded drill, or cordless drill/driver. Drill presses afford you more control over drilling tasks than the other two drills, and they can handle larger bit diameters. However, you can still do clean, relatively accurate work with a hand drill if you don't have a drill press. Whichever tool you use, try to drill as carefully as you can, holding the tool so the bit meets the workpiece surface squarely. A quick way to check for square when using a handheld drill is to hold the tool against the blade of a combination square with the head of the square resting on the workpiece.

For drilling holes freehand, mark the centerpoint of your hole, and tap a dimple into the wood at the reference mark with a scratch awl or nail. Set the tip of the bit in the dimple. Start drilling at slow speeds to

Drill presses are handy for boring holes that are either perpendicular or at an angle to the workpiece. Tilting the drill press table changes the drilling angle.

score the entry hole and register the bit tip, then increase the tool speed to clear chips from the hole efficiently.

Drilling holes with a drill press involves first setting the motor speed appropriately for the size and type of bit you're using as well as the material being drilled. Most drill press motor speeds are changed by unlocking and shifting the motor forward and moving a drive belt to different pulleys on two large clusters inside the machine. A few drill presses now have variable speed with a dial for adjusting chuck speeds. Check inside the pulley housing on top of the machine for a chart that indicates the right belt configuration to use for the speed you need. Larger bits require slower speed settings.

Tighten bits securely in the drill press chuck. Use the hand lever to lower the quill—the vertical shaft that contains the chuck—and engage the bit in the workpiece. If you're drilling all the way through a workpiece, be sure the bit lines up with a hole in your drill press table (if your machine table has a center hole). Or place a piece of scrap material underneath the workpiece and use this as a backer when the bit passes through the workpiece. It helps minimize tearout on the back side of the workpiece, and it keeps the bit from drilling into the machine table.

If you don't own a drill press, one way to improve your accuracy for drilling straight holes with a portable drill is to guide the tool with a square.

When drilling holes larger than ½ inch, hold workpieces securely against a fence or scrap of wood clamped in place. Otherwise, the rotation of the chuck can pull a workpiece out of your hands and spin it forcefully around. With smaller bits, you can safely drill holes without the fence, but keep your hands and shirtsleeves well clear of the spinning chuck and bit.

DRILL BITS & DRILLING ACCESSORIES FOR WOODWORKING

Garden-variety twist bits drill holes through wood, but they leave a ragged edge around the entry hole. Several other bit options shown here produce cleaner edges and remove waste just as efficiently. Other drilling accessories cut larger holes, circles, plugs, and countersinks for recessing screwheads.

Brad-point bits (A) have a center spur for locating the exact centerpoint of a hole, and two sharpened spurs on the ends of the cutting flutes score a clean entry hole. Brad-point bits are designed exclusively for drilling wood. They come in sizes ranging from ⅛ inch to 1 inch in diameter.

Forstner bits (B) have a circle-shaped cutting head with sharpened rims or serrated edges for shearing clean entry holes. The center cutting area consists of a pair of chisel-shaped paddles that remove most of the waste in large chips. Forstner bits range in diameter from ¼ inch to 2 inches and are intended for use in a drill press. Use slower speeds when drilling with these bits, and withdraw the bit often from the hole to help clear the chips.

Spade bits (C) have flat cutting heads with a long center spur and sharpened edges on either side. Some spade bits have scribing spurs on the corners for making cleaner entry holes. Although spade bits are intended for drilling wood, they're better suited for rough carpentry jobs than fine woodworking applications.

Countersink/counterbore bits (D) feature a twist bit or tapered bit mounted to a counterbore collar. The collar has tapered cutting surfaces that enlarge the entry hole for recessing screw heads. Driving the bit so just the tapered cutters of the collar score the hole creates a countersink. Countersinks allow screws to be driven flush or slightly below the surface of a workpiece. By drilling the collar deeper into the wood, you can form a counterbore to recess a screwhead entirely below the surface, then conceal the screw with a wood plug.

Hole saws (E) have a steel cup machined around one edge with saw teeth, and the cup is mounted to a center mandrel that holds a twist drill bit. The twist bit centers the hole, and the cup saws a circular cutout. Hole saws are used more frequently in plumbing and carpentry applications than woodworking, but the range of cup sizes and relatively clean cutting capabilities make them handy for woodworking tasks as well. Hole saw diameters range in size from 1¼ inches up to more than 4 inches.

Circle-cutters (F) also drill large holes, but the mandrel holds an adjustable rod and chisel-shaped cutter rather than a sawtooth cup. To change the hole diameter, move the rod and cutter in or out from the mandrel. Circle cutters are designed for drill press use. At slow speeds and with a sharp cutter, they'll score holes with clean edges or create perfect wheel shapes from the cutout material. Toymakers use circle cutters to make wheels this way.

Plug cutters (G) form round wood plugs used to fill counterbore holes. They are typically sold in sets for drill press use, with each cutter sized to make a different diameter plug. Sharpened surfaces on the cutter score and remove material around the plug so the plug is formed inside the cutter opening. Once a cutter bores the plug, you remove the plug by breaking it out with a chisel or by sawing the board through its thickness to cut the plug free.

Countersinks (H) can be used in a handheld drill or drill press for scoring a conical depression around a drilled hole to recess screwheads. Countersinks with one or two cutting flutes cut smoother surfaces than those with flutes all around the cutter. The former are designed for wood and the latter for other materials, like soft metals and plastics, as well as wood.

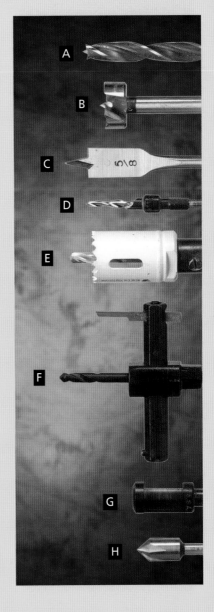

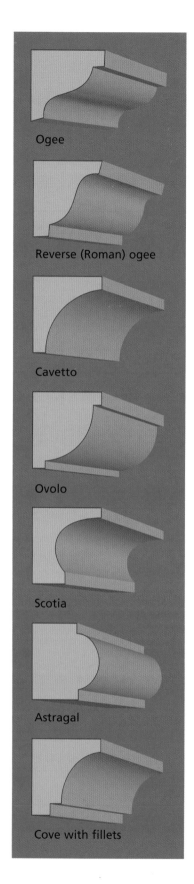

Ogee

Reverse (Roman) ogee

Cavetto

Ovolo

Scotia

Astragal

Cove with fillets

Shaping decorative edges with a router

Woodworkers tend to use routers for shaping the ends and edges of workpieces into lots of different decorative profiles. As edge-forming tools, routers are the next best things to dedicated shaper machines. All that's required for the setup is chucking the bit and setting the depth, and within a few seconds you can turn an ordinary board into a finished work with a classically profiled detail.

You can form decorative edges in a multitude of different shapes and sizes using common router bits. Typical router bits for edge-forming include roundover or chamfer, bullnose, and cove. Scores of other specialized profiles are available, too, including the classical Greek and Roman profiles shown to the left. Depending on the application, you can even combine two different bit cuts to make a customized shape. Most edge-forming router bits are bearing-guided. With piloted bits, the bearing determines the side-to-side depth, so all you have to set up is the vertical position of the bit, which establishes how much of the bit's cutting edges will enter the workpiece. At full depth, the bit will cut its full profile. At a partial depth, you'll get a segment of the bit shape instead. Both options can produce attractive edges.

Edge-forming techniques are simple, but because this is finish work you often get only one chance with a cut. If you're new to routing or using an unusual bit for the first time, make a few practice cuts on scrap to get the hang of using the bit and router before actually routing your final workpiece.

Edge-forming with handheld routers. The key to smooth edge-forming lies in keeping even pressure on the bearing against the stock while maintaining the proper feed rate. If you hesitate at corners or the ends of the cut, you'll burn the wood. You also need to keep the router from tipping. In handheld work, less than half of the router's base is supported by the workpiece, so it's easy to let the tool tilt sideways and spoil the cut. An offset subbase provides greater stability for edge cuts than a standard base.

SETTING DEPTH FOR PROFILE CUTS

An easy way to see what you'll be cutting away with a decorative edge-forming bit is to use a scrap cut from the workpiece material. Place the scrap on the router base so its edge touches the bit's pilot bearing. The cutter's profile will show what the cut will look like.

Tearout is another vital consideration with edge-forming. If you're routing the perimeter of a workpiece, follow the conventional (counterclockwise) feed direction (see page 111), and start and finish the cut in the middle of an end-grain edge. Sweep into the cut initially to prevent burning (see A sweeping start, below). The objective with this technique is to remove any tearout that occurs on the end-grain cut when you make the subsequent long-grain cut. If you're routing only one edge, clamp a scrap piece to the work at the finish of the cut. This prevents tearout and keeps you from accidentally cutting into the adjacent edge.

A SWEEPING START

When starting an edge cut, it's easy to leave a burn mark if you push the router straight in until the base contacts the edge guide or bearing, then move it sideways to make the cut. There's just enough hesitation to burn the wood. Instead, start with a curved, sweeping motion so the bit reaches its full cutting position a few inches from the end of the workpiece. Run to the end of the cut using the same feed direction. Complete the cut by returning to the beginning and making a second pass, again sweeping into the workpiece but with an opposite feed direction, to finish off the first few inches. Typically this final pass is a climb cut, so be careful. Make sure the router base is supported by the board at the beginning of the motion.

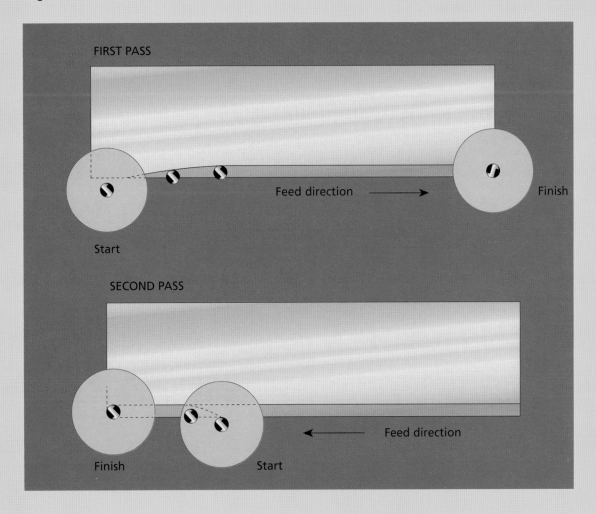

FIRST PASS

Feed direction ⟶

Finish

Start

SECOND PASS

⟵ Feed direction

Finish

Start

Create different profiles with the same bit by adjusting the bit depth or running the bearing along a template mounted beneath the workpiece. In this photo, it's made of hardboard.

Dips and bumps in the workpiece (like this knot) will transfer to the router cut. Either smooth the workpiece or use a straightedge guide instead of a bearing bit.

The bane of bearings. As a guide system, the main drawback of a bearing is that it transfers any defects in the workpiece (or template) edge to the surface of the cut. There are three ways to deal with this: The most obvious solution is to joint or re-saw the edge of the workpiece before routing to provide a perfectly smooth surface for the bearing. Another solution is to use an edge guide. With this method, set the guide just inside of the bearing so the guide controls the cut instead of the bearing. The guide will bridge minor defects in the workpiece edge for a smoother cut. A third option is to make the cut on the router table using a fence.

Edge-forming with router tables & templates. You can use almost any type of edge-forming bit on the router table. The advantage here is that a router table provides more support for the workpiece. Instead of guiding the router over the wood, you slide the wood along the router table and through the bit. (Read more about using a router table on page 121.) You can also use templates to assist in forming decorative profiles, especially when the router bit bearing needs to ride below the workpiece in order to form the full bit shape. By placing a template below the workpiece, the bit has a surface to ride against. (Read more about using templates with routers beginning on page 114.)

Making test cuts. Making test cuts is an essential step with most decorative profiling work. Even after a careful setup, you won't know exactly how the cut will go until you try it out. The test cut also gives you a feel for the setup and how the wood reacts to the bit, which is your best indicator for finding the proper feed rate.

FEEDS AND TOOL SPEEDS

The direction and rate at which you move the router through a cut are critical factors in the quality of the work. These variables are referred to as the *feed direction* and *feed rate*. Another factor that is equally important in certain situations is the tool speed; that is, the rotational speed of the router bit—a factor that can be controlled only on variable-speed routers. There are a few rules of thumb for determining the correct feeds and speeds, but, as with all woodworking techniques, experience is the best teacher.

An offset router base attached to the router can add helpful extra support when guiding a router around a workpiece for making decorative cuts.

CONVENTIONAL FEED DIRECTIONS

The conventional feed moves the router opposite to the work forces of the rotating bit. In handheld routing, the bit spins clockwise when viewed from above, so the router is fed from left to right. This is the safer method of the two because the force of the router is countered by the force of the operator, resulting in a more balanced, controlled motion. For most routing, the conventional feed direction is the proper method.

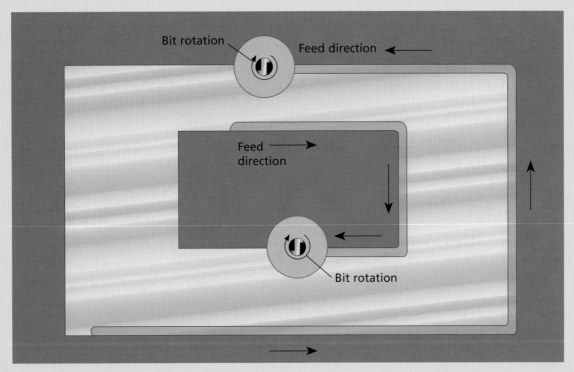

Bit rotation

Feed direction

Feed direction

Bit rotation

Inside and outside edge cuts

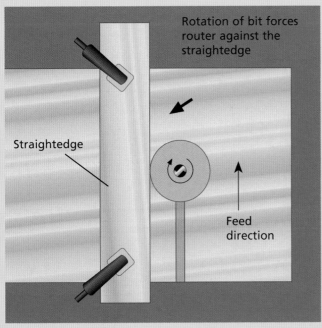

Rotation of bit forces router against the straightedge

Straightedge

Feed direction

Cuts using a straightedge

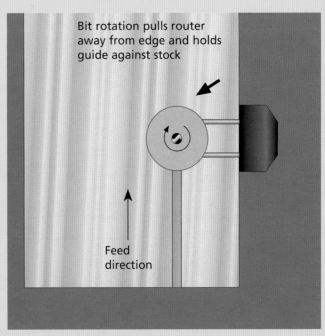

Bit rotation pulls router away from edge and holds guide against stock

Feed direction

Cuts using an edge guide

When edging three sides of a piece, begin with a sweeping cut in the end grain. Complete the end with a climb cut. Edge the long-grain side. Edge the second end grain side using a backer board (below right).

Feed direction. There are two ways you can feed the router: the conventional feed and a feed that is known as the *climb cut*. The conventional feed moves the router opposite to the work forces of the rotating bit. In handheld routing, the bit spins clockwise when viewed from above, so the router is fed from left to right. This is the safer method of the two because the force of the router is countered by the force of the operator, resulting in a more balanced, controlled motion. For most routing, the conventional feed direction is the proper method.

The climb cut goes with the bit's rotational force as the router is moved from right to left. With the bit pulling it along, the router has a tendency to climb away from you (hence the name), making it more difficult to control the tool. Despite this disadvantage, the climb cut is commonly used for select operations,

When edge-forming the entire perimeter of a board, start with the cross-grain cuts first. The tearout will be removed when making the long-grain cuts.

If only the cross-grain ends are being routed, use a scrap board clamped firmly against the exit side of the cut to prevent tearout.

because it produces less tearout than conventional feeding and offers a smoother finish with some difficult woods. However, it is considered a dangerous practice and should always be done with care and a great deal of awareness. Always make a very light pass when climb cutting, to minimize the potential for the bit to grab the wood and pull the router.

Feed rate. The ideal feed rate for any cut is based on five main factors: 1) the material (its hardness, density, grain properties, etc.), 2) the router bit (characteristics such as size, number of flutes, sharpness, and cutter complexity), 3) the depth of the cut (see How deep should the cut be?, below), 4) the power of the router motor, and 5) the tool speed. Generally, hard wood, large bits, deep cuts, and less power require slower feed rates.

When it comes down to routing, however, the best way to judge your feed rate is by the quality of the cut. Feeding the router too fast stresses the motor and bit and typically produces a rough cut, torn fibers, or excessive tearout. And the motor will sound overloaded if the feed rate is too fast. Feeding too slowly creates excessive friction, resulting in burnishing or burn marks in the wood. Your test cuts will tell you whether your feed rate is good. Once you start making the

How deep should the cut be?

Proper cutting depth for edge profiling is determined by the material, the size, type, and sharpness of the bit, and by the power of the router motor. Cutting too deeply stresses the motor and bit and may burn the wood and prematurely dull the bit. It can also be unsafe because the bit can grab too much wood and cause you to lose control. On the other hand, overly shallow cuts are prudent but may require many passes to reach the finished depth. Knowing the right depth for each cut is something that comes through experience, but here are some general guidelines to follow, based on a midsize, handheld router:

• Limit edge-forming cuts to the equivalent of ⅜" square of material. That translates to a ⅜" cutting depth for a ⅜" rabbeting bit, or a ¼" depth for a ½" straight bit.

• Make very light passes—1/16" or so—when using large bits that remove a lot of material, such as raised panel cutters.

Heavy-duty routers can remove more material with less trouble than midsize tools, although they still are limited by the bit's capability. In any case, it's a good practice to go light on the first pass when routing new material.

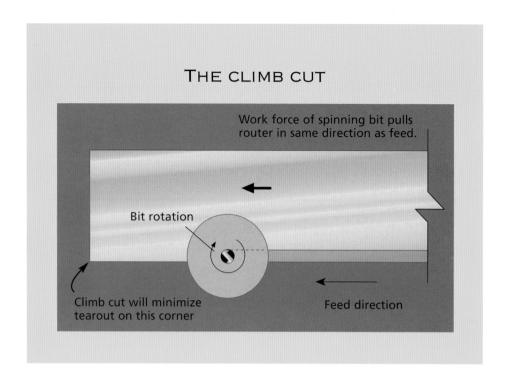

THE CLIMB CUT

Work force of spinning bit pulls router in same direction as feed.

Bit rotation

Climb cut will minimize tearout on this corner

Feed direction

real cut, it's important to keep the feed rate constant. If you stop moving the router or slow down too much, even for an instant, the wood will burn.

Tool speed. Standard routers run at an average speed of about 24,000 rpm. This rate is acceptable for most router bits up to about 1 inch in diameter. Bits 1 inch and larger typically require slower speeds, because the greater diameter translates to more travel along the wood at a faster rate. Thus a slower spin is needed to ensure safety and prevent burning. To run large bits, you must use a router with variable speed, which can be set at anywhere from 8,000 to 24,000 rpm, on average. Bit manufacturers often recommend a tool speed for their larger bits. The chart below shows general guidelines for safe routing speeds. Note that bits over 1¾ inches in diameter should be used only on a router table.

Shaping parts using router templates

Template routing exploits the router's unique ability to make patterned cuts. The procedure is perfectly simple: affix a template to the workpiece, then rout around the edges of the template to create an exact copy. Virtually any shape is

Templates allow routers to make very precise patterned cuts.

SAFE ROUTER SPEEDS

Bit diameter	Maximum tool speed
Up to 1"	24,000 rpm
1¼" to *2"	18,000 rpm
*2¼" to 2½"	16,000 rpm
*2¾" to 3½"	12,000 rpm
*recommended for router table use only	

possible, and the router will duplicate the template accurately every time. In addition to cutting shapes, you can use templates to make precise cutouts, excavations, holes, and slots, and to create inlays. Custom work with shopmade templates greatly expands the creative possibilities of routing. On the more practical side, commercial templates help take the guesswork (and fear) out of construction cuts that leave no room for error, such as hinge-mortising and countertop installations.

Template basics. There are two main types of setups in template routing. The difference lies in the bits used. If you make the cuts with a bearing-guided pattern bit or flush-trimming bit, the bearing travels along the template edge and the bit trims the workpiece flush, creating an exact duplicate. The alternative setup involves a nonpiloted bit used with a template guide (see next page). In this configuration, the guide follows the template while the exposed portion of the bit below makes the cut. The finished workpiece has the same shape as the template, but is a slightly different size, due to the offset between the outside of the template guide and the cutting edge of the bit. You compensate for the offset by making the template slightly smaller or larger than the finished workpiece. The following chart summarizes the pros and cons of the different configurations.

A flush-trimming bit with a bottom bearing rides along a template placed below the workpiece.

TEMPLATE ROUTING SETUPS

Setup	Advantages	Disdvantages
Pattern bit (bearing at top of bit)	• Template is same size as workpiece • Plunge cuts possible • Multiple cuts possible on thick stock	• Full bit extension required with thin template
Flush-trimming bit (bearing at bottom of bit)	• Template is same size as workpiece • Easy setup on router table, reduced bit exposure	• All cuts are full depth
Template guide	• Greatest bit selection • Can use multiple bits with same guide • Plunge and shallow cuts possible, with guide always contacting template	• Template size must account for offset • No exact duplication of objects

A template guide eliminates
the need for a pilot bearing on
the bit. Using a template
guide does result in an offset
between the size of the template and the final size of the
workpiece.

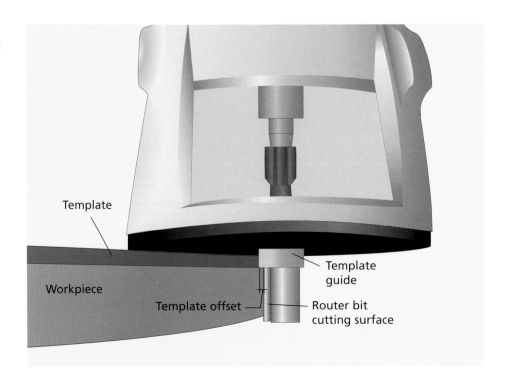

Template

Workpiece

Template offset

Template
guide

Router bit
cutting surface

TEMPLATE GUIDES

Template guides, also called collar guides, are metal fittings that attach to the router's subbase and have a cylindrical collar that surrounds the bit. The collar rides along a template to control the cut, eliminating the need for a pilot bearing. There are guides made for specific router brands, as well as universal systems that are compatible with several different router makes. Ask about which systems will work for your router. Guides may attach with a locknut, screws, or a twist-lock fitting.

Template guides come in a range of sizes, each with three important dimensions: the inner and outer diameters of the collar and the distance the collar projects from the subbase. The collar's inner diameter must be larger than the overall diameter of the bit (dovetail bits are an exception, because their cutters remain below the collar). For template work, the smaller the outer diameter of the guide, the better it will be at following fine detail and making sharp turns. The collar projection, which ranges from about $\frac{5}{32}$" to over $\frac{1}{2}$", is important because the template must be thicker than the projection. However, you can grind down or hacksaw a little off the collar projection without affecting the guide's performance.

To allow for the offset of the template guide, add or subtract the offset dimension from your template size.

Template edges must be perfectly smooth. Any irregularities will transfer to the finished piece. Use a file or sanding block to smooth or straighten corners.

Making your own templates. Templates are easiest to make using thin, ¼- to ½-inch sheet materials, including plywood, hardboard, MDF, and plastic. The best material thickness to use depends on the application. The thin edges of ¼" hardboard are easy to cut and smooth, but the template won't withstand long-term use as well as ½-inch plywood or MDF. Voids in plywood edges can be a problem, so use cabinet-grade material if possible. Also consider the bit setup to make sure the template isn't too thick to permit a full cut or too thin for your template guide. If you're using a pattern bit, a thick template will give you some control over the depth of cut.

How you make the template also depends on the bit setup. Working with a

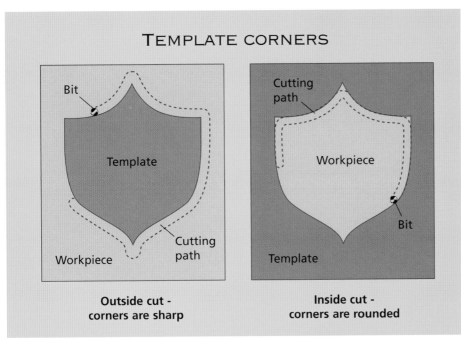

TEMPLATE CORNERS

Bit

Template

Workpiece

Cutting path

Outside cut – corners are sharp

Cutting path

Workpiece

Template

Bit

Inside cut – corners are rounded

Cutting around the outside edge of a template with a flush-cutting bit results in an exact match (left). Cutting around the inside of a cutout template results in rounded corners due to the radius of the bit or the template guide collar (right).

template guide requires an extra step when laying out the template, but otherwise the procedure is the same. Keep in mind that the quality of the template translates directly to the quality of the finished workpiece, so make the template with care. Start by drawing a full-size outline of the pattern onto your template stock. The sharpness of the corners is determined by whether the cut is around the outside of the template or within a cutout in the template (see page 117). If you're using a template guide, re-trace the pattern outline, adding or subtracting the offset of the guide. Make the outline smaller for outside cuts, larger for inside cuts. Cut the template along the outline using a jig saw, band saw, scroll saw, or coping saw. Smooth all the lines with a file and sandpaper. Any bumps or dips left on the template will show up on your workpiece.

Template routing techniques. Template cuts can be made with a handheld router or on the router table. Minimize wear on your router by tracing the template outline onto the workpiece and trimming most of the waste with a saw before routing. For a template guide setup, trace around the template with a compass to add the offset. Saw the workpiece to within ¹⁄₁₆ to ¹⁄₈ inch of the outline. Clamp the template and work securely. If conventional clamps will get in the way, use hot glue or double-sided tape to stick the template to the workpiece and the workpiece to your bench. Use the same methods for the router table, or build a jig to hold the work as you move it over the bit.

With a handheld router, make the template cut using a conventional feed: feed the router counterclockwise for outside template cuts, clockwise for inside cuts. A plunge router fitted with a pattern bit or template guide allows you to plunge into interior cuts and make partial-depth interior groove cuts. For stock that is thicker than bit capacity, use a pattern bit and make two passes. On the second pass, the bearing follows the cut made in the first pass. You can also make the second pass with a flush-trimming bit, cutting from the other face of the stock.

To remove excess stock before routing, use a compass to mark slightly outside the final dimensions of the workpiece.

Use a band saw or jig saw to cut along the rough outline, then attach the template and rout the final cut.

Template cuts on the router table involve the same techniques used for handheld edge-forming. You can use a pattern or flush-trimming bit or a template guide setup. For a pattern bit or template guide, stick the template to the bottom of the workpiece. A flush-trimming bit works with the template on top of the stock, making it easier to watch the bearing as it follows the template. Always use a bit guard and a starting pin or fulcrum to stabilize the workpiece.

Creating decorative inlays. Inlay work adds a distinctive touch of craftsmanship to any piece. Most often used as decoration, inlays can also hide knots and other stock defects. Installing an inlay is a basic template-routing operation. It's a job for a handheld router (preferably a plunge router) and an inlay kit—a set with a template guide, a bushing that fits over the guide's collar, and a bit, typically a ⅛-inch down-spiral bit. The bushing creates on offset equal to the bit diameter. Inlay kits are commonly available through bit manufacturers.

When cutting thick material using a template and a flush-trimming bit, adjust the bit depth so the bearing runs along the template for the first cut. For successive cutting depths (shown), the bearing will run along the previously cut stock.

The inlay process involves cutting a recess using a shopmade template and the inlay kit with the bushing in place. Then, you cut the inlay insert, this time without the bushing, using the same template used to make the recess. Glue the insert into the recess and sand it flush to complete the detail.

Start by making the template. Use a material that's just slightly thicker than the inlay kit's bushing; a thick template would require greater extension of the fragile ⅛-inch bit, increasing the chance of breakage. The overall size of the template

Inlay kits make it possible to create fine decorative panels, like the one shown here.

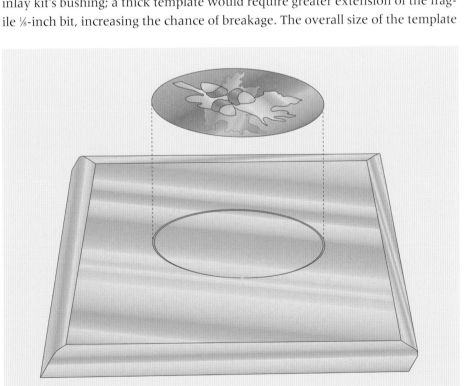

must provide adequate support for the router base. Draw the outline of the inlay onto the template stock, then enlarge the outline by a margin equal to the offset (⅛ inch in this example). The inner outline is the actual size of the inlay. Make sure any inside corners or curves on the outer pattern have a radius that's no smaller than the radius of the bushing. Cut the template to the outer pattern line, and file and sand the edges smooth.

Rout the recess next. Secure the template to the workpiece with clamps or double-sided tape. Set up your router with the template guide, bushing, and inlay bit. Set the bit depth to cut just shy of the thickness of the insert stock. If the inlay is small, you can rout the entire recess with the inlay bit: work outward from the center to clear away the material. For larger inlays, rout along the perimeter of the template cutout with the inlay bit to establish the outline of the recess, then switch to a larger straight bit to clean out the rest of the recess. In either case, rout along the template edges twice to make sure the recess is complete.

Cut the insert using the inlay bit and template guide without the bushing. Lay the insert stock over a scrap board to protect your workbench. To keep the insert from coming free and possibly getting damaged as the bit finishes the cut, place a strip of double-sided tape between the insert stock and the scrap backer. Clamp or tape the template over the insert stock. Set the bit depth to cut completely through the stock. Make the cut by carefully following the edges of the template cutout. Any deviation from the edge will misshape the insert. Check the fit of the insert in the recess. Brush an even coating of glue over the recess floor and sides. Tap the insert into the recess using a mallet or a hammer and block. After the glue dries, sand the insert flush to the workpiece surface.

Manufactured templates. Commercially made router templates are available for a variety of jobs that require a high degree of accuracy. The most popular router templates are hinge mortisers. These range from simple plastic plates that you clamp to the door edge, to precision rack systems that help you make perfectly spaced mortises on both the door and the jamb.

Once you have determined the size and shape of the inlay, size the template to allow for the template guide offset.

For large inlays, rout the outline with the inlay bit, then remove the remaining waste with a large straight bit.

Secure the inlay to scrap wood with tape. Use the inlay bit and template guide without the bushing to cut the inlay to size.

Apply glue to the bottom of the recess and the back of the inlay piece, and join the pieces.

You can also find pre-made router templates for forming plaques, decorative cutouts for picture frames, raised-panel door shapes, and letter and number templates for making custom signage.

Making parts with a router table

Router tables add considerably to the versatility of routing. With the tool secured below the table and the bit exposed above, you can use both hands to run the workpiece past the bit, often without hold-downs or special clamping. The fence provides the means for controlling the cut, just like a table saw fence does. Together with the flat, stable surface of the tabletop, the fence allows for safe, accurate cuts with quick setup (many cuts require only two settings—bit depth and fence adjustment). Using a bearing-guided bit, you can rout without a fence and take advantage of the tabletop's broad surface for support. A basic shopmade version can be inexpensive and easy to build, and may be all you'll ever need. Or you can buy one of the many commercial tables available.

Advantages of table routing. While router tables aren't ideal for every task, the great majority of work done by handheld routers can also be accomplished on the table, and often more safely and efficiently than with a portable tool. Which setup is better for a specific job? The deciding factor in many cases is the size of the workpiece: if it's too small to support the base of a handheld router, consider working on the table; if it's too big to maneuver easily on the table, use a handheld router.

Tables clearly are the better choice (and in some cases, the only choice), when routing with large bits. As a general rule, bits over 1¾ inches in diameter are much safer to use in table-mounted routers. Big bits can be hard to control with handheld routers, especially on edge-forming operations. When using large bits on the router table, cover as much of the bit as possible with the fence, and cut incrementally with light passes. Also make sure to adjust the tool's speed based on the bit's diameter (see Safe router speeds, page 114) or as recommended by the bit manufacturer. Many large bits are designed for use in a router table only.

Router tables generally have bit guards, making cuts on narrow stock much safer.

Having a fence to work from offers several advantages. First, it keeps the workpiece in line and allows you to focus on the feed and other critical aspects—in contrast to handheld operations, where you have to remain constantly aware of keeping the router upright. A tall fence provides support for running workpieces on edge or vertically, simplifying cuts that would require complicated setups for handheld work. The fence controls the depth of cut when using nonpiloted bits but can also produce superior results with bearing-guided cutters. By setting the fence just in front of the bearing, you eliminate the transfer of defects from the workpiece edge to the cut.

A commercial benchtop table with frame-style open base, flip-up guard, two-piece fence, vacuum port, and base-mounted switch. Always clamp the base to the supporting workbench for safest use.

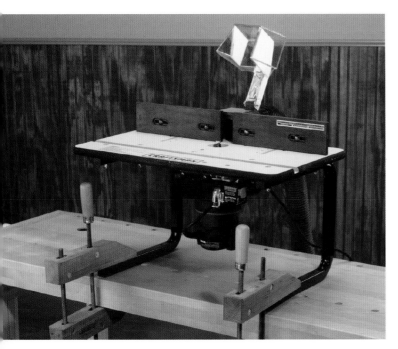

Building a router table. The essential design criteria for any router table are simple: The table must be smooth and flat, and the fence must be straight and square to the table. As long as those requirements are met, you can use almost any materials and include any features you like. You can double-up sheets of MDF or melamine particleboard for making a worktop, use a piece of heavy-gauge sheet metal or laminate-covered countertop, or simply buy a commercially made router tabletop and mount it to a base of your choice. The base could be as simple as a framework of shop lumber or as elaborate as a cabinet with storage drawers for supplies and an enclosed area to conceal the router and contain dust.

Buying a commercial router table. Commercial tables are available as clamp-on tabletop, benchtop,

If the base of a router table is enclosed, you can run a vacuum hose into the cabinet to collect dust and chips.

and floor models. In terms of quality, the overall field runs wide, as does the price range. When shopping, look closely at the main components—the table-top, the fence, and the base—and compare the usability features, such as fence adjustments and overall versatility. There are a lot of great tables to choose from, as well as a few design features to avoid. Safety features, like bit guards, starting pins, and reducer rings, should be available as accessories if they aren't standard equipment.

Router table safety. The main safety concerns with table routing involve exposure to the bit, feeding techniques, and trapping the workpiece (which can cause kickback and other unpleasant outcomes). Understanding feed directions and keeping your hands away from the cutter are your best defenses against trouble. As with handheld routing, safe work on the table starts with the setup. If a cut seems tricky or potentially risky, stop and rethink the setup. There's probably a better way to do it, or it might be safer to make the cut with a handheld router.

Bit safety. You can cover bit safety and reduce exposure risk by following a few rules of thumb. First, set the bit depth to expose only what is necessary to make the cut. Use the fence and proper hole size in the table to close in around the bit as

RULES OF SAFE TABLE ROUTING

- Unplug the router before changing bits or adjusting bit height.
- Feed the work against the rotation of the cutter.
- Never trap the work between the bit and the fence or table.
- Use push sticks, sleds, or hold-downs as needed to keep cuts safe.
- Beware of the emerging bit.
- Make light passes with large bits and use the recommended tool speed.
- Start bearing-guided cuts against a starting pin or fulcrum.

Whether you build or buy your router table, a miter gauge slot is a good feature to have. It can be used to hold clamps and featherboards. Or you can use your table saw miter gauge to support work as you push it past the bit.

much as possible, and make a zero-clearance fence when appropriate. In all cases where a bit guard can be used, do so.

Second, prepare for the unexpected. If you're pushing a workpiece toward the cutter and something slips or the work is suddenly zipped from your grasp, where will your hands go? Stay well balanced during a cut and make sure the force you're applying to the workpiece won't bring your hands near the cutter if something goes wrong. During the cut, the bit is often concealed by the work and can emerge unexpectedly from the end of the workpiece. For this reason, never push from the back edge of stock where your fingers could end up anywhere near the cutter.

Feed direction. If you're not familiar with the principles of feed direction and feed rate, see Feeds and tool speeds, starting on page 110. The conventional feed direction for router table work is opposite that of handheld routing for the simple reason that the router is upside down, thus reversing the bit's rotation relative to the user. In handheld work, the bit spins clockwise and the proper feed is to move the router from left to right over the workpiece. In table routing, the bit spins counterclockwise and the conventional feed is moving the workpiece from right to left along the fence.

DEDICATING A BASE

If you're using a midsize fixed-base router in your table, buy an extra base and leave it permanently mounted to the table. Some manufacturers offer a simplified, handleless base for this purpose.

With the conventional feed, the working forces of the bit pull the workpiece against the fence and push it back toward you (the user), giving you more control. Feeding left to right is a climb cut, and the bit's action forces the work away from the fence and you. If the bit grabs during a climb cut, it can pull the work from your hands and send your fingers toward the bit. Keeping this in mind,

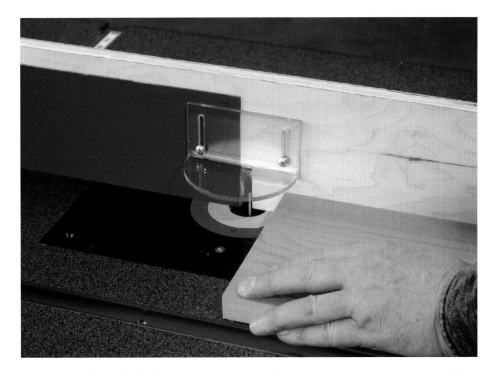

This safe setup includes a bit guard and minimal clearances around the bit. For a full-thickness cut, the bit depth needs to extend only $\frac{1}{16}$" above the top face of the workpiece. (Here, the router table is being used as a jointer. See page 128 for more on edge-jointing.)

you can make safe climb cuts if you take all measures necessary to control the work and make very light passes.

Trapping the workpiece. Trapping the work between the bit and fence is a dangerous situation that must always be avoided. Trapping creates an especially hazardous climb cut in which the board, pinched between the immovable fence and spinning bit, can be shot across the shop at an astonishing rate. In most situations, you'll avoid trapping the workpiece by keeping the work between yourself and the bit.

Trapping can happen three different ways. One is setting the fence away from the bit and feeding the board between the fence and the bit (see pages 126 and

The standard feed direction using a router table pushes the workpiece against the fence. A climb cut on the router table can grab the workpiece and pull your fingers toward the bit.

127). The second way trapping happens is when using a router table to widen grooves on a workpiece. This can fool you because while you think you're making a conventional left-to-right feed, you're actually climb cutting and trapping the work against the fence. Avoid this dangerous setup by machining the wall of the groove that is farther from the fence. The third instance of trapping occurs when the bit is raised and the workpiece is fed between the bit and the table-top, trapping it again.

Fence

Bit

Feed direction

Bit rotation

Workpiece

Table

When making multiple passes cutting a groove or dado, be careful not to trap the bit. The correct method is to machine the wall away from the fence (right), not the side near the fence (left).

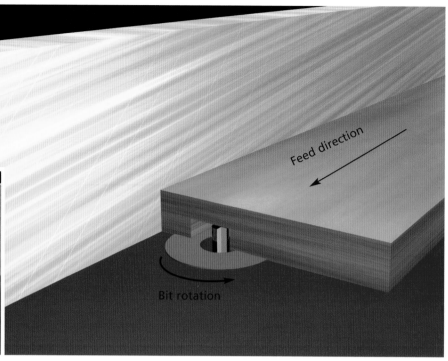

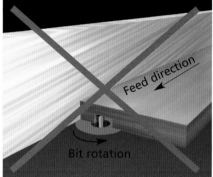

Keeping your hands clear. Push sticks, sleds, and hold-downs such as featherboards help you push the work safely past the bit and are especially useful for small and narrow stock that might endanger your fingers. A push stick can have almost any design and be made with scrap wood. For narrow work, a solid stick with a notched end will suffice. For routing larger stock, attach a handle to a scrap block (make sure the block has square corners) to make a push sled that doubles as a backer board to prevent tearout. Trim the block or move the handle to a new block when the old one has seen too many cuts. A simple L-shaped sled helps support stock set on edge. Glue two scrap pieces of plywood or lumber together so they're square, and discard the sled when it gets chewed up. Use

A good rule of thumb: Make sure your thumb will be well clear of the bit when it emerges from the workpiece during a blind cut.

featherboards—either shopmade or manufactured—as a second pair of "hands" can help you keep the work in line.

Routing without a fence. Always use a starting pin (or fulcrum) for bearing-guided work without a fence. When initiating a cut into a bearing-guided bit, the cutter can grab the workpiece, resulting in a gouge and possibly yanking the work from your hands. The starting pin helps prevent this by acting as a stabilizing point until the work makes contact with the bit's bearing. Commercial mounting plates often come with a metal or plastic starting pin that fits into holes in the plate. You can add a pin to a shopmade table by installing a threaded insert into the top or by clamping on a pointed board to act as a fulcrum. Locate the starting pin 2 to 4 inches from the bit. Remember, if a task calls for a starting pin, you should also use a bit guard.

To make the cut, anchor the work against the pin, then carefully pivot it into the bit until it contacts the guide bearing. Complete the cut while keeping the work in contact with the bearing. If convenient, you can use the starting pin for extra stability, but don't let it distract you from the cut. Be very mindful of feed direction here. Always move the work against the rotation of the bit.

Trapping the wood between the bit and the fence creates a dangerous situation where the wood will be pinched and likely kicked back.

The correct way to cut an edge using a table router and fence. The bit is on the fence-side edge of the board and fingers are protected by the bit guard.

A starting pin is often standard on commercial mounting plates. A bit guard is a must when doing this type of routing.

If you don't have a starting pin, a pointed board clamped to the tabletop can act as a fulcrum.

Edge-jointing. Smoothing and squaring up an edge is an easy operation on the router table. To remove about ¹⁄₁₆ inch of material from an edge, set up a straight bit for a full-thickness cut. Clamp or adhere a plastic laminate shim on the outfeed side of the fence, then set the fence so the bit will cut flush with the laminate face. Run the stock through as many times as needed to create a clean, square edge, just like a jointer.

To set up for edge-jointing, glue or clamp a plastic laminate shim to the outfeed side of the fence. Use a straightedge to align the bit's cutting edge with the laminate. This will remove ¹⁄₁₆" of material with each pass.

Making stopped cuts. A stopped cut is any interior cut that begins or ends at a point inside from the workpiece edge. A blind cut is a stopped cut where both ends stop short of the edge. You can make many types of stopped cuts with accuracy on a router table. However, because blind cuts have no access from the workpiece edge, you must plunge the work down onto the spinning bit to initiate the cut—a potentially risky operation that must be done carefully and always with a stop block as an anchor. As a rule, blind cuts are safer and cleaner with a handheld plunge router.

To set up a stopped cut on the router table, load the bit (use a plunge-cutting type) and use a straightedge or square block to mark the front and back edges of the bit (from the tips of the cutters). Mark onto the fence or table or onto a piece of tape. On the workpiece, mark the beginning and end of the cut. Line up the leading mark on the workpiece with the left (front) bit mark and clamp a starting block to the fence or table at the trailing end of the workpiece. For blind cuts, line up the other two marks and clamp a stop block at the other end.

A push sled with a notch safely holds small stock for table routing. A handle grip keeps fingers away from the blade.

An L-shaped sled supports stock on edge for cuts like this tenon shoulder cut. Because you cannot use a bit guard on these cuts, use clamps to keep your fingers a safe distance away from the bit.

For safety, make the cut incrementally with a series of light passes. Anchor the end of the workpiece against the starting block. Keeping the work firm against the fence, slowly pivot it down onto the bit. Once you make contact, move the work back and forth slightly until the bit reaches full depth, then move the work from right to left until it contacts the stop block. Turn the machine off and pause until the bit stops before lifting the work from the bit at the end of the cut. It's critical to keep constant pressure against the fence during all stages of the cut.

Featherboards and push sticks improve router safety. Featherboards can be clamped onto the fence, or you can use T-bolts and knobs in the miter slot. Push sticks can be purchased or made from scrap lumber.

To set up a stopped or blind cut on the router table, begin by marking the front and back edges of the bit on the fence and tabletop.

Line up the workpiece stopping line with the back of the bit. Clamp a stop block in front of the workpiece. For blind cuts, move the workpiece to align the starting line with the front edge of the bit. Clamp a starting block behind the workpiece.

To make the cut, raise the bit to the desired height (it is best to make multiple shallow passes). Place the heel of the workpiece against the starting block and lower the workpiece onto the spinning bit. Slide the workpiece to the stop block. Turn off the machine before lifting the work.

A stopped cut simply requires a stop block rather than both a start and stop block. Feed the workpiece along the fence in normal fashion.

TROUBLESHOOTING POOR CUTS

Here are some of the more common routing problems and suggestions for correcting them.

Burning
- Make sure bits are sharp.

- Don't hesitate during the cut. Pay special attention to points where you naturally tend to slow down, especially at the beginning or end of a cut and when routing around corners. Also try starting with a sweeping motion (see A sweeping start, page 109).

- Make light passes. Cutting too deeply in a single pass forces a slower feed rate, which commonly leads to burning.

Practicing on scrap wood will help you determine the correct feed rate. The hard oak (left) and soft pine (right) show the results of cutting too slowly (top), too fast (middle), and just right (bottom).

Tearout
- When cutting across the grain, clamp a sacrificial piece of wood as a backer to the exit side of the cut.

- When routing the perimeter of a board, or adjacent perpendicular sides, make the cross-grain cuts first. This allows you to clean up the tearout when you make the long-grain cuts.

- Prevent top-side tearout (usually in the form of fuzz) from making a rough ride for the router by using a template or straightedge and a template guide. This lifts the router subbase off the surface of the workpiece for a smoother ride and cleaner cut.

Problems with bearing-guided bits
- When a cut is flawed due to a rough workpiece edge, either clean up the edge and re-rout, or switch to a setup with a straightedge guide and a pattern bit or template guide. A base-mounted edge guide can help bridge minor dips in the workpiece edge.

- If the uncut edge of a workpiece is burnished or scored, check the travel of the bearing, and replace it if necessary. Don't use edging bits with solid pilots.

- When rounding over the top and bottom of plywood, make sure the bearing is indexing from the same surface. Inconsistencies in the plies can produce poor results.

- Avoid deflection or runout from long, skinny, flush-trimming bits by switching to a pattern bit or template-guide setup.

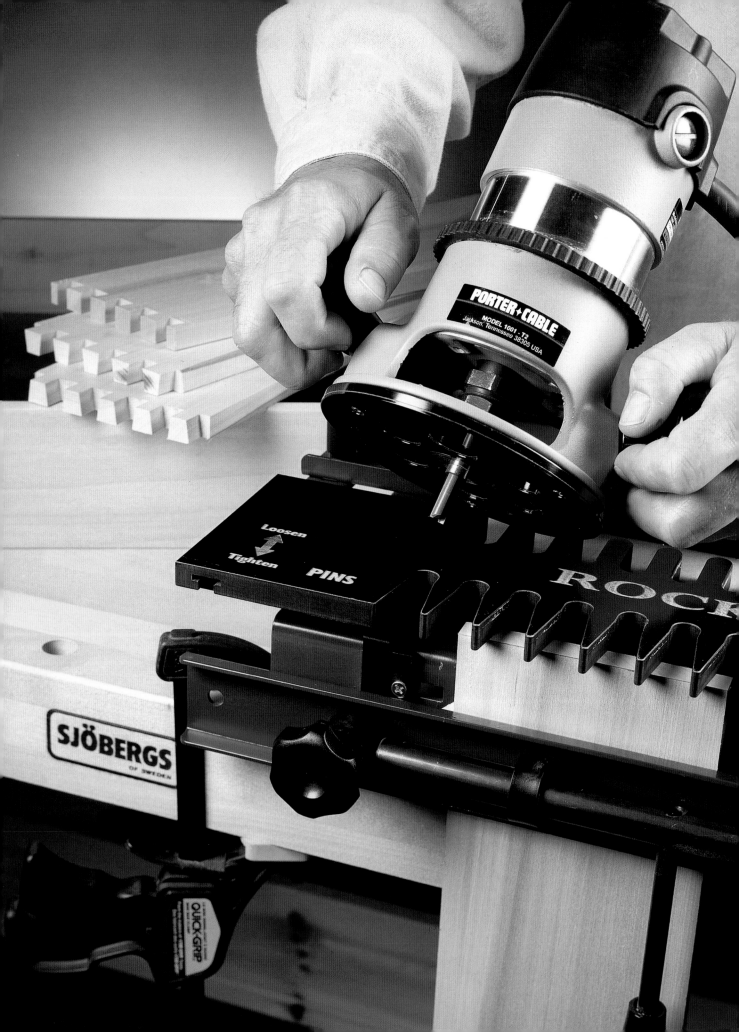

Chapter 6
MAKING WOOD JOINTS

Through centuries of woodworking, craftspeople have refined furniture and cabinetry joints to accomplish a few basic purposes. First of all, joints are structural elements of a project: they help to bear the loads and resist the natural forces of tension, compression, racking, and sheer that affect two workpieces functioning together. By machining two parts so they interlock, friction helps hold the pieces together so the joint doesn't rely entirely on the glue's adhesive strength. When parts are intertwined, each part benefits from the grain strength of the other. Joints also allow wood to expand and contract with changes in humidity so it doesn't crack or distort. And joinery can contribute a delightfully artistic touch where two pieces of wood intersect, by making the most of contrasting grain, color differentiation, and geometric shape.

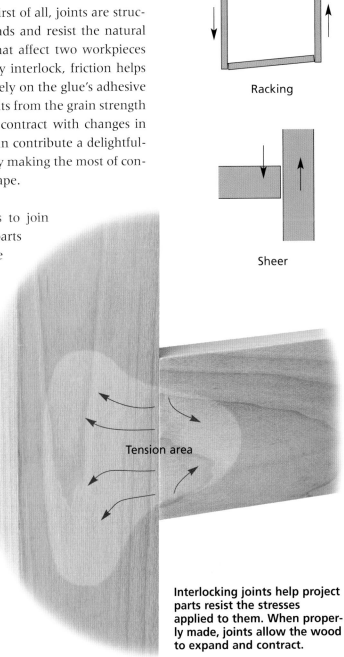

Racking

Sheer

Tension area

To fulfill these purposes, there are numerous ways to join wood. The simplest method is to simply glue two flat parts together and allow the glue bond to do all connective work. Other joints, such as rabbets and dadoes, have interlocking parts so the strength of the wood helps contribute to the connection. These interlocking styles are usually reinforced with glue and screws or nails. Some joints fit together with a third wood member, such as a biscuit, spline, or dowel. A few interlocking joints have pins or pegs that lock the parts together in the event the glue bond fails. In this chapter, you'll learn how to make some of each type.

Regardless of which joint style you make, the mating parts must be cut accurately to form durable, snug-fitting connections. Joint cutting is also the time to be meticulous in your machine, blade, and bit setups. The tolerance between properly fitting joint parts is extremely small, and often a joint that fits loosely can't be tightened up with screws or strengthened by squeezing on more glue. You'll usually have to start over with new workpieces to get a proper fit, so it pays to work carefully the first time.

Interlocking joints help project parts resist the stresses applied to them. When properly made, joints allow the wood to expand and contract.

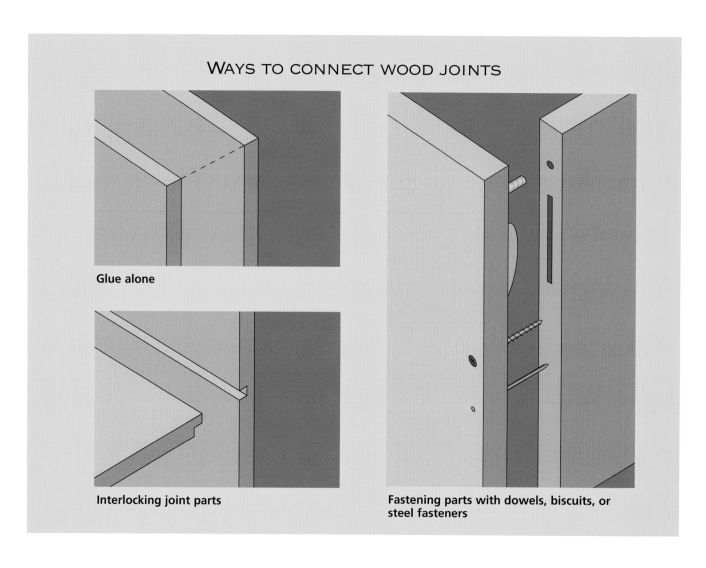

Glue alone

Interlocking joint parts

Fastening parts with dowels, biscuits, or steel fasteners

Tool options for jointmaking

Most woodworking joints can be made with a table saw, router, and a few different blades and bits. We'll show how to build a range of joints with both machines here. In some examples, you'll be able to choose either a table saw or a router to build the joint, because the essential cutting techniques are possible with either machine. Choose the tool you're most comfortable with or the one that offers better control or convenience. If you're building a project where you're still cutting parts as well as building joints, you may want to leave your table saw set up with the standard blade and use a router for making joints.

JOINTMAKING WITH A ROUTER

Router joinery involves holding the tool freehand or with the router mounted in a router table (for more on using a router table, see page 121). You won't need a bunch of different bits to cut most of the joints in this chapter. Straight bits in sizes ranging from ¼ inch to ¾ inch will take care of nearly all the cutting work you'll need to do, especially if you have a router table. A piloted rabbeting bit is a helpful bit to own as well, especially if it comes with an assortment of interchangeable bearings in different diameters. By switching the bearing, you can cut rabbets of various widths using the same bit. For router-cut dovetails, you'll need a dovetail jig and a couple sizes of dovetail bits. Some dovetail

The two primary power tools for building joinery are the router and table saw. Depending on your application, the tools can be used interchangeably to make the same joint. As shown here, a router and scrap fence clamped in place can cut a dado or a rabbet, but so can a table saw outfitted with a dado blade.

jigs come with the appropriate bits for use with the jig. If yours doesn't, be sure to follow the manufacturer's recommendations for the correct bits to use with your dovetail jig.

JOINTMAKING WITH A TABLE SAW

When you cut joint parts with a table saw, the cuts you'll make are different than ordinary rip and crosscuts. Instead of cutting all the way through the workpiece, you'll typically only remove part of the thickness, edge, or end of a workpiece and leave the rest as a connection point for the other half of the joint. These types of non-through cuts are made by nibbling away material with repetitive passes over the blade or by setting the blade low and making a pair of cuts to slice away a portion of the wood.

A general-purpose table saw blade will do the work accurately but slowly. A better alternative for cutting joinery with a table saw is a dado blade. Dado blades are essentially saw blades with adjustable cutting widths. There are two primary dado blade styles: stacked dado blades and wobble dadoes. Stacked dado blades consist of a pair of carbide-tooth saw blades that sandwich one or more chipper blades in between. The outer blades create the side walls of a cut, while the chippers shear away the rest of the waste. Chippers have only two to six carbide teeth, with each tooth mounted on its own wing of the blade. The chipper blades are manufactured in various thicknesses so you can "stack" them to produce cuts of different widths. You'll get a set of them in a range of thicknesses with the outer blades.

Wobble dadoes don't have chipper blades. Instead, a single saw blade is mounted on a large hub that holds the blade at a skewed angle. When the blade spins, the wobbling action removes all the waste material in the cut. The center hub is adjustable and marked for dialing the blade to different cutting widths. Twisting the hub changes the blade pitch and, in turn, the cutting width. Some wobble dadoes have two blades that form a V configuration on the hub. Stacked

TYPES OF NON-THROUGH CUTS

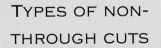
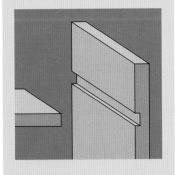
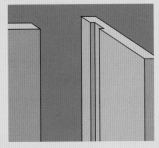

Unlike ripping or cross-cutting, making joinery with a table saw involves cutting part way through a workpiece. Making these cuts will usually require removing the saw's guard, which increases the chances for kickback.

Dado blades come in two styles: stacked sets (left) or wobble dadoes (right). Stacked sets come with variable-thickness chipper blades that fit between a pair of conventional-looking saw blades to make cuts of different widths. To change the cutting width on a wobble dado, you turn a dial on the blade's hub.

dado sets have more components than wobble dadoes, and they're generally quite expensive—upwards of $200. However, the higher price is usually a good value since stacked dadoes tend to make cleaner, more flat-bottomed cuts than wobble dadoes. Whichever style you buy, select a dado that has a smaller diameter than the maximum blade size your saw can handle. For 10-inch table saws, buy an 8-inch-diameter blade.

TABLE SAW SAFETY

Making joints with a table saw presents some unique safety concerns. Non-through joinery cuts don't pass all the way through the workpiece, so you'll have to remove your table saw's blade guard and splitter to cut them. The risk of kickback increases without a splitter in place, and so do your chances of getting cut. The best option to increase safety is to invest in an aftermarket blade guard that can be used without a splitter, but high cost may make this unrealistic for you. In that case, exercise extreme caution if you have to operate your saw with the guard and splitter removed. Use push sticks to keep your hands well away from the blade.

Working with a dado blade poses other safety issues. Dado blades remove more material than standard blades, so you'll have to apply more force to push workpieces through the cut. Instead of forcing the work, which is both harder on your saw motor and more dangerous for you, make cuts in several shallow passes, raising the dado blade higher with each pass. You'll want to use featherboards, clamps, and other hold-down devices to keep workpieces firmly against the saw table and miter gauge or rip fence. Otherwise the increased feed resistance during dadoing will tend to lift the workpiece off the saw table as it's cut, making kickback more likely and affecting accuracy as well.

SETTING UP A DADO BLADE

Dado blades require a different setup procedure than standard blades. Since a dado is designed for cutting channels that vary in both width and depth, both of these dimensions need to be set on the dado blade to make an accurate cut. Wobble-style dado blades are particularly tricky because the blade doesn't spin in a flat orbit like stacked dado blades do, so you can't simply measure off the two outermost cutters to determine the blade's cutting width.

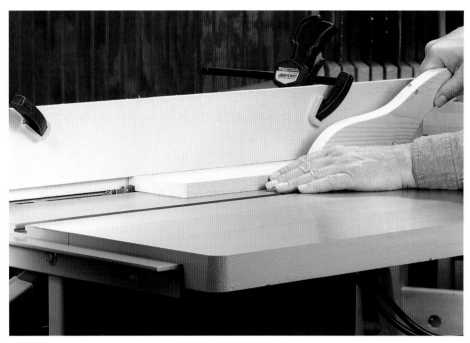

For setting up stacked dado blades, first install the outer cutting blade that goes against the arbor flange. Make sure the beveled teeth face away from the chipper blades you'll install next. (Most stacked dado blades have outer blades milled with teeth that face the same direction.) Slide on the chipper blades in a combination that will add up to the cutting width you need when added to the thicknesses of the outer two blades. You may need to insert a few shims between the chippers to micro-adjust the final cutting width. Shims are often included with the dado blade, or you can use sheets of paper, plastic, or metal with an arbor hole cut in the center. Arrange the chipper blades so the teeth don't touch one another or the teeth on the outer blades. Distribute the chippers evenly around the arbor to help balance the dado when it spins. Install the other outer blade with the tooth bevels facing away from the chippers, and tighten the assembly using both the arbor washer and nut. If your arbor isn't long enough to allow both the washer and nut to fit, pull off a few chippers to make more room. Never saw without the arbor washer in place.

To set a wobble-style dado, follow the manufacturer's instructions for twisting the center hub to set the cutting width. The hub has indicator marks for adjusting it to various cutting-width settings. Install the arbor washer and nut.

Make height adjustments as you would with a standard blade by raising or lowering the dado. If the cutting width needs to change, add or remove chippers for a stacked dado, or adjust the hub on a wobble dado. Then make test cuts on scrap until the blade matches the cutting dimensions you need. Making test cuts will also help you see if the rip fence is set the correct distance away from the blade for the joint cuts you need to make.

If you don't have a blade guard that works independently of the splitter, you'll have to remove it for making non-through cuts. One way to protect yourself in these instances is to clamp a thick hold-down to the rip fence above the blade to shield it.

TIP

Cut a piece of test scrap to determine the height and width settings of the dado blade as well as its position relative to the rip fence. Use it to mark a strip of tape on the saw table for easier workpiece alignment.

Butt joints

No other joint is faster or easier to make on a table saw than the common butt joint. Essentially, all it takes to make a butt joint is a pair of flat, smooth workpiece surfaces. Any pairing of workpiece faces, edges, or ends makes a butt joint.

Edge-to-edge butt joints form wider panels from narrower boards. Face-to-face butt joints build thick blanks for table and chair legs or lathe turnings. A butt joint combining the end of one workpiece and the edge of another creates right-angle joints for cabinet face frames. Pair the end of a workpiece with the face of another to make simple shelving or the corner joints for boxes.

What butt joints offer in simplicity they sacrifice in strength. Edge-to-edge and face-to-face joints are stronger than the other options because long face and edge grain responds well to glue. Glue bonds less effectively to the open pores of end grain regardless of the grain direction on the mating surface, and end-grain to end-grain joints are the weakest of all. Whenever end grain is combined with edge or face grain, the glue joint will eventually fail because each workpiece will expand and contract at different rates with changes in humidity.

For edge- and face-glued butt joints, glue alone forms a sufficient bond to keep the joint together. You may want to install biscuits, dowels, or splines to make edge-glued butt joints easier to keep aligned during clamping. Otherwise, wet glue can act as a lubricant under clamping pressure and cause the parts to slip out of position. All other butt joint variations should be glued and reinforced

BUTT JOINT VARIATIONS

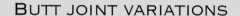

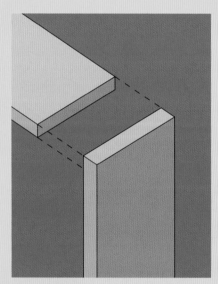

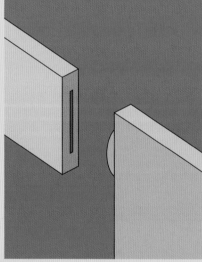

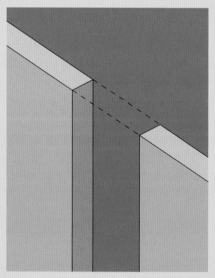

Butt joints that marry the end of one workpiece with the face of another workpiece form a right angle. This style, common in box and cabinet construction, needs to be reinforced with mechanical fasteners as well as glue to provide strength.

Butt joints that combine the end of one workpiece with the edge of another are sometimes used to make cabinet face frames. A biscuit inserted between the joint parts reinforces the connection.

When long grain is paired with long grain, the result is a strong edge-to-edge butt joint for making larger wood panels from narrower boards. Glue alone provides sufficient holding power here.

with mechanical fasteners such as screws, nails, staples, dowels, biscuits, or splines driven through both members of the joint.

Cutting butt joints on the table saw is a simple matter of making flat, square rip and crosscuts using a combination blade or specialized blades for ripping and crosscutting. Check your fence and blade settings carefully for square before cutting the parts. If your blades cut cleanly, you may be able to build the joint as soon as the wood is cut without further tooling. However, it's a good idea to shave off any blade marks and square up the sawn edges using a sharp hand plane or a jointer, especially for edge-to-edge joints bonded only with glue. Flat, square edges here will produce almost invisible seams.

Splined butt joints. Splines are a good way to convert the flat mating surfaces of a butt joint into interlocking parts. Splines also contribute additional wood surfaces inside the joint for more area. This adds strength.

Unless a butt joint is connecting faces with faces or edges with edges, reinforce the butt joints with mechanical fasteners such as screws or nails as well as glue.

Splines are thin strips of wood or plywood inserted into a pair of matching slots that cross the butt joint. One slot is cut into each member of the joint, usually with a standard blade in a table saw. The width of the spline is typically equal to the thickness of the workpieces. Spline thickness should be about one-third the board thickness. So, for butt joints in ¾-inch stock, splines should be milled ¾-inch wide and ⅛- to ¼-inch thick. Larger splines don't add much to joint strength, and they can even weaken the joint if the slots are too wide or deep.

To make splined butt joints, cut the spline slots first. Center the slot locations on the thickness of the joint parts when possible for greatest strength. Using either a standard saw blade or a narrow dado blade, set the cutting height to one-half the spline width plus ½₂ inch more to provide a "well" for excess glue. This height will center the spline across the joint. Cut edge and end spline slots with workpieces standing on edge or on end against the rip fence. For end cuts on narrow workpieces, clamp a runner to the workpiece so it rides on top of the rip fence to provide additional support, or use a tenoning jig (see pages 140 and 162). Saw slots into the faces of workpieces using either the rip fence or miter gauge as you would to make standard rip or crosscuts.

Wood splines can be used instead of biscuits to join edges or ends. Despite their slender thickness, splines add considerable strength to the joint.

Cut the spline stock after you've cut the slots so you can carefully match the spline proportions to the slots. If you're making splines from solid wood, rip them off the edge of a board. Choose a piece of spline stock with a thickness that matches the spline width you need. If you accidentally cut splines that are too wide or thick to fit the slots, do not try to rip or joint them to correct the error. The spline proportions will be too small to make these machining corrections safely. Reset the rip fence for a more accurate cut, and rip new splines.

Use a tenoning jig to cut spline slots in the ends of narrow workpieces. Center the workpiece carefully over the blade, or the joint won't align when assembled.

To cut spline slots along the edge of a workpiece, use the rip fence. Set the blade height slightly higher than necessary to provide a well for excess glue to seep into.

TIP

When cutting end- or edge-grain spline slots, it's important that the slot is exactly centered on the workpiece. You can ensure centered slots by passing the workpiece along the rip fence twice—one pass with each face against the fence. This way, any misalignment of the cutter will still make a centered, although slightly wider, spline slot.

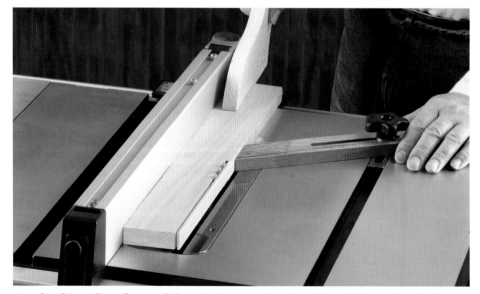

Cut the thin splines from solid stock, ripping them in strips off the edge of the workpiece. Adjust the rip fence carefully so the spline is the correct thickness to fit the slots.

Rabbet joints

Rabbets are two-sided channels cut along the edge or end of a workpiece. Their shape forms an offset tongue that can be used to form partially interlocking joints. Inside this rabbet channel, the cut that forms the side of the tongue is called the *cheek*, and the other cut forms the rabbet's *shoulder*. When the ends or edges of two workpieces are milled with matching rabbets and combined at right angles, the result is a double rabbet joint. You can also cut a rabbet with a cheek wide enough to completely conceal the flat end or edge of another workpiece and make an overlap rabbet joint. Both overlap and double rabbet joint styles are often used for building boxes and cabinet carcases. Overlap rabbets are especially useful because the rabbets hide the end grain of back and top panels. Secure these joints with a combination of glue and brads, nails, or staples.

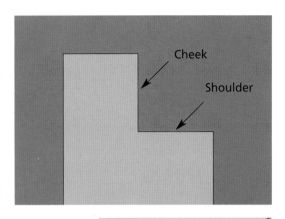

A third rabbet joint style—the shiplap—mates pairs of matching rabbets to form an interlocking flat joint for panel construction. You'll see shiplaps used on back panels where the boards aren't glued together. The stepped effect of the joint hides board edges when they shrink. Shiplaps are a stronger option than edge-glued butt joints for building panels because the cheeks and shoulders are self-aligning if they're cut carefully, and they contribute more surface area for glue.

Rabbet joints are easy to make with either a router or a table saw. Using a hand-held router, you can cut a rabbet with a piloted rabbeting bit or a straight bit and edge guide. If you're cutting a rabbet along a large workpiece that would be cumbersome to lift, opt for a handheld router to make the rabbet. In cases where the workpiece is more manageably sized, you can cut the joint on a router table, which offers better control. All it takes is a straight bit and the router table fence or a piloted rabbeting bit with or without a fence. Rabbeting on the table saw can be done with a dado blade or a standard blade. Either way, make sure the workpiece you're rabbeting on the table saw is easy to lift and slide over the saw table. If it's unwieldy, a router is the better tool to use.

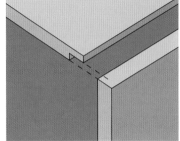

Rabbet joint

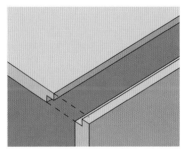

Double rabbet

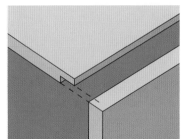

Overlap rabbet

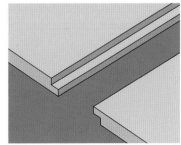

Shiplap rabbet

Cut wide rabbets with a straight bit and right-angle jig or clamped straightedge.

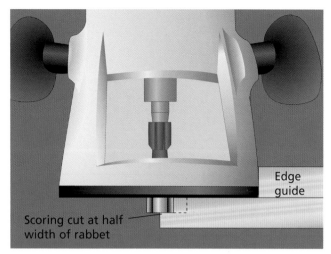

Scoring cut at half width of rabbet

Edge guide

To reduce tearout when making a rabbet cut, limit the first cut to half the diameter of the bit.

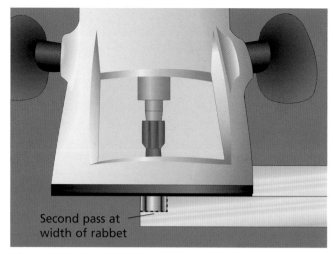

Second pass at width of rabbet

Then, move the edge guide and make a second pass to complete the rabbet.

Rabbeting with a handheld router. The most basic rabbeting technique calls for a handheld router and a piloted rabbeting bit. The rabbet's width is set by the bit bearing, while the depth is set by you. Common rabbeting bits cut ¼-, ⅜-, or ½-inch rabbets. However, you can change the bearing to yield a different cutting width or buy a rabbeting bit set (see bottom left photo, this page). To cut a rabbet wider than your bit will allow, you have to use a setup with a straight bit. Cut deeper rabbets by making successively deeper passes with a piloted or straight bit.

Rabbeting with a straight bit requires an edge guide, straightedge, or right-angle jig. The rabbet depth is set by the cutting depth of the bit. The width is determined by the placement of the guide or jig, so the rabbet can be as wide as you need. Tearout is a concern for any rabbet cut because you're cutting two surfaces that are vulnerable to splintering and chipping. Usually, the best way to minimize tearout is to make a narrow initial cut, or score, followed by a full-width final cut. This works because a narrower pass cuts a more gradual angle at the leading cutter edge. If you're still tearing out using a conventional feed, try a climb cut for the scoring pass, then a conventional feed for the final pass. Using a bit that's at least twice as big as the rabbet width (½"-diameter bit for a ¼" rabbet, for example) also helps reduce tearout.

Some rabbeting bits come with a single pilot bearing, but rabbeting bits with multiple bearings of different sizes are far more versatile.

Rabbeting on the router table. Rabbeting on a router table offers the usual advantages over handheld routing: less telegraphing of defects from the stock edge (when using a fence), ease of working small or narrow stock, and no risk of ruining the cut due to a tipped router. Always use a fence for straight work. For curved workpieces, you can omit the fence and use a bearing-guided bit and starting pin.

With a standard fence setup, use a straight, spiral, or piloted rabbeting bit. For straight or spiral bits, adjust the fence to the desired rabbet width, and adjust the bit height to equal the depth of cut. When using a rabbeting bit, set the fence even with the bit's bearing, or beyond the bearing to make a more narrow cut. Note: Never trap the work under the bit by cutting into the top side—bowed stock or lifting during the cut will ruin the cut and can break the bit.

Making a stopped rabbet with a router. Stopped rabbets run short of one or both ends of a workpiece and are good for hiding the edges of panels and construction joints. Cut them like standard rabbets, but use stop blocks to index the ends of the cut. With a handheld router, clamp blocks across the work (perpendicular to the rabbet), allowing for the distance between the edge of the subbase and the bit. Initiate the cut by pivoting the workpiece into the spinning bit—make a sweeping cut (see page 109) with a conventional feed until you reach the far stop block. Then come back and sweep into a climb cut to finish up the remaining few inches of the rabbet. On a router table, set up the cut with marks and stop blocks. For more on making stopped cuts with a router, see page 128.

Rabbeting on a table saw. Rabbets can be cut on a table saw using either a standard blade or a dado blade. Dado blades require a bit more setup time, but one pass over the cutter forms both the cheek and shoulder cuts without resetting the blade height or rip fence position. To cut rabbets with a dado blade, install a sacrificial fence on the rip fence and set the blade width ⅛ to ¼ inch wider than the rabbet cheek will need to be. Raise the blade and move the rip fence until the amount of blade that projects out from the fence equals the shoulder and cheek dimensions. For rabbets that follow the edge of a workpiece, pass the workpiece through the dado blade on its face like a rip cut. Install a featherboard directly over the dado blade and a second featherboard to the saw table adjacent to the blade to keep the workpiece tight against the table and fence as you make the cut. You can also cut edge rabbets with workpieces standing on edge, but orient the workpiece so the tongue is cut outside the dado—not between the fence and blade. Test your setup on scrap before cutting your actual workpieces to be sure the rabbet proportions are accurate.

Use the miter gauge to support workpieces for cutting rabbets on board ends. Make the cut with workpieces face down. Support the workpiece from behind with the miter gauge. In this situation, you can safely use the miter gauge and rip fence simultaneously.

SACRIFICIAL RIP FENCES

Oftentimes, jointmaking involves setting the rip fence on a table saw close to or even touching the dado blade. This is a typical scenario for making rabbet or tenon cuts. Without some form of modification, this blade setup is clearly unsafe and will damage both the blade and the rip fence surface. The remedy is to clamp or fasten a flat, smooth wood scrap to your rip fence. In this book, we'll call it a sacrificial fence. A piece of hardwood, plywood, or medium-density fiberboard makes a sturdy sacrificial rip fence. With the fence installed, you can raise the blade and cut a recess into the wood fence to provide clearance for the spinning dado blade. This way, you can set the blade so its exposure matches the dimensions you need for cutting the joint while having it partially buried in the sacrificial fence. The metal fence is safe from the blade, and you can set up the dado blade for a variety of width cuts without changing the arrangement of the chippers.

To make the original recess cut in the sacrificial fence, slowly raise the blade into it, but first be sure the metal fence isn't crossing the cutting path of the blade. Keep the rip fence locked in place.

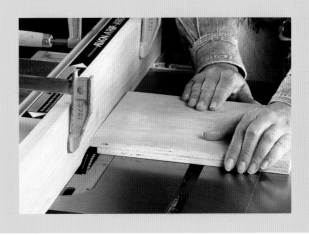

CUTTING EDGE RABBETS WITH A STANDARD BLADE

For rabbets that follow an edge, cut the rabbet cheek with the workpiece standing on edge against the rip fence.

Complete the rabbet with the workpiece face down on the saw table to make the shoulder cut. Be sure to adjust the blade height first, if necessary.

CUTTING END RABBETS WITH A STANDARD BLADE

To cut a rabbet into the short end of a workpiece with a standard blade, make the cheek cut with the workpiece clamped on end in a tenoning jig.

Switch to the miter gauge for making the shoulder cut. Use a zero-clearance throat plate in the saw, if possible, to keep the small waste piece from dropping down into the blade slot when it is cut loose.

Cutting rabbets with a standard saw blade is a two-step operation (see facing page). One cut forms the cheek and a second cut makes the shoulder. Mark the rabbet shape on the workpiece before you cut it to serve as an index for setting the blade height and fence position. It doesn't matter which cut you make first, but if you're milling a series of rabbets on a number of workpieces, work efficiently by making all like-sized cuts before resetting the saw for the second cuts.

For edge rabbets, form the cheek by standing the workpiece on edge against the rip fence. Then reset the fence and cut the shoulder with the board flat on the saw table. Arrange this second cut so the wastepiece will fall on the side of the blade opposite the fence. Do not make the shoulder cut with the waste piece between the blade and rip fence, or it could wedge inside this tunnel when it's cut free and kick back. Be careful to reset the blade height as well if you are cutting overlap rabbets where the cheeks and shoulders are different sizes.

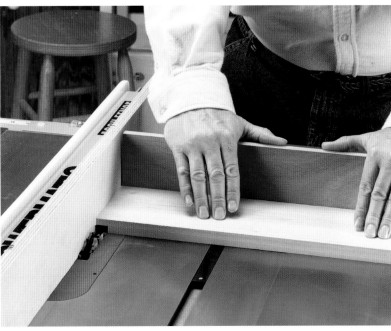

A dado blade can also be used to cut short end rabbets. Back up the workpiece with the miter gauge, and bury the blade partially in a sacrificial rip fence. Since this is a non-through cut, both the rip fence and miter gauge can be used in tandem safely.

If you're cutting rabbets on short board ends, you'll need to cut the cheeks with the workpiece standing on end. When the workpiece is long or particularly

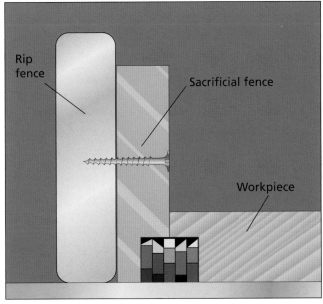

To cut rabbets along the edges of a workpiece with a dado blade, set the blade partially in a sacrificial fence and pass the board face down over the blade. If the rabbet follows a wide end or edge, feed it by hand against the rip fence.

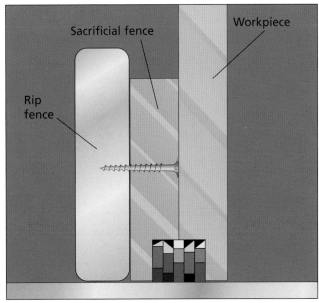

When rabbets follow a long edge of a narrow workpiece, you can run the workpiece on edge against the sacrificial fence. For wide workpieces, make the sacrificial fence taller than shown here to provide sufficient support.

narrow, clamp the board in a tenoning jig and make the cut this way rather than running it on end against the rip fence. If it rocks or teeters, the work-piece could bind the blade and kick back. You can also make this short end cut safely by attaching a tall auxiliary rip fence and supporting the workpiece from behind with a wide piece of scrap. Cut the shoulder with the workpiece on its face and against the miter gauge. Use a stop block clamped to the rip fence to index the shoulder cut, or line up the cut by eye. Either way, do not use the rip fence to support the workpiece during the shoulder cut.

Joints with dadoes and grooves

Dadoes are non-through cuts that cross the width of a board, in from the board ends. If you make the same non-through cut along the length of a board, fol-lowing the long grain, the cut is called a groove. Grooves also refer to centered cuts made into the edges or ends of a workpiece. Both dadoes and grooves can be made with a standard blade, dado blade, or router and straight bit.

Dadoes and grooves can be combined with flat-edged or rabbeted workpieces to form numerous different joints. Among them are housed dadoes, blind dadoes, rabbet-and-dadoes, and tongue-and-groove joints. There are more dado and groove joints than are shown here, but these four examples serve a broad range of design applications and are sturdy and simple to make.

Making housed dado joints. A good way to strengthen a bookcase or cabi-net with fixed shelving is to lock the shelves into the sides of the case with dadoes. The simplest way to do this is to leave the shelf ends flat and square and fit them into dadoes that match the shelf thickness. This way, the shelves are "housed" in the dadoes. One downside to this joint is the ends of the shelves show along the front edge of the bookcase or cabinet sides, but you can easily hide them behind a face frame, solid-wood edging, or veneer edge tape.

To build these joints, set up the width of the dado blade carefully. The dadoes should be a hair wider than the shelf thickness so the parts fit together easily, but not so wide as to leave a gap. Set the blade height for about one-third the thick-ness of the workpieces receiving the dadoes. Experiment on scraps to test the fit of the shelves in the dadoes before cutting dadoes across the actual workpieces. To make the dado cuts, guide your workpiece over the blade using the miter gauge as a backup. With the saw turned off, line up the blade carefully with your layout lines before beginning the cut. Always use the miter gauge to support workpieces that are narrower than they are long. Otherwise, the narrow board end tends to pivot away from the fence as you slide the workpiece along, which binds the dado blade and can lead to kickback. But if the dado runs across a workpiece that's wider than it is long, you can cut it without the miter gauge by guiding the workpiece end along the rip fence.

You can also cut housed dado joints using a large straight bit in a router. This router method is particularly effective on long, narrow workpieces that would be difficult or impossible to guide over a table saw. To cut them, first lay out your dado locations carefully with a long rule and pencil. Clamp a piece of wide, flat-edged scrap to the workpiece to guide the router along the cut. Install a straight bit in the router that matches the exact thickness of the shelving.

Rabbet

Groove

Dado

Dadoes are non-through cuts that cross the grain. Grooves follow the grain. Rabbets can follow or cross the grain, but they always occur along board ends and edges.

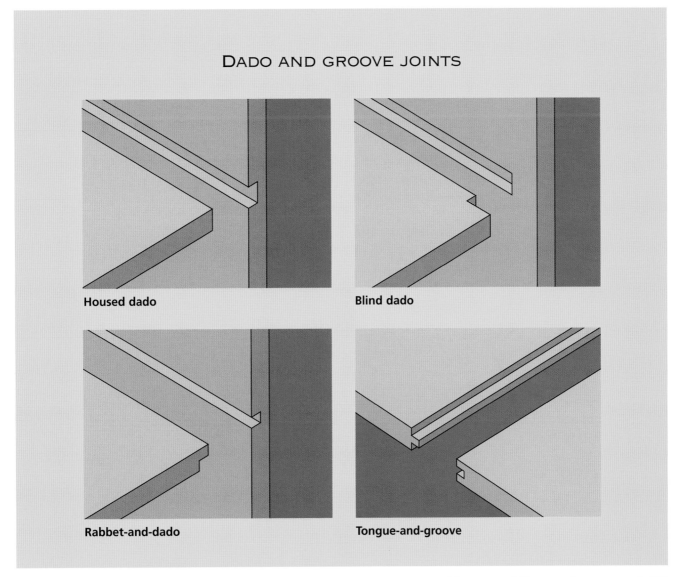

DADO AND GROOVE JOINTS

Housed dado

Blind dado

Rabbet-and-dado

Tongue-and-groove

Housed and blind dado joints can be cut with a dado blade on the table saw by guiding workpieces from behind with the miter gauge.

Note: For ¾-inch plywood shelving, the material thickness is often slightly less than ¾ inch. These days, ¾-inch plywood is actually closer to ²³⁄₃₂ inch. Straight bits are sold specifically for cutting undersized plywood. Use an undersized plywood-cutting straight bit for a perfect fit.

Once the bit is installed, measure the distance from the cutting edges of the bit to the edge of the router base, and set the scrap straightedge this same distance away from your dado layout lines on the workpiece. Position the straightedge to the left or right of the layout lines. Set the router in place against the straightedge and check the orientation of the bit on your layout lines to be certain things line up. If you're cutting dadoes deeper than ¼ inch, make the dado cuts in two passes of increasing depth. This practice prevents overloading the router motor or stressing the bit. To make each dado cut, guide the router along the straightedge, pulling the tool through the workpiece toward you if the straightedge is left of the router. Push the router across the workpiece from front to back if the straightedge is clamped to the right of the cut.

Even though housed dado joints "capture" the shelving in the side panels, it's still a good idea to reinforce these joints with glue and drive finish nails into the shelves through the bottom of the dadoes. Long shelves can bow, and the deflection can pull the shelf ends out of the dadoes unless they are locked in place.

Making blind dado joints. For bookcases or cabinets without face frames, blind dadoes are a convenient way to hide the shelving joints along the edges. This joint still captures the shelving in full-width dadoes, like housed dadoes do, but the dadoes stop short of the front edges of the bookcase or cabinet sides, hiding the shelf ends. The front corners of each shelf are notched so the shelf can wrap around the stopped dadoes and still line up with the front edges of the side panels.

You can cut stopped dadoes on a table saw, but the setup is involved. If you're

SHIMMING A DADO BLADE

If your outer blades and chippers form a too-tight fit for the shelving, no matter which combination of chippers try, an easy way to get extra "wiggle room" is to insert a few paper or metal shims between the chipper blades. Usually, one or two shims will do the trick. This widens the dado blade just enough for the plywood to slide snugly into place.

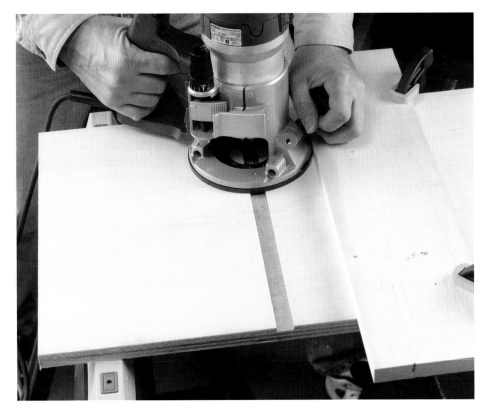

To cut a dado for a blind dado joint, run the router against a straightedge, pulling it toward you until the bit reaches the "blind" stopping point of the cut.

making a large bookcase or cabinet, sawing these stopped dadoes is also diffi-cult to do accurately. It's easier to use a large straight bit in your router and guide the router against a clamped straightedge, just as you would for making housed dadoes. Lay out the dado cuts on your workpieces, and clearly mark the dadoes where the cuts must end to form the blind corner. Use the same offset-ting procedure as described in the housed dado instructions to establish the position for clamping the straightedge guide in place. Set up the straightedge on the left side of the dado layout lines. Arrange the workpiece on the bench so the blind ends of the dado cuts are closest to you.

Cut each dado starting at the back "open" edge of the workpiece and pulling the router along the straightedge rather than pushing it. Slow down the cut when you are a few inches from the "blind" stopping point. Complete the cut by pulling the router more slowly along the straightedge, stopping the tool as soon as the bit reaches the end of your layout lines. Once all the dadoes are cut, square up the curved portion with a sharp chisel. Trim away the front corners of the shelving so the shelves fit fully in the dadoes and the front edges of all the parts line up.

Making rabbet-&-dado joints. When rabbets are paired with dadoes, the combination creates a strong, interlocking joint that has several woodworking applications. Rabbet-and-dadoes are often used like housed or blind dadoes to fit shelving into bookcase or cabinet side panels. The advantage of this joint over the housed dado is that you can use any conventional ⅜-inch straight bit in a router to mill the dadoes into the bookshelf or cabinet. No special under-sized bit is required. The shelf ends receive the rabbets, which are typically cut to fit the dadoes after the dadoes are milled. For ¾-inch material, make the rab-bet tongues ⅜ inch thick and ¼ inch long.

Mill the dadoes by guiding your router and straight bit against a straightedge, or use a dado blade in the table saw and guide the workpieces with the miter gauge. These procedures are outlined in the housed dado joint description (see page 146). Cut the rabbets using the same methods as were described for making rabbets with a table saw or router and rabbeting bit (see page 143). Which tool option you use is really up to you. You can expedite the process by cutting half the joint—either the dado or the rabbet—with a router and the other half on the table saw.

It doesn't really matter which half of the joint you cut first, the rabbets or the dadoes. The more failsafe approach is to cut the dadoes first, then cut the rabbets to fit the dadoes. If you cut the rabbets first, it's harder to refine the shape of a dado accurately or easily. It's always a good idea to first make test cuts on scrap to inspect your router bit or saw settings before committing to the project workpieces.

When cutting the rabbet tongues, make them a hair shorter than ¼ inch so there's a bit of extra room in the bottom of the dado for excess glue to migrate. Drive short brads at an angle down through the shelves and into the bookcase or cabinet sides to lock the joint parts.

Making tongue-&-groove joints. Tongue-and-groove joints feature a centered tongue that fits into a matching groove on the edges or ends of the other joint part. Since the tongue has twice the number of cheeks and shoulders as a standard rabbet, it contributes more surface area to the joint for an even stronger glue bond. The interlocking nature of this joint makes it a good choice for assembling large panels for tabletops or for making back panels in cabinets and cupboards. It's also used on occasion to join the rails and stiles of small doors. In these instances, the grooves are cut along the full inside edges of all four door frame parts. This way the groove can hold a panel or pane of glass as well as connect the four frame parts.

Lay out the joints so the tongues are one-third the thickness of their workpieces. When the tongues and grooves are situated along the edges of boards, make the tongue lengths and widths match. Tongues measuring ¼ × ¼ inch are sufficiently strong on ¾-inch stock. If you are building cabinet doors, make the tongues on the ends of the door rails longer—½ inch is a good length for standard 1× lumber.

A dado blade will mill all the parts of these joints quickly and easily. Start by cutting the grooves. On ¾-inch material, set the dado blade for a ¼-inch cutting width and raise it to the appropriate height for your tongue length. Set the fence ¼ inch from the inside blade face for this operation. Guide workpieces along the rip fence when they are cut into a board edge. If you are cutting grooves into the end of a workpiece, first attach a tall auxiliary fence to your rip fence to provide additional support for long workpieces. Make the auxiliary fence 8 to 10 inches wide and attach it just as you would a sacrificial rip fence.

It isn't safe to groove the ends of a narrow workpiece without some form of backup support. A simple solution is to use a large piece of flat-edged scrap wood held against the rip fence behind the workpiece. Slide both the workpiece and the backup board along the rip fence to cut the groove. An even safer, more accurate method for cutting end grooves on long, narrow workpieces is to clamp the workpiece on-end in a tenoning jig that rides in the saw's miter slot. (For more on tenoning jigs, see page 162.)

When cutting the grooves, it's important that they are exactly centered on the workpiece edges or ends. You can form a centered groove by carefully setting the fence in relation to the blade, but there's an easier way to get the same result. Set the fence so the blade is close to centered on the workpiece, then pass it through the blade two times, flipping the workpiece from one face to the other after making the first pass. This way, even if the blade is slightly off-center on the first cut, the second pass will automatically center the groove. Be aware that this technique will create a slightly wider groove than if you make it in just one pass.

Once the groove is cut, make the tongue. The dado height you set for cutting the groove is nearly perfect for cutting the tongue to length, but lower the blade about 1⁄32 inch so the tongue won't bottom out in the groove. Install a sacrificial fence on the rip fence and slide the fence over until it just touches the blade. The blade should still move freely. In this position, the dado will cut a cheek and shoulder accurately in one pass with the blade fully exposed. Cut one side of the tongue on a piece of test scrap, then flip the scrap to the other face and make a second pass to complete the tongue. Check the fit of the tongue and groove. The parts should slip together easily with just a slight bit of resistance.

To cut the groove for a tongue-and-groove joint along the edge of a workpiece, set up the dado blade and fence so the blade is roughly centered on the workpiece thickness. Make two passes along the rip fence, flipping the board from one face to the other to center the groove exactly.

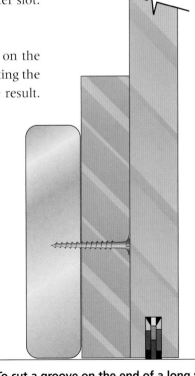

To cut a groove on the end of a long workpiece, guide it against a tall auxiliary rip fence and support it from behind with a large piece of scrap. The extra support will keep it from rocking or tipping during the cut.

Often, your test fit will require a bit of refinement. If the tongue is too thin, reposition the rip fence a hair closer to the dado blade and cut another tongue on more scrap. **NOTE:** *In this situation, you may have to lower the blade completely and cut a blade recess into the sacrificial fence (see page 143). Use the previous test scrap as a quick reference for resetting the blade height.* Correct overly thick tongues by moving the fence slightly further away from the blade to cut a wider shoulder. A single light tap on the fence might shift it just enough to perfect the fit.

If you'd rather use a router to cut tongue-and-groove joints, you can make both the tongue and the groove cuts on a router table. On 1× lumber, install a ¼-inch straight bit to establish the groove width, and set the router fence ¼ inch from the bit. Raise the bit so its height matches the groove depth you need. For ¼-inch-deep grooves, mill the groove in one pass, moving the workpiece across the router table from right to left. Keep the workpiece tight to the fence at all times. If you are cutting deeper grooves, make the first pass at ¼-inch cutting height, then repeat with more passes, raising the bit about ¼ inch each time until you reach the groove's full depth.

Switch to a wider straight bit for making the tongue. Set the router table fence over the bit, just as you would with a dado blade and sacrificial rip fence, so the portion of the bit that is exposed matches the cheek and shoulder dimensions you need. Set up the fence and bit to mill the cheek and shoulder with the workpiece face-down. Use a push stick to guide the workpiece and hold it securely against the fence and table. Push the workpiece across the router table from right to left. Flip the workpiece over and repeat the cut to form the second cheek and shoulder. Make these cuts on test scrap first to ensure the tongue you make will fit the groove. Lower the bit slightly to make wider tongues, or raise the bit to trim thinner tongues.

Another option for cutting the tongues is to use a piloted rabbeting bit and guide the router freehand over the workpiece. Follow the same procedure as you would for cutting rabbets with this bit. Select a bearing for the bit that will allow it to cut the proper cheek and shoulder sizes.

Cut the tongue in two passes with a dado blade, flipping the workpiece end-for-end with each pass. Be sure to have a sacrificial fence installed for this operation to protect the rip fence and blade.

Tongue-and-groove joints can also be made on the router table. Here, a ¼-inch straight bit cuts the groove. Use a wider bit for milling the tongue, and make it in two passes, as you would if cutting with a dado blade.

Making lap joints is easy with a router and a simple shopmade jig.

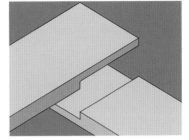

Corner half-lap

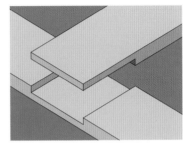

T half-lap

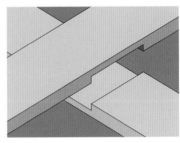

Cross half-lap

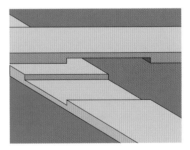

Angled half-lap

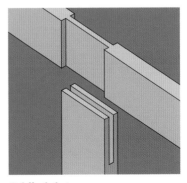

Bridle joint

Lap joints

Lap joints combine a wide rabbet with a dado or a wide pair of dadoes together so the workpieces cross at full width and the faces of the mating parts are flush. They're the simplest kinds of frame joints and a good choice for quick, strong connections where it's acceptable for the wood joints to show. Typically, lap joint dadoes are cut halfway through the thickness of their parts. They're also cut wide enough to house a rabbet tongue or a matching dado that's as wide as the mating workpiece.

Lap joints may connect workpieces of equal or differing thickness, depending on the application, but the former type are more common. When the workpiece thicknesses aren't the same, of course only one pair of workpiece faces will be flush. Choose lap joints for building strong table and bench frameworks where legs meet stringers and aprons. The joints are interlocking and provide large, long-grain surface areas for gluing.

Lap joints take many forms, as shown at right. Corner half-laps combine two matching rabbets arranged at 90°. T half-laps couple an end rabbet on one workpiece with a dado on the other workpiece. Cross half-laps and angled half-laps form an intersection where two wide dadoes lock together at 90° or another angle. Another less common lap joint hybrid is the bridle joint. Here, a pair of wide dadoes are milled into opposite faces of one workpiece. A deep end slot is cut into the mating workpiece to create two outboard tongues. The tongues fit around the dadoes.

To cut cross-laps, use guides clamped to both sides to trap the router base.

When cutting square corner half-lap joints, gang the workpieces and cut from the ends inward.

Basic lap joints are easy to cut with a handheld router and shop-made jig or straightedge clamped in place. You can also cut them on the router table with a straight bit against the fence or using a table saw and dado blade.

Cutting half-laps with a handheld router. Mark the width of the stock onto the workpieces, then gang them together to make both cuts at once. Use a straight bit that makes a clean bottom cut. For end-laps, set up a right-angle jig so the fence will stop the router at the marks. Cut from the ends inward, making successive passes until reaching full depth of cut. Use test cuts to determine the proper bit depth for the final cut. If the lap is long, clamp a block to the workbench to support the router base. To cut a cross-lap joint, use two right-angle jigs (or straightedges) to trap the router base and limit the cuts.

Cutting half-laps on the router table. Load a straight bit and set the height at about ⅛". Mark the stock width onto the workpieces, then adjust the fence so the outer edge of the bit will cut at the line. Cut both workpieces at once, using a sled

HALVING THE WORKPIECE

Here's an easy way to find the correct bit depth for making half-lap joints. With each bit setting, make test cuts on both sides of the stock. When the two cuts meet, the bit is set to cut away exactly half of the stock.

or backer board if necessary. Cut from the ends of the stock, working inward until the pieces meet the fence. Re-cut at deeper bit settings until you reach full depth. If necessary, clean up the lap cheeks with a chisel.

Cutting lap joints on the table saw. There are no special cutting techniques for making lap joints. Set the dado blade for a wide cut to remove waste material more quickly, and mill the dadoes or trim the rabbet cheeks and shoulders in several side-by-side passes. For lap joints on workpieces with matching thicknesses, you can use the same blade height setting to machine both workpieces if you set the cutting height carefully. To help minimize tearout and to provide more workpiece support, back up the dado cuts with an auxiliary miter fence. It helps to mark the dado cutting width on the saw table so you can line up the cuts accurately (see Tip, page 137).

Lap joints unavoidably form cross-grain connections. If the workpieces expand and contract significantly, the glue bonds will eventually fail. Reinforce the glue joint with dowels, screws, or bolts driven though both members if the joints will be subjected to moisture or extreme twisting or racking stresses.

Mortise and tenon joints

Mortise-and-tenon joints are arguably the strongest examples of interlocking joinery. Furniture builders have used them for centuries in situations where strength and stress resistance are paramount. You'll find mortise and tenons used most commonly to attach chair and table legs to aprons, rails, and stretchers.

A dado blade and miter gauge make quick work of cutting the notched half of a bridle joint. Make the notch in a series of side-by-side passes.

Cut the tongue of the lap joint as you would a wide rabbet using a tenoning jig and miter gauge. Make the tongue in two passes with a standard blade—one for the cheek and another for the shoulder. Or use a dado blade and nibble the waste away.

MORTISE & TENON VARIATIONS

Mortise-and-tenon joints come in a variety of styles for different situations. The common variations shown here are made using the same techniques as for the classic joint, with specific modifications as noted.

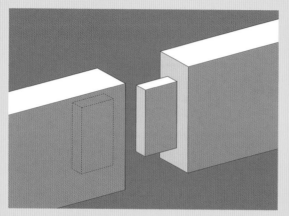

Square mortise: Mortise is squared at corners (with a chisel) to match tenon.

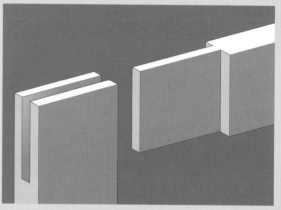

Bridle joint (or open mortise): Mortise continues through end of stock. Often used where table aprons meet legs. Intersecting tenons can be mitered to increase length.

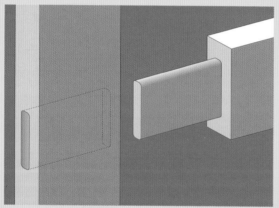

Through mortise: Mortise continues through back of stock. Used as decorative effect.

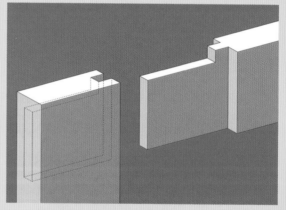

Haunched tenon: Haunch on outside edge of tenon prevents twisting. Commonly used in cabinet door construction.

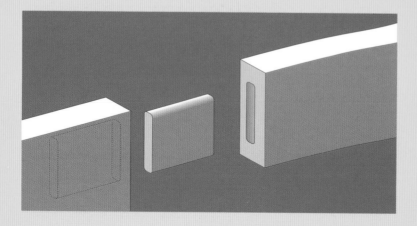

Loose tenon: Both mating pieces receive same-size mortise. Separate tenon glued inside. Good for hard-to-cut pieces or angles.

These critical connections are subject to the full gamut of racking, sheer, and tension forces as furniture is moved about and loaded down. Mortise and tenons keep chairs and tables standing tall by taking full advantage of those factors that contribute most to joint strength—namely large surface areas for glue and fully interlocking parts.

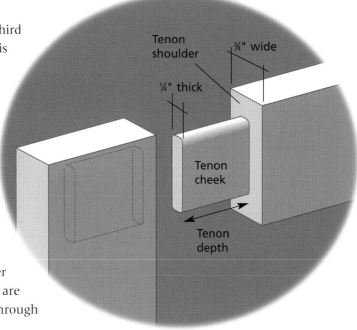

Blind mortise-and-tenon joint

Tenon shoulder

¾" wide

¼" thick

Tenon cheek

Tenon depth

As far as proportions go, tenons are usually one-third the thickness of the workpiece. Their length is determined mostly by the width of the workpieces that house them and the joint style itself—mortise and tenons take many forms. Some tenons stop halfway or less through the mortised workpiece, while other joint designs extend the tenon all the way through and even beyond the mortised workpiece. Tenons have two to four pairs of cheeks and shoulders, depending on the joint style, and all these cheek and shoulder faces form gluing surfaces. "Through" tenons are often wedged in place from the opposite end or across their width for greater strength. Even joints with fully concealed tenons are frequently locked with pegs or dowels driven through the mortise walls and into the tenons.

Mortises are simply the holes that fit the tenons. Depending on how you make the joint, mortises may have square or rounded ends.

Tool options for mortise & tenon joints. A plunge router is commonly used for mortising, because it lends itself perfectly for making progressively deeper cuts to form mortises. However, a drill press outfitted with a Forstner bit or a mortising attachment and hollow-chisel bits are also good options for making mortises.

Tenons can be cut in several different ways, with fixed-base, plunge, or table-mounted routers as well as with a table saw and dado blade. Handheld router operations generally require a jig that holds the workpiece vertically while the router cuts around the end to form the tenon. Or you can rout them with the router guided against a straightedge.

In most cases, it's easiest to cut the mortises first, then cut the tenons to fit the mortises. This allows you to trim away the tenon gradually and "sneak up" on a tight-fitting joint. Use a plunge-cutting straight or spiral bit for mortising with a router. Size the mortise so it's about ⅓ the thickness of the stock that will receive the tenon. For example, a door frame with ¾"-thick rails should have ¼"- or ⁵⁄₁₆"-wide mortises cut into the stiles.

Routing mortises with an edge guide. A commercial edge guide on a plunge router makes for an easy mortising setup (if you don't have an edge guide, use a fixed straightedge or fence to guide the router base). Start by

Mark the outline of the mortise on the workpiece.

Use the mortise outline to set up the edge guide and stop blocks. Side supports ensure stability while making the cut.

To cut a mortise wider than the bit diameter, use a saddle jig or two straightedges to guide the cut.

marking the center of the mortise on the workpiece, then measure from the centerline and mark the mortise's outer edges. Mark the ends of the mortise. If you're working with narrow stock, clamp extra pieces to either side of the workpiece to support the router's base. Load the bit and set the plunge depth to equal the full depth of the mortise. Place the router on the work and sight the bit against the pencil marks to set the guide fence. Also set up stop blocks that will contact the router base at the ends of the cut. Make the cut incrementally with ⅛" passes, cutting the full length of the mortise with each pass. Keep the router upright and the guide fence tight to the work throughout the operation, removing waste chips with a vacuum or air hose as needed.

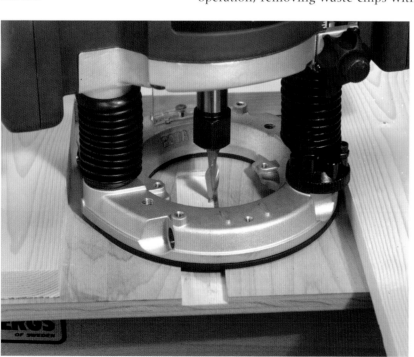

Routing mortises with a shop-made jig. An alternative to mortising with an edge guide is to use a slotted jig. One design works with a template guide to control the router; another uses stop blocks fixed to the jig.

To make the template-guide jig, fasten a straight fence to the underside of a ¼" MDF or hardboard base. On the router table, cut a slot through the base that matches the outside diameter of your template guide. The length of the slot equals the mortise length plus 2 times the offset of the template guide to the bit. Locate the slot so the jig can be centered on the thickest stock you're like-

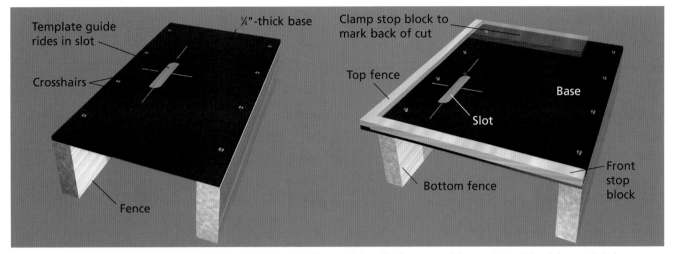

Mortising jig for use with a template guide (above left). Mortising jig for use with mortising bits (above right).

ly to use. Add crosshairs marking the center of the slot to help position the jig. For thinner stock, place shims between the fence and workpiece.

The stop-block jig has a fence on the bottom side of its base and one on the top side. Attach these so they are parallel to each other. Also attach a front stop block to the top side, perpendicular to the fences. Using the top fence and stop block to guide your handheld router, cut the slot using your mortising bit. The front end of the slot will always mark the front end of the mortise. To set up the jig, clamp it to the work (using shims, if necessary, to center the slot over the work), then clamp a stop block behind the router to mark the back end of the mortise.

Routing tenons. Making classic, four-sided tenons is easiest on the table router. All you need is a fence, a straight bit, and a push sled or miter gauge. Since you're cutting tenons to fit existing mortises, it's best to err on the side of making them too big, then nibble them down for a good fit. Use the mortises to test-fit each tenon, and make adjustments carefully—any change in the bit depth has a doubled effect because you always cut from both sides.

Mark the length of the tenon onto the stock: it should be 1/32" to 1/16" shorter than the mortise depth, to leave a little room for glue. Set the fence using the marks. Adjust the bit height to cut about 1/8" for the initial pass. Make the cheek cuts using the push sled or block to keep the work square to the fence and back up the work to prevent tearout. Nibble away the end of the

Use shims with the mortising jigs to center the workpiece in the slot.

If you cut numerous mortises of the same size in the same stock, create a permanent jig by screwing in stop blocks and spacers, rather than clamping them.

When cutting tenons, make the initial cheek cuts with the bit set at ⅛" depth. Use a sled or miter gauge to keep the work square.

Use the mortised workpiece to set the bit height for the final cheek cuts.

stock and work toward the fence with successive passes. Cut on both sides of the stock to keep the tenon centered. Reset the bit height for the final passes, using the mortise as a gauge. Test-fit and recut as needed to achieve the proper thickness.

Mark the tenon for the width cuts, set the bit height, and make the cuts in light passes as with the cheek cuts. Because the bit guard must be removed for this cut, be very aware of your hand placement in relation to the bit. Complete the tenon by rounding over its square corners with a file. To protect the shoulders, file to within ⅛" of them, then clean up the rest with a chisel.

Cutting tenons on a table saw. Typically, only the tenon portion of a mortise and tenon joint can be cut on a table saw. The process for cutting tenons on a

Cut the tenon to width, making light passes. Use an L-shaped push sled to support the work.

Use a file to slightly round the tenon, being careful not to mar the shoulder.

If you don't have a tenoning jig or dado blade, you can cut tenons with a standard blade and miter gauge. Start with the shoulder cuts indexed off a stop block clamped to the rip fence. Remove the waste out to the end of the tenon in side-by-side passes.

table saw is straightforward and simple to do with either a standard saw blade or a dado blade. Cheek and shoulder cuts can be made with a standard saw blade in two ways: First, cut the tenon cheeks and shoulders with the workpiece lying flat on the saw table and against the miter gauge. Use a stop block clamped to the rip fence to index the first shoulder cut, then form the cheek by

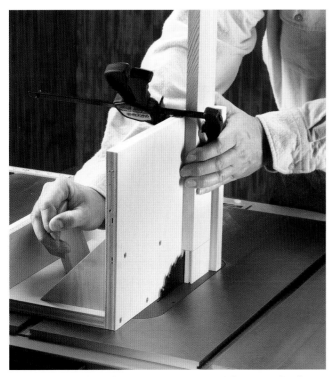

A second method for cutting tenons with a standard blade is to make the long cheek cuts with the workpiece clamped on end in a tenoning jig. Set the blade height so it cuts each cheek in one pass.

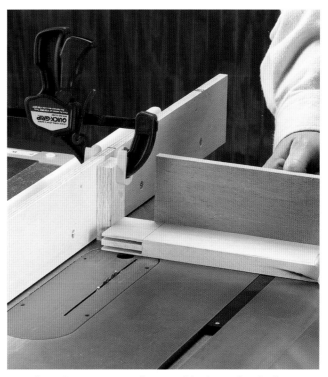

Use the miter gauge and a stop block on the rip fence to trim off the waste in a pair of shallow shoulder cuts. Position the stop block so the workpiece clears it before making contact with the blade.

A dado blade cuts tenons more efficiently than a standard blade. Cut the cheeks and shoulders along the long faces of the workpiece in a series of side-by-side passes. Use a miter gauge to support the workpiece from behind and a stop block clamped to the rip fence to index the blade for making the shoulder cuts. Be sure the workpiece clears the stop block before it makes contact with the dado blade. If the tenon has cheeks and shoulders on the short edges of the workpiece, stand it on-edge against the miter gauge to make these cuts.

making side-by-side passes over the blade out to the end of the workpiece. Flip the workpiece over to cut the second shoulder and cheek. If the tenon has cheeks and shoulders on the board ends as well as the faces, stand the workpiece on edge against the miter gauge to cut the narrow cheeks. You may need to change the blade height for cutting the end cheeks, but keep the rip fence stop block where it is so the shoulder cuts line up all around.

A quicker method for cutting long cheeks is to stand the workpiece on end against a tenoning jig and use a standard blade. Set the blade height so the teeth cut to the shoulder line, and be sure to account for the thickness of the blade when lining things up so it cuts on the waste side of the tenon layout line. If the tenon has four shoulders and cheeks, cut the

TENONING JIGS

Cutting tenons with the workpiece standing on-end is a balancing act unless you support the part firmly. It's difficult to move a narrow end over the blade without the workpiece shifting position either away from the fence or forward and back. You can either build a shop-made jig (see page 161, lower left) or buy a fabricated jig instead. Commercial jigs slide in the saw's miter slots on a metal bar. These heavy-duty jigs are typically made of cast iron and steel, and they're outfitted with a back-up fence for supporting the work as well as a stout clamp for holding the part securely against the jig body. Most jigs have a number of screw-type adjusters that allow you to move the workpiece laterally in relation to the blade, as well as tip it from side to side or front to back for cutting angled tenons. Expect to pay about $100 for a metal tenoning jig, which should pay for itself over a lifetime of hard use.

narrow end cheeks with the workpiece face clamped against a tall auxiliary fence on the miter gauge. Once you've made all the cheek cuts, trim the shoulders using the miter gauge with the workpiece laying flat or on edge. Install a stop block on the rip fence to index these shoulder cuts. Be sure to reset the blade height carefully so you trim just to the saw kerfs you cut for the cheeks.

A dado blade cuts tenon cheeks and shoulders more efficiently than a standard blade because it removes more material with each pass. Use the same multiple-pass technique as you would with a single blade to cut tenons with the workpiece flat on the saw table. Clamp a stop block to the rip fence to index the shoulder cuts, and make these cuts first. Then remove the remaining waste in a series of additional passes working out to the end to form the cheeks. Stand the workpiece on edge to cut end cheeks.

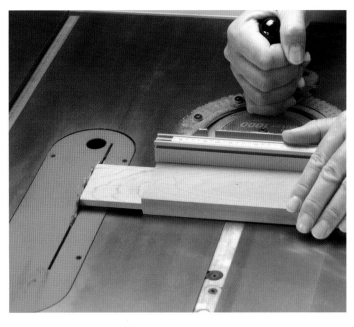

Once you've cut both parts of a mortise and tenon joint, assemble the joint to examine the fit. The tenon should slide into the mortise with moderate friction, and the shoulders should seat against the mortised workpiece. There should be no need to pound the joint together. If the shoulders don't touch the mortise, trim a bit off the end of the tenon to improve the fit.

Fitting the joint together. Once the mortise and tenon are routed or cut to rough shape, try to slip them together. Using a file, chisel or a sharp shoulder plane, pare down the tenon faces and edges until the tenon slips into the mortise with just a bit of friction. Do this trimming work a little at a time, and check your progress frequently by test-fitting the parts. Make the tenon length slightly shorter than the mortise depth so there's room for excess glue to pool at the bottom. Apply a thin coating of glue inside the mortise and on the tenon surfaces to glue up the joint. Keep the surfaces around the mortise free of glue.

One method for making mortises is to drill a series of side-by-side holes with a Forstner bit or brad point bit in the drill press. Back the workpiece up with a clamped straightedge or a fence on the drill press table.

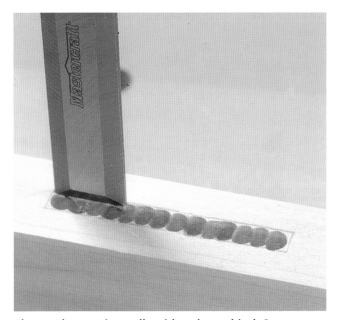

Flatten the mortise walls with a sharp chisel. Square up the ends with a narrower chisel. Check your progress with a square to be sure the mortise remains straight from top to bottom.

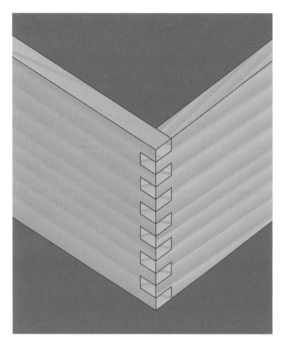

Box joints combine a series of matching pins and slots to create an attractive and sturdy connection.

Box joints

When you're building a chest, drawers, or boxes, box joints (sometimes called *finger joints*) can make the corner connections both strong and attractive. This joint combines equally spaced pins and matching slots, so it has the look of through dovetails without all the angles. It gets its strength principally from the gluing surfaces sandwiched between the pins and slots. Box joints are simple to make with a dado blade or router table and a shop-made jig. If you build the jig carefully, the joint should slide together smoothly with no further tooling.

Build this joint starting with the jig. It consists of an auxiliary miter fence with a pin attached that matches the size of the joint slots. The pin is offset one pin width away from the dado blade or router bit and acts like a spacer for creating the pin and slot pattern. To make the jig on the table saw, clamp a fresh auxiliary fence to your miter gauge, and install a dado blade. Set the width of cut to match the pin width. You can choose any width you like, but ¼-, ⅜-, and ½-inch pins are typical. Raise the blade so it will cut the full depth of the pins—they should be as tall as the mating workpiece is thick. Use an auxiliary miter fence that's about 18 inches long and at least 6 inches wide. You'll be cutting the joint workpieces on end, so the fence must be tall enough to provide adequate support.

With the fence clamped in place so it's roughly centered on the miter gauge, cut one slot through the fence. Glue a hardwood pin into this slot so it projects ¾ inch in front of the fence. Reset the fence on the miter gauge, sliding the pin

Make the box joint jig by clamping a new auxiliary fence to your miter gauge and cutting a pin slot through it with a dado blade.

Install a hardwood pin into the slot and shift the fence over so the distance between the pin and the dado blade matches the pin thickness. Measure this distance carefully, and fasten the jig to the miter gauge.

Make the first pin on the workpiece by setting its edge against the jig pin and passing it through the blade. Hold or clamp the workpiece to the jig, whichever affords you better control.

Once the first pin and slot are made, slip the slot over the jig pin and cut the second pin and slot. Repeat this process to cut the rest of the pins and slots across the workpiece.

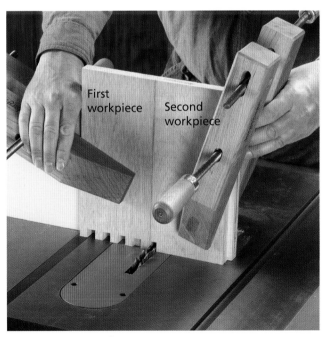

The mating workpiece needs to have a slot along its edge so it will mesh with the first workpiece. To set up this cutting pattern, fit the first pin of the first workpiece between the blade and jig pin to fill this space, and butt the second workpiece against the first. Now the blade will cut a slot on the second workpiece instead of a pin. Make this cut, remove the first workpiece, and cut the remaining pins and slots in the second workpiece.

exactly one pin width away from the dado blade. The spacing here is crucial. If you have a piece of extra hardwood pin stock, use this as a spacer between the pin on the jig and the dado blade to set the fence position. Screw the fence to the jig again, and try the following procedure on scrap before you cut your actual workpieces. If the joint parts don't fit properly when you finish cutting your scrap test pieces, the culprit is an inaccurate gap between the blade and jig pin. Reset the fence slightly to perfect the gap spacing, and try more test cuts.

To cut the pins and slots, butt the first workpiece against the pin with the board standing on end. Clamp or hold it firmly to the fence, and slide the jig through the blade to cut the first pin. If the workpiece is clamped firmly, slide the jig back across the blade to prepare for the next pass. If you're holding the workpiece instead, remove it and slide the jig back. Reposition the workpiece on the jig so the slot you've just cut straddles the jig pin, then cut the second pin and slot. Repeat this procedure to cut all the remaining pins and slots on this workpiece end. When you're finished, flip the board end over end to cut a matching pattern of pins and slots on the other end.

Form the mating part of the joint by fitting the first slot you cut in the first workpiece over the jig pin so one pin on that board fills the gap between the blade and the jig. Butt the other workpiece against its mate. This way, the second board will receive a slot along the edge for the first cut and not a pin. Slide both workpieces over the blade to cut the initial slot, then remove the first workpiece. Slip the slot of the second workpiece over the jig pin, and make a second pass to cut its first pin. Repeat the technique across the board, then flip it end over end and use the first workpiece to set the first slot cut.

When all the joints are cut, they should fit together snugly, but without force or gaps between the slots and pins. If so, the joints are ready for glue.

Follow the same procedure for cutting box joints on the router table with a straight bit and jig instead of the dado blade. See the setup below.

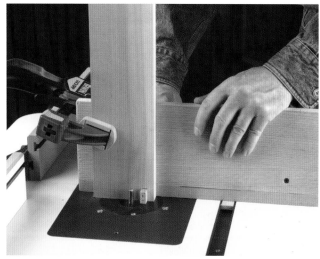

Follow the same procedure shown on page 165 for making box joints on the router table. Use a straight bit and miter gauge outfitted with a box joint jig.

Leave the first workpiece in place after making the last cut. Position the second workpiece against the first to make its first cut.

Dovetail joints

Dovetails are traditional joints typically used for building box frames, such as drawer boxes and carcasses. Their connections are made up of interlocking tails and pins that yield an exceptionally strong joint with undeniable visual appeal. Dovetail joints in particular have been regarded by furniture makers for centuries as symbols of craftsmanship and quality construction.

The best way to rout dovetails is with a handheld router and a commercial dovetail jig. Executing the joints successfully can be relatively easy or time-consuming and frustrating, depending on the jig you buy.

Types of dovetails. The two main styles of dovetail joints differ mostly in appearance. With a through dovetail, the tails and pins are visible in the assembled joint. With a half-blind dovetail, only the faces of the tails are visible. Half-blinds are used most commonly for drawer construction, because the pin board (always the front and back piece of the drawer box) retains an uncut outer face. Drawers also benefit from the mechanical connection of a dovetail: when you pull on a pin board, the joint holds together even without being glued. Through dovetails are used for all sorts of boxes but especially when the builder wants to show off the construction.

Dovetail jigs. Commercial dovetail jigs come in three classes. Half-blind jigs cut only half-blind joints, through jigs cut only through joints, and combination jigs cut both types as well as a varying number of other joints, such as sliding dovetail and rounded finger joints. Most jig manufacturers offer accessory templates for cutting box joints or small dovetails.

While the designs vary quite a bit, all dovetail jigs use a similar system. The work is clamped into the jig and the router, fitted with a dovetail bit, makes the cuts following a finger template. Some templates work with a template

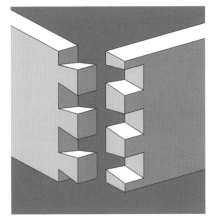

Through dovetail joint

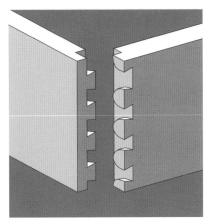

Half-blind dovetail joint

DOVETAIL JIGS

Before you buy a dovetail jig, talk with woodworkers you know or the salespeople at woodworking stores about the jig they prefer. There are dozens on the market, and some are much easier to use than others. Another way to shop wisely is to read dovetail jig reviews in woodworking magazines or visit the chat rooms of woodworking groups on the Internet. This is one accessory that requires careful selection to avoid headaches later on.

A half-blind dovetail jig sets up to cut the pins and the tails at the same time.

Cutting through dovetails requires separate cuts.

guide, while others are made for a bearing-piloted dovetail or flush-trimming bit. Often the bit and template guide are included with the jig, or the manufacturer specifies the right type to use. With half-blind jigs, the pins and tails are cut at the same time. Pins and tails for through joints are made separately. The procedure for setting up a dovetail jig is specific to the model. Consider these features when shopping for a jig:

• Construction: For any type of jig, a solid, rigid template is best. Many are heavy aluminum or phenolic resin. Plastic templates can have flexing problems, and router bases may not glide smoothly over them. Board clamps should hold the work firmly. Big knobs or handles for tightening clamps are a plus.

• Adjustable templates: Some jigs have cutting templates with adjustable fingers, allowing you to vary the spacing between pins and tails. Standard (non-adjustable) templates may be reversible for different dovetail sizes. If you think you may want custom spacing, buy the adjustable style.

• Ease of use: All dovetail jigs require careful setups, but some are simpler to learn and use than others. The tradeoff is that a more complex jig may offer greater versatility.

• Capacity: The maximum size of stock that jigs can accommodate ranges between 12" and 36" wide and up to 1½" thick.

SLIDING DOVETAILS

A sliding dovetail essentially is a tongue-and-groove joint in which both the groove and tongue are dovetail shaped, creating a strong, interlocking connection without the need for fasteners or glue. Use them for adjustable shelves, custom box lids, casework, or table leg-to-post connections. You can make the cuts with a handheld router, using an edge guide, a right-angle jig, or a T-square. Because the joints can be long, it's a good idea to cut first with a straight bit that matches or is slightly smaller than the neck (narrowest part) of the dovetail bit, then make a final pass with the dovetail bit.

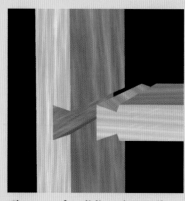

Closeup of a sliding dovetail joint.

Cut the groove for a sliding dovetail, using a right-angle jig.

Clamp 1½" blocks against both sides of workpiece and use an edge guide to cut the tail for a sliding dovetail.

Rail-and-stile joints

Rail-and-stile joinery, also called *cope-and-stick,* is a form of decorative frame construction used for making frame-and-panel cabinet doors and traditional wall paneling. Specialty router bits allow you to cut the frame joints along with the profiled edges and continuous groove that receives the panel. Panels can be flat, or you can use special bits to mill the edges of thicker panels with decorative profiles for a classic raised panel assembly.

Rail-&-stile bits. These are available in three styles. Matched bit sets include two bits—one stile cutter and one rail cutter. They are the easiest type to use and generally require the shortest setup time, so they're usually worth the extra cost. A reversible rail-and-stile bit can make both cuts, but you must disassemble and reverse the cutters to do so, and setting up the cuts can be trying. A third type is the stacked bit, which has the rail and stile cutters stacked on the same arbor. Instead of reversing the cutters, you raise and lower the stacked bit to make the two cuts. Rail-and-stile bits come in a range of decorative profiles, and all should be used only on the router table.

Panel cabinet doors made with rail-and-stile joinery are common in fine cabinetry and can be created with three bits (inset). Standard rail-and-stile frames are ¾" thick, but most bits can also cut ⅝" to ⅞" stock.

Cutting rail-&-stile joints. When preparing the stock for your project, make extra pieces to use for test cuts and for a backer piece used when milling the rail ends. To simplify assembly, you can cut all the pieces a little long—trim the rails to length after making the stile cuts, and trim the stiles flush to the rails after the glued frame has dried. Be aware that the longest point on the rail piece is the tongue. To get the proper dimensions, add the length of the two tongues to the desired rail length. Because the tongues are typically ⅜", this will add ¾" to the length of the rail. Some woodworkers like to make their door frames using stock about ⅛" wider than the final dimensions, so they can trim the doors to fit after they're assembled.

Start by making test cuts using scrap pieces cut from the good stock. Note: All four pieces of a frame have their inside edges milled with the stile cutter, while only the ends of the rails are cut with the rail cutter. Load the stile bit and set the height to cut the desired reveal (typically ¾₂" to ⅛"). Using a thin straightedge, adjust the fence so it's flush with the bit's bearing. Rout two test pieces face-down, using hold-downs and a sled or push stick as needed for safe operation.

Change to the rail bit. Using one of the stile test pieces as a gauge, set the bit height so the tongue-cutting portion of the bit is aligned with the stile's groove. Position the fence so it's flush with the bit bearing, then rout an end of one of the test pieces using a push sled to stabilize the work. The

Make the stile cuts, using featherboards to stabilize the long, thin stock.

To set the height of the rail bit, use one of the stile test pieces as a gauge. Align the tongue-cutting portion of the bit with the stile's groove.

Cut a rail end edge along a scrap piece to form a backer for cutting the rail ends. Fit the stile cutout into the scrap, and feed the rail into the bit, outer side first.

bit's configuration determines whether the stock should be faceup or facedown. Check the fit of the joint. If it shows gaps or isn't flush, adjust the fence and make more test cuts.

Once the fit is acceptable, make a backer piece using the rail bit to mill the long edge of a scrap piece. Use the backer to prevent tearout when cutting the ends of the rails. Also keep the final test pieces for setting up the bits for the real cuts. Cut the finish frame pieces following the same sequence used for the test cuts. Make the stile cuts on all of the frame pieces, then make the end cuts on the rails, using the rail bit.

Making raised panels. Raised panels are made with a single router bit on the router table. The bit cuts a profiled reveal into the face of the panel and creates a flat tongue along the perimeter that matches the groove in the rail-and-stile frame. Because there's no accurate method for indexing panel cuts, it's best to cut gradually and test the panel in the frame grooves until you achieve a good fit.

Use scrap pieces of stock to create a test joint to get the proper fit.

If you're building frame-and-panel doors, decide whether the front panel face will be flush to the front of the frame, project beyond the frame, or be recessed. The back of the panel can be flush, which requires cuts on the back side, or be left flat to create an inset from the back of the frame. Most cabinet doors with ¾"-thick frames have ⅜"- or ¼"-thick panels. You can use a solid panel (usually only if the doors are narrow) or panels made from glued-up boards.

Cutting raised panels. Determine the size of each panel by measuring the frame it will fill. To calculate the width, measure between the inside edges of the stiles, then add twice the groove depth from each side. Subtract ³⁄₁₆" to ¼" from the width to allow for expansion. (If the panel is wider than 12", subtract an additional ⅛" for each additional 12" of panel width.) To calculate the panel's length, measure between the

inside edges of the rails, add twice the groove depth, then subtract $\frac{1}{16}$"
from the total to provide some wiggle room during assembly. Cut the
panels to size.

Set up the router table with a raised panel bit (see Raised panel bits,
below). If you're using a vertical bit, adjust the bit height to equal the
desired amount of reveal, then set the fence to expose about $\frac{1}{8}$" of the
cutter. With a horizontal bit, set the fence flush with the bearing, and
adjust the bit height for a $\frac{1}{8}$" cut. Rout the panel with the front face
against the fence (or facedown on the table), cutting the end-grain edges first,
then the long-grain edges. If you're using $\frac{3}{4}$"-thick stock and want it to be flush
at the back, rout the back-side edges after completing the front.

Test the fit against a frame piece to make sure the setup is accurate, then move
the fence or raise the bit and make another pass. Repeat the process until the
tongue of the panel fits easily but snugly into the frame grooves. If you're making back-side cuts, stop routing the back side when the back face is flush with
the frame.

**Dry-fit the rails and stiles and
measure the diagonals to
make sure it is square.
Measure the inside dimensions
of the frame plus the panel
slots cut by the rail and stile
bits to determine the overall
panel size. Then subtract an
expansion allowance from the
overall panel width and $\frac{1}{16}$"
from the length.**

RAISED PANEL BITS

There are two main types of raised panel bits, both of which are available in a variety of decorative profiles. Horizontal raised panel bits (left, below) are large, flat cutters, commonly $3\frac{1}{2}$" in diameter, that cut with
the panel facedown on the table. The sheer size of these bits creates some challenges. They typically require
a $2\frac{1}{2}$ hp router with variable speed and should be run at about 10,000 rpm. Vertical raised panel bits (right,
below) are tall and are less than half the diameter of horizontal bits. You can run them in a $1\frac{1}{2}$ hp router, often
at the standard tool speed. They are generally considered safer to use than horizontal panel bits. However,
because the panels are cut on-edge, vertical bits can be difficult to use with large panels. With any type of
raised panel bit, it is critical for safety and cut quality to make the cuts incrementally, removing at most $\frac{1}{8}$" of
material with each pass.

**When using a horizontal bit (inset), set the fence
flush to the bit bearing. Use hold-downs and a
push sled as needed for a safe cut. Adjust the bit
height to make the cuts incrementally.**

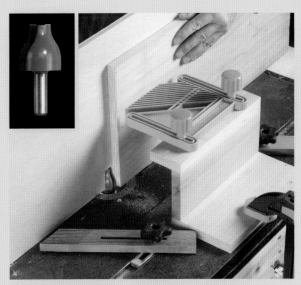

**Cut panels with a vertical panel bit (inset) using a
tall fence for support. A raised featherboard helps
keep the panel tight to the fence. Control the
depth of cut with the fence adjustment.**

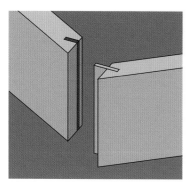

Splined bevel joint

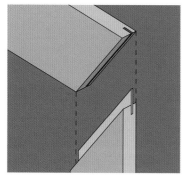

Splined miter joint

Splined bevel and miter joints

End-grain to end-grain surfaces often come together when you join workpieces with either miters or bevels. Glue alone can't form a strong connection because the open wood pores wick too much glue away from the mating surfaces. If you're making mitered picture frames or boxes with beveled corners, a spline inserted between the joint parts strengthens the connection immensely. Splines can also add a bit of decoration to the joint if you make them from wood that contrasts with the joint parts.

Both beveled and splined miter joints can be cut easily on the table saw. If you're building with ¾-inch-thick stock, the splines only need to be ⅛-inch thick, so you can cut spline slots with a standard blade. For thicker workpieces, switch to a dado blade to cut wider slots. In both of these joint styles, the splines extend the full length of the joints, but the kerfs are cut in different fashions. For splined bevels, the workpiece rests face down and is cut with the blade tilted. The workpieces of a splined miter joint stand on their mitered ends against a simple jig that supports them at an angle for the slot cuts.

For splined bevel joints that form 90° corners, first cut the beveled ends on the workpieces with the blade tilted at 45° (see page 101). To cut the spline slot, set the workpiece on the saw table with the beveled angle facing down. Tilt the blade to 45° so it faces the beveled workpiece. Raise the blade so it projects ⅜ inch above the table. Slide the rip fence to the side of the blade opposite its tilt direction. Using the rip fence as an index for the end of the workpiece, adjust the fence and workpiece so the blade will cut into the beveled end of the work-

Locate the spline in a beveled spline joint so it's near the inside corner. This position keeps the outside corner from breaking when the joint is stressed.

Use the rip fence to index the location of the spline slot on the beveled end of the workpiece. Cut the slot with a standard blade using the miter gauge to support the workpiece from behind.

piece near its inside corner (see bottom left photo, previous page). Back up the workpieces with the miter gauge and an auxiliary fence when you cut the spline slot in each part.

Making the spline slots on a miter joint requires cutting the workpieces along their mitered ends against the rip fence. There's no way to tackle this cut safely by simply feeding the workpiece along the rip fence and over the blade. Instead, clamp the workpiece flat against a larger backer board so the mitered end is aligned with the bottom edge of the backer. A piece of plywood makes good backer material. Attach a strip of wood to the backer board so it braces the mitered workpiece at 45°. With the blade set square and raised to ⅜ inch, run this jig against the rip fence equipped with a tall auxiliary fence to cut the spline slot. Adjust the rip fence before you make the cut so the blade is centered on the thickness of the workpiece, which centers the spline on the joint.

To cut spline slots for a mitered spline joint, fashion a tall jig with a clamp and fence to hold the workpiece at the miter angle securely. Slide the jig along a tall auxiliary rip fence to cut the slot.

Rip splines from the edge of a piece of ¾-inch lumber, just as you would for building splined butt joints (see page 139). Cut the splines carefully, and sand the faces if necessary so the splines slide smoothly into the joint slots. Glue and clamp the joints, then trim the splines flush with a hand saw.

Glue splines into their slots, leaving the splines a bit long. When the glue dries, trim the splines with a fine-toothed back saw and sand them flush.

Chapter 7
ASSEMBLY & FINISHING

With your project parts carefully milled, all that stands between you and the satisfaction of a completed piece of furniture is assembly and finishing. In the big scheme of woodworking, most of the hard work is behind you. However, careful assembly and finishing can make or break your project. Here's where a well-crafted collection of parts becomes that wonderful project you had in mind—or it's the stage in which you'll wish you had done a bit more planning, followed your drawings more carefully, or machined your parts with greater precision. It's not too late to get it all right, but don't hurry the assembly stage. If necessary, remake a few less-than-perfect parts to ensure your project will go together without a hitch and result in something you'll be proud of.

In this chapter, you'll learn about gluing and clamping methods, dry-assembly, and installing fasteners. Before that, however, we'll cover the basics of good sanding techniques so parts are smooth and ready for finishing once assembly is complete.

After the glue dries, this chapter will cover what you'll need to know to apply a protective and beautiful finish to your project. Most bare wood needs a barrier against the environment to protect it, enhance its beauty, and keep it looking great for years to come. There are many different wood finishes available, and some are easier than others to apply. However, finishing doesn't have to be difficult. All it takes is choosing the correct finish to meet your needs and a little application know-how. You'll learn it here.

Sanding basics

If your project surfaces remain fully accessible once you put the pieces together, you can skip the sanding until just before applying finish. But in many instances, such as building boxes, drawers, or chair and table frame-work, it's much easier to sand the parts prior to assembly. Sanding serves to level the wood surfaces so parts meet evenly. It removes dings, nicks, and swirls or minor burn marks left by saw blades and router bits. On a microscopic level, sanding provides "tooth" to the wood, so finishes have something to adhere to. But at its most basic level, sanding abrades

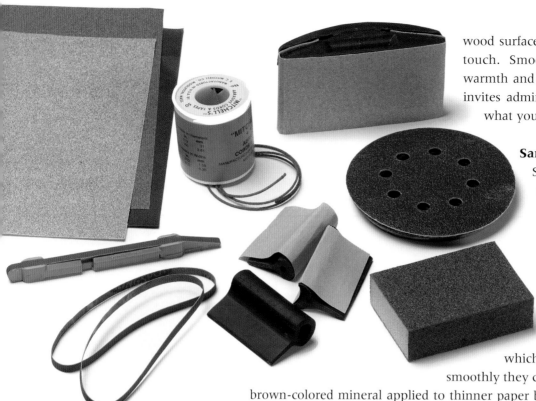

wood surfaces so they feel smooth to the touch. Smoothness contributes to the warmth and completeness of a project. It invites admirers to touch and appreciate what you've worked so hard to make.

Sandpaper options & grits.

Sandpaper is nothing more than natural or synthetic grit applied to different kinds of heavy paper or cloth backing. The three principal grit types are garnet, aluminum oxide, and silicon carbide. All three come in a variety of different grit sizes, from fine to coarse, which influence how quickly and smoothly they cut wood. Garnet is a natural, brown-colored mineral applied to thinner paper backing. It tends to wear out more rapidly than the synthetic options, but it is useful for hand-sanding situations. You won't find it in disk or belt form for power sanders because it tends to clog up quickly. Aluminum oxide is a synthetic material with tougher working characteristics than garnet. The particles fracture during use to expose new, sharp cutting edges. Aluminum oxide is applied to backing papers that are suitable for both hand- and power-sanding wood. Silicon carbide, the toughest grit type, is also a synthetic material. Typically you'll find it on fine-grit sandpapers over 150-grit. Silicon carbide sandpaper is intended for wet sanding finishes between coats or to prepare metal for painting.

A variety of sanding products takes some of the chore out of sanding. In addition to conventional sandpaper, you can find sanding blocks, sponges, contour sanders, sanding cord, and sanding belts.

In addition to flat-sheet paper, there are a variety of other sanding tools made for hand-sanding. Rubber or wood sanding blocks make it easy to hold sheet sandpaper and level a surface evenly. You'll also find foam sponges with sandpaper grit applied, for sanding irregular or contoured surfaces. Sanding grit even comes on a spool for cleaning up thin reveals and narrow routed details.

Choosing grits. Grit numbers refer to industry standards that regulate the size of the grit particles. As the number increases, the grit size gets smaller. Low numbers are for heavy stock removal, and high numbers are intended for finer smoothing jobs.

For smoothing away imperfections on bare wood, 60-grit paper is the coarsest grit you should ever need to use. Start with this grit if your workpieces have deep scratches or burn marks left by sawing and routing. Once the large blemishes are sanded away, switch to 80-grit paper to remove the abrading left by the 60-grit paper. If your project parts are relatively smooth to begin with and you need to remove just light milling marks or scratches, start with 100-grit paper. Once you've smoothed away the noticeable imperfections, switch to 150- or 180-grit paper and sand again. As you move into progressively finer grits, you'll still leave scratches—that's how sandpaper does its job. But the scratch marks become so tiny that you can't see or feel them in the wood. Most experts agree that you can stop sanding after carefully working the surfaces with 180-grit or 220-grit paper. The scratches at this stage won't be noticeable under any wood finish. Continuing with even finer-grit papers can actually burnish the wood surface, which means the wood pores close up and inhibit the adhesion of the finish. Believe it or not, you can actually sand too much.

Sanding in four stages. Here's an easy four-step technique to follow for sanding by hand or with portable sanders. Follow this approach and your workpieces will be set for assembly or finishing, whichever stage you are at with your project. First, sand all the surfaces of a workpiece in one direction, moving the sandpaper at roughly 45° to the long grain. For reasonably smooth wood without major blemishes or scratches, use 100-grit paper for this angled sanding work. *NOTE: Always sand in the general direction of the grain. Sanding across the grain inevitably leads to scratches that are difficult to remove.* Sand in broad, overlapping strokes, keeping power sanders moving across the workpiece at all times. Once you've sanded the entire workpiece, switch to the opposite direction at 45° and sand the surfaces again with 100-grit paper to remove the scratches left in the first sanding stage. Next, remove the angled scratch marks by sanding with the grain using 100-grit paper. Switch to 150-grit and repeat all three steps. To ensure that all power sander scratches are removed, finish up with a light sanding by hand using 180- or 220-grit paper. Sand with the grain only on this last step.

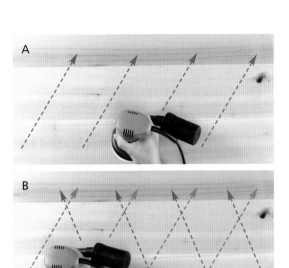
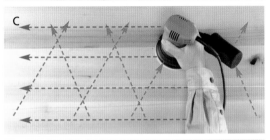

A

B

C

D

The four stages of sanding include: A) sanding at a 45° angle to the grain; B) sanding at the opposite 45° angle; C) sanding with the grain to remove the crossgrain sanding scratches; and D) removing the long-grain power-sanding scratches by hand sanding. Follow this four-step process for each grit, moving to progressively finer grits up to 180- or 220-grit.

CHECKING FOR SCRATCHES

If you think you're finished sanding a workpiece, one way to be sure is to dampen the surfaces by wiping with mineral spirits. Mineral spirits will highlight any scratches that should be attended to without raising the wood grain. Shine a light across your dampened workpiece. If you can see scratches now, they'll usually show up later under a stained or clear finish. Keep sanding, and wipe the surfaces again with mineral spirits to check your progress. It's worth the effort.

Gluing and clamping basics

Unless the parts of your project are moveable or designed to be disassembled for storage or transport, you'll generally glue them together permanently. Sometimes you can simply spread glue between two joint parts and secure the joint with nails, screws, or other mechanical fasteners while the glue is still wet. In most cases, you'll want to hold the parts immobile with clamps while the glue cures. Here's a general overview of the issues you'll need to consider when using glue and clamps.

Choosing a glue. Unless you are building regularly and using large amounts of glue, it's a good practice to buy only a reasonable amount of the glue you really need, use it as soon as possible, and then buy more glue from fresher stock. Some glues have a "shelf life" of only a year or two before thickening and losing their adhesive properties. Containers that hold from 8 ounces to a quart of glue are more than enough for assembling average to large projects. Leave the gallon-size jugs for the pros who use it constantly.

If you buy only one type of wood glue for your projects, make it yellow wood glue. Technically called aliphatic resin glue, yellow wood glue will perform almost all wood-to-wood gluing situations exceptionally well, provided the surfaces are clean, flat, and smooth. It's the most common woodworking glue, available in formulations for both interior and exterior applications. Yellow wood glue cleans up with soapy water when it's still wet and spreads easily. It also has a moderately long "open time," which is the time you have to alter the connection or disassemble the parts before the glue sets and cures. You can even buy it blended with a dark pigment so it hides better under the finishes of darker-colored woods, such as walnut.

Glue application & clean-up. For gluing edge and face joints, apply a bead of glue over each part surface and spread the glue out into a thin film that covers the full contact area. Use a paint or foam brush, a scrap of wood, or even your finger to do this. Aim for a thinner, rather than thicker, film on both surfaces. Too much glue will simply squeeze out of the joint and be wasted when you apply clamps. Wet glue also acts as a lubricant between two parts. The more glue that's present, the more slippery the parts will be.

Press the parts together until the surfaces meet fully and the joint parts are flush. For gluing board edges or faces together where the parts meet but do not interlock, slide them back and forth to drive glue into the wood pores. Apply a few clamps across the joint where possible, and tighten the clamps just enough to close any small gaps that may be present between the parts. Over-tightening the clamps can break the wood, distort the joint, or force too much glue out of the joint and compromise the bond strength. If it seems to take too much clamping pressure to close a joint, the joint parts need more flattening with

Aliphatic resin wood glue isn't just yellow anymore. For gluing up darker woods, like walnut, brown-tinted glue blends in better.

The secret to a strong glue joint is to coat both mating surfaces with an even, thin layer of glue. Be sure the parts to be joined are smooth, flat and clean, first.

tools, or you may have trapped a bit of debris between the parts. Pull the parts open and inspect them. Clean off the glue, if necessary, and check the part fit again. Clamps are not a remedy for fixing misfitting parts.

When gluing up individual boards to make larger panels, install the clamps both above and below the panel in an alternating pattern. This way, the clamping pressure is distributed more evenly. Too much clamping pressure on one face will warp the wood.

One way to tell you have a well-glued and clamped joint is when it shows a thin line of glue or tiny glue beads along the seam between the joint parts. If the joint drips excessively, you've either applied the glue too heavily or the clamps are overly tight. Wait a few minutes until the excess glue moves out of the joint. Recheck the part alignment to ensure that the joint parts haven't slipped during clamping. After 15 to 30 minutes, scrape off the congealed glue with an old wood chisel or putty knife. Wipe up any remaining residue with a water-dampened rag, switching to a fresh area of the rag with each swipe. Once the glue dries, you'll have to remove any remaining squeeze-out or smears by sanding, chipping, or using a sharp paint scraper.

When gluing dowels into holes or tenons into mortises, be aware that glue has a hydraulic effect if it is compressed into a tight space. Its volume can only be reduced so much. The glue will keep joints from closing if there isn't extra room inside the joint for the excess to escape. Drill your dowel holes and cut your mortises a bit deeper than necessary so the excess glue has room to pool, and apply

WHERE NOT TO APPLY GLUE

Glue bonds are beneficial for strengthening most wood joints, but not all of them. Limit the use of glue or avoid it altogether when the grain patterns of two workpieces cross. Two examples of this situation are where solid-wood tabletops meet the aprons that cross the tabletop width, and where wood panels fill the inside area of a wood-framed cabinet door. In both cases, long-grain parts (the aprons and top and bottom door rails) cross the grain direction of large panels (the tabletop and door panel).

Wood expands and contracts most across the wood grain. Long grain moves the least. If you apply glue all along these cross-grain joints, the wide tabletop or door panel is trapped by the end aprons or top and bottom door rails and cannot move freely with changes in humidity. Eventually, either the glue joint will break as the wood attempts to move, or the wood panel will split along the grain.

There are several ways to attach cross-grain joints that still allow for wood movement. One method is to glue short blocks of wood along the joint but not at the ends. Or install short buttons of wood with a rabbeted tongue into long slots in the long-grain part. The buttons screw to the panel. As the panel expands and contracts, the button slides along the slot. A third alternative is to drive screws along the joint into slotted holes on the long-grain part (shown below). Orient these screw slots so they cross the grain of the wide panel—the same direction the panel will move. This way, the panel can slip past the screw shanks without restriction. Rock a drill from side to side to elongate these screw holes into slots. You can also nail or peg a cross-grain joint, but leave the last few inches of each end of the joint unfastened so the ends of the panel can move.

the glue evenly but sparingly. Buy fluted or spiral-cut dowels or score the sides of smooth dowels by scraping them through the teeth of a pair of pliers. This way, the glue and excess air will have channels to flow back up to the surface and escape.

Clamp options. There are a variety of different clamp styles for securing workpieces during assembly. For gluing up wide panels or closing joints on long parts, you'll want to own at least a half dozen long pipe or bar clamps. Both styles feature moveable clamp heads that fit onto either a steel bar or a length of black ½- or ¾-inch gas pipe. One clamp head slides along the bar or pipe for making coarse adjustments, while the other clamp head has a hand screw mechanism for final tightening. It is fixed on the end of the bar or pipe. Pipe clamps are particularly versatile, because you can install the clamp heads on pipes of any length. For general woodworking applications, buy the pipe in 3- or 4-foot sections with threaded ends. If you need longer clamps, connect two shorter pipes together with inexpensive threaded couplings.

For clamping workpieces less than 2 feet wide or long, have a selection of shorter bar clamps on hand. Most clamps of this sort have a fixed head on the end of the bar and a sliding head on the other. Some tighten up with a threaded shaft outfitted with a twist handle. Others have a squeeze grip to draw the adjustable head closer to the fixed head. The squeeze-grip style bar clamps have a quick-release lever that loosens the clamp. Pipe clamps have a series of spring-loaded slip plates that serve the same quick-release function.

C-clamps in the 4- to 6-inch size range are great for clamping small parts or holding jigs in place on router tables and table saws. Inexpensive metal or plastic spring clamps are also handy to have for low-strength clamping situations. Buy the type with pivoting plastic jaws or rubber-lined jaws. Wood screws, which operate by turning two threaded shafts in opposite directions, are not only helpful for closing joints but also do double duty as makeshift vises for holding parts vertically or horizontally during tooling operations.

Band clamps are helpful for securing the staves of round cylinders or holding odd-shaped assemblies together, such as chair legs and rails. These clamps have an adjustable nylon strap that cinches up with a ratcheting mechanism. In a pinch, a length of surgical tubing, a piece of rope, or even strips of packing tape can become band clamps.

Corner clamps are handy for securing two mitered parts together. Picture framers swear by them. Each joint part clamps separately, and the clamp body holds the parts squarely until the glue dries or while you install fasteners across the joint.

Dry-fitting and staging

Before slathering glue onto your carefully crafted and sanded workpieces and clamping them together,

Wood clamps come in all shapes and sizes, from large bar and pipe clamps intended for clamping panels and casework to smaller C-clamps, wood screws, and spring clamps for smaller frame and part assembly or machining clamp aids. Even packaging tape or heavy rubber bands can provide clamping pressure when needed.

USING PADS AND CAULS

Clamps exert tremendous pressure on workpieces, so much so that the clamp contact surfaces can easily dent softer woods. If your clamps lack protective pads, be sure to slip scraps of soft wood between the clamp heads and the workpieces before tightening the clamps. Sections of hardboard or even adhesive felt tabs for furniture work well for this purpose.

When gluing up wide panels using several narrower boards, oftentimes one or more of the boards will slip out of alignment as you tighten the clamps. One way to keep the board faces aligned is to squeeze them between pairs of cauls clamped above and below the panel. Cauls can be made from strips of any stiff, flat scrap material. Plywood or hardwood pieces 2 to 3 inches wide make great clamp cauls. A pair of cauls installed over each end of a panel is usually sufficient. Use short bar clamps to hold the cauls in place and long pipe or bar clamps to pull the panel together width-wise. Cover the edges of the cauls with painter's tape to keep them from sticking to glue.

plan how you want the assembly process to go. Think about the process of gluing and clamping like an exercise in woodworking surgery. In order for parts to go together as you hope, you must work methodically and neatly, but not slowly. Once the glue is spread, you'll have a limited time to assemble and clamp things together before the glue starts to set.

One way to prevent gluing and clamping headaches is to dry-fit the parts ahead of time. Be sure all the joints fit together easily without glue. If you have to reach for a mallet to pound things closed now, you'll probably have to do it again when you apply glue. Fix those too-tight joints before opening the glue bottle. As you slip the parts together dry, plan the order in which you'll assemble them. Stage some glue-ups ahead of others, even if it means turning one gluing operation into a two-day affair. Better to allow some stages of the glue-up to dry than try to do too much gluing at once. Write the gluing order down if need be; then follow it carefully. Sometimes it helps to label your parts, especially if several workpieces look alike but don't assemble interchangeably. If one piece must mate with another piece, mark them so there's no confusion.

Rehearsing your gluing and clamping procedure and dry-fitting the pieces is a good opportunity to arrange all the hardware and supplies you'll want to have close at hand. Install the clamps on the dry-assembled parts to make sure they'll work properly, then open the clamps a bit wider than necessary when you remove them. Lay them within arm's reach of where they'll be installed. Have a bucket of warm, soapy water and a sponge close by for wiping up squeeze-out and drips as well as to keep your hands clean while you work. Be sure there are shop towels or paper towels nearby, too.

Line your benchtop with waxed paper, sheet plastic, or plastic trash bags if it isn't top-coated with varnish, to keep glued parts from sticking to it. If your benchtop is small and you have many parts to glue up, spread out some parts and supplies on another table to reduce the clutter so you'll have ample room to work.

Before opening the glue bottle to begin a glue-up, dry-fit all parts of the project and install clamps to rehearse the best sequence for assembly.

Installing nails and screws

Once your project has passed through the gluing and clamping stage of assembly, you may need to reinforce the joints with additional mechanical fasteners, such as nails and screws. Unless you are gluing edges to edges or faces to faces, all other butt joints should be reinforced with nails or screws. Rabbet and dado joints also benefit from a few nails or screws driven across the parts.

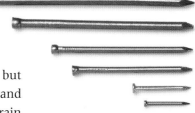

Finish nails and brads come in a range of sizes. Keep an assortment of sizes on hand for general project assembly.

Types of nails for woodworking. There are lots of different nail styles, but for woodworking, finish nails are the best choice. The nail heads are small and easy to conceal with wood putty, and their slender shanks penetrate wood grain easily without splitting it. You'll find finish nails sold in a range of lengths and shaft thicknesses. The nails are sized by the pennyweight system, which pairs a number with the letter "d." The number refers to the nail length and gauge, while the "d" means penny. Pennyweight sizes start at 2d (1 inch) and go up from there. Keep a range of finish nail sizes on hand for all your fastening needs. You'll find that 3d (1¼-inch) up to 8d (2½-inch) sizes are most useful for fastening common 1× and 2× material.

For tacking thin or fragile workpieces together, use brad nails or wire nails instead of finish nails. Either option comes in lengths shorter than 1 inch, and the shanks are much thinner than 2d finish nails. Use a small tack hammer to drive these tiny nails. Hold them in place with a needle-nosed pliers to start nailing, and tap them gently to keep from bending or jarring them off a straight course.

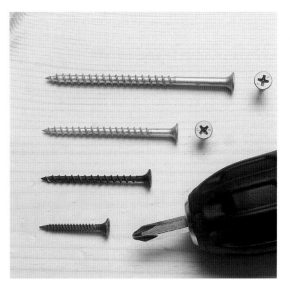

Installing finish nails. Use a medium-weight claw hammer with a smooth face for driving finish nails. On softwoods such as cedar and pine, you can often hammer them in without drilling pilot holes first. For hardwoods, don't skip the pilot hole. Drill the hole with a twist bit that's slightly smaller than the nail shank thickness to give the nail a good friction fit in the wood.

Various types of construction and woodworking screws are worth having in your shop. Be sure to use corrosion resistant screws for projects that will encounter moisture.

Once you've driven the nail and the head is flush with the wood surface, tap the head below the surface with a nailset to conceal it. Nailsets are made with tips of different sizes and are sold in sets or individually. With the nail head recessed, fill the divot with matching wood putty or a wax-based putty stick to hide it. ***NOTE***: *If you are staining the project, wait until after the stain is applied, then use putty that's tinted to approximately the same stain color to hide the fastener head.*

Common screws for woodworking. Several screw styles can be used almost interchangeably for general woodworking. Wallboard screws and deck screws have become widely popular woodworking screws as well as construction fasteners. Both styles have coarse threads that bite quickly into wood. Wallboard screws should be used only for interior woodworking projects, because they have no weather-resistant surface finish. Deck screws can be used for interior or exterior projects. Their galvanized or plasticized coatings stand up well to the elements, but they also can be hidden beneath putty or

You can conceal recessed nailheads with tinted wood filler or putty before applying finish. Press it into the nailhead holes with a putty knife and remove the excess. If you're going to stain the project, apply the wood filler after staining.

wood plugs like wallboard screws. You can also find deck screws made of stainless steel, which is impervious to corrosion. Wallboard and deck screws are sold by length, not by gauge. Keep a supply of sizes ranging from 1¼ inches to 3 inches in your shop.

In the fine woodworking arena, most professionals choose flathead wood screws over construction screws. Wood screws have thicker shanks and finer threads, and the top portion of the shank has no threads. The bare shank prevents the top half of the joint from lifting away from the bottom half as the screw is driven home.

Wood screws are made of several metals, including bright or brass-coated steel, solid brass, and stainless. They're sized by gauges ranging from 0 to 12. Both the shank thickness and the screw length increase as the number of the gauge goes up. You'll find wood screws sold by both gauge and length. For most uses, #6- to #10-gauge wood screws will serve your needs. Choose Phillips-style or square-drive screw head patterns over slotted styles made for flat-blade screwdrivers. Flat-blade screws are harder to drive without stripping the head or marring your work with the screwdriver tip.

Installing screws. You'll never regret drilling pilot holes for any type of screw you drive into a woodworking project. Pilot holes prevent splits, even if the holes aren't necessary. If you are using self-tapping screws, you can skip the pilot hole. Always drill pilot holes before driving flathead wood screws or when installing any screw style into hardwood. Pilot holes are wise precautions for softwoods, too.

To drill a pilot hole, use a countersink bit that has a slightly smaller diameter than the screw shank you are installing. Make sure the overall length of the countersink portion and the bit does not exceed the screw length—slightly shorter is even better. Drill the pilot hole until the countersink portion of the bit engages the wood. If you want the screw head to stop flush or slightly below the wood surface, drill a little deeper until the countersink makes a tapered recess for the screw head. You can also continue drilling until the countersink flutes are buried ¼ inch or so into the wood, then cover the screw head with putty, or cap it with glue and a short dowel or wood plug.

If you use a cordless drill/driver to drive screws, set the drill's clutch for drill-only mode so it won't disengage under excessive torque. Stop driving the screw as soon as the screw head seats, to prevent snapping the screw. For soft brass screws, drive a steel screw of the same size into the pilot hole first, then back it out and replace with the brass screw. Use a lower torque setting on the drill to keep it from over-driving and breaking the screw.

When drilling into softwoods, you'll seldom need to lubricate the screw to drive it home. On hardwoods, rub the tip of the screw threads with beeswax or paste furniture wax first to make the screw easier to drive. If any wax ends up at the surface of the screw hole, remove it with mineral spirits before applying finish. Otherwise, the finish won't stick.

Why apply a wood finish?

If you appreciate the natural look, smell, and feel of unfinished wood, you might wonder why you should apply a finish at all? There are a number of important reasons. First, finishes protect and seal wood from water. A topcoat of varnish, shellac, paint, or other finishing material slows down the rate of moisture exchange between the atmosphere and the wood. Joints stay tighter, warpage is reduced, and glue bonds last longer.

Finishes also help seal wood pores against stains that develop from spills, dirt, and grime. The surface coating provides added protection from scratches and scuffs as well. Some even provide a degree of UV protection to help slow the bleaching and damaging effects of sunlight.

Finally, finishes help you to change or enhance the color and texture of wood. You can turn pine from blonde to mahogany red/brown, and give oak a highly glossy surface or a matte sheen. Finishing provides one final degree of design control to a woodworking project.

A good way to hide recessed screwheads is to drill counter-bored holes and cap them with wood plugs. Use plugs of the same wood species as the project to help them blend in.

Notice in these two oak samples how an oil finish leaves a matte finish with the wood pores open, while the varnished finish creates a smoother film on the surface that hides the wood's texture.

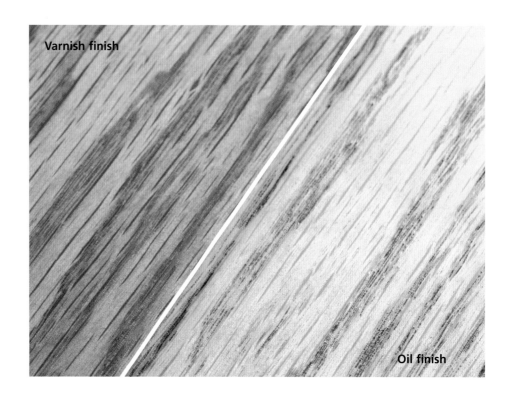

Varnish finish

Oil finish

Preparing surfaces for finishing

Thorough sanding is the best way to ensure that finished surfaces feel smooth and the topcoat layers apply evenly. A few other tasks also fall under the heading of surface preparation. Before coloring the wood or applying a topcoat, clean up any excess glue on the wood surface, and fill dents, holes, and other imperfections. If you're going to use a water-based dye, stain, or varnish, you'll want to raise the grain before finishing and sand again lightly.

After you are finished with your final sanding, thoroughly clean off all sandpaper residue and dust by vacuuming the wood or blowing off the surfaces with compressed air. Either of these methods is more effective than brushing off the wood or wiping it with a rag. It is imperative to remove all loose surface debris to ensure that stain and finish will go on smoothly and bond securely to the wood.

A walnut stain on white oak (top) offers a darker color than a clear finish on actual walnut.

Cleaning up dried glue. Even if you apply glue to your project with a surgeon's care, eventually you're going to end up with a little extra squeezing out here or there around joints. Even the smallest amount of extra glue will show up like a traffic light under a colored or clear finish, so it's important to remove all traces of dried glue before proceeding with stains and topcoats. Wipe your project down with mineral spirits, just as you would to check for surface scratches (see page 177), and the dried glue will show up as discolored areas on the wood. It's a good idea to do this clean-up in stages, wiping down and removing glue on one part of the project before moving on to the next. That way you won't miss any spots.

The obvious method for removing dried glue is to scrape or sand it away. For blobs of glue, use a sharp chisel and gently chip or pare off the glue with the flat back of the chisel against the wood. Hold the blade as flat as possible against the wood to keep the cutting edge from digging in. Sanding off glue takes longer, but it works better for removing smears. Use the next coarser grit than you used for the final sanding to cut through and sand off the glue, then smooth the area out with finer-grit sandpaper. Check your progress by wiping with mineral spirits to ensure you've removed all the glue and sanding scratches. For the final touch-up sanding, be sure to sand with the grain.

Another option for removing dried glue is to re-dissolve it, scrub the softened glue with a synthetic scrubbing pad, and wipe off the residue. Use acetone, toluene, or xylene solvents to soften yellow wood glue. You'll find these chemicals sold in the paint section of your home center or hardware store. Warm water also works, but the stronger solvents offer the added advantage of not raising the wood grain. Acetone also removes hot-melt glue and contact cement. There are no effective solvents for removing polyurethane glue or epoxy. Your only option is to scrape and sand them off.

Dried glue won't absorb transparent colored finishes like stain or dye, and it will show up under them. Remove all traces of dried glue before finishing.

Filling dents, holes & other imperfections. You can easily dent bare wood just by dropping it or applying too much clamping pressure. If all the wood in a damaged area is intact but simply compressed, steam out the dent. To do this, wet the damaged area with a few drops of water, cover with a small piece of clean cloth, and heat the cloth with a hot soldering iron or the tip of a clothes iron (see page 188). As the water on the wood boils, it will swell the wood fibers and virtually eliminate the dent. Be sure to sand the area after it dries to smooth the raised grain.

For repairing holes, use slivers of scrap wood that match the project wood, coat them with a dab of glue, and tap them into the hole. Try to match the grain direction as best you can with these wood plugs. For filling end-grain holes, use end-grain scrap. Face-grain holes should be filled with face-grain scrap. The advantage to using real wood is that the damaged area will take finish just like the surrounding wood and blend in well.

A variety of wood doughs, putties, and fillers are also available for filling holes, cracks, and other small imperfections. Basically, these products are mixtures of finely ground wood powder and sawdust blended with glue or lacquer to hold the material

If you'd rather not scrape or sand dried glue off, you can also dissolve the excess with a solvent. Use the solvent sparingly, wiping with a synthetic scrub pad. Too much solvent can weaken the glue joint.

Minor dents are easy to remove from bare wood by steaming. Heat a water-dampened cloth in the repair area with the tip of a soldering or clothes iron, and the steam will swell out the blemish.

together. Most come premixed and ready to use in various wood-tone colors. Although they seem like a convenient solution for making repairs, they don't absorb wood stain well. The patch will be visible, just like a glue smudge, if you apply the filler before staining. If you're planning to stain the project, do this first, then fill the holes with wood putty tinted to blend with the wood stain.

Work carefully to keep the repair area as small as possible. The less putty there is to blend with the finish, the easier it will be to conceal. If the putty has a strong solvent smell when wet, it has a lacquer base. Clean up excess lacquer putty with acetone or lacquer thinner. For products with latex bases, use water to clean up wet putty, and acetone, toluene, or xylene to remove dried putty. Work carefully when cleaning up the excess to keep from removing the wood stain around the repair.

If you fill nailheads after applying stain, choose a tinted wood putty or filler with a color that closely matches the stain color.

If you have small nail holes to fill, don't worry about concealing these prior to applying finish. After the topcoat dries fully, fill the holes with colored wax. Wax crayons in various wood finish colors are sold in the finishing section of your home center. You can also experiment with ordinary color crayons in the various brown tones. Press a small chip of wax into the hole with a fingernail or paint scraper blade and smooth it with your fingertip. Your body heat will soften the wax and blend it in. Scrape away the excess carefully.

Coloring wood with stains

The topcoat layer of a finish doesn't add much color to the wood. Its primary purpose is to form a protective barrier. To change the color, you'll need to apply stain before the topcoat. Most of the wood you see in furniture has been color-altered with a stain. Stain gives you creative control over how your completed project looks in three ways: First, it allows you to choose the basic color of the wood from a wide range of color tones. If you'd prefer your mahogany project to look more red or brown than the natural wood, a stain provides the means for making the color shift. Second, it enhances the natural grain pattern in the wood. This is highly desirable in some woods, such as curly maple or quartersawn oak, that have interesting wavy or flake patterns in the grain. It's not always advantageous in other woods, such as pine or soft maple, because the grain density of these woods varies significantly in the same board. Certain types of stains can make the wood look splotchy and uneven. A third reason for staining is that it blends wood with contrasting heartwood and sapwood so the light and dark areas are less pronounced.

The components that give a stain its color are pigments, dyes, or a combination of the two. Pigments are finely-ground particles of colored earth or synthetic chemicals suspended in a liquid. Dyes contain much smaller molecules of color rather than visible particles.

RAISING THE GRAIN

No matter how smoothly you sand wood surfaces before finishing, water-based dye, stain, or varnish will still raise the wood grain. Here's why: Water-based finishing products soak into the surface fibers of raw wood and cause them to swell up. Once the wood swells, it feels rough and the smoothing effect of sanding is lost. The solution is to raise the grain before applying finish, sand the rough grain off, and then proceed with finishing. To do this, wet your project with distilled water and a damp rag, and let the wood dry for a few hours. Sand lightly with the same grit of paper you used for your final sanding. The paper need not be from a fresh sheet. Used sandpaper abrades less and leaves smaller scratches. Sand just until the wood feels smooth. This step knocks off the raised wood fibers at the surface so the grain can't rise again.

Pigments color wood by filling the open pores on the surface. The more pigment that gets trapped in the pores, the darker the grain appears. Once the pores are filled with pigment, the wood can't be made darker with more pigment. Usually one application of pigment stain fills the pores. Pigment-based stains are more effective for coloring open-grained woods, such as mahogany or oak, than for denser, closed-grained woods, such as hard maple. If the pores are too small to trap the pigment, the wood color won't change as much as more open-pored woods.

The liquid component of pigment-based stains keeps the pigment suspended and helps the particles of color flow onto the wood easily. There's also a binding agent in the liquid that acts like glue to hold the particles in the pores. Binders are made of water-based acrylic, oil, varnish, or lacquer, depending on the stain chemistry.

Dye stains work differently than pigment-based stains. Since dyes are molecules of color rather than larger particulates, they absorb into the wood's cells. Dyes saturate both open-grained and tight-grained woods relatively evenly. They also color both face and end grain consistently, unlike pigment stains that make end grain much darker. The higher the concentration of dye, the darker the

Some woods, such as walnut, have markedly lighter sapwood than heartwood. In some cases, the sapwood will be almost white. Stain will help blend these light and dark areas together so they're less noticeable.

wood color becomes. Dyes can make wood darker than pigments because the coloring action isn't limited by the depth of the surface pores.

Dye stains are commonly sold in powdered form rather than a liquid. You won't find dye powders sold in a hardware store or home center, but they're widely available from woodworking supply catalogs. Dye powders are formulated into both wood tone shades and primary colors. Depending on the chemistry of the powder, dyes need to be mixed with either water or denatured alcohol to create the liquid for staining. The solvent dissolves the dye and helps it flow over the wood. The particular solvent you need to use will be labeled clearly on the container of dye powder. As long as dye powders have the same solvents, you can mix them in any combination you like to make your own custom colors.

Some dye stains are sold premixed as "NGR," or non-grain-raising stains. The main advantage to an NGR stain is that unlike water-soluble dye stains, which raise the grain, NGR stains do not.

Most of the ordinary premixed stains you'll find on the shelves of the hardware store or home center are pigment-based. Some manufacturers mix both pigments and dye into one solution to produce more even coloring characteristics. You can't easily tell on the label whether a premixed stain is only pigment or a mixture of both pigment and dye. Use the stain as though it is primarily pigment-based.

When to use pigments vs. dyes. Both pigment and dye stains are easy to apply. If you are choosing between the two, think in terms of the results you want. One issue to consider is the grain pattern of the wood you are finishing.

Oak, for example, has distinctively porous and non-porous face grain. The difference in density between the open-pored and closed-pored regions is what gives stained oak its prominent, face-grain pattern. Using pigment stain on oak dramatizes the difference between the open pores and closed pores. The pigment lodges in the open pores, producing dark areas, but it shades the closed-grain areas much less. A dye stain, on the other hand, saturates both the open- and closed-pored areas more evenly, with less light and dark variation.

On certain woods, such as pine, birch, and soft maple, the grain pattern isn't as regular and attractive as oak. There can be inconsistent, open-pored areas that aren't easy to see until the stain is applied. Pigment stains make these irregular areas obvious as darker, uneven splotches. For these woods, dye stains blend the surface grains more evenly and minimize splotching. On woods with dramatic figure, such as fiddleback maple, curly cherry, and quartersawn oak and sycamore, dye stain highlights the unique figure. Pigment stains, which don't saturate into the wood fibers, often obscure this depth and contrast. So, dye stains generally are more effective on highly figured woods.

Dye stain offers more flexibility than pigment stain when it comes to changing the intensity and color once you've stained the project. To lighten a too-dark dye stain, remove the excess color by wiping down the wood surfaces with the same solvent you used to mix the dye powder. The solvent reactivates the dye, and a cloth or paper towel draws it out of the wood cells.

Dye stain   **Pigment stain**

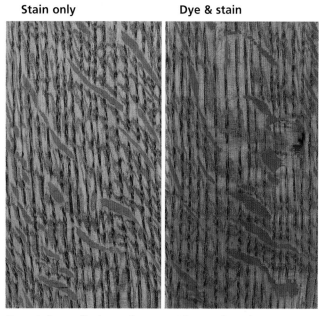

Pigment stain (right) becomes trapped in the open pored areas of oak and darkens them more than dye stain (left). Dye produces more even coloring.

Dye stain   **Pigment stain**

Stain only   **Dye & stain**

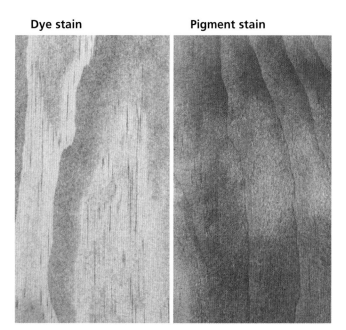

Notice how the pigment stain (right) penetrates unevenly on this pine sample, producing splotches. The left sample was colored with dye, which reduces splotching.

Dye stain applied as a base coat beneath a pigment stain will reveal the contrast of highly figured woods better than pigment stain alone.

Gel stains

If you are staining large vertical surfaces and are concerned about drips, or if you are working with pine or soft maple with inconsistent grain pattern, try a gel stain instead of a liquid. Gel stains are also a great way to match end grain with face grain. Gel stains consist of pigments or dyes suspended in a thick binder of varnish or water-based acrylic. The material typically has the consistency of petroleum jelly and will not flow like a liquid. The coloring agent, whether pigment or dye, doesn't penetrate as deeply into the open pores or cells, and it provides more even coverage on all types of wood. The thinner surface penetration helps minimize blotching and darker end-grain color. However, gel stain can be difficult to control when wiping into corners or crevices. The excess varnish will leave streaks or fill crevices unless it is thoroughly wiped clean. Also, your range of color options is more limited with gel stain than when using conventional, liquid-based pigment or dye stains.

If dye tone or color isn't what you want, you can modify the color by wiping down the project with a different color dye stain or reapplying the same dye and not removing the excess. More dye intensifies the color and tone. Adding a different color dye will blend with the base dye to form a new color.

You can also wipe a coat of pigment stain over the dried dye stain to dramatize the open-grain areas. This is a great technique for finishing figured wood. Use a pigment stain with a different solvent than that of the dye stain to keep the dye from lifting out of the wood. An oil-based pigment stain is a good choice for wiping over water-based dye stain.

One disadvantage to dye stains is that alcohol-based dye stains can fade if wood surfaces are subjected to direct sunlight. Water-based dye stains are more lightfast, but even these will fade to a lesser degree over time.

Pigment stains are more difficult to lighten once they are in the wood. The binder acts as a sealing coat over the pigment and holds the pigment in the pores. If you wipe the wood down with the clean-up solvent for the stain while the stain is still wet, it's possible to remove some of the pigment and lighten the color. Once the stain dries, you'll have to sand out the color.

If you'd like to darken the wood with pigment stain after applying the first coat of stain, apply a second coat and leave the excess on the wood rather than wiping it off. The binder bonds the pigment to the open-pored areas and produces a darker look overall. However, extra pigment will obscure the grain pattern to some degree.

The best way to see what you'll get when using pigment stain versus dye stain

Aniline dye stains are usually sold in powdered form. To prepare them for use, mix the powder with either distilled water or alcohol, depending on the dye chemistry.

is to try both options on a large sample of the same wood you're using for the project. This offers you a chance to try your hand with both stain types and experiment before you commit the stain to the project.

Applying stains

To prepare a pigment stain for application, just stir the can thoroughly. This suspends the pigments and mixes the binder and solvent together. To mix a dye stain, measure and add the dry powder to the appropriate solvent slowly while stirring. For water-based dye, use warm distilled water and stir the mixture until all the powder is blended into solution. Cool water works too, but the powder takes longer to dissolve and can leave clumps.

Pour the stain into a clean, nonmetal container. (The stain can react with metal and discolor.) For dye stains, strain the material through a disposable paper paint strainer first to remove any undissolved powder. Prepare enough dye stain to complete your entire project. If you have to mix more midway through, you may introduce color shifts. During the application process, sawdust and other debris will inevitably get mixed with your stain. It's best to dispose of the excess rather than pour it back into the stain can when you are through. Seal the extra stain in a lidded container to keep the solvent from evaporating. Otherwise the binder will thicken and the color intensify as the solvent flashes off. If you'd rather dispose of the extra stain instead of saving it, take oil stains to a hazardous waste drop-off. Water- or alcohol-based dye stains can be safely flushed down the drain with plenty of water.

You can apply stain with a brush, clean rag, or even disposable shop towels. Brushing on stain floods the surface more quickly than wiping, which can help if the stain has a tendency to dry quickly. Wiping on stain is a good way to avoid drips, especially if your project has vertical surfaces.

With the wood surface clean, dry, and smooth, brush or wipe on the stain. Try to cover a complete surface of your project with stain before removing the excess, but don't stain more than one surface at a time to prevent premature drying. Flow the stain on in a moderately heavy coat so the wood surface is thoroughly wet. It doesn't matter if you apply the stain with or across the grain. A heavy flow of pigment stain or dye will fill the pores and color the wood regardless of grain direction. Once the stain is on the wood, wipe off the excess with a clean rag, exposing clean surfaces of the rag as you wipe the surface dry. Work your way across the surface steadily and quickly, wiping each stroke nearly dry before moving onto a new wet area. The goal is to achieve an even-colored film of stain without leaving wiping marks behind. If one dry area looks lighter than another dry area, try wiping your stained rag over the lighter area to apply a bit more stain. If some areas dry prematurely before you have a chance to wipe off the excess, try wetting the unwiped areas with the appropriate clean-up thinner (for pigment stains) or the solvent (for dye stains) and then wiping these areas to remove surplus stain.

You'll notice that staining the end grain of wood with pigment stains typically results in a darker color. End grain exposes more wood pores than face or edge grain, which traps more pigment. To help blend the end and face grain color, you may need to apply another coat of stain to the face grain and leave on the excess. This will produce a more even color from face to end grain, but it won't match the two exactly.

Apply stain with a brush or rag to flood the surface, then wipe off the excess with a clean rag.

Once you've applied stain, it might reveal surface scratches not removed with sanding. Sand these areas again to remove the scratches, then restain.

CHOOSING A BRUSH FOR FINISHING

Brushes are made with either animal-hair or synthetic bristles. You can also find foam-pad brushes. Synthetic bristle brushes perform well with all oil- or water-based stains and topcoats. Avoid using natural-bristle brushes with water-based stains and finishes because the bristles swell and tangle. Foam-pad brushes are inexpensive and save you the hassle of cleaning after use, but they tend to harden or dissolve when used with solvent finishes. Use foam pads with water-based finishes instead.

Brushes between 1½ and 3 inches wide are the most practical sizes for finishing. Choose brushes with bristles about 2 to 3 inches long and with an overall bristle pattern that tapers to a point. Brushes with square edges tend to flow finish unevenly and leave streaks. Look closely at the bristle tips as well. Those that taper to points or splay into fine flagged tips carry more finish than square-tipped bristles.

Synthetic bristles work with all finishes, natural bristles work well for oil-based finishes, and foam brushes work well for water-based finishes.

Tapered brushes apply stains more evenly than square brushes.

Once the excess stain is wiped off and you are pleased with the color, allow the surfaces to dry thoroughly before proceeding with a topcoat of clear finish. After staining, if you notice milling marks or scratches you missed during sanding, remove them now by sanding. Start with a grit one step coarser than your final sanding grit, then switch to the final grit to remove the new sanding scratches. Reapply stain to these areas and blend the color in with the surrounding stain color to hide the repair. It's easier to fix these imperfections now than after the final finish is applied.

Applying a topcoat

There are many finish options for the final topcoat. Among them are wax, oil, wipe-on mixtures of oil and varnish or thinned varnish, unthinned varnish, shellac, and lacquer. Wax alone or a concentrated oil such tung oil or boiled linseed oil are too soft to provide adequate protection from dirt, water penetration, and other incidental surface abrasions. On the other end of the spectrum, lacquer provides a highly durable and protective topcoat, but it's best applied with special spray equipment, and the vapors are both flammable and harmful to breathe. For our purposes here, we'll concentrate on applying the easier, reasonably durable finishes that fall between these extremes: wiping finishes, shellac, and varnish.

WIPE-ON FINISHES

Many, many blends of wiping finishes are marketed to consumers as easy-to-apply, rapid-drying topcoats. The biggest advantage to using a wipe-on finish is that you can apply these products without ever lifting a brush. All it takes to apply the product is a clean, lint-free rag and some elbow grease. Wipe-on finishes are made from a variety of different ingredients. Some are blends of tung, linseed, or other oils combined with varnish and mineral spirits. Others are basically varnish thinned with mineral spirits so they flow more easily but provide better protection than oil/varnish blends. The product labels rarely identify exactly what concoctions are inside the bottle or can, but you'll know you are dealing with a wipe-on finish if the product name combines tung oil with varnish, or if the product calls itself a "finish." Products called "Danish," "Scandinavian," or "Nordic" oil finishes are all wipe-on finishes, too.

Wipe-on finishes are not as durable as varnish or shellac that forms a protective film on the wood's surface. The finish coat is extremely thin and leaves the wood pores largely exposed. However, for projects that don't require a high level of resistance to moisture or abrasion, wipe-on finishes provide a quick, no-fuss topcoat. Most produce a flat or satin sheen. If you don't want your project to look plasticized or coated with finish, wipe-on finishes may be good options. The downside to wipe-on finishes is that some cure to only a soft coat-

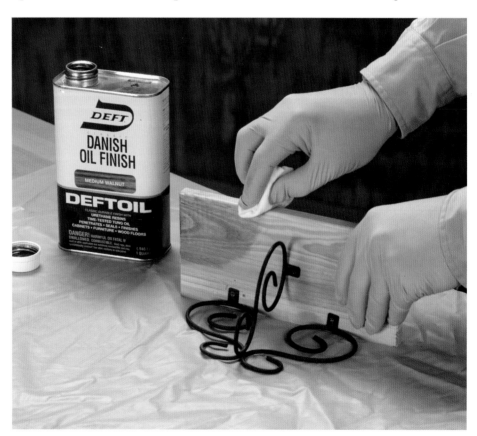

Wipe-on finishes are quick and easy to apply with a clean rag. Allow surfaces to dry between coats of finish.

Bare wood

Untinted wipe-on finishes leave wood looking wet but not shiny. Their thin consistency soaks into wood pores rather than building to a thick film.

Test a wipe-on finish for varnish. If a dried drop of finish dents easily, it is mostly oil. The harder it dries, the more varnish it contains.

ing. The more coats you apply and the thicker the topcoat gets, the softer it will feel. Wipe-on finishes that have a higher percentage of varnish than oil will cure harder, but the varnish is still so thin that it takes several coats to build up the same level of protection as one coat of brushed-on, unthinned varnish.

Applying a wipe-on finish. Pour a small amount of finish onto a clean, lint-free rag and wipe on the finish until the surface is wet. Allow the finish a few minutes to flow into the pores, then wipe off the excess and allow the surfaces to dry. Leaving excess finish on the wood may seem like an easy way to expedite the finishing process, but it really just prolongs the curing time. You'll get more coats of finish on the wood in less time by wiping off the residue. In humid weather, apply the finish in a well-ventilated but dry area. It can help to run a dehumidifier to lower humidity levels so the finish cures more rapidly. The drier and warmer the air, the faster the finish will cure.

Once the first layer of finish cures, you can apply additional coats of finish to help protect the wood. This is especially effective for thinned varnishes that cure hard even when built up in multiple layers. One way to help identify whether you are using an oil/varnish blended finish or a thinned varnish finish is to put a drop of finish on a piece of scrap, spread it slightly, and allow it to cure. If the drop hardens to the point that you can't dent it with a fingernail, you're using a varnish thinned with mineral spirits. If the finish remains slightly soft, even after curing, it's an oil/varnish blend.

SHELLAC

Another finish that's easy to apply and more durable than wipe-on finishes is shellac. Shellac is a natural resin harvested from purified bug secretions that are dried into thin sheets and broken into flakes. Used for centuries as a fine furniture finish, shellac is nontoxic in dry form, and it creates a reasonably durable surface film for projects that do not come in contact with water or alcohol. Shellac is usually brushed or sprayed onto wood. The finish can be built up into

Shellac builds to a smooth film and fills wood pores. Amber shellac casts an orange tone, and garnet is more reddish, while blonde shellac cures clear.

as many layers as you like for improved surface protection or if you prefer a highly smooth surface on your project. One big advantage to using shellac over some other finishes is that you don't have to sand between one coat and the next. Each new coat of finish partially dissolves the coat beneath and fuses to it for a strong bond.

Another attribute of shellac is that it forms an effective barrier against water vapor exchange in the wood. Shellac helps to reduce the amount of expansion and contraction that always occurs in wood with changes in humidity. You'll appreciate this benefit on projects with doors and drawers. In summer months, less wood expansion means doors and drawers won't swell enough to stick and bind in their openings.

Shellac does have a few downsides. It can be damaged by water, which leaves whitish stains on the wood. These are the familiar drinking glass rings you've probably seen on tabletops finished with shellac. Shellac dissolves in the presence of concentrated alcohol, lye, and ammonia. It also softens when exposed to high heat. Use another finish for kitchen or bathroom projects.

Shellac has a natural orange color, but it's also available in formulations with the orange color bleached out. Orange shellac gives wood a warm, amber color when it dries, while bleached varieties cure nearly clear. Most shellac has a percentage of naturally occurring wax in the mixture, which imparts a slightly cloudy tone to the finish. Some finishing techniques use shellac as a sealing coat under other finishes, like varnish. In these cases, the natural wax can cause adhesion problems with the varnish, so shellac is also sold in "dewaxed" form for use as an undercoat.

You'll find shellac sold in dry flakes or as a premixed liquid in cans and aerosols. Flake shellac must be mixed with denatured alcohol to dissolve the flakes and prepare it for use. The advantage to starting with flakes over premixed varieties is that the flakes have a much longer shelf life. Dry flake shellac will last for several years or more, but a can of premixed liquid shellac is only good for about one year, and even less after it's opened. As liquid or aerosol shellac ages, it takes longer to cure and eventually won't cure at all. If you buy liquid shellac rather than flakes, you can check its freshness with a fingernail test just like you would with a drop of wipe-on finish (see page 197).

Shellac is sold as premixed liquid, in aerosol form, or as dry flakes, as shown below.

Garnet

Blond

Preparing shellac for use. Mixing dry flake shellac with alcohol is called "cutting" the shellac. "Cut" refers to the number of pounds of shellac that are dissolved into one gallon of denatured alcohol. This quantity of alcohol is only a universal starting point. Actually, you can mix any quantity of shellac you need, no matter how small, using smaller increments of shellac and alcohol. Premixed liquid shellac is commonly sold in 3- to 5-pound cuts. The higher the number, the greater the percentage of shellac in alcohol and the thicker the

Blend shellac flakes in a non-metal container with denatured alcohol to prepare it for use. The ratio of flakes to solvent establishes the mixture's "cut."

mixture is. For general finishing, a 2-pound cut is ideal. It spreads easily with a brush and produces an even surface film with each coat. You can obtain this blend by diluting premixed shellac with denatured alcohol or by mixing flake shellac in the correct proportions with alcohol. Information is printed on the shellac can for diluting premixed shellac for a variety of cuts. If the can doesn't specify how to make thinner cuts, mix ½ part alcohol to one part premixed shellac for making a 2-pound cut.

When you're starting with flake shellac, here's how to prepare a reasonable quantity of 2-pound cut for finishing smaller projects: Combine 1 pint of denatured alcohol with ¼ pound (4 ounces) of shellac flakes. Mix the two together in a glass or plastic container. Metal containers will react with the shellac and discolor it. Stir the solution thoroughly until all the flakes are dissolved in the alcohol and then stir periodically during use to keep the shellac from clumping.

Once the shellac and alcohol are thoroughly blended, strain the liquid through a disposable paint strainer into a clean container to remove bits of undissolved shellac. Keep the container covered with a tight lid when not in use to prevent the alcohol from absorbing water from the air. Label the container with the date you prepared it in case you need to store an unused portion for use later.

Applying a shellac finish. The alcohol solvent in shellac evaporates quickly, which is good for efficiency's sake but somewhat challenging if you have a large surface to cover. The trick to brushing shellac is to keep the surface wet. The area you are brushing should touch the area you've just brushed along a wet edge. This way, the brush won't drag over partially dried shellac and leave ridges. Move the brush in long, overlapping strokes in the direction of the wood grain. Keep the brush moving over the wood, and reload the brush as soon as the shellac stops flowing out smoothly. You can use either a synthetic or natural bristle brush and get good results. If the 2-pound cut seems too thick to brush easily over the bare wood, thin it to a 1-pound cut instead. A thinner cut may also be helpful if you notice small bubbles appearing in the finish that don't pop as the

Strain freshly blended shellac through a paper filter to remove bits of undissolved shellac before use.

Brush on shellac in long, overlapping strokes keeping the edges between the strokes wet. Allow each coat to dry thoroughly before reapplying.

shellac cures. However, be aware that a thinner cut will dry faster than a thicker cut—it contains more alcohol.

After you've brushed on the first coat, allow at least two hours of drying time before applying the second coat. Then brush the second coat right over the first with no further prep work. Alcohol in the second coat will dissolve the first coat slightly, and the two layers of finish will bond together well. Apply as many additional coats of shellac as you like to "build up" the surface smoothness.

VARNISH

Of all the topcoat options available to consumers, varnish is the usual choice, and it's a good one. It forms a tough, protective film on the wood surface, and some varieties are highly resistant to wear, heat, acids, and solvents. Varnish is easy to apply with a brush, but it cures much more slowly than shellac. Once cured, varnish behaves like a coating of plastic over the wood, sealing the pores and helping to reduce wood movement. Another advantage to varnish is that you can buy it formulated to cure to flat, satin, or gloss sheens. This way, you can use varnish to simulate a "close-to-the-wood" finish that doesn't shine, a finish with just a bit of sheen to it, or a highly wet-looking finish. You can reduce the sheen of gloss varnish by rubbing the cured finish with #0000 steel wool and mineral spirits to whatever level of sheen you prefer.

The term varnish encompasses a variety of products, but they can be broken into three broad categories: alkyd varnish, polyurethane varnish, and water-based acrylic or water-based polyurethane. The first two varnish types are made by combining various oils with blends of synthetic resins and metallic driers to help accelerate the curing process. Water-based varnishes are mixtures of acrylic or polyurethane and water. Oil-based varnishes are more resistant to water, solvents, and heat than water-based products, but the wet varnish creates unpleasant fumes as it cures. Oil-based varnishes take on a yellowish tint as they age, and the polyurethane can leave an amber tint. Polyurethane also degrades in the presence of ultraviolet sunlight. Over time, poly varnish will eventually peel off the wood if its exposed to direct sunlight. Some polyurethane formulations have UV additives to help counteract this tendency.

Varnish dries to various surface sheens including satin, semigloss, and gloss. However, a gloss varnish can be dulled to lesser sheens by rubbing it with steel wool or fine abrasives.

Among the oil-based varnishes, you'll find some labeled as "spar" or "marine" varnishes intended for outdoor applications. These blends are made with oils that prevent the varnish from curing to a hard film like other varnishes made for interior projects. The softer cure of a spar varnish makes it more flexible. This characteristic is important for wood exposed to the elements because the wood expands and contracts more than it would if stored indoors. Soft varnish is better able to move with the wood. For a tougher finish, go with an interior varnish.

Oil-based varnishes also come in gel forms with working characteristics similar to gel-based stains (see page 192). The varnish wipes on with a cloth instead of brushing. It's handy for use on vertical surfaces where liquid varnishes could drip, run, or sag. The best areas for applying gel varnish are flat, open surfaces without small details or inside corners. The gel can be difficult to apply evenly in these areas and can leave globs. Wipe them off while they're still soft.

The popularity of varnish with consumers is evident in the wide range of products available. You'll find stain/varnish mixes, water- or oil-based formulations, aerosols, gels, and wipe-on varnish.

Water-based varnish has different characteristics than its oil-based cousins. It is more susceptible to damage from solvents, water, and heat. It dries to a highly scratch-resistant coating, much harder than oil-based polyurethane and about equal to alkyd varnish. You'll need to raise the grain and sand the wood smooth before applying water-based varnish (see page 189). Otherwise, the varnish will raise the grain as it soaks into the surface. Water-based polyurethane dries clear and takes no yellowish cast over time, although some finishers feel that it leaves wood looking dull and without depth. Probably the biggest advantage to using water-based varnish is its low solvent content. It emits significantly fewer bad-smelling fumes, and the curing varnish isn't a fire hazard as the solvents evaporate. Clean-up is also easier. Wash brushes in warm, soapy water before the varnish cures.

Applying a varnish finish. Both oil- and water-based varnishes can be applied with a synthetic bristle brush. Use natural-bristle brushes with oil-based varnishes only. Water-based varnish will swell and tangle natural bristles. Because varnish cures slowly, especially oil-based varnish, it's important to work in a clean, dust-free environment. Otherwise, bits of dust in the air will settle on the varnish before it cures and leave tiny rough spots on the surface. It's a good idea to apply varnish away from the workshop in another room to avoid these dust issues. Work in a well-ventilated area. If you are sensitive to concentrated solvent fumes, wear a cartridge-style respirator.

The lower solvent content of water-based varnish makes it easier on your nose, but it's more likely to leave undissolved bits in the can. Strain it through a paper filter before using.

For the first coat of finish, many experts thin oil-based varnish to a 50/50 mixture with mineral spirits. The thinned varnish spreads more easily with a brush over bare wood. If you're using water-based varnish, there's no need to thin the first coat. Its composition is thinner than oil-based varnish right out of the can, and it flows easily. Strain water-based varnish through a paper filter before applying it. The low solvent content makes water-based varnish more likely to have bits of undissolved solids in the liquid.

With either varnish, pour off a small amount of finish from the can into a clean container and load the brush from this container. To brush on the varnish, start a few inches in from the ends of the surface and brush out to the ends. Apply these short brush strokes with the grain. Starting in from the end and working outward helps you avoid leaving extra varnish right on the ends of the surface where it can run or drip. Once both ends of the surface are covered, brush the bare area in between in long, overlapping strokes. When the whole surface is covered with wet finish, drag just the tips of the bristles over the surface in long strokes to level any ridges and dips. This technique is called "tipping off" the finish, and it also helps pop small bubbles in the surface film before they cure hard. Skim the bristles against the edge of the container to remove any excess after each tip-off stroke. Let the first layer of finish cure hard.

When the varnish is dry, sand it lightly with 280-grit paper. For water-based varnish, this sanding knocks off any grain nibs that may have raised up through the first coat of finish. On oil-based varnish, especially polyurethane, sanding between coats is crucial. It abrades the varnish film just enough so the next coat can form a mechanical connection to the coat underneath. Varnish is not like shellac, which partially dissolves the finish layer beneath and forms a chemical connection. Clean off the sanding dust with a vacuum or compressed air.

Apply the next coat of varnish, just as you did for the first coat, keeping a wet edge and brushing with the grain. After this coat dries hard, prepare it for another coat by sanding lightly with 320- or finer-grit sandpaper to scuff the surface film. You can also use a fine-textured synthetic scrub pad for this purpose. Look for pads colored grey or white—the green ones are too coarse. Clean the surfaces before brushing the varnish. For most applications, two to three coats of varnish builds a sufficiently durable finish. However, you can apply as many coats as you like, provided you sand lightly between coats.

Apply varnish by brushing short strokes out to the edges of a workpiece first. This minimizes drips and sags along the edges. Then fill in the center area with long, even strokes, tipping off the finish when it's fully applied.

PAINTED FINISHES

If wood grain and texture aren't important for a project, paint makes a wonderful finish. It provides durable protection against surface abrasions, spills, and degradation from UV sunlight. Now that all paint is lead-free, it's child-safe when dry, and you can't beat the vibrant color choices. Exterior paint is the best of all finishes for outdoor wood projects; it will outlast spar varnish if applied correctly. Paint usually won't peel unless it is applied without a primer coat, used over wet wood, or subjected to standing water.

Both oil- and water-based paints are good choices for wood. Oil-based paints take longer to dry, but some experts prefer them because of their smooth-flowing and leveling tendencies. Acrylic latex paint is just as durable as oil-based paint, and it comes in the same sheen options. Latex paint is also easy to clean up with soapy water. Some experts also argue that latex paint provides a more flexible coating over wood than oil paint, so it won't crack or peel as the wood moves.

All varieties of lumber you'll find at the home center can be painted. Closed-grain woods such as birch, maple, and poplar provide the smoothest surface for paint. If you paint cedar, pine, or redwood, use a primer fortified with additives that help seal in natural oils and pitch to keep the these substances from bleeding through the paint and staining it. Many exotic woods, such as teak, cocobolo, and rosewood, are extremely oily and are not good candidates for a painted finish.

Prepare bare wood for paint just as you would for stains and clear topcoats. Sand the surfaces thoroughly up to 150- or 180-grit, remove all dust, and raise the grain if you're using a water-based paint. Apply the recommended primer for the paint with a bristle or foam brush. Primer serves several important purposes: It levels the wood surface, seals the pores, and allows the paint to bond fully with the wood. Never skip the primer, or you'll compromise the finish.

Once the primer dries, topcoat with two or more coats of paint. You only need to apply enough coats of paint to form an even surface color. Protective properties of paint don't improve with more than a few layers. Apply each coat sparingly so it dries quickly and doesn't drip or sag. There's no need to sand between coats.

Painted finishes always begin with a base layer of primer. Use a primer that's compatible with the oil- or latex-based paint you will use as a topcoat.

When the primer dries, overcoat with paint. One or two coats should be enough to produce an even surface color.

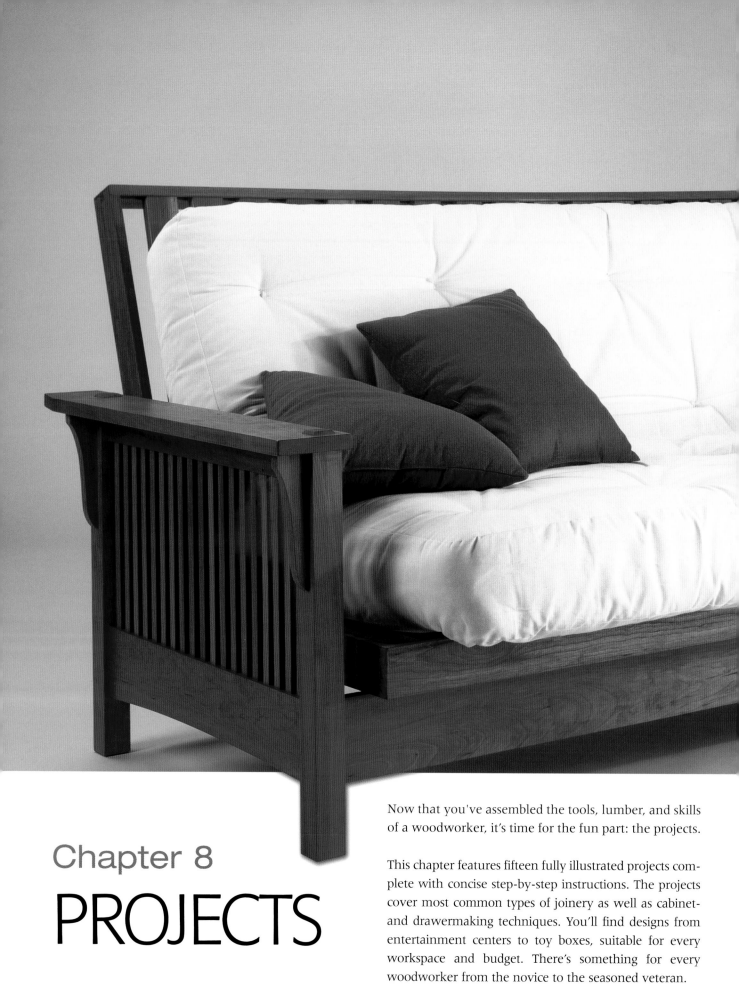

Chapter 8
PROJECTS

Now that you've assembled the tools, lumber, and skills of a woodworker, it's time for the fun part: the projects.

This chapter features fifteen fully illustrated projects complete with concise step-by-step instructions. The projects cover most common types of joinery as well as cabinet- and drawermaking techniques. You'll find designs from entertainment centers to toy boxes, suitable for every workspace and budget. There's something for every woodworker from the novice to the seasoned veteran.

Along with an exploded isometric drawing, each project has detailed materials and shopping lists, including hardware and fasteners. You'll also find precise elevation and detail drawings and patterns to help you make exact cuts and build strong joints.

Of course, all of these plans can serve as inspiration for your own designs. You may want to modify and redesign elements of these projects to suit your own

skills and tastes. Whatever you choose to do, the material from the previous chapters will serve you well.

Note: All of the hardware and fasteners specified for these projects can be found at woodworking retailers, such as those listed on page 303.

Bed frame

This bed frame is based on a timeless Mission-style design. The exposed tenons and tenon keys and the narrow vertical slats are hallmarks of the early-20th-century furniture maker and designer Gustav Stickley. For a small fraction of the cost a manufactured reproduction, you can build this classic American bed.

As a piece of furniture in your bedroom, the bed is substantial and impressive, but in your workshop, it is a fairly straightforward proposition and an excellent chance to polish your craft. Careful work with a router, drill, and chisels on the mortises and tenons—especial-

ly the angled mortise-and-tenon joints—is essential for a sturdy and stable finished product.

Most Mission-style furniture was built with quartersawn oak, but other hardwoods are also suitable to this design. Contrasting grain or coloring on the tenon keys is a typical Mission detail and one you can easily reproduce.

The plan is measured for a queen-size mattress and box spring. A standard king-size mattress is 16 inches wider, and could be accommodated by scaling up the headboard and footboard accordingly.

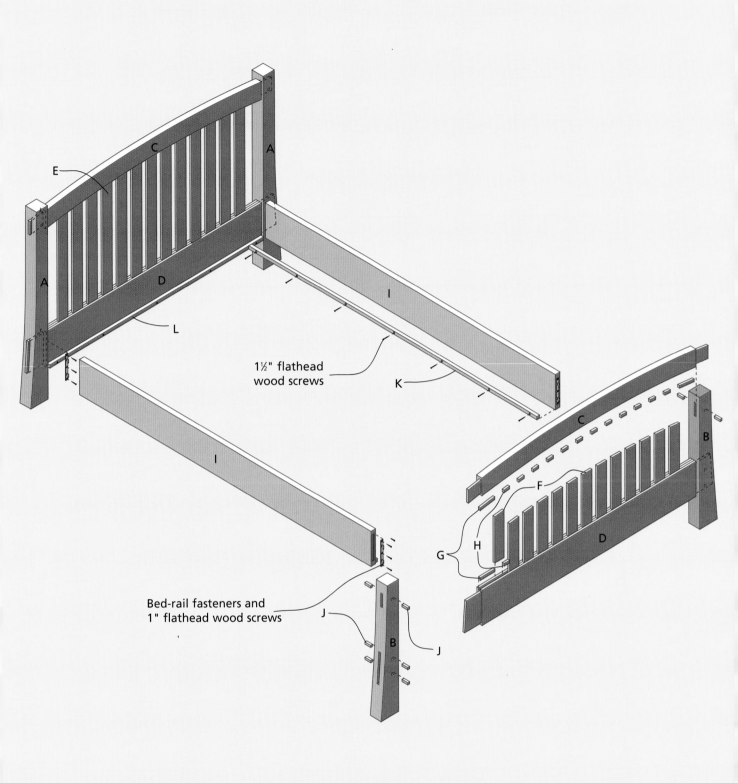

E

C

A

A

D

L

1½" flathead
wood screws

I

K

I

C

F

B

H

G

D

Bed-rail fasteners and
1" flathead wood screws

J

B

J

Shopping List
Total board feet required: 84
Dimensional lumber: 1 x 1" x 10' (1 required)
Dimensional lumber: 1 x 1" x 8' (2 required)

Materials List					
Key	Part name	Qty.	Thickness	Width	Length	Material
Overall dimensions (68"w × 84½"d × 44½"h)					
A	Headboard legs	2	3"	4¾"	44"	Solid wood or glue up
B	Footboard legs	2	3"	4¾"	30"	Solid wood or glue up
C	Top rail	2	1½"	6"	65⅝"	Solid wood or glue up
D	Bottom rail	2	1½"	8"	67¾"	Solid wood or glue up
E	Headboard slat	13	½"	2½"	* 26½"	Solid wood
F	Footboard slat	13	½"	2½"	* 12½"	Solid wood
G	Long rail spacers	8	½"	9/16"	4"	Solid wood
H	Short rail spacers	48	½"	9/16"	1½"	Solid wood
I	Side rails	2	1¼"	8"	78½"	Solid wood or glue up
J	Tenon key	24	½"	½"	1 5/16"	Solid wood—contrasting appearance
K	Long box spring blocking	2	¾"	¾"	78"	Solid wood—dimensional lumber
L	Short box spring blocking	2	¾"	¾"	58"	Solid wood—dimensional lumber
* Indicates oversized part. Cut to exact size during assembly.					
Hardware					
	Bedrail fasteners	4		⅝"	6"	
	Flathead wood screws				1½"	

Headboard & Footboard Elevations

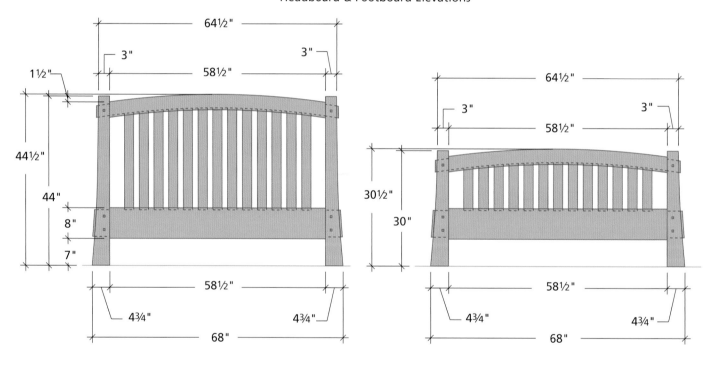

Rail Dado Detail

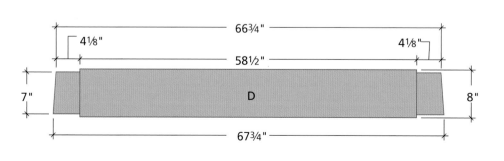

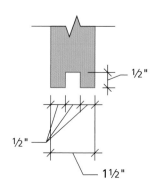

Leg Detail

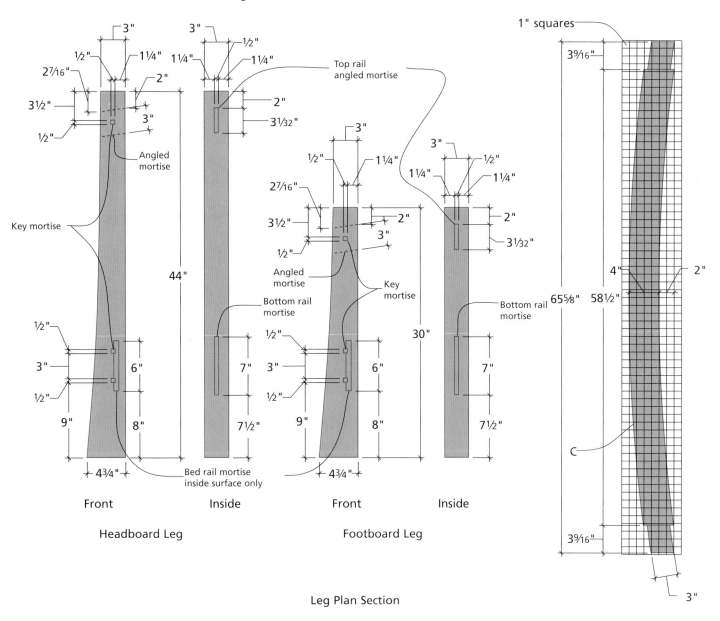

Rail Pattern

1" squares

Top rail angled mortise

Angled mortise

Key mortise

44"

Bed rail mortise inside surface only

Front   Inside

Headboard Leg

Angled mortise

Bottom rail mortise

Key mortise

30"

Bottom rail mortise

Front   Inside

Footboard Leg

3⁹⁄₁₆"

65⁵⁄₈"   58½"

4"   2"

C

3⁹⁄₁₆"

3"

Leg Plan Section

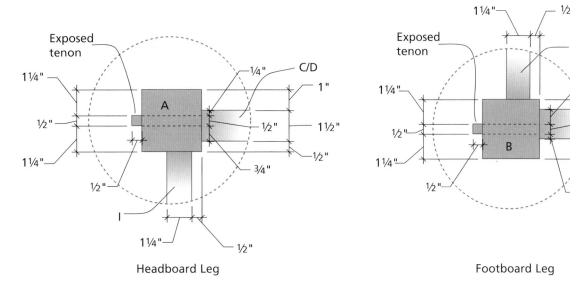

Exposed tenon

C/D

A

I

Headboard Leg

Exposed tenon

I

C/D

B

Footboard Leg

A   Machining the Legs

Step 1. If necessary, glue up the leg stock and machine the headboard legs (A) and the footboard legs (B) to size.

Step 2. Cut the tapers on the legs (3" at the top and 4¾" at the bottom) per the leg detail drawings.

B   Machining the Top, Bottom & Side Rails

Step 1. If necessary, glue up stock and machine the top rails (C) and the bottom rails (D) to size according to the detail drawings.

Step 2. Cut the arcs on the top rails per the rail pattern.

Step 3. Machine tenons on all the rails using a router. Note that the tenons are offset. See the leg detail drawings for tenon specifications.

Step 4. Machine a ½ × ½" dado in the top edges of the bottom rails and the bottom edges of the top rails. Use a router on the top rails and use a table saw and/or a router on the bottom rails.

Step 5. Machine headboard slats (E) and footboard slats (F) to rough length.

Step 6. Machine the long rail spacers (G) and the short rail spacers (H). Try to choose wood that matches the rails in color and grain orientation.

Step 7. If necessary, glue up stock and machine the side rails (I).

C   Laying Out Slats on the Bottom Rails

Step 1. Starting with the long rail spacers, glue and clamp one at each end of the bottom rail dado, making sure it is flush at the end of the rail.

Step 2. Place a slat into the dado, tight against the long rail spacer you just glued in.

Step 3. Glue and clamp a short rail spacer tight against the slat.

Step 4. Remove the slat and proceed in this manner until you have all the rail spacers glued and clamped in place.

Step 5. The spacers should sit slightly above the top edge of the bottom rails. Flush them up with a belt sander.

D   Mortising the Legs & Side Rails

Step 1. Lay out the top and bottom rail mortises on the legs using the leg detail drawings. It is most important that the outside of the mortise is the exact size of the tenon. Mark the tops of the mortises by drawing the outline of the mortise on the front faces of the legs. Use a hand drill or drill press (at an angle) and chisels for the top rail mortises. Use a drill press and chisels for the bottom rail mortises. Check the fit using the rails previously machined with tenons.

Step 2. Lay out the bed-rail fastener mortises on the legs and side-rail ends. The width and depth of the mortise will depend on the hardware you choose. Note that the mortises on the side rails are centered on the side rail ends.

Step 3. Mortise for the bed-rail fasteners using a chisel and a small trim router set for the depth of your bed-rail fastener hardware.

E   Assembling the Headboard & Footboard

Step 1. Dry fit the headboard and footboard pieces using clamps to hold the assembly together. Do not insert the slats. Mark the locations for the tenon keys using the leg detail drawings.

Step 2. Drill a ½"-diameter hole at the tenon-key locations. There are 3 holes on each leg.

Step 3. Mark a line on the top and bottom rails that represents the depth of the dado (½"). Use this line to cut the slats (E and F) to exact size. Make sure that they are a little shorter than the actual length required. Mark a number on the rails and on each slat so you can install the slats in their proper positions when you do final assembly.

Step 4. Take apart the headboard and footboard assemblies and reassemble them with the slats in place.

Step 5. Fit the rail spacers into the top rails. Make angled cuts as necessary. It is all right for the spacers to stick out slightly below the dado. Note that the fit doesn't need to be as exact as the bottom rail spacers. Clamp and glue in place, making sure no glue squeezes out on the slats.

Step 6. Take apart the headboard and footboard assemblies, and using a belt sander, flush up the spacers with the bottom edge of the top rail.

Step 7. Square out the tenon-key holes (on the legs and on the rail tenons) using a chisel, making sure to keep the size on the outside surface the same as the tenon key.

Step 8. Cut the tenon keys (J) to size. They should be a little long so you can flush them up with the legs after gluing them in place.

Step 9. Sand all pieces with an appropriate grit sandpaper.

Step 10. Glue and clamp the headboard assembly and the footboard assembly together.

Step 11. After the glue has dried, sand the tenon keys flush with the legs.

F   Attaching the Side Rails & the Box-spring Blocking

Step 1. Attach bed-rail fasteners to the previously mortised legs and side-rail ends using the specified hardware.

Step 2. Connect the side rails to the legs using bed-rail fasteners.

Step 3. Machine the long box-spring blocking (K) and the short box-spring blocking (L) to size.

Step 4. Attach the box-spring blocking to the bottom and side rails using 1½" flathead wood screws and glue. The location of the rails is determined by the thickness of your box spring. The illustration shows the blocking flush with the bottom of the rails. Position the blocking ¼" in from the ends of each rail.

Step 5. Detach the side rails from the headboard and footboard.

G   Applying a Finish

Step 1. Make sure all pieces have been sanded with at least 180-grit sandpaper.

Step 2. Apply a finish of your choice to all surfaces.

Step 3. Reassemble the bed.

Bedside table

This deceptively simple bedside table in a Shaker style packs a great deal of woodworking skill and detail into a small package—ideal for a smaller shop or a tight budget. The angled and tapered legs lend grace to the table, while the wide top and shelf make it a solid and highly practical piece.

Precise mitering and beveling of the legs and aprons will ensure that the finished piece is stable and sturdy. The single drawer is a showcase for that most prized of joinery techniques: dovetailing.

Almost any wood is suitable for this piece, but it is worth taking particular care in selecting stock with attractive grain and figure for the glued-up top and shelf.

The 28-inch height of this table is a standard height for such a table, but you may want to adjust the height to suit and add an inch or two to the leg lengths if you have a particularly thick mattress and box spring.

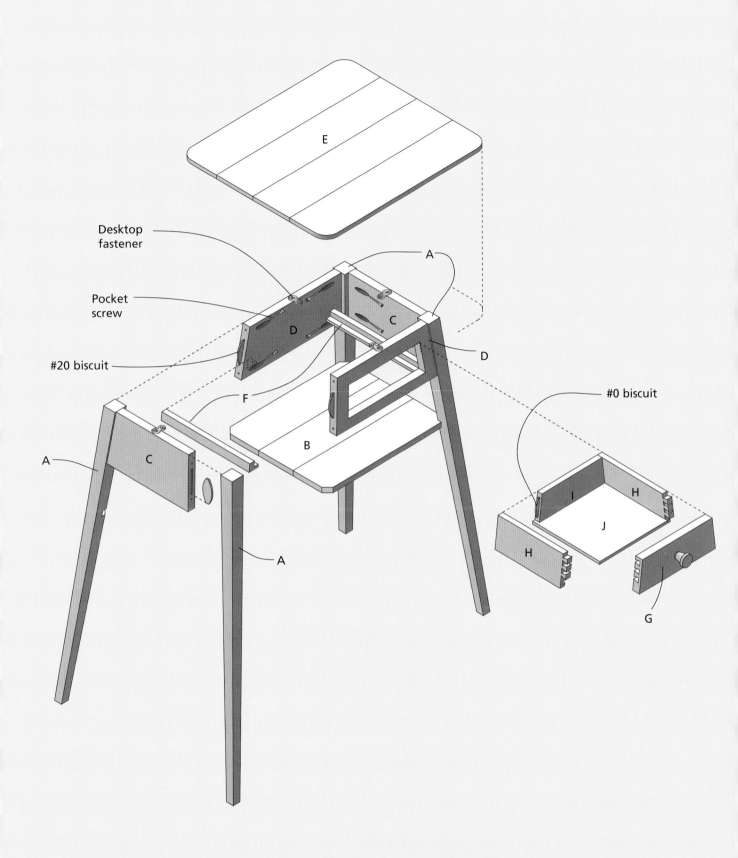

Desktop
fastener

Pocket
screw

#20 biscuit

A

A

A

D

C

D

F

B

E

A

C

D

#0 biscuit

I

H

H

J

G

Shopping List
Total board feet required: 9
Plywood required: ¼ x 12 x 12"

Materials List						
Key	Part name	Qty.	Thickness	Width	Length	Material
Overall dimensions (18"w × 16"d × 28"h)						
A	Leg	4	1¼"	1¼"	27 9/16"	Solid wood
B	Shelf	1	½"	11¼"	13¼"	Solid wood (glue-up)
C	Side apron	2	¾"	5"	9 3/16"	Solid wood
D	Front/back apron	2	¾"	5"	11 3/16"	Solid wood
E	Top	1	¾"	16"	18"	Solid wood (glue-up)
F	Drawer guide	2	¾"	1"	10"*	Solid wood
* Indicates oversized. Cut to fit.						
Drawer (8 7/16"w × 8"d × 3"h)						
G	Drawer front	1	¾"	3"	8 7/16"	Solid wood
H	Drawer side	2	½"	3"	7¾"	Solid wood
I	Drawer back	1	½"	2½"	7 7/16"	Solid wood
J	Drawer bottom	1	¼"	7¾"	7 15/16"	Plywood
Hardware						
	Drawer pull	1				
	Desktop fasteners	4				
	Joining biscuits					#0 and #20
	Pocket screws				1¼"	
	Nylo tape					

Elevation Detail

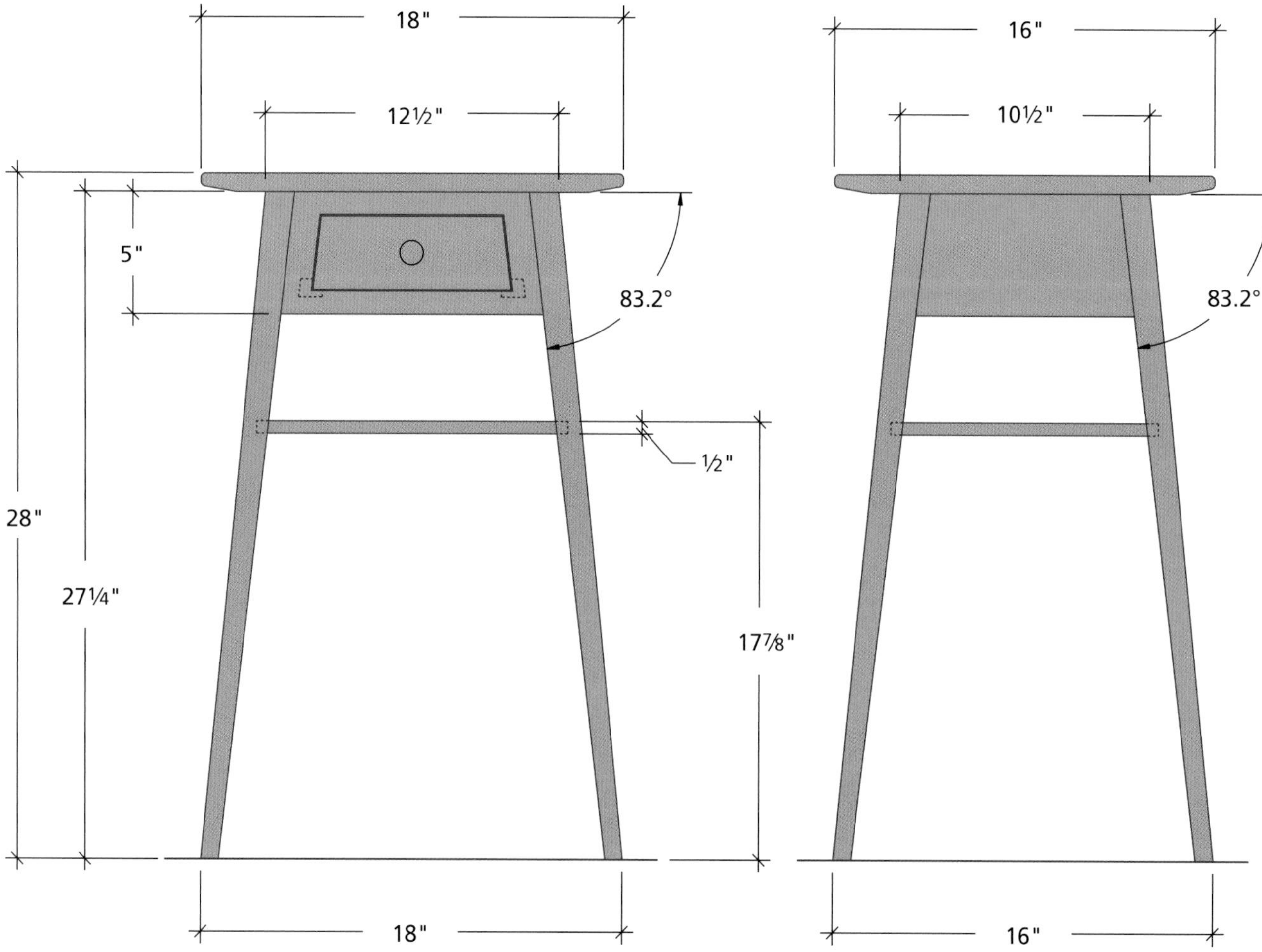

Dovetail Diagram

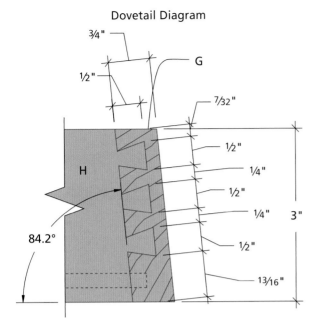

Apron Detail

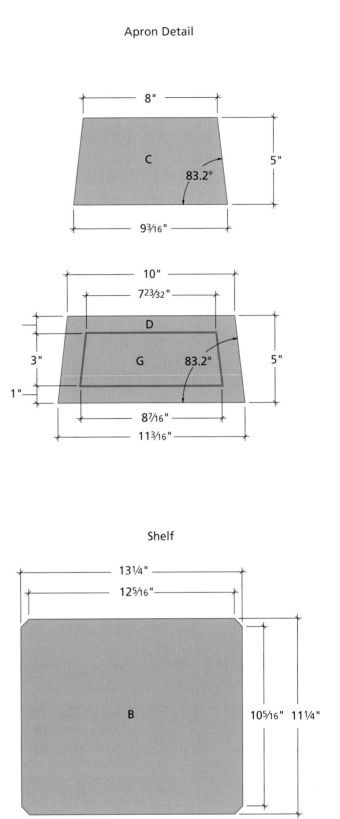

Top Edge Detail

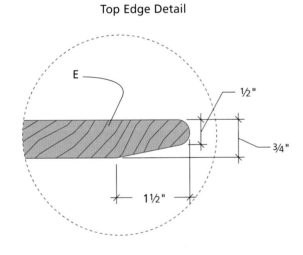

Drawer Guide Detail

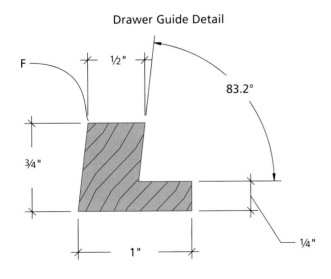

A   **Machining the Legs**

Step 1. Machine the legs (A) to approximate size, leaving them 1" longer than the final length. (It's a good idea to make a test leg—or even a whole set—out of dimensional lumber.)

Step 2. Cut the legs to finished length. Miter cut each end at approximately 6.8°. Note that the cuts are parallel to each other.

Step 3. Taper the legs on two inside surfaces only. The legs taper from 1¼" at top to ¾" at bottom. It's a good idea to label the legs on top.

Step 4. Notch the legs for the shelf. Mark the legs so the top of the shelf will be 17⅞" above floor. This is approximately 18" from the bottom inside corner of the leg to the top of the notch. It is most important that the legs are all notched in the same place to the same depth, approximately ⅜" deep and ½" wide. You may want to use your test legs to make sure your notches make a good fit.

B   **Machining the Aprons, Drawer Front & Shelf**

Step 1. After gluing up a blank, machine the shelf (B) to size. Do not clip the corners of the shelf.

Step 2. Machine the side aprons (C) and the front and back aprons (D) to size. See the patterns for angles on the aprons (see apron detail). Note that the aprons all have top and bottom edges beveled at approximately 6.8°.

Step 3. Lay out the drawer front on the front apron per the detail drawing (see apron detail). If you want to use the cut-out as the drawer front (G), drill a small hole (⅟₁₆") at one of the corners. Make sure to drill the hole outside of your cut lines. Use a scroll saw or jig saw with a thin blade to cut the drawer front out of the apron. Make cuts as straight as possible to maintain a small reveal between the apron and the drawer front. Use the tool of your choice to clean up edges.

C   **Dry-fitting the Legs, Aprons & Shelf**

Step 1. Mark the side aprons and legs for #20 biscuit slots, and machine the slots. It's helpful to mark which apron end goes with which leg. Note that the side aprons are set in ⅛" from the outside face of the legs. Dry-fit the legs and side aprons using #20 biscuits and pocket screws.

Step 2. Mark the front and back aprons and the leg assemblies for #20 biscuit slots, and machine the slots. Note that the front and back aprons are set in ⅛" from the outside face of the legs. Dry-fit the parts using #20 biscuits and pocket screws.

Step 3. Measure the distance between the shelf notches and notch or "dog ear" the shelf accordingly. It is a good idea to make a test shelf made of plywood or particle board first to ensure a good fit before notching the actual shelf.

Step 4. Detach one leg assembly and fit the shelf between legs. Reassemble to check the fit of all parts.

Step 5. Machine the center of each apron to accept a desktop fastener, and attach the fasteners.

D   Machining the Top

Step 1. After gluing up a blank, machine the top (E) to size.

Step 2. Cut a bevel on all the edges by running the piece on edge through a table saw set for an approximately 10.5° bevel. Refer to the drawing for details (see top edge detail). Make sure to use a zero-clearance insert in the saw and a high fence to give you stability.

Step 3. Cut a 1¼" radius at the corners with a jig saw or band saw.

Step 4. Complete the bevel at the corners of the top using a belt sander or block plane.

Step 5. Radius the top edge using a router fitted with a ¼" radius bit and a bearing. Clean up the edge using a sanding block or small hand sander.

E   Building the Drawer & Drawer Guides

Step 1. Machine the drawer guides (F) to approximate size. Machine the beveled outside face (83.2°, see drawer guide detail) with a table saw. Reduce the blade depth to ½" and make a parallel cut ½" away from the first angled cut. Complete the rabbet by making a 90° cut, ½" deep, leaving ¼" material.

Step 2. Machine the drawer front (G) if necessary. Machine the drawer sides (H), drawer back (I), and drawer bottom (J) to size per the materials list. See the dovetail diagram for a detailed view of the drawer side joint.

Step 3. Machine a ¼ × ¼" dado in the drawer sides and front ¼" from the bottom edge. Note that the drawer front has a blind dado, stopping ⅜" from each end.

Step 4. Cut dovetails in the sides and the drawer front using a router and a 14° dovetail bit. Use the dovetail diagram to lay out the dovetails or lay out your own design.

Step 5. Align the sides and back. Mark and machine slots for #0 biscuits.

Step 6. Glue and clamp the drawer box together. After the glue has dried, attach drawer bottom by sliding it in from back and fixing it in place with ¾" screws driven into the bottom edge of the drawer back. Run a bead of hot-melt glue between the drawer sides, front, and back and the drawer bottom.

Step 7. Mark and drill the front for the drawer pull of your choice.

F   Sanding, Assembling & Finishing

Step 1. Finish sand all the parts of the table with 180-grit or finer sandpaper.

Step 2. Assemble the table as follows:

a. Attach side aprons to the legs with glue and pocket screws.

b. Attach the front and back aprons and the shelf to the leg assemblies. No glue is necessary for the shelf.

c. Cut the drawer guides to correct size, and miter the ends at 83.2°. Clamp in place to test drawer alignment. Attach guides to the aprons with glue and predrilled finish nails.

d. Center the top on the lower assembly, and attach it with desktop fasteners.

Step 3. Apply the finish of your choice.

Step 4. After the finish has dried, attach the drawer pull.

Step 5. Use nylo tape on the drawer guides to give a proper reveal between the drawer front and the front apron.

Breakfront bookcase

Perhaps no other piece of furniture captures Craftsman-style woodworking better than glass-doored breakfront bookcases such as this one. In the early part of the 20th century, freestanding and built-in variations on this design were integral parts of the bungalow-style homes built by Frank Lloyd Wright and Gustav Stickley.

While the materials list for this project is long, the plans divide the bookcase into several manageable sections to be completed separately and attached to the carcass.

Assembly will require a variety of cabinetmaking skills. Take time to check the pieces for square and to dry-fit before final assembly. In particular, the back panel of this bookcase is a highlight rather than an afterthought, and it will require careful work with a router and rail-and-stile bits.

Designed with adjustable shelves, this cabinet is perfect not only for storing books, but also for displaying china or collectibles. If you plan to use the cabinet for display, you might want to incorporate small, low-voltage lights into the design.

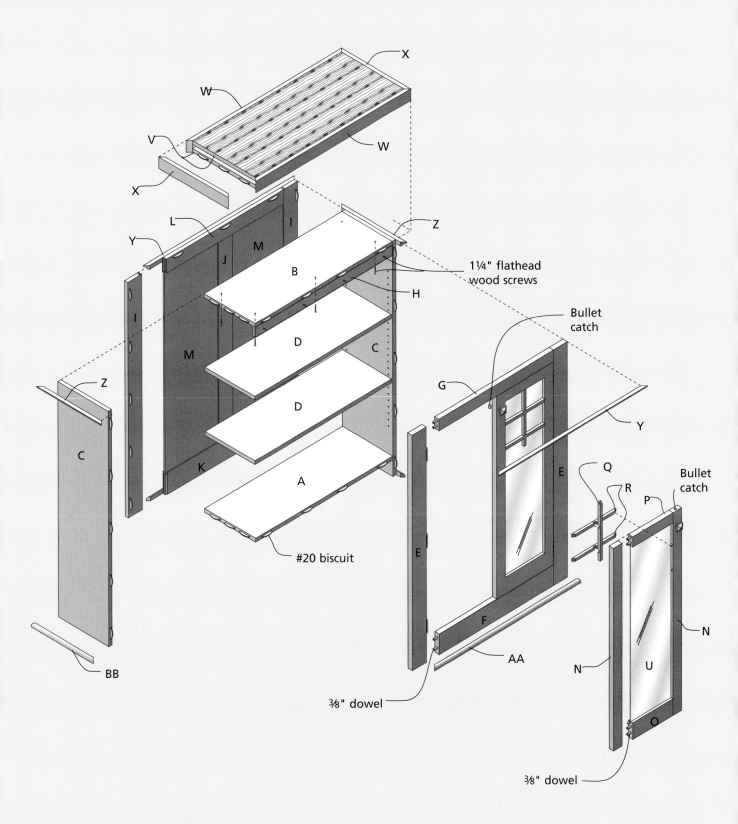

X

W

W

V

X

L

I

M

J

M

Y

I

M

K

Z

C

BB

B

D

D

A

#20 biscuit

H

1¼" flathead
wood screws

Bullet
catch

G

E

C

Y

Q

R

Bullet
catch

P

N

E

U

N

F

N

O

AA

⅜" dowel

⅜" dowel

Shopping List
Total board feet required: 20
Plywood required: ¼ x 30 x 48"
Plywood required: ¾ x 12 x 96"
Plywood required: ¾ x 48 x 72"
Glass required: ⅛ x 10¹/₁₆ x 35" (2 required)
Veneer tape required: ⅞" x 6'
Base shoe molding required: ½ x ¾" x 10'
Top molding required: ½ x ¾" x 10'

Materials List						
Key	Part name	Qty.	Thickness	Width	Length	Material
Overall dimensions (36"w × 16"d × 48 ¼"h)						
A	Bottom	1	¾"	11¾"	32"	Plywood
B	Interior top	1	¾"	11¾"	32"	Plywood
C	End	2	¾"	11¾"	46"	Plywood
D	Adjustable shelf	2	¾"	11½"	31⅞"	Plywood
E	Face frame stile	2	1"	3¼"	46"	Solid wood
F	Face frame bottom rail	1	1"	4"	27"	Solid wood
G	Face frame top rail	1	1"	2¼"	27"	Solid wood
H	Door stop	1	½"	2"	32"	Solid wood
Back panel (33½"w × 46"h × ¾" thick)						
I	Back panel stile	2	¾"	3¼"	46"	Solid wood
J	Back panel middle stile	1	¾"	3¼"	39½"	Solid wood
K	Back panel bottom rail	1	¾"	4¼"	27½"	Solid wood
L	Back panel top rail	1	¾"	2¾"	27½"	Solid wood
M	Back panel	2	¼"	12⅝"	39¾"	Plywood
Door (13¹³⁄₃₂"w × 39⅝"h × 1" thick)						
N	Door stile	4	1"	2"	39⅝"	Solid wood
O	Door bottom rail	2	1"	3¼"	9¹³⁄₃₂"	Solid wood
P	Door top rail	2	1"	2"	9¹³⁄₃₂"	Solid wood
Q	Door vertical mullion	2	½"	½"	11⅜"	Solid wood
R	Door horizontal mullion	4	½"	½"	10⁵⁄₃₂"	Solid wood
S	Long glass stop	4	⁵⁄₁₆"	⅜"	35⅛"	Solid wood
T	Short glass stop	4	⁵⁄₁₆"	⅜"	10⁵⁄₃₂"	Solid wood
U	Glass	2	⅛"	10¹⁄₁₆"	35"	Tempered glass
Top (16"w × 36"l × 2¼" thick)						
V	Top/bottom	2	¾"	14½"	34½"	Plywood
W	Long edge	2	¾"	2¼"	36"	Solid wood
X	Short edge	2	¾"	2¼"	16"	Solid wood
Y	Long top molding	2	¾"	¾"	35"	Solid wood
Z	Short top molding	2	¾"	¾"	15"	Solid wood
AA	Long base shoe	2	½"	¾"	34½"	Solid wood
BB	Short base shoe	2	½"	¾"	14½"	Solid wood
Hardware						
	Knob	2	1¼"	1¼"		
	Hinge	6				Non mortise hinge
	Shelf pin	8	¼"			
	Bullet ball catch	2				
	Joining biscuit					#20
	Dowel					⅜" dia.
	Flathead wood screw					1¼"
	Pins/nails					¾"/1"

Elevation Detail

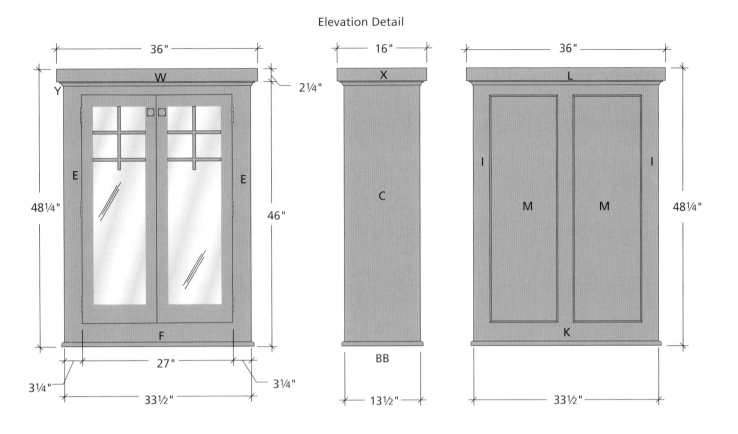

Door Detail

Plan Section Detail

Top Edge Detail

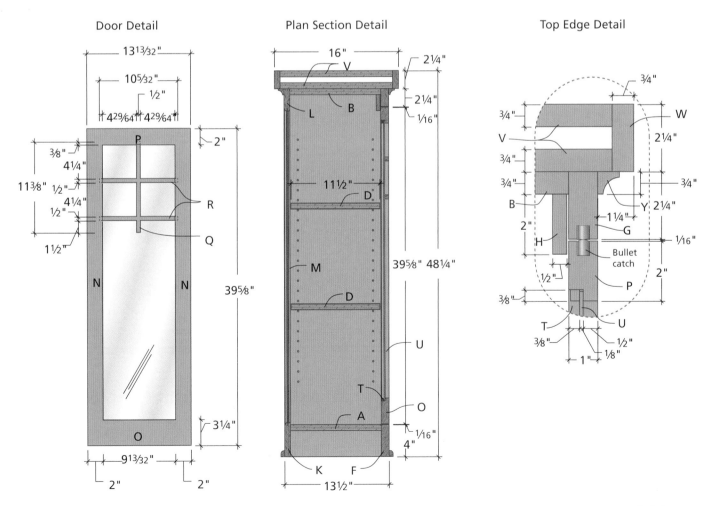

A   Building the Cabinet Carcass

Step 1. Machine the bottom (A), the interior top (B), the ends (C), and the adjustable shelves (D) to size from ¾" plywood.

Step 2. Apply veneer tape to one long edge of each adjustable shelf.

Step 3. Drill ¼" shelf-pin holes in the ends; 25 holes, 1¼" on center, starting 9⅜" from the bottom gives a wide range of adjustability, but you can place the holes differently according to your needs. Mark and drill the holes 1" in from the front and back edges.

Step 4. Lay out and machine the top, bottom, and ends for #20 biscuit slots. The bottom is located 4" from the bottom of the ends, and the top sits flush with the top edges of the ends (see plan section detail).

Step 5. Sand all interior surfaces with 180-grit sandpaper.

Step 6. Insert #20 biscuits and glue and clamp the carcass, making sure front and back edges are flush. Avoid squeezing out any glue on the inside of the cabinet.

B   Building the Face Frame & Attaching It to the Carcass

Step 1. Machine the face frame stiles (E), the face frame bottom rail (F), and the face frame top rail (G) from 1" solid stock.

Step 2. Mark and machine the face frame rails and stiles for ⅜" dowels per the drawing.

Step 3. Dry-assemble the face frame, and verify its fit with the carcass.

Step 4. Mark and machine the front edges of the ends and back faces of the face frame rails and stiles for #20 biscuit slots per the drawing.

Step 5. Insert ¾" dowels and glue and clamp the face frame together. Wipe any glue squeeze-out from the corners. Make sure the face frame is square.

Step 6. Attach the face frame to the carcass with glue and #20 biscuits. Clamp securely.

Step 7. Machine the door stop (H) from ½" solid stock.

Step 8. Attach the doorstop to the top inside face of face frame with 1¼" flathead wood screws (see top edge detail).

C   Building the Back Panel & Attaching It to the Carcass

Step 1. Machine the back panel stiles (I), the back panel middle stile (J), the back panel bottom rail (K), and the back panel top rail (L) from ¾" solid stock.

Step 2. Using a router and a rail-and-stile bit of your choice (round shown), machine all the stiles and rails on one long edge. Machine the back panel middle stile on both edges.

Step 3. Using the opposite profile rail-and-stile bit, route the ends of the rails and of the middle stile.

Step 4. Machine the back panels (M) from ¼" plywood. Sand both faces with

180-grit sandpaper.

Step 5. Insert #20 biscuits and glue and clamp the back panel assembly.

Step 6. Dry-fit the back panel assembly to the carcass back, and mark the backs of the rails and the side stiles and the edges of the top and end for #20 biscuit slots as illustrated in the drawing. Machine the biscuit slots.

Step 7. Glue and clamp back panel assembly to the carcass.

Step 8. Sand all exterior surfaces with 180-grit sandpaper.

D Building & Attaching the Doors

Step 1. Machine the door stiles (N), door bottom rails (O), and door top rails (P) to size from 1" solid stock.

Step 2. On the door stiles and rails, route a ⅜-wide × ½"-deep rabbet on the back inside edge for the glass. On the stiles, the rabbet will be blind.

Step 3. Mark and machine the stiles and rails for ⅜" dowels per the drawing.

Step 4. Machine the door vertical mullions (Q) and the door horizontal mullions (R) to size from ½" solid stock.

Step 5. Use a router to create half-lap joints on the mullions. Refer to the door detail for locations. Note that the vertical mullions fits over the horizontal mullions. Machine ⅜-wide × ½"-deep rabbets on both ends of the horizontal mullions and on the top end of the vertical mullions.

Step 6. Mark and machine the back sides of doors for ⅜-wide × ¼"-deep mortises to fit the mullions. See the door detail for locations. Use a chisel to remove the material. Dry-fit the window mullions.

Step 7. Glue and clamp window mullions to doors.

Step 8. Machine the long glass stop (S) and the short glass stop (T) to size, and fit them to the doors but do not attach. This will be done after the finish has been applied to the cabinet.

Step 9. Attach the hinges to the doors and the cabinet following the hinge manufacturer's specifications.

Step 10. Attach the doors to the cabinet.

Step 11. Mark and machine the tops of the doors and the face frame for bullet catches per the manufacturer's specifications. Install the bullet catches.

E Building & Attaching the Top & Attaching the Moldings

Step 1. Machine the top and bottom panels (V) from ¾" plywood.

Step 2. Machine the long edge (W) and the short edge (X) to width. Miter it and check for fit with the top and bottom panels.

Step 3. Mark and machine the long and short edges and the top and bottom panels for #20 biscuits.

Step 4. Insert #20 biscuits and glue and clamp the edges to the top and bottom panels, making sure the joints are tight.

Step 5. Finish sand the top panel surface, edges, and the perimeter (approximately 2" wide) of the bottom panel with 180-grit sandpaper.

Step 6. Attach the top to the carcass with 1¼" flathead wood screws, driven up from inside the cabinet. There should be a 1¼" overhang on all sides of the cabinet.

Step 7. Miter the long top molding (Y) and the short top molding (Z), and fit them to the cabinet (see top edge detail). Once the fit is tight, attach the moldings with 1" nails.

Step 8. Miter the long base shoe (AA) and the short base shoe (BB), and fit them to the cabinet. Once the fit is tight, attach the base shoes with 1" nails.

F Applying a Finish & Installing Decorative Hardware

Step 1. Do any final sanding with 180-grit sandpaper. If you are using wood knobs, attach them at this time.

Step 2. Apply the finish of your choice. Don't forget to finish the glass stops and the adjustable shelves.

Step 3. After the finish has dried, attach the door knobs if you haven't done so already.

Step 4. Have the glass (U) cut to size.

Step 5. Attach glass to the doors using the glass stops and ¾" nails.

Step 6. Install the adjustable shelves using shelf pins.

Console vanity

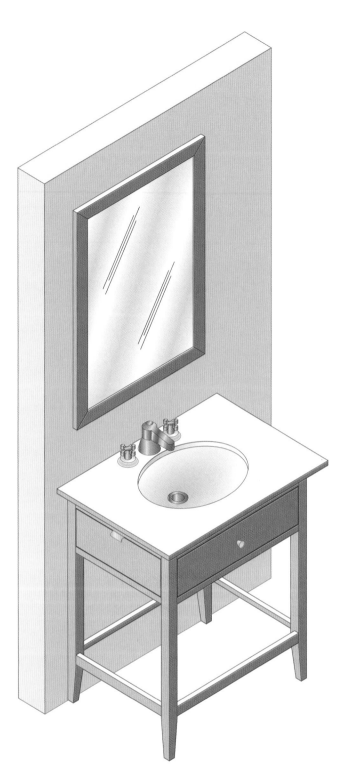

Manufactured bathroom vanities are almost literally a dime a dozen, but unless you shell out for custom work, they don't offer much in the way of choice. For a woodworker, this needn't be an obstacle.

This design allows you to build a stylish and functional vanity with the wood and finish of your choice and with whatever countertop and basin you like—all for a fraction of the cost of a high-end custom model.

By building your own vanity, you can build it to match the rest of the trim in your bathroom. You can also customize the height of the basin for the unique needs of a family member or to fit the bathroom.

The joinery used to build this vanity is basic but strong and well within the reach of most woodworkers. Take extra time and care when laying out and dry-fitting the biscuit and dowel joints on the legs and rails to ensure the finished vanity is square and stable.

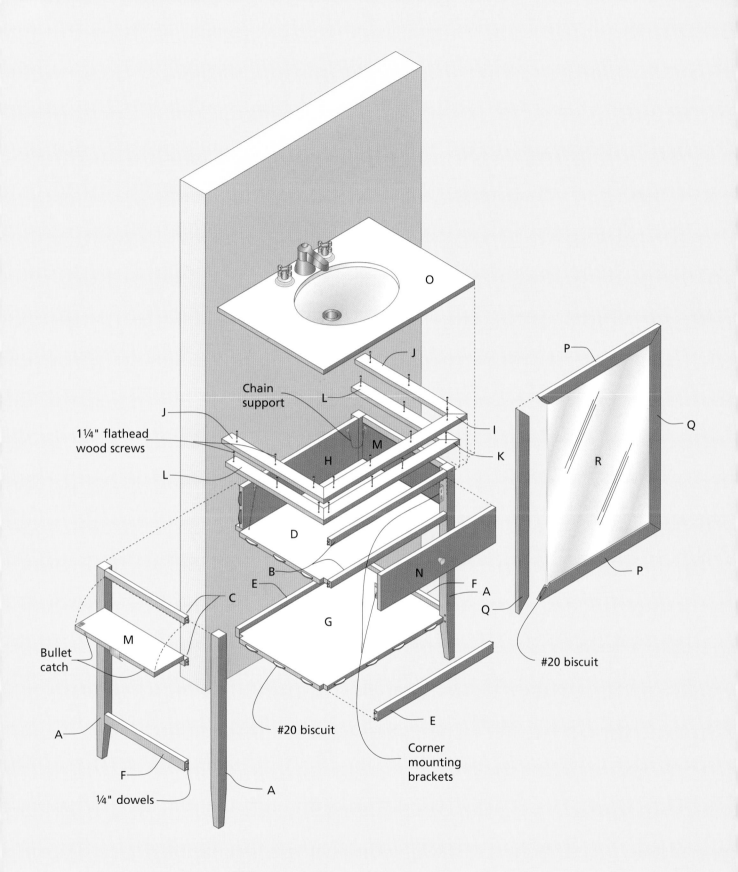

Chain
support

1¼" flathead
wood screws

Bullet
catch

¼" dowels

#20 biscuit

Corner
mounting
brackets

#20 biscuit

J

L

J

L

H

M

D

B

E

C

M

A

F

A

G

E

N

F

A

Q

O

I

K

P

Q

R

P

Shopping List
Total board feet required: 13
Plywood required: ¾ × 48 × 36"
Countertop required: ¾ × 21 × 30"
Mirror required: ¼ × 20⅝ × 30⅝"

Materials List

Key	Part name	Qty.	Thickness	Width	Length	Material
Overall dimensions (30"w × 21"d × 34"h)						
A	Leg	4	1½"	1½"	31¾"	Solid wood or glue-up
B	Front rail	2	¾"	1"	23"	Solid wood
C	End rail	4	¾"	1"	16"	Solid wood
D	Middle shelf	1	¾"	18¼"	24½"	Plywood
E	Front/back bottom rail	2	¾"	1½"	23"	Solid wood
F	End bottom rail	2	¾"	1½"	16"	Solid wood
G	Bottom shelf	1	¾"	17½"	24½"	Plywood
H	Back	1	¾"	7"	23"	Plywood
I	Front upper trim	1	¾"	2"	28½"	Solid wood
J	End upper trim	2	¾"	2"	20¼"	Solid wood
K	Front lower trim	1	¾"	2"	27"	Solid wood
L	End lower trim	2	¾"	2"	19½"	Solid wood
M	Tilt-down front	2	¾"	5⅞"	15⅞"	Solid wood or glue-up
N	Fixed front	1	¾"	5⅞"	22⅞"	Solid wood or glue-up
O	Top	1	¾"	21"	30"	Granite, marble, or engineered stone
Mirror (24"w × 34"h × ¾" thick)						
P	Frame top/bottom	2	¾"	2"	24"	Solid wood
Q	Frame end	2	¾"	2"	34"	Solid wood
R	Mirror	1	¼"	20⅝"	30⅝"	Mirror
Hardware						
	Knob at front	1				
	Pull at sides	2				
	Mirror retaining clip	4				
	Hanging brackets for mirror	2	⅛"	1½"	1⅞"	
	Hinges at tilt-down sides	2 pr.		½"	2⅜"	Soss-style hinge
	Chain support	2				
	Bullet catch	4				
	Corner mounting bracket	2				
	Dowels					¼"-dia.
	Joining biscuit					#20
	Flathead wood screw					1¼"

Mirror Edge Detail

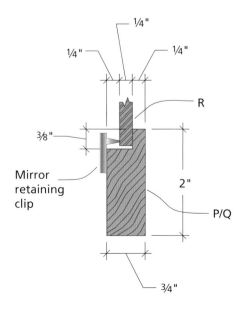

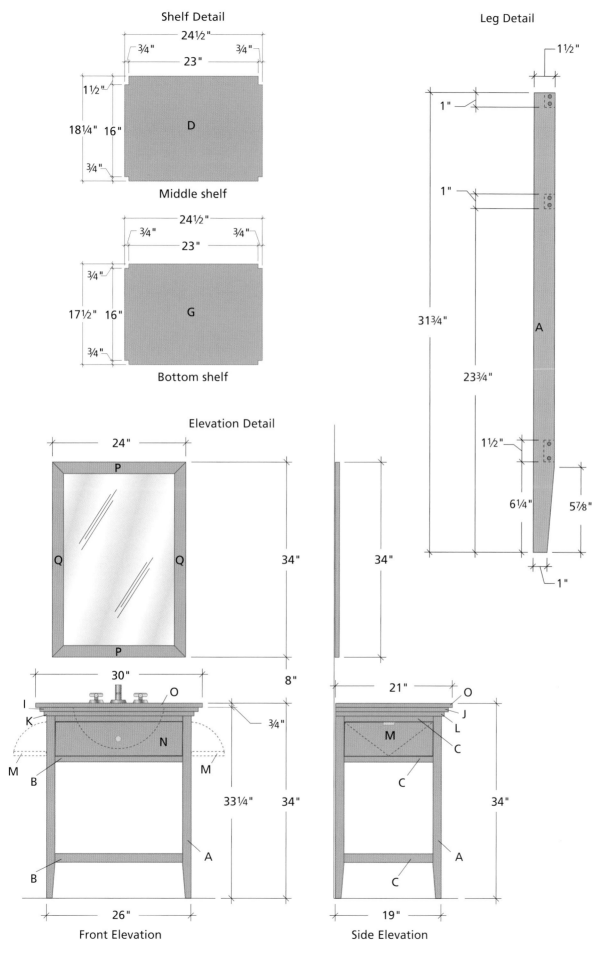

Shelf Detail

24½"
¾" · 23" · ¾"
1½"
18¼" · 16"
¾"

D

Middle shelf

24½"
¾" · 23" · ¾"
¾"
17½" · 16"
¾"

G

Bottom shelf

Leg Detail

1½"
1"
1"
31¾"
23¾"
1½"
6¼" · 5⅞"
A
1"

Elevation Detail

24"
P
Q · **Q**
34"
P
8"

34"

Front Elevation

30"
I
K
O
N
M · **M**
B
¾"
33¼" · 34"
A
B
26"

Side Elevation

21"
O
J
L
M
C
C
34"
A
C
19"

CONSOLE VANITY 227

A Machining the Legs & Assembling the Ends

Step 1. Machine the legs (A) to size.

Step 2. Cut the taper on 2 adjoining faces of each leg (see leg detail).

Step 3. Machine the front rails (B), the end rails (C), the front/back bottom rails (E), and the end bottom rails (F) to size.

Step 4. Mark the legs for rail locations (see leg detail), and machine the legs and the rails for ¼" dowels. All rails are flush with the outside faces of the legs.

Step 5. Machine the middle two end rails for Soss-style hinges per the manufacturer's specifications.

Step 6. Machine the back (H) to size.

Step 7. Mark and machine the back and legs for #20 biscuits per the drawing. The back should be flush with the tops and inside faces of the legs.

Step 8. Dry-fit the entire assembly.

Step 9. Insert #20 biscuits, and clamp and glue the end rails between the legs.

B Machining Shelves & Attaching the Ends

Step 1. Machine the middle shelf (D) and the bottom shelf (G) to size.

Step 2. Notch each of the shelves per the drawing pattern (see shelf detail).

Step 3. Mark and machine the fronts of the shelves and the front and back rails for #20 biscuits. The middle shelf should be flush with the top of the rails, and the bottom shelf should be flush with the bottom of the bottom rails.

Step 4. Insert #20 biscuits, and clamp and glue the front and back rails to the shelves. Only the bottom shelf gets a back rail. Make sure the ends of the rails are flush with the notches.

Step 5. Mark and machine the ends of the shelves and the end rails for #20 biscuits.

Step 6. Dry-fit the whole assembly.

Step 7. Insert #20 biscuits, and glue and clamp the shelves and back to the end assemblies.

Step 8. Using 1¼" flathead wood screws, secure the back to the middle shelf.

Step 9. Sand using 120-grit sandpaper.

C Machining Fixed Front & Tilt-down Sides

Step 1. Machine the tilt-down sides (M) and the fixed front (N) to size.

Step 2. Check fit. There should be an even ¹⁄₁₆" reveal at each front.

Step 3. Sand using 120-grit sandpaper.

Step 4. Attach the fixed front using corner mounting brackets.

Step 5. Machine the tilt-down fronts for Soss-style hinges per manufacturer's specifications. Make sure they align with the end rails previously machined.

Step 6. Drill the top of the tilt-down fronts for bullet catches per the manufacturer's specifications.

Step 7. Drill the fronts for drawer pulls. A pull mortised into the top of the tilt-down front is shown.

Step 8. Fit the tilt-down fronts to the console vanity. Attach support chains to the back and the tilt-down fronts.

D   Machining the Top Trim

Step 1. Machine the front lower trim (K) and the end lower trim (L) to width, leaving slightly long for miters.

Step 2. The lower trim sits flush with the back and overhangs the ends and front by ½". Cut miters and attach to the legs and top rails with 1¼" flathead wood screws. Use glue at miters.

Step 3. Machine the front upper trim (I) and the end upper trim (J) to width, leaving slightly long for miters.

Step 4. The upper trim sits flush with the back and overhangs the lower trim by ¾". Cut miters and attach to lower trim with 1¼" flathead wood screws. Use glue at miters.

E   Building the Mirror

Step 1. Machine the frame top/bottom (P) and the frame ends (Q) to width, leaving slightly long to fit miters.

Step 2. Machine a ⅜"-wide × ½"-deep rabbet on one edge of each piece (see mirror edge detail).

Step 3. Miter pieces to make a frame with outside measurements of 24 × 34".

Step 4. Machine each miter for a #20 biscuit.

Step 5. Dry-fit, and check for square. Insert #20 biscuits, and glue and clamp together, making sure miters are tight.

Step 6. Sand with 120-grit sandpaper.

F   Sanding, Assembling & Finishing

Step 1. Finish sand all parts with 180-grit sandpaper.

Step 2. Apply a finish.

Step 3. After the finish has dried, attach decorative hardware.

Step 4. Have a countertop (O) cut from the material of your choice. At the same time, select your sink and have a cut-out made for it in the countertop.

Step 5. Attach the top to the vanity using silicone. Make sure the silicone is dry before moving vanity.

Step 6. Have a mirror (R) cut to size.

Step 7. Attach the mirror to the frame using mirror retaining clips.

Step 8. Attach hanging brackets to the mirror and wall. Mount the mirror to wall. Position the vanity and connect fixtures and plumbing.

Entertainment center

Most manufactured entertainment centers are either outrageously expensive or poorly designed and constructed. This attractive cabinet-style design is neither. High-quality materials and strong joinery guarantee a solid piece of furniture to house your television and other electronics.

Little details like pocket doors that disappear completely within the frame, adjustable component shelves, and three drawers spacious enough for 180 CDs and DVDs have all been included in the design.

The television compartment will accommodate most screens up to 27 inches (larger for LCD- or plasma-type screens), but be sure to measure your television before you build. You can always adjust the plan drawings to accommodate a larger screen size.

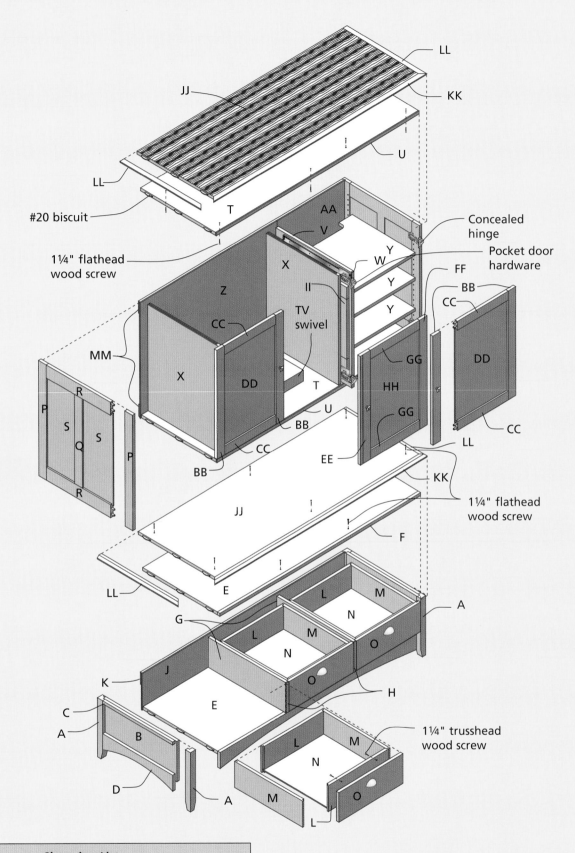

LL

KK

JJ

U

#20 biscuit

1¼" flathead wood screw

T

AA

V

X

Z

II

CC

TV swivel

MM

X

DD

T

U

BB

CC

BB

P

R

S

Q

S

R

P

Concealed hinge

Pocket door hardware

Y

W

Y

Y

FF

BB

CC

DD

GG

HH

GG

EE

CC

LL

KK

JJ

1¼" flathead wood screw

F

LL

E

G

L

M

N

A

L

M

N

O

K

J

L

M

N

E

O

H

C

A

B

D

A

L

M

N

M

O

L

1¼" trusshead wood screw

Shopping List
Total board feet required: 30
Plywood required: ¼ × 48 × 96"
Plywood required: ¼ × 48 × 60"
Plywood required: ¾ × 48 × 96" (3 required)
Black melamine required: ¾ × 48 × 72"
Veneer tape required: ⅞" × 35'

Materials List					
Key	Part name	Qty.	Thickness	Width	Length	Material
Overall dimensions (63½"w x 24"d x 45"h)						
Lower cabinet (63"w x 23¾"d x 14¾"h)						
A	Leg	4	1½"	1½"	14¾"	Solid wood or glue-up
B	Lower side panel	2	¾"	21¾"	10"	Plywood
C	Lower side rail - top	2	¾"	¾"	20¾"	Solid wood
D	Lower side rail - bottom	2	¾"	4"	20¾"	Solid wood
E	Lower top/bottom	2	¾"	22¼"	60"	Plywood or black melamine
F	Lower top edge	1	¾"	⅞" *	61" *	Solid wood
G	Lower vertical divider	2	¾"	22¾"	7½"	Plywood or black melamine
H	Vertical divider edge	2	¾"	⅞" *	8" *	Solid wood
I	Lower front rail	1	¾"	4"	60"	Solid wood
J	Lower back	1	¼"	9"	60½"	Plywood
K	Lower nailing cleat	2	½"	3"	60"	Scrap
Drawer box - 3 @ (19"w x 21"l x 6½"h)						
L	Drawer box front/back	6	¾"	6½"	18¼"	Plywood w/ veneer edge or black melamine
M	Drawer box side	6	¾"	6½"	21"	Plywood w/ veneer edge or black melamine
N	Drawer bottom	3	¼"	20"	18"	Plywood or black melamine
O	Drawer front	3	¾"	7⅜"	19⅜"	Solid wood or glue-up
Upper cabinet (62"w x 23¼"d x 28¾"h)						
Upper side panel 23¼"w x 28¾"h x ¾"thick)						
P	Upper side stile	4	¾"	2¼"	28¾"	Solid wood
Q	Upper side middle stile	2	¾"	2¼"	22¼"	Solid wood
R	Upper side rail	4	¾"	3¼"	18¾"	Solid wood
S	Upper side panel	4	¼"	9"	23"	Plywood
T	Upper top/bottom	2	¾"	22¼"	60½"	Plywood
U	Upper top/bottom edge	2	¼"	⅞" *	61" *	Solid wood
V	Upper vertical divider	1	¾"	22¼"	27¼"	Plywood
W	Vertical divider edge	1	¼"	⅞" *	28" *	Solid wood
X	TV partition	2	¾"	21¼"	27³⁄₁₆"	Plywood w/ veneer edge
Y	Adjustable shelf	3	¾"	21"	19½"	Plywood w/ veneer edge
Z	Back - left	1	¼"	40⅝"	28¾"	Plywood
AA	Back - right	1	¼"	20⅜"	28¾"	Plywood
Door "a" - 2 @ (19⅝"w x 27⅛"h x ¾"thick)						
BB	Door "a" stile	4	¾"	2¼"	27⅛"	Solid wood
CC	Door "a" rail	4	¾"	2¼"	15⅛"	Solid wood
DD	Door "a" panel	2	¼"	15⅞"	23⅜"	Plywood
Door "b" - 1 @ (20³⁄₁₆"w x 27⅛"h x ¾"thick)						
EE	Door "b" left stile	1	¾"	3¹⁄₁₆"	27⅛"	Solid wood
FF	Door "b" right stile	1	¾"	2¼"	27⅛"	Solid wood
GG	Door "b" rail	2	¾"	2¼"	14⅞"	Solid wood
HH	Door "b" panel	1	¼"	15⅝"	23⅜"	Plywood
II	Follower strip	2	¾"	3"	22¾"	Solid wood
Lower/upper top (24"w x 63½"l x ¾"thick)						
JJ	Horizontal panel	2	¾"	23¼"	62"	Plywood
KK	Horizontal edge - long	2	¾"	1¼"	63½"	Solid wood
LL	Horizontal edge - short	4	¾"	1¼"	24"	Solid wood
MM	Upper nailing cleat	4	½"	3"	60½"	Scrap
*Indicates oversized part.						
Hardware						
	Drawer slides	3 pr.				
	Pocket door slides	1 set			20"	
	Pocket door hinge set	2				
	Door hinge	2				
	TV swivel (no platform needed)	1	2¾"	25½"	14½"	
	Door knob	3	¹³⁄₁₆"	1"	1"	
	Drawer pull	3		3"	⅞"	
	Shelf pin	12				
	Dowels					⅜" diameter
	Joining biscuit					#20
	Flathead wood screw					1¼"
	Trusshead wood screw					1¼"

Elevation Detail

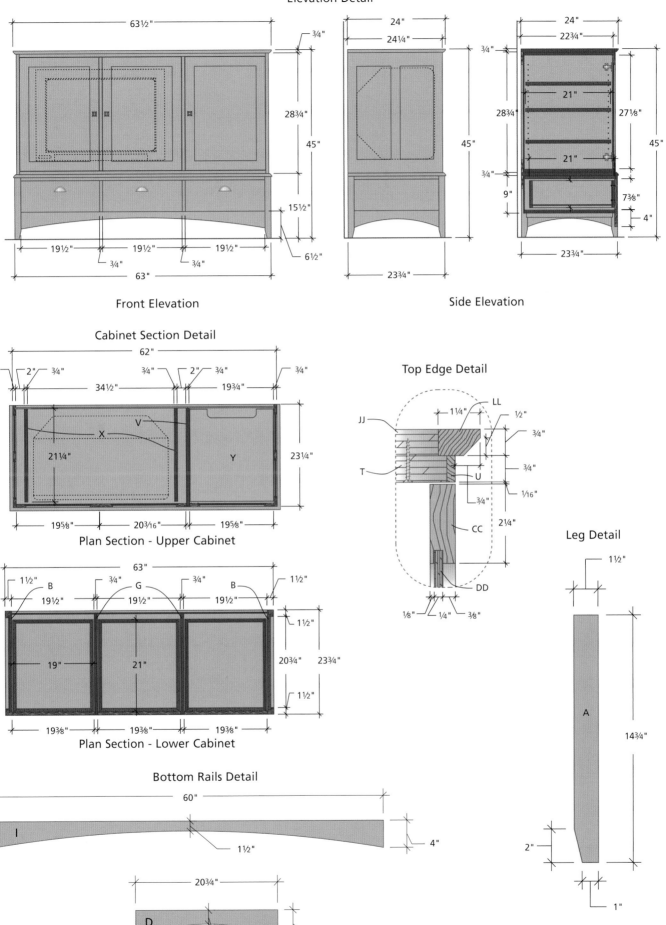

Front Elevation

Side Elevation

Cabinet Section Detail

Top Edge Detail

Plan Section - Upper Cabinet

Leg Detail

Plan Section - Lower Cabinet

Bottom Rails Detail

ENTERTAINMENT CENTER 233

A Constructing the Lower Unit Carcass

Step 1. If necessary, glue up leg stock, and machine legs (A) to size.

Step 2. On each leg, create taper at the bottom on two inside faces (see leg detail).

Step 3. Route a ¾-wide × ½"-deep rabbet on the inside edge of each leg for the lower side panel. The rabbets should extend down 10" from the top of each leg.

Step 4. Machine a ¼ × ¼" dado for the lower back on the inside faces of the two back legs. The dado should be ½" in from the back edge and extend down 9" from the top of the leg.

Step 5. Cut the lower side panels (B) to size from ¾" plywood.

Step 6. Fit the lower side panels into the leg rabbets, and attach them with 1¼" flathead wood screws, making sure the tops are flush.

Step 7. Machine the top lower side rails (C) and the bottom lower side rails (D) from ¾" solid stock.

Step 8. Cut arcs on the bottom lower side rails (see bottom rails detail).

Step 9. Glue and clamp the rails between the legs. The top of the bottom rail should be 6½" from the bottom of the leg.

Step 10. Cut the lower top and bottom (E) and the vertical dividers (G) to size from ¾" plywood.

Step 11. Machine to size edging for the entire project: lower top edge (F), lower vertical divider edges (H), upper top and bottom edges (U), and upper vertical divider edge (W). Edging is oversized in both width and length for trimming after it has been applied. All pieces are ¼" thick except for the lower top edge which is ¾" thick.

Step 12. Glue and clamp edges to the lower top and the lower vertical divider. After the glue has dried, trim the top, bottom, and ends flush.

Step 13. Lay out the vertical divider locations on the top and bottom (see cabinet section detail).

Step 14. Machine the lower bottom and the lower side rails for #20 biscuits per the drawing.

Step 15. Drill pilot holes in the lower top and bottom for screwing in vertical dividers.

Step 16. Insert #20 biscuits, glue, screw, and clamp the carcass together.

Step 17. Cut the front rail (I) to size from ¾" solid stock.

Step 18. Cut the arc on the front rail (see bottom rails detail).

Step 19. Mark and machine the front edge of the lower bottom and the back face of the front rail for #20 biscuits.

Step 20. Insert #20 biscuits and glue and clamp the front rail to the carcass.

Step 21. Cut the lower back (J) to size from ¼" plywood.

Step 22. Attach the lower back to the carcass by sliding it into the leg dados and screwing 1" flathead wood screws into the lower top, bottom, and vertical dividers. Make sure carcass is square.

Step 23. Machine the nailing cleat (K) to size, and attach it at the top of the carcass using hot-melt glue or panel adhesive.

Step 24. Finish sand the exterior surfaces using 180-grit sandpaper.

B Building & Attaching the Drawers

Step 1. From ¾" plywood, cut the drawer box fronts and backs (L) and drawer box sides (M) to size.

Step 2. Apply veneer tape to the top edge of each piece.

Step 3. Route a ⅜" × ⅜" rabbet in the inside edge of the ends of each piece.

Step 4. Machine a ¼ × ¼" dado ½" up from the bottom inside edge. This ½" is critical since the drawers use bottom-mount slides.

Step 5. Cut the drawer bottoms (N) from ¼" plywood.

Step 6. Glue and screw all the drawer boxes together using 1¼" flathead wood screws driven through the front and back. Turn the drawer box over and run a bead of hot-melt glue between the drawer sides, front, and back and the drawer bottom.

Step 7. If necessary, glue up solid stock for the drawer fronts (O) and machine them to size.

Step 8. Attach each drawer front to a drawer box using 1¼" trusshead wood screws. Drawer fronts should extend ½" below the drawer box and should be centered from side to side.

Step 9. Following manufacturer's specifications, do any additional machining for the drawer slides, and attach them to the drawer box and cabinet.

Step 10. Check the fit of the drawer fronts, and adjust as needed to create a uniform 1⁄16" reveal.

C Machining the Upper Frame & the Panel Sides

Step 1. Machine the upper side stiles (P), upper side middle stiles (Q), and upper side rails (R) to size from ¾" solid stock.

Step 2. Machine a ¼-wide × ⅜"-deep dado on the edge ⅜" in from the front face on one long edge of each piece, except for the middle stile which gets both edges machined. Stop the dado approximately 1" from the ends of the upper side stiles.

Step 3. Mark and machine the upper stiles and rails for ⅜" dowels. You should be able to get two dowels in the end of each piece.

Step 4. Cut the upper side panels (S) to size from ¼" plywood.

Step 5. Dry-fit the upper side frame and panel assemblies, and check for square.

Step 6. Insert the dowels, and glue and clamp the upper side frame assemblies together, minimizing glue squeeze-out on the inside corners by the panels.

Step 7. Machine a ¼ × ¼" deep dado for the back of each panel ½" in from the back edge.

Step 8. On the inside face of the right panel, drill holes for ¼" shelf pins; 19 holes, 1¼" on center, 1¾" in from the edges is a useful spacing, but you can modify the plan to suit your electronics.

Step 9. Finish sand the frame and panel assemblies using 180-grit sandpaper.

D Machining the Upper Frame & the Panel Doors

Step 1. Machine the A-door stiles (BB), A-door rails (CC), B-door left stile (EE), B-door right stile (FF,) and B-door rails (GG) to size from ¾" solid stock.

Step 2. Machine a ¼-wide × ⅜"-deep dado on one long edge of each piece, ⅜" in from the front face (see top edge detail). Stop the dado approximately 1" from the ends of the door stiles.

Step 3. Machine a ¹⁄₁₆ × ¹⁄₁₆" dado on the B-door left stile, ¾" in from the left edge. This reveal is designed to align with the reveal in the lower carcass between the vertical divider and the drawer.

Step 4. Mark and machine all the door stiles and rails for ⅜" dowels. You should be able to get two dowels in the end of each piece.

Step 5. Cut the A-door panels (DD) and B-door panel (HH) to size from ¼" plywood.

Step 6. Dry-fit the door frames and panels.

Step 7. Insert the dowels and glue and clamp the doors together, minimizing glue squeeze-out on the inside corners by the panels.

Step 8. Finish sand doors using 180-grit sandpaper.

E   Constructing the Upper Unit Carcass

Step 1. Machine the upper top and bottom (T), upper vertical divider (V), TV partitions (X), and adjustable shelves (Y) to size from ¾" plywood.

Step 2. Mark and drill holes for ¼" shelf pins in the upper vertical divider. Make sure the markings match up with the holes in the right upper side panel.

Step 3. Glue and clamp edges to the upper top and bottom and upper vertical divider. After the glue has dried, trim the top, bottom, and ends flush.

Step 4. Create a wire chase at the back of adjustable shelves. The illustration show a 2"-wide slot, 4" in from the ends and with rounded corners, but you can adjust this for your needs.

Step 5. Apply veneer edging to the front edges of the TV partitions and adjustable shelves. Finish sand all parts with 180-grit sandpaper.

Step 6. Lay out the TV partitions and upper vertical divider locations on the upper top and bottom (see cabinet section detail). For the TV partitions only, the biscuits will only be glued in the top and bottom and will act as guides for the the TV partitions. The TV partitions will have a continuous groove on their ends (blind in the front edge). The TV partitions are slightly undersized and will be removable in case you need to get at the pocket door hardware.

Step 7. Machine the upper top and bottom and the upper divider for 4 #20 biscuits per the drawing. Machine a blind dado slightly wider than the width of your biscuits in the top and bottom edges of the TV partitions. The dado should stop 1" from the front edge. Dry-fit #20 biscuits and make sure the partition slides freely. Machine a ¾" deep, 10"-long cable chase in the back edge of the right TV partition

Step 8. Drill pilot holes in the top and bottom for screwing in the vertical divider.

Step 9. Finish sand all the interior surfaces with 180-grit sandpaper.

Step 10. Insert #20 biscuits, glue, screw, and clamp the carcass together.

Step 11. Machine the left back (Z) and the right back (AA) to size from ¼" plywood.

Step 12. Attach the backs to the carcass by sliding them into the dados and screwing 1" flathead wood screws into the upper top, bottom, and vertical divider. The backs should meet on the vertical divider. Make sure the carcass is square.

Step 13. Machine the upper nailing cleats (MM) to size and attach them at the top and bottom of carcass using either hot-melt glue or panel adhesive.

F   Attaching Interior Fittings & Assembling the Cabinet

Step 1. Cut the horizontal panels (JJ) to size from ¾" plywood.

Step 2. Machine the long horizontal edges (KK) and the short horizontal edges (LL) to size from ¾" solid stock, leaving extra length so you can fit the miters around the horizontal panels.

Step 3. Miter the edging around the horizontal panels.

Step 4. Mark and machine for the edging and the horizontal panels for #20 biscuits.

Step 5. Insert #20 biscuits, and glue and clamp the edging to the horizontal panels.

Step 6. Finish sand the top and bottom surfaces with 180-grit sandpaper.

Step 7. Route a ½ × ½" chamfer on the bottom of the upper horizontal panel edge and the top of the lower horizontal panel edge.

Step 8. Attach the lower horizontal panel to the lower carcass with 1¼" flathead wood screws per the drawing. The panel should be flush in the back and overhang the sides and the front by ¼".

Step 9. Attach the upper carcass to the lower horizontal panel with 1¼" flathead wood screws driven through the bottom of the upper carcass. The upper carcass should be flush in the back and have a ¾" overhang on the front and sides.

Step 10. Attach the upper horizontal panel to the upper carcass with 1¼" flathead wood screws, driven through the top of the upper carcass. The upper horizontal panel should be flush in the back and overhang the upper carcass on the sides and front by ¾".

Step 11. Drill holes in the upper backs as necessary for power cables.

G   Applying the Finish & Installing the Decorative Hardware

Step 1. Do any final sanding using 180-grit sandpaper, and apply the finish of your choice.

Step 2. After the finish has dried, attach the door knobs and drawer pulls.

Step 3. Install the pocket door hardware. Machine follower strips (II) to size per hardware manufacturer's specifications.

Step 4. Install the hinges for the far right door per the manufacturer's specifications.

Step 5. Attach all the doors.

Step 6. Slide in the TV partitions.

Step 7. Follow manufacturer's instructions and attach a TV swivel to the cabinet.

Step 8. Install the adjustable shelves using shelf pins.

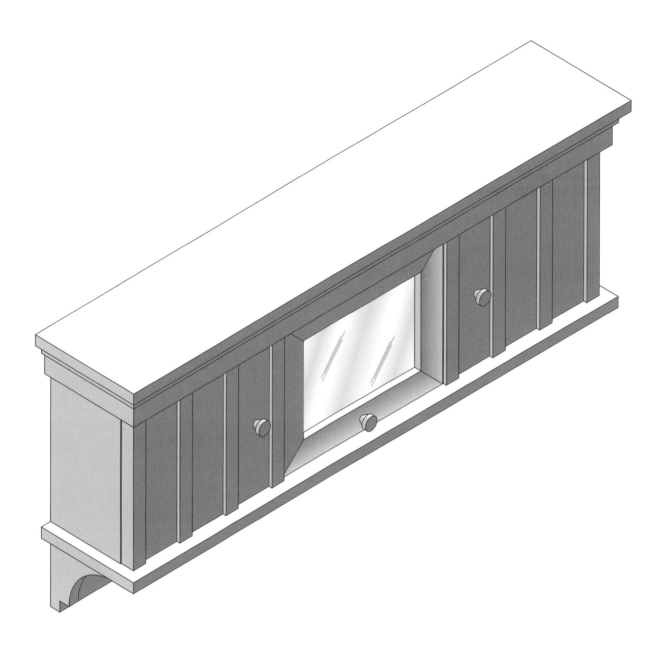

Entry cabinet

The simplicity of this small piece of cabinetry belies its usefulness. Placed in an entryway or back hall, it's an attractive and formidable clutter-fighting catchall for keys, cell phones, sunglasses, hats, bags, and jackets. And the mirror in the center door gives you one last chance to avoid heading off to the lumberyard with your safety glasses on and sawdust in your hair.

The materials and the space required for this piece are minimal, making it an ideal project for a smaller work-space. If assembled from inexpensive softwood and ply-wood stock, it's an excellent piece for a beginning woodworker. More advanced woodworkers can make this cabinet a showpiece for their craft by selecting wood with distinctive grain and figure for the facing pieces or by getting creative with tinted finishes.

Instead of a mirror, you might want to include a piece of cork, chalkboard, or dry-erase board for leaving messages.

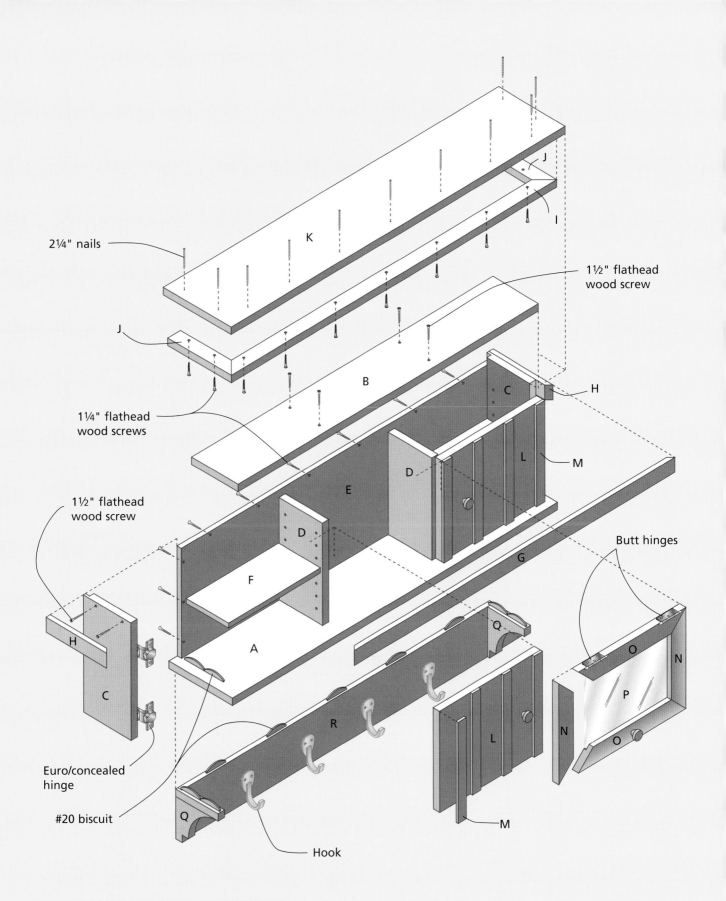

2¼" nails

1½" flathead wood screw

1¼" flathead wood screws

1½" flathead wood screw

Euro/concealed hinge

#20 biscuit

Hook

Butt hinges

K

J

I

B

J

C

H

D

E

D

L

M

F

G

A

H

C

Q

Q

O

N

R

P

O

L

N

M

Materials List						
Key	Part name	Qty.	Thickness	Width	Length	Material
Overall dimensions (40"w × 8"d × 19"h)						
A	Bottom	1	¾"	7½"	39"	Solid wood or glue-up
B	Interior top	1	¾"	6¼"	36"	Solid wood or glue-up
C	End	2	¾"	5¹¹⁄₁₆"	11¾"	Solid wood or glue-up
D	Vertical divider	2	¾"	5³⁄₁₆"	10¼"	Solid wood or glue-up
E	Back	1	½"	37"	11½"	Solid wood or plywood
F	Adjustable shelf	2	½"	5"	11"	Solid wood or plywood
G	Lower trim—front	1	½"	1½"	38½"	Solid wood
H	Lower trim—end	2	½"	1½"	7¼"	Solid wood
I	Upper trim—front	1	¾"	1½"	39"	Solid wood
J	Upper trim—end	2	¾"	1½"	7½"	Solid wood
K	Top	1	¾"	8"	40"	Solid wood or glue-up
End door (12¼"w × 10⅛"h × 1" thick)						
L	Door panel	2	¾"	12¼"	10⅛"	Solid wood or glue-up
M	Door batten	8	¼"	1"	10⅛"	Solid wood
Middle door (12⅞"w × 10⅛"h × ¾" thick)						
N	Mirror door stile	2	¾"	1¾"	10⅛"	Solid wood
O	Mirror door rail	2	¾"	1¾"	12⅞"	Solid wood
P	Mirror	1	¼"	10"	7¼"	Beveled mirror
Q	Bracket	2	¾"	5"	5"	Solid wood
R	Bracket back	1	½"	5"	37"	Solid wood or plywood
Hardware						
	Hinges—end doors	4				
	Hinges—middle door	2				
	Hooks	4				
	Mirror retaining clips	4				
	Shelf pins	8				¼" dia.
	Knobs	3				
	Flathead wood screws					1¼", 1½"
	Nails/pins					2¼"
	Joining biscuits					#20

Mirror Frame Detail

Bracket Detail

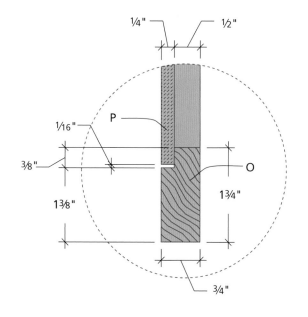

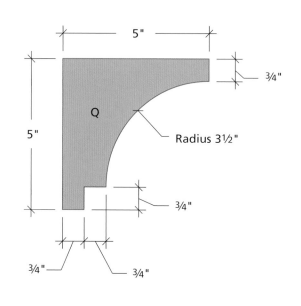

Front Detail

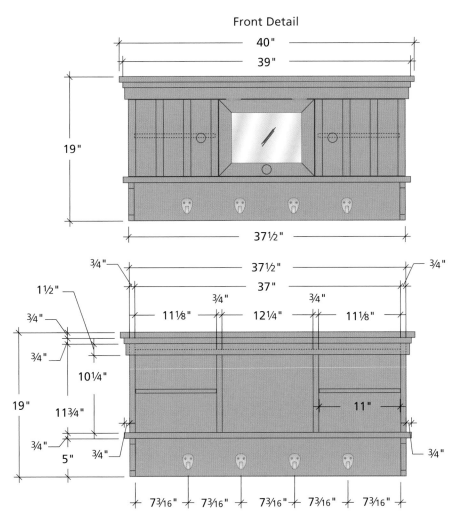

40"

39"

19"

37½"

¾"   37½"   ¾"

37"

1½"

¾"   11⅛"   ¾"   12¼"   ¾"   11⅛"

¾"

10¼"

19"

11"

11¾"

¾"

5"   ¾"   ¾"

7³⁄₁₆"   7³⁄₁₆"   7³⁄₁₆"   7³⁄₁₆"   7³⁄₁₆"

Side Detail

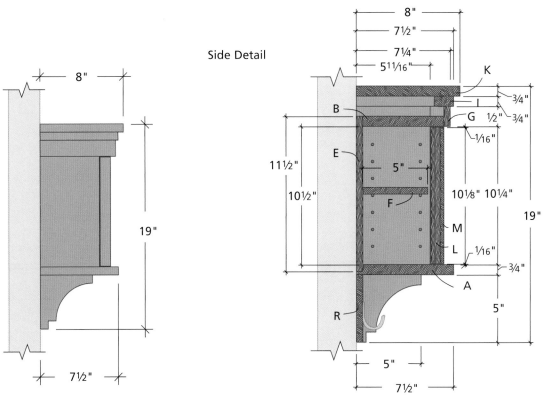

8"

8"

7½"

7¼"

5¹¹⁄₁₆"

K

B   G   ¾"

11½"   E   ½"   ¾"

10½"   1/16"

5"   10⅛" 10¼"   19"

F

M

L   1/16"

A   ¾"

19"   R   5"

7½"   5"

7½"

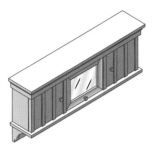

A Building the Cabinet Carcass

Step 1. Machine the bottom (A), the interior top (B), the ends (C), and the vertical dividers (D) to size from ¾″ solid stock. On the wider parts, glue up as needed.

Step 2. Machine a ½ × ½″ rabbet on the back inside edge of each end.

Step 3. Drill ¼″ shelf pin holes in the ends and the vertical dividers. A good spacing is 7 holes, 1¼″ on center and ¾″ in from the front and back edges. Lay out all the holes from the bottom edge of the part. Only drill holes on one face of each vertical divider.

Step 4. Lay out the end and vertical divider locations on the bottom, and machine for #20 biscuits (see front detail). You should be able to get two biscuits in each part.

Step 5. Lay out and drill pilot holes in the interior top and the ends per the drawing.

Step 6. Dry-fit all the pieces, and screw together. Drill pilot holes for screws if using hardwoods. Check for square.

Step 7. Disassemble and finish sand all interior surfaces with 180-grit sandpaper.

Step 8. Glue, screw, and clamp the carcass together, making sure you hold the vertical dividers ½" in from the back edge.

Step 9. Machine the back (E) and adjustable shelves (F) from ½" solid stock or from plywood (veneer the front edges of the shelves if you use plywood). Finish sand with 180-grit sandpaper.

Step 10. Fit the back to the carcass, and drill pilot holes into the ends, the interior top, and the vertical dividers. Attach with 1¼" screws.

Step 11. Machine the lower front trim (G) and lower end trim (H) to width from solid stock. Miter to fit, then glue and clamp to the carcass, making sure the trim is flush with the top edges.

B Building the Top & Attaching It to the Carcass

Step 1. Machine the top (K) from ¾" solid stock. Glue up stock if necessary to obtain width.

Step 2. Machine the upper front trim (I) and the upper end trim (J) to width from ¾" solid stock.

Step 3. Miter the pieces to fit around the bottom face of the top, creating a ½" reveal at the front and the sides.

Step 4. Attach the upper trim pieces to top with 1¼" flathead wood screws. Keep the screws 1" back from the front edge of the upper trim pieces.

Step 5. Attach the top assembly to the carcass using 2¼" nails. Drill pilot holes if using hardwoods. Nails should be driven 1" in from the front and side edges so they go into the center of the lower trim pieces.

C Building the Bottom Bracket Assembly & Attaching It to the Carcass

Step 1. Using the drawing provided, machine the brackets (Q) to shape (see bracket detail).

Step 2. Machine a ½ × ½" rabbet on the back inside vertical edge of each bracket.

Step 3. Machine the bracket back (R) to size. Note that the grain is running horizontally on this piece. If you used plywood earlier, then do the same here and veneer the bottom edge.

Step 4. Attach the bracket back to the brackets using 1¼" flathead wood screws. Drill pilot holes if using hardwoods.

Step 5. Mark and machine the bracket assembly and the carcass for #20 biscuits per the drawing.

Step 6. Insert #20 biscuits, and glue and clamp the bracket assembly to the carcass.

D Building & Attaching the Doors

Step 1. Machine the door panels (L) to size from solid stock. Glue up if necessary to obtain width. Sand the panels with 180-grit sandpaper.

Step 2. Machine the battens (M) to size from ¼" solid stock.

Step 3. Glue and clamp the battens to the door panels. There should be 2¾" between the battens.

Step 4. Per manufacturer's specifications, machine the sides for European-style hinges. Make sure the hinges used are for a full-overlay application.

Step 5. Attach the end doors to the cabinet.

Step 6. Machine the mirror door stiles (N) and the mirror door rails (O) to width from ¾" solid stock, keeping extra length to fit miters.

Step 7. Machine a ⅜-wide × ¼"-deep rabbet in the stiles and rails for the mirror (see mirror fram detail).

Step 8. Cut miters in the rails and stiles and fit the pieces together, making a 12⅞ × 10⅛" door.

Step 9. Attach the hinges to the door and the cabinet following the manufacturer's specifications. Attach the door to the cabinet.

E Applying a Finish & Installing Decorative Hardware

Step 1. Do any final sanding with 180-grit sandpaper. If you are using wood knobs, attach them at this time.

Step 2. Apply the finish of your choice to cabinet and the adjustable shelves.

Step 3. After the finish has dried, attach door knobs if you haven't done so already.

Step 4. Have the mirror (P) cut to size. Attach the mirror to the mirror door using flush-mount retainers.

Step 5. Attach the hooks to the cabinet (see front detail).

Step 6. Install the adjustable shelves using shelf pins.

Freestanding mirror

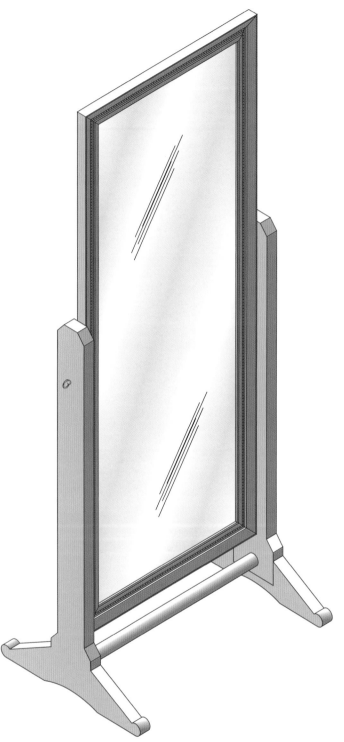

Freestanding tilting mirrors, also known as cheval mirrors, are not often seen in homes today. This is a pity, because they are both attractive and quite useful.

This mirror is simple in its design, and although the project requires only a small amount of lumber, the end result is substantial and attractive.

Machining and assembling the mirror frame will challenge your tool and layout skills, and careful work with the router and table saw in creating and shaping the molding pieces will reflect well on you in the end.

Almost any wood will work well in this project, though you may wish to choose stock based on the varieties of rope molding you can find. You can also add detail to the piece by using beveled mirror glass, though this will likely triple the cost of the mirror glass.

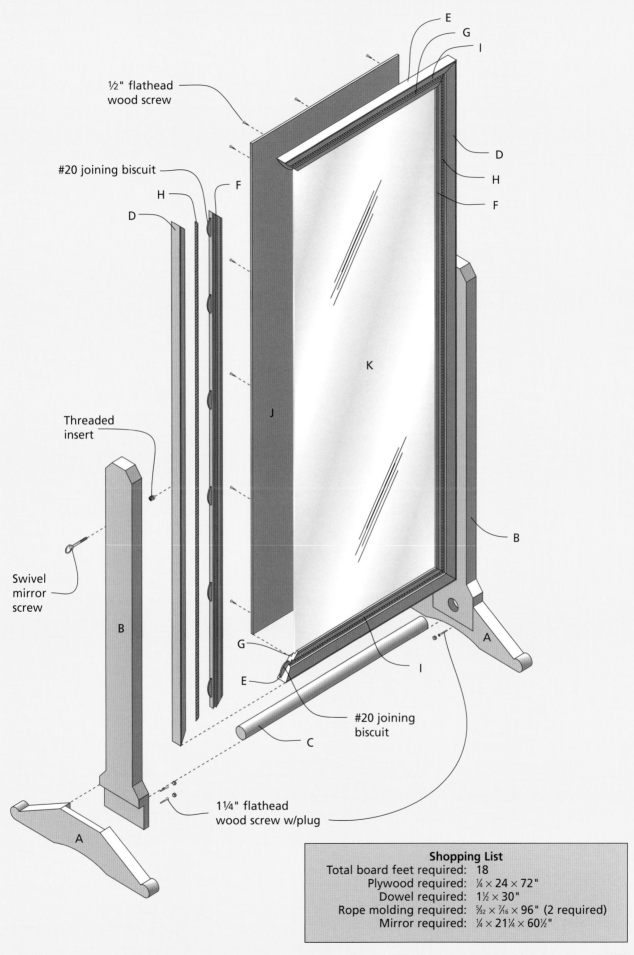

½" flathead
wood screw

#20 joining biscuit

Threaded
insert

Swivel
mirror
screw

E

G

I

D

H

F

F

H

D

B

J

K

B

A

G

E

#20 joining
biscuit

C

I

A

1¼" flathead
wood screw w/plug

Shopping List
Total board feet required: 18
Plywood required: ¼ × 24 × 72"
Dowel required: 1½ × 30"
Rope molding required: ⁵⁄₃₂ × ⁷⁄₁₆ × 96" (2 required)
Mirror required: ¼ × 21¼ × 60½"

Materials List

Key	Part name	Qty.	Thickness	Width	Length	Material
Overall dimensions (29"w × 21"d × 72"h)						
A	Foot	2	1½"	4¾"	21"	Solid wood or glue-up
B	Upright	2	1½"	6"	44¼"	Solid wood or glue-up
C	Dowel	1	1½" diameter	27½"	solid wood	
D	Long outer molding	2	1¼"	1¼"	66" *	Solid wood
E	Short outer molding	2	1¼"	1¼"	27" *	Solid wood
F	Long inner molding	2	⅞"	1³⁄₁₆"	66" *	Solid wood
G	Short inner molding	2	⅞"	1³⁄₁₆"	27" *	Solid wood
H	Long rope molding	2	⁵⁄₃₂"	⁷⁄₁₆"	66" *	Rope molding
I	Short rope molding	2	⁵⁄₃₂"	⁷⁄₁₆"	27" *	Rope molding
J	Mirror backer	1	¼"	22⅛"	61⅜"	Plywood
K	Mirror	1	¼"	21¼"	60½"	Mirror
* indicates oversized length. Miter to fit after combining inner and outer moldings.						
Hardware						
	Swivel mirror screws w/ inserts	1 pr.	⅜" dia.		2⅝"	
	Wood plugs		⅜" dia.			
	Joining biscuits				#20	
	Flathead wood screws				½", 1¼"	
	Nylon washers	4				

Frame Molding Detail

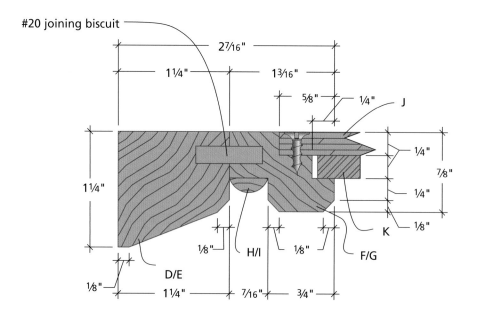

Elevation Detail

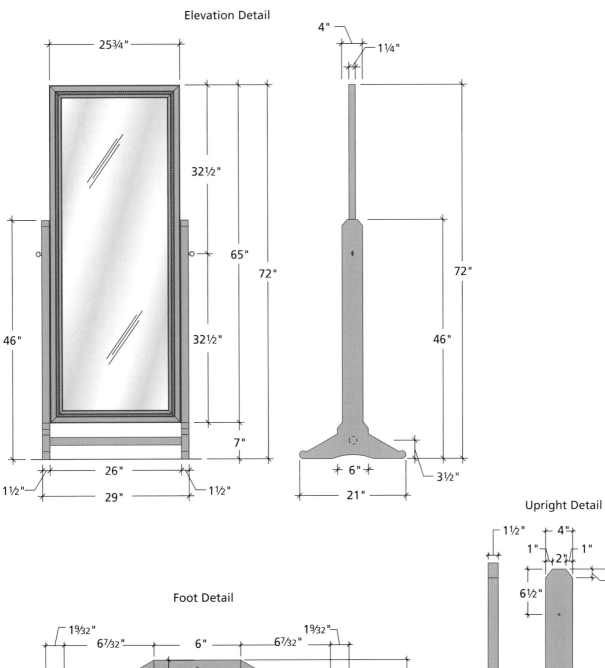

25¾"

32½"

65"

72"

46"

32½"

7"

26"

29"

1½"   1½"

4"

1¼"

72"

46"

6"

21"

3½"

Foot Detail

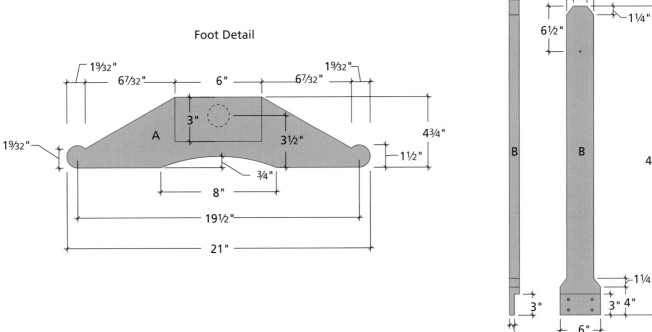

1⁹/₃₂"

6⁷/₃₂"   6"   6⁷/₃₂"

1⁹/₃₂"

1⁹/₃₂"

3"

A

3½"

4¾"

1½"

¾"

8"

19½"

21"

Upright Detail

1½"

4"

1"   1"

2"

6½"

1¼"

B   B

44¼"

1¼"

3"

3" 4"

6"

¾"

A   Building the Supports

Step 1. If necessary, glue up solid stock for the feet and uprights.

Step 2. Machine the feet (A) to size using the drawing (see foot detail). Use a band saw or jig saw to make the curved and angled cuts.

Step 3. Machine the uprights (B) to size using the drawing (see upright detail). A bandsaw or jigsaw is most useful for making the angled cuts.

Step 4. Machine for a half-lap joint between the foot and the upright. Use a chisel to mark the perimeter and a router to remove the material (in several passes). On the uprights, use a crosscut sled on a table saw. The depth of the mortise is ¾".

Step 5. Dry-fit the upright to the foot. Check for gaps and square.

Step 6. Glue and clamp the upright to the foot. Use four 1¼" wood screws to secure the joint. Recess the screws so you can cover them with a wood plug.

Step 7. After the glue has dried, mark the locations of the holes for the mirror swivel screws. The holes are located 6½" below the top of the upright. Follow the manufacturer's specifications for the size of the hole to be drilled.

Step 8. Mark the dowel hole locations on the feet, and drill 1½" diameter holes, ¾" deep. The holes are centered from side to side and are 3½" from the bottom of the feet.

Step 9. Finish sand all surfaces of the supports with 120-grit sandpaper.

Step 10. Cut the dowel (C) to size.

Step 11. Glue and clamp the dowel between the supports. Until the mirror frame is screwed to the supports, you will have to be careful with this assembly; clamp a board to the top of the uprights to provide additional support.

B   Machining Mirror Frame Moldings

Step 1. Machine the long outer moldings (D) and the short outer moldings (E) to size.

Step 2. Use a table saw set to 21° to make the angled cut on the front (see frame molding detail).

Step 3. Machine a ⅛" chamfer on the inside front edge.

Step 4. Machine the long inside moldings (F) and the short inside moldings (G) to size.

Step 5. Machine the rabbets for the mirror backer, the mirror, and the rope moldings. Machine a rabbet for the mirror (¼-wide × ½"-deep) first, then the mirror backer (⅝-wide × ¼"-deep), and lastly the rope rabbet (7/16-wide × ⅜"-deep).

Step 6. Machine a ⅛" chamfer on the front edges.

Step 7. Mark and machine the inner and outer moldings for #20 biscuits.

Step 8. Insert #20 biscuits, and clamp and glue the outer moldings to the appropriate inner moldings.

Step 9. Finish sand all surfaces with 120-grit sandpaper.

C | Assembling the Mirror Frame

Step 1. Miter the molding assemblies to create a frame that has outside dimensions of 25¾ × 65". Make sure miters fit tightly and that the frame is square.

Step 2. Mark and machine each miter joint for a #20 biscuit. Machine the biscuits at the back portion of the frame.

Step 3. Drill a hole through each edge of the long moulding assemblies, per the manufacturer's specifications, for the threaded insert. The hole should be centered horizontally and vertically on the assembly.

Step 4. Insert #20 biscuits, and glue and clamp the frame together. Minimize glue squeeze-out at the front of the frame, and immediately clean up any excess glue with a wet cloth.

Step 5. After the glue has dried, clean up the miters and finish sand as needed.

Step 6. Miter and fit the long rope molding (H) and the short rope molding (I) to the mirror frame. Glue and clamp in place.

Step 7. Cut the mirror backer (J) to size from ¼" plywood.

Step 8. Dry-fit the mirror backer to the mirror frame.

Step 9. Mark and drill countersunk holes for attaching the backer to the mirror frame. Wait until after you have applied a finish to attach.

Step 10. Finish sand the outside surface of the mirror backer with 120-grit sandpaper.

D | Applying a Finish & Installing Decorative Hardware

Step 1. Finish sand the mirror supports, mirror frame, and mirror backer with 180-grit sandpaper, and apply a finish.

Step 2. Have a mirror (K) cut to size. The mirror is sized so there is a ¹⁄₁₆" gap between it and the frame on all sides.

Step 3. Place the mirror and the mirror backer. Attach the mirror backer to the frame with ½" flathead wood screws. Screws can be left exposed or covered with screw caps.

Step 4. Attach the mirror frame to the supports with the swivel mirror hardware. Place black nylon washers between the mirror frame and the supports to fill the ⅛" gap.

Step 5. Tighten the swivel mirror hardware until you have the desired amount of friction.

Futon couch/bed

Most futons are poorly designed, cheaply constructed, shabbily finished pieces that are destined for a short, hard life in a college dorm room.

Not this futon. This piece includes fine-furniture details like Mission-style through tenons and narrow vertical slats on the arms. Exposed dovetail joinery in the frame will highlight your jointmaking skills and give the futon a solid foundation. Heavy-duty hardware and roller tracks guarantee this futon can make the trip from couch to bed and back again. All told, this is a piece of furniture sturdy enough to last and nice enough for the living room.

This futon couch/bed is designed to accommodate a full-size futon mattress (54 × 75"). Mattresses are available in a variety of thicknesses and coverings from furniture and bedding stores or online.

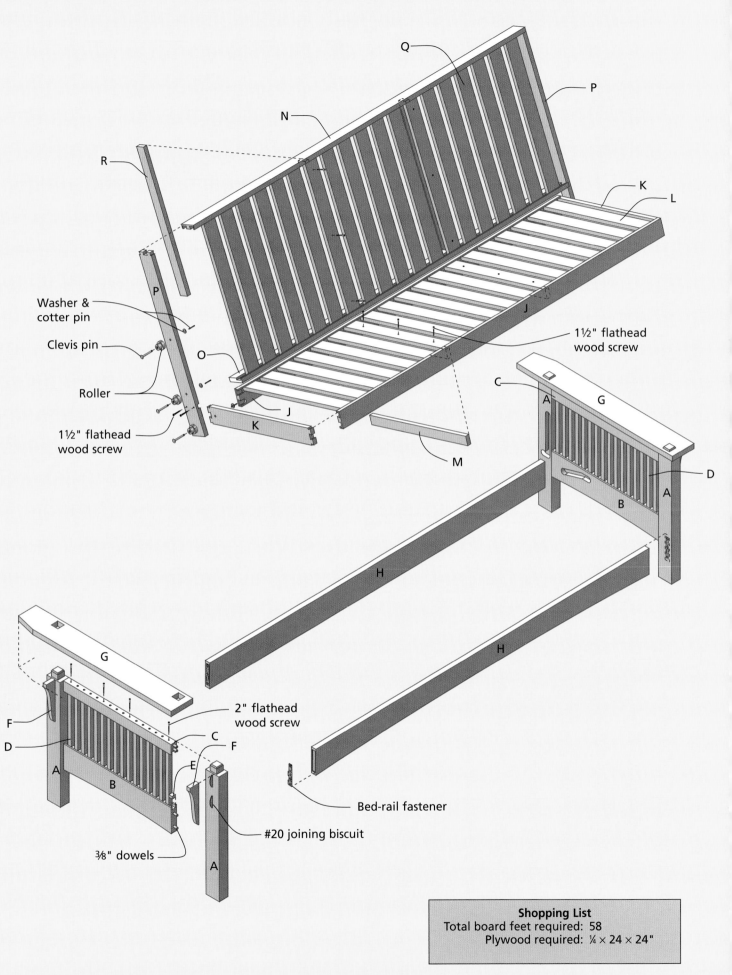

Q

P

N

R

K

L

Washer &
cotter pin

Clevis pin

P

O

Roller

J

1½" flathead
wood screw

1½" flathead
wood screw

C

A

G

K

J

A

B

D

K

M

H

2" flathead
wood screw

G

F

H

D

C

F

A

B

E

Bed-rail fastener

#20 joining biscuit

⅜" dowels

A

Materials List

Key	Part name	Qty.	Thickness	Width	Length	Material
\multicolumn{7}{Overall dimensions (86½"w X 36½"d X 32⁹⁄₁₆"h)}						
\multicolumn{7}{Leg/arm assembly (5"w X 36"l X 25¼"h)}						
A	Leg	4	2"	3"	25¼"	Solid wood or glue-up
B	Bottom rail	2	1¼"	5"	24¾"	Solid wood
C	Top rail	2	1¼"	2"	24¾"	Solid wood
D	Spindle	32	¾"	¾"	11⅛"	Solid wood
E	Spindle spacer	34	½"	¾"	¾"	Solid wood
F	Bracket	4	¾"	2"	8"	Solid wood
G	Arm	2	1"	5"	36"	Solid wood
H	Front/back rail	2	1"	5"	77⅛"	Solid wood
I	Routing template	1	¼"	17"	17"	Plywood
\multicolumn{7}{Seat assembly (25"w X 74¼"l X 3"h)}						
J	Seat front/back	2	¾"	3"	74¼"	Solid wood
K	Seat end	2	¾"	3"	24½"	Solid wood
L	Seat slat	19	¾"	2½"	24¼"	Solid wood
M	Seat support	2	¾"	1⅞"	23½"	Solid wood
\multicolumn{7}{Back assembly (32"w X 76"l X 3"h)}						
N	Back top	1	¾"	3"	76"	Solid wood
O	Back bottom	1	¾"	3"	75¼"	Solid wood
P	Back end	2	¾"	3"	31¾"	Solid wood
Q	Back slat	19	¾"	2½"	26⅝"	Solid wood
R	Back support	2	¾"	1⅞"	25⅞"	Solid wood
\multicolumn{7}{Hardware}						
	Futon roller kit	1 set				Available from Rockler, item #38437
	Bed-rail fasteners	4 sets	⅛"	⅝"	4"	
	Dowels		⅜"			
	Joining biscuits				#20	
	Flathead wood screws				1½", 2"	
	Cotter pins	6				

Dovetail Detail

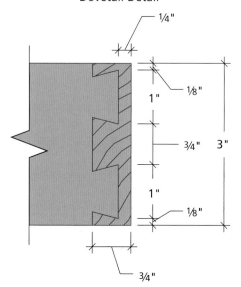

Slat Dado Detail

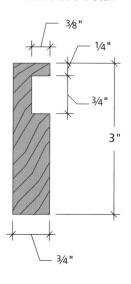

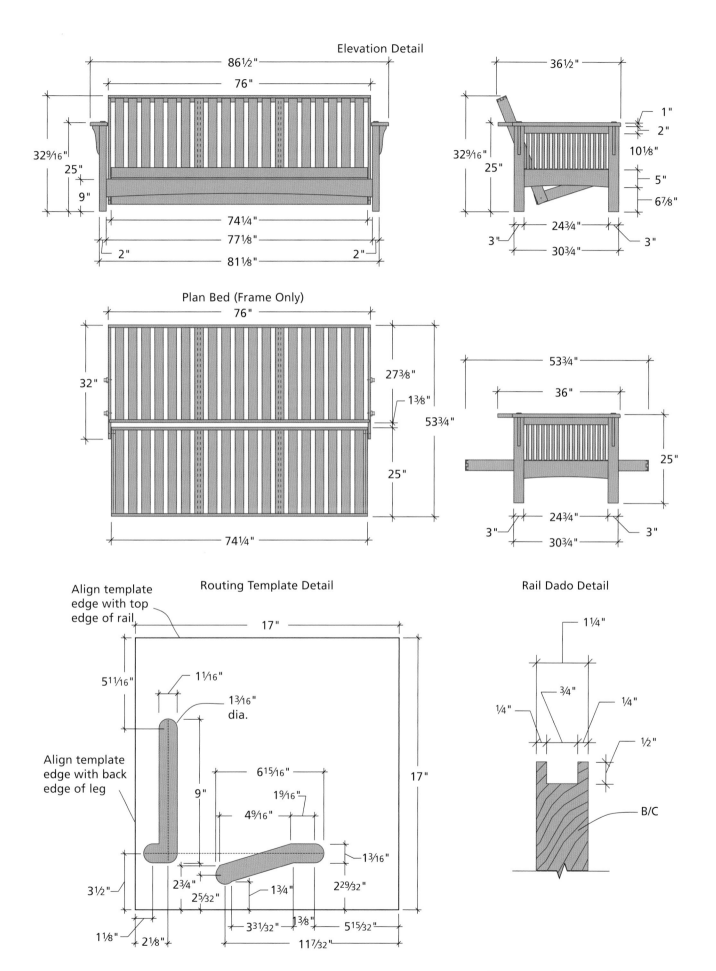

Elevation Detail

Plan Bed (Frame Only)

Routing Template Detail

Align template edge with top edge of rail

Align template edge with back edge of leg

Rail Dado Detail

Futon Couch/Bed 253

Rail Detail

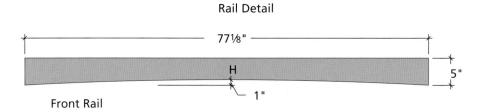

77⅛"

H

5"

1"

Front Rail

Bracket Pattern

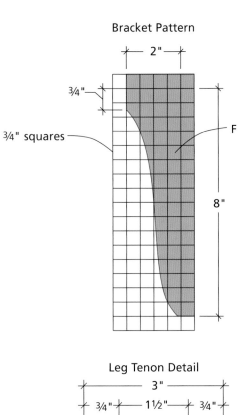

2"

¾"

¾" squares

F

8"

24¾"

B

5"

½"

Bottom Rail

End Detail

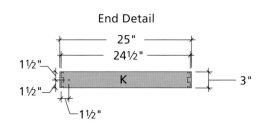

25"

24½"

1½"

K

3"

1½"

1½"

32"

31¾"

¾"

4⅝"

3"

P

1½"

1½"

7¼"

1½"

16⅝"

Leg Tenon Detail

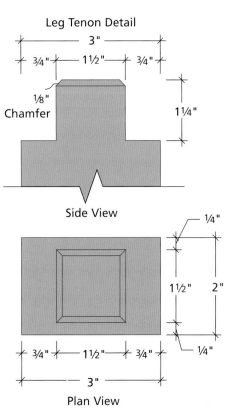

3"

¾"   1½"   ¾"

⅛"
Chamfer

1¼"

Side View

¼"

1½"   2"

¼"

¾"   1½"   ¾"

3"

Plan View

Arm Detail

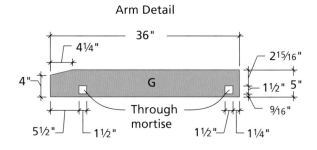

36"

4¼"

2¹⁵⁄₁₆"

4"

G

1½"   5"

9⁄16"

Through
mortise

5½"

1½"

1½"   1¼"

Step 1. Machine the legs (A) to size.

Step 2. Cut a tenon on the top of each leg per the drawing (see leg tenon detail).

Step 3. Rout a ⅛" chamfer on the top edges of each tenon.

Step 4. Machine the bottom rails (B) and the top rails (C) to size.

Step 5. Rout a ¾-wide × ½"-deep dado on the bottom edge of the top rail and the top edge of the bottom rail (see rail dado detail).

Step 6. Machine an arc on the bottoms of the bottom rails (see bottom rail detail).

Step 7. Mark and machine the rails and the legs for ⅜" dowels. You should be able to fit 2 dowels per joint. Note that the rails are flush with the inside faces of the legs. The top rail is flush with top of leg (the shoulder of the tenon). The bottom of bottom rail is 6⅞" from the bottom of leg.

Step 8. Dry-fit the rails to legs.

Step 9. Machine spindles (D) and the spindle spacers (E) to size. Make sure the spindles and spindle spacers are exactly ¾" (use calipers to be sure).

Step 10. Glue the spacers in the dado in the bottom rail. Start at one end by gluing and clamping a spacer in the dado. Dry-fit a spindle in place. Then glue another spacer in place. Continue until the end of the bottom rail. Adjust the length of last spacer as necessary so it is flush with the end of the bottom rail.

Step 11. Insert ⅜" dowels, and glue the end assembly together. Place the rails on a table with their inside faces down. Fit the spindles between the spindle spacers on the bottom rail. Place some ¼" scrap beneath the spindles to keep them level. Slide the top rail over the spindles (don't worry about the alignment of the spindles). Glue and clamp the rails to the legs.

Step 12. Mark the top rail and drill countersunk holes for 2" flathead wood screws that will secure and align the spindles. Using the extra ¾" spacer to space the top of the first spindle, drill and screw one spindle at a time, working from one end to the other. Make sure the spacer is the same length as your lower spindle spacers (exactly ¾").

Step 1. Cut the routing template (I) to size from ¼" plywood.

Step 2. Using router template detail, mark the pattern on the plywood template.

Step 3. Cut out the pattern by drilling holes and using a jig saw for straight lines. Use a rasp as necessary to clean up.

Step 4. Clamp the routing template to the inside face of the end assemblies (make sure to orient the template as indicated in the drawing). Align the template with the back edge of the leg and the top edge of the top rail. Position the clamps so they won't interfere with the router.

Step 5. Using a router fitted with a template guide, rout out the roller recess. Rout in ¼"-deep increments, finishing at a depth of ¾".

Step 6. Repeat on the other end assembly, making sure to orient the template correctly.

Step 7. Lay out and cut the brackets (F) to size from ¾" solid stock (see bracket pattern).

Step 8. Mark and machine the brackets and the legs for #20 biscuits. Each bracket should get 2 biscuits. The bracket is flush with the top of the leg and centered on the 3" outer face of the leg.

Step 9. Finish sand all surfaces of the end assemblies and the brackets with 120-grit sandpaper.

Step 10. Insert #20 biscuits, and glue and clamp the brackets to the end assemblies.

Step 11. Machine the arms (G) to size (see arm detail).

Step 12. Machine 1½ × 1½" through mortises in the arms (see arm detail). Use the legs with the previously machined tenons to check the accuracy of the mortises.

Step 13. Route a ¹⁄₁₆" radius on the top-face edges of each arm.

Step 14. Finish sand the arms with 120-grit sandpaper.

Step 15. When you are satisfied with the fit, glue and clamp the arms to the end assemblies.

Step 16. Machine the front and back rails (H) to size.

Step 17. Lay out and cut an arc on the front rail (see rail detail).

Step 18. Mark and machine the inside faces of the legs and the ends of the front and back rails for the bed-rail fasteners per the manufacturer's specifications. Note that the tops of the rails are located 9" from the bottom of the leg and the outside faces of the rails are set in ½" from the outside faces of the legs.

Step 19. Attach the bed-rail fasteners to the legs and the rails with screws suggested by the manufacturer.

Step 20. Finish sand all exposed surfaces of the front and back rails with 120-grit sandpaper.

C   Assembling the Seat

Step 1. Machine the seat front and back (J) and seat ends (K) to size.

Step 2. Machine dovetails on each end of the seat front and back and the seat ends according to the drawing (see dovetail detail).

Step 3. Machine a ¾-wide × ⅜"-deep dado in one face of the seat top and bottom, ¼" in from the top edge. Make sure to stop the dado 1" from each end so it doesn't ruin the beautiful dovetails you just cut!

Step 4. Drill a ⁵⁄₁₆" hole in each seat end for the pivot pin (see end detail).

Step 5. Machine the seat slats (L) and the seat supports (M) to size.

Step 6. Finish sand all exposed surfaces of the seat parts with 120-grit sandpaper.

Step 7. Glue and clamp the seat front and back to the seat ends, with the seat slats in place (don't worry about the spacing of the seat slats).

Step 8. Using temporary spacer blocks and working from left to right, position each slat and secure it with two 1½" flathead wood screws driven in from the back side of the seat frame. The first seat slat has ⁷⁄₁₆" of space between it and the seat end. Each subsequent seat slat has 1¹¹⁄₃₂" of space between it and the next seat slat. Make sure to predrill and countersink the wood screws.

Step 9. Clamp the seat supports in the correct locations, under the seventh slat from each end, and attach them with 1½" flathead wood screws driven through the seat slats.

D   Assembling the Back

Step 1. Machine the back top (N), the back bottom (O), the back ends (P), the back slats (Q), and the back supports (R) to size.

Step 2. Machine dovetails on each end of the back top and the back ends

(see dovetail detail). Do not dovetail the back bottom.

Step 3. Machine a ¾-wide × ⅜"-deep dado in the back top and bottom, ¼" in from the front edge (see slat dado detail). Make sure to stop the dado 1" from each end of the back top. The dado on the back bottom can be a through dado.

Step 4. Machine a ¾-wide × ⅜"-deep dado in the back ends. This dado runs across the grain 4⅝" from the bottom of the end (see end detail).

Step 5. Drill three ⁵⁄₁₆" holes in the outside face of each back end for the pivot pin and futon rollers (see end detail for spacing).

Step 6. Glue and clamp the back top and back bottom to the back ends, with the back slats loosely in place in the dados.

Step 7. Use two predrilled and countersunk 1½" flathead wood screws at each end to fix the back bottom to the back ends.

Step 8. Using temporary spacer blocks and working from left to right, position each back slat and secure it with two 1½" flathead wood screws driven in from the bottom face of the back bottom. The first back slat is 1⁵⁄₁₆" from the back end. Each subsequent back slat has 1¹¹⁄₃₂" of space between it and the next back slat. Make sure to predrill and countersink the wood screws.

Step 9. Clamp back supports in the correct locations, under the seventh slat from each end, and attach them with 1½" flathead wood screws driven through the back slats.

E   Sanding, Finishing & Assembling

Step 1. Finish sand all the parts of the futon with 180-grit sandpaper.

Step 2. Apply a finish to the project. If you are using oil as a finish, do not use oil on the slats that the futon cushion will rest against. Finish those slats with a harder finish.

Step 3. Assemble the futon in the following manner:

• Attach rollers to the seat back following the manufacturer's specifications.

• Use clevis pins with futon roller hardware to attach the back assembly to the seat assembly.

• Attach the front and back rails to one end assembly.

• Block up the other ends of the front and back rails so they are level and in the correct position to accept the other end assembly.

• With the back-and-seat assembly in the bed position (fully reclined), slide the rollers into the recess. The back-and-seat assembly should be resting on the rails.

• Place the other end assembly into position and secure with bed rail fasteners. Make sure the rails are solidly seated by hitting with a mallet or dead-blow hammer. Test to make sure the rollers move smoothly and the futon changes positions easily.

Step 4. To go from the bed to the couch position:

• Pull the seat frame front slightly forward to unlock the rollers from the indented portions of the roller recess.

• Push the seat frame front back and down until seat frame and back frame are locked in the couch position, with the rollers in the indented portions of the slots.

Step 5. To go from couch to bed position:

• Lift the center of the seat frame front slightly and pull forward to unlock the rollers from the indented portions of the slots and move the rollers into the straight sections of the roller recess.

• Move to the rear of the couch and carefully push down and forward on the back frame top until the back frame and seat frame are resting flat on the rails.

• Pull the back frame top toward you until you hear the rollers lock into the indented portions of the roller recess. Note: The bed may fold in the center if the rollers are not locked into the indented portions of the slots.

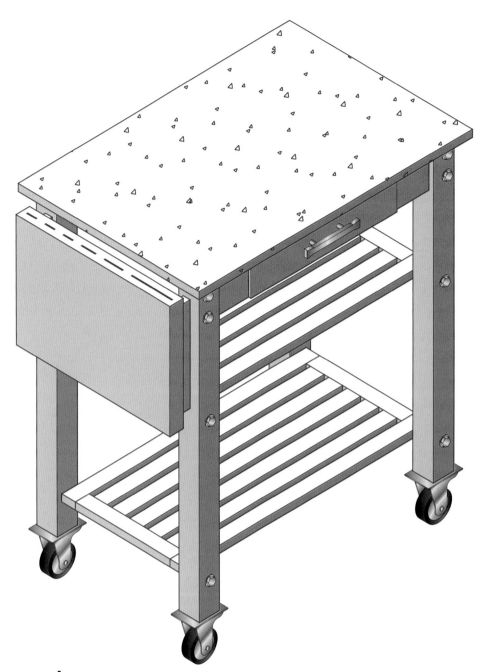

Kitchen cart

Ample storage and workspace are the twin goals of any kitchen design, and this cart can help any kitchen come closer to both those goals.

The design and construction of this piece are straightforward but very functional. There's storage for large items like pots and pans on the shelves and for kitchen gadgets in the drawer. A knife block keeps knives close at hand but safe from damage. The top makes for a sturdy and easy-to-clean worksurface.

Pay especially careful attention to laying out the holes for the dowels and the bolts so the drawer will track

smoothly and the cart will be stable. And it's a good idea to use corrosion-resistant hardware for any kitchen project.

This cart is attractive and inexpensive if built from an affordable hardwood like ash or birch. Stone is a good choice for a cutting surface, and its substantial weight helps to stabilize the cart, but you could also use butcher block or a laminate or metal product to match your countertops.

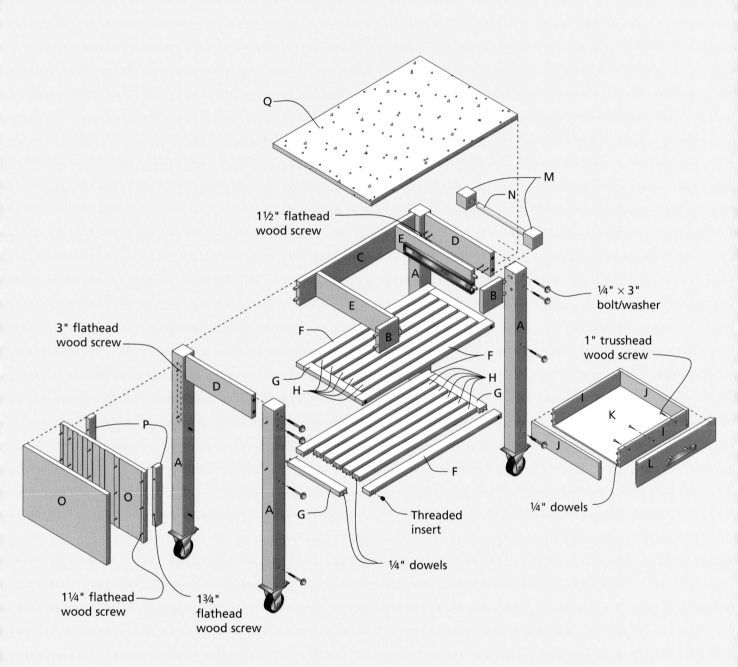

Q

1½" flathead
wood screw

M

N

¼" × 3"
bolt/washer

C

E

D

A

B

E

F

B

F

3" flathead
wood screw

D

H

H

G

G

1" trusshead
wood screw

P

A

I

J

K

A

G

F

O

O

A

J

I

Threaded
insert

L

¼" dowels

1¼" flathead
wood screw

1¾"
flathead
wood screw

¼" dowels

Shopping List
Total board feet required: 21
Plywood required: ¼ × 24 × 24"
Baltic birch plywood required: ½ × 3 × 60"
Dowel rod required: ¾ × 12"
Countertop required: ¾ - 1¼ × 20 × 30"

Materials List

Key	Part name	Qty.	Thickness	Width	Length	Material
Overall dimensions (20"w × 32¼"l × 36"h)						
A	Leg	4	2¼"	2¼"	31"	Solid wood or glue-up
B	Front apron	2	¾"	4"	4"	Solid wood
C	Back apron	1	¾"	4"	23½"	Solid wood
D	End apron	2	¾"	4"	13½"	Solid wood
E	Stretchers	2	¾"	4"	15½"	Solid wood
Shelf (13½"w × 27"l × ¾" thick)						
F	Frame front/back	4	¾"	1½"	27"	Solid wood
G	Frame end	4	¾"	1½"	10½"	Solid wood
H	Frame slat	10	¾"	1½"	24"	Solid wood
Drawer box (14½"w × 14"l × 3"h)						
I	Drawer box front/back	2	½"	3"	13½"	Baltic birch
J	Drawer box side	2	½"	3"	14"	Baltic birch
K	Drawer bottom	1	¼"	13½"	14"	Plywood
L	Drawer front	1	¾"	3⅞"	16"	Solid wood
M	Towel bar ends	2	2"	2"	2"	Solid wood or glue-up
N	Towel bar rod	1	¾" Dia.		11"	Dowel rod
O	Knife holder panel	2	¾"	17"	12"	Solid wood
P	Knife holder stand-off	2	¾"	1¼"	10"	Solid wood
Q	Stone top	1	¾" - 1¼"	20"	30"	Marble, granite, or engineered stone
Hardware						
	Casters	4				Use heavy-duty casters that swivel and lock
	Drawer slides	1 pr.			14"	
	Drawer pull	1				
	Threaded inserts	16				
	Bolt with washer	16				¼" × 3"
	Trusshead screws					1"
	Flathead wood screws					1¼", 1½", 1¾", and 3"

Plan Section Detail

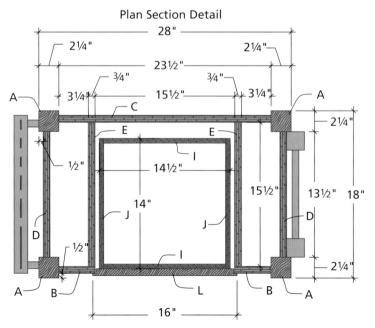

Elevation Detail

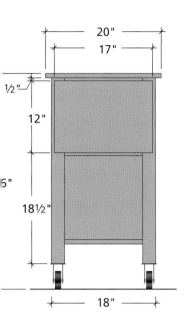

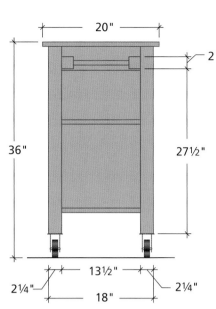

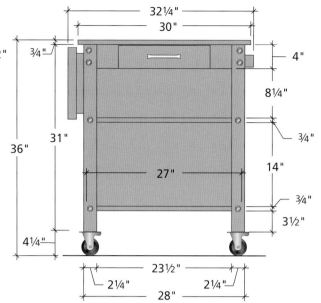

Shelf Detail

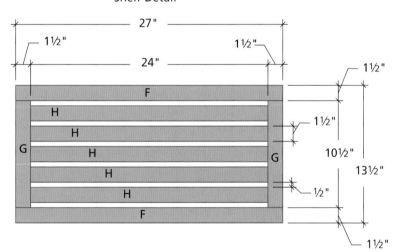

Leg Detail

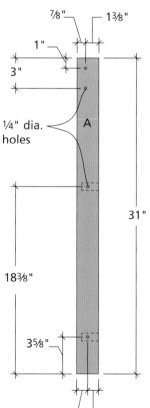

¼" dia. holes

Knife-Block Detail

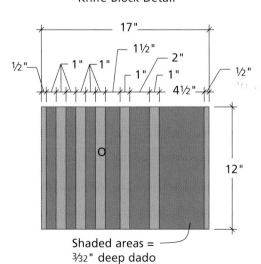

Shaded areas = ³⁄₃₂" deep dado

A   Machining & Assembling the Legs & Aprons

Step 1. If necessary, glue up stock and cut the legs (A) to size. It's also a good idea to glue up extra for the towel bar ends (M).

Step 2. Machine the front aprons (B), the back apron (C), the end aprons (D), and the stretchers (E) to size from ¾" solid stock.

Step 3. Drill ¼" holes in each leg (see leg detail).

Step 4. Clamp the end aprons between the legs so the tops of the aprons are flush with the tops of the legs and ½" back from the outside face. Using the top two holes you drilled in the legs, drill ¼" holes in the ends of the aprons for the threaded inserts.

Step 5. Enlarge the holes for threaded inserts per the manufacturer's specifications, and place the threaded inserts into the ends of the end aprons.

Step 6. Using the plan section detail, lay out locations for ⅜" dowels for the front aprons, back apron, and stretchers. You should have two dowels per joint.

Step 7. Drill holes for ⅜" dowels.

Step 8. Finish sand the outside surfaces of all the pieces with 180-grit sandpaper.

Step 9. Insert ⅜" dowels, and clamp and glue the front aprons, stretchers, and back apron together.

Step 10. Using ¼ × 3" bolts, attach the end aprons to the legs.

B   Building & Attaching the Knife Holder & Towel Bar

Step 1. Machine the towel bar ends (M) to size.

Step 2. Cut the towel bar rod (N) to length from a ¾" dowel.

Step 3. Drill a ¾"-diameter hole ¾" deep in the center of one face of each towel bar end.

Step 4. Glue and clamp the towel bar rod between the towel bar ends, keeping the faces of the ends parallel.

Step 5. Attach the towel bar assembly to the end apron using 1½" flathead wood screws. It should fit between the legs and sit ¼" above the bottom of the end apron.

Step 6. Glue up ¾" solid stock and machine the knife holder panels (O) to size.

Step 7. Using the drawing provided (see knife-block detail) or a layout of your own, machine ³⁄₃₂" deep slots for knives. Slots should be machined in one piece only.

Step 8. Drill pilot holes through the slotted knife holder panel per the drawing (see page 259).

Step 9. Join the two knife-holder panels together using 1¼" flathead wood screws and glue. Apply glue around the outside edge only, being careful not to get glue squeeze-out in the knife slots.

Step 10. Machine the knife-holder stand-offs (P) to size.

Step 11. Attach the stand-offs to the knife-holder panel with 1¾" flathead wood screws. The stand-offs should be located ½" in from the outside edges of the panel and centered top to bottom.

Step 12. Attach the knife holder to the leg assembly with 3" flathead wood screws. Center the knife holder on the leg assembly with the top of the stand-offs 1½" below the top of the legs.

C   Building & Attaching the Shelves & Apron Assembly

Step 1. Glue and clamp the apron assembly to the two leg assemblies. In the drawing, the knife holder is on the left and towel bar is on the right relative to the drawer, but you can reverse this orientation.

Step 2. Machine the frame fronts and backs (F), the frame ends (G), and the frame slats (H) to size from ¾" solid stock.

Step 3. Lay out and machine all parts for ¼" dowels per the drawing. You should be able to get two dowels in each end.

Step 4. Dry-fit the shelf assemblies, and check for square.

Step 5. Insert ¼" dowels, and glue and clamp the shelf assemblies.

Step 6. Finish sand the shelf assemblies with 180-grit sandpaper.

Step 7. Clamp the shelves to the legs (see elevation detail), and using ¼" holes previously drilled, continue the hole into the shelf frame.

Step 8. Enlarge the holes and insert threaded inserts per the manufacturer's specifications.

Step 9. Attach the shelves to the legs with ¼ × 3" bolts.

D   Building the Drawer & Attaching the Drawer Slides

Step 1. Machine the drawer box front and back (I), the drawer box sides (J), and the drawer bottom (K) to size.

Step 2. Machine a ¼ × ¼" dado in the inside faces of the front, back, and sides, ¼" from the bottom edges.

Step 3. Finish sand all drawer parts with 180-grit sandpaper.

Step 4. Align the parts and machine for ¼" dowels, two per joint.

Step 5. Insert ¼" dowels, and glue and clamp the drawer box together. After the glue is dry, turn the drawer box over and run a bead of hot-melt glue between the drawer sides, front, and back and the drawer bottom.

Step 6. Attach the drawer slide hardware to the drawer and kitchen cart per slide specifications.

Step 7. Machine the drawer front (L) to size.

Step 8. Machine a ⅜"-wide × ½"-deep rabbet in each end.

Step 9. Align the drawer front on the drawer box, leaving a ⅛" reveal at the top of the drawer front. Attach with 1" truss head screws.

Step 10. Drill the drawer front for a drawer pull.

E   Applying a Finish & Attaching Decorative Hardware & the Top

Step 1. Finish sand any remaining parts of the kitchen cart with 180-grit sand paper and apply a finish.

Step 2. After the finish has dried, attach decorative hardware and casters.

Step 3. Have the stone top (Q) cut to size.

Step 4. Attach the top to kitchen cart with silicone. It should overhang the legs by 1" on each side. Allow the recommended time for the silicone to dry before using.

Library table

It's difficult to imagine a woodworking project more useful and straightforward than this library table. Every house should have one.

The table's few design details are subtle but attractive. The chamfered square legs, the prominant side stiles, and arched lower rails are Mission hallmarks.

The woodworking techniques required are not advanced, but they will build an impressive and attrac-tive piece of furniture. Pay careful attention to accuracy when marking and machining the biscuit joints on the legs and frame to ensure the table will be square and stable.

For such a large piece, this project requires surprisingly little lumber and minimal cutting, making it a good choice for a new woodworker.

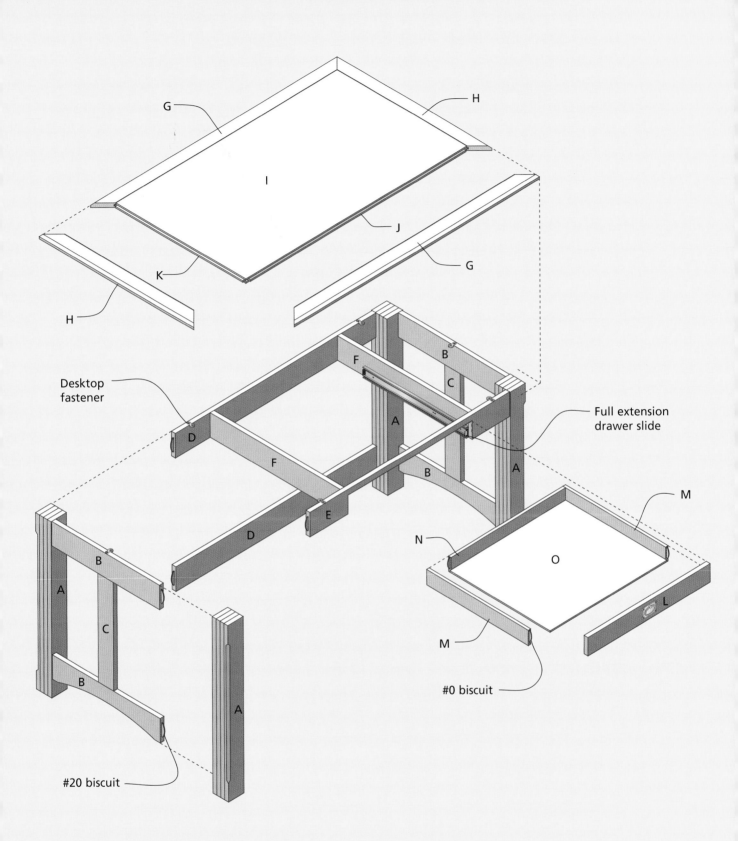

G

H

I

J

K

G

H

Desktop
fastener

F

B

C

D

A

F

B

A

D

E

B

A

B

C

Full extension
drawer slide

M

N

O

L

M

B

A

M

#0 biscuit

#20 biscuit

A

Materials List					
Key	Part name	Qty.	Thickness	Width	Length	Material
Overall dimensions (48"w × 30"d × 29½"h)						
A	Leg	4	3"	3"	28¾"	Solid wood or glue-up
B	Side rail	4	¾"	4"	21"	Solid wood
C	Side stile	2	¾"	3"	17¾"	Solid wood
D	Back rail	2	¾"	4"	39"	Solid wood
E	Front apron	1	¾"	4"	39"	Solid wood
F	Drawer stretcher	2	¾"	4"	25¼"	Solid wood
G	Long top edge	2	¾"	2½"	48"	Solid wood
H	Short top edge	2	¾"	2½"	30"	Solid wood
I	Top center panel	1	¾"	25"	43"	Plywood
J	Long top spline	2	¼"	¾"	42"	Solid wood or plywood
K	Short top spline	2	¼"	¾"	24"	Solid wood or plywood
Drawer dimensions (24"w × 20¾"d × 3"h)						
L	Drawer front	1	¾"	3"	24"	Solid wood or cut-out of front apron
M	Drawer side	2	½"	2½"	20"	Solid wood
N	Drawer back	1	½"	2½"	22⅛"	Solid wood
O	Drawer bottom	1	¼"	20"	22⅝"	Plywood
Hardware/supplies						
	Sidemount drawer slides	1 pr.		20"		
	Drawer pull	1				
	Desktop fasteners	6				
	Joining biscuits					#0 and #20

Top Edge Detail

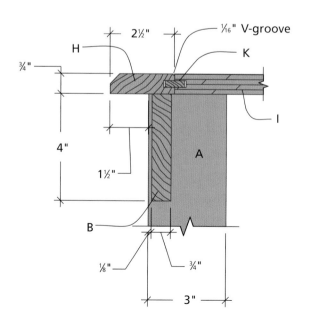

Elevation Detail

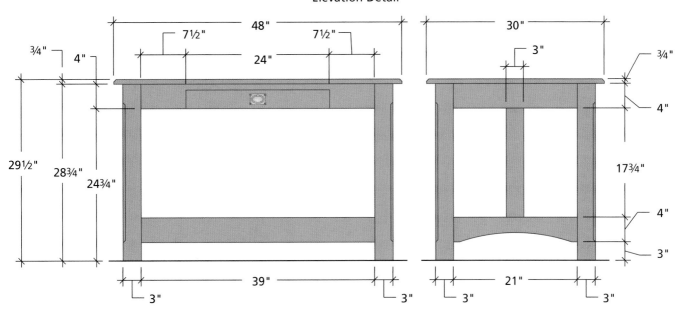

Lower Side Rail Pattern

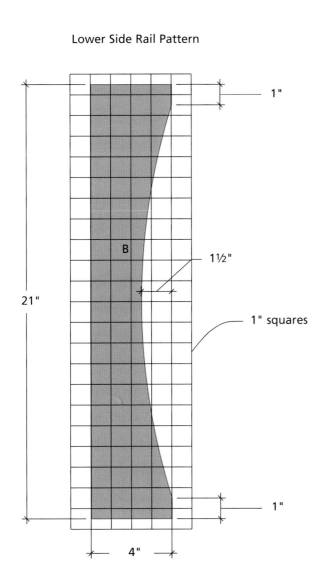

1" squares

Leg Detail

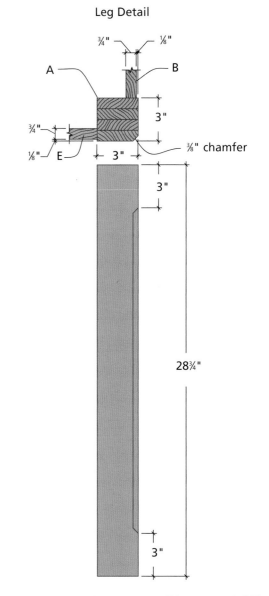

⅜" chamfer

A Building the Leg Assemblies

Step 1. If necessary, glue up stock and machine the legs (A) to size.

Step 2. Machine a ⅜" chamfer on one corner of each leg, stopping 3" from the top and bottom.

Step 3. Machine the side rails (B) and the side stiles (C) to size.

Step 4. Cut an arc on the bottom of the two side rails according to the pattern (see lower side rail detail).

Step 5. Mark one face of each side rail and stile as the outside face. Mark and machine the legs, rails, and stiles for #20 biscuits, centering the side stiles between side rails.

Step 6. Insert #20 biscuits, and glue and clamp the side rails and stiles together. After the glue has dried, sand both sides of the assembly with 120-grit sandpaper.

Step 7. Align the side stile and rail assemblies between the legs, and mark and machine for #20 biscuits. Note that the assembly will be set in ⅛" from the faces of the legs and flush with the tops of the legs.

Step 8. Sand the faces of the legs you will be joining to. Insert #20 biscuits, and glue and clamp the side stile and rail assemblies to the legs.

B Building & Attaching the Back Rail & Apron Assembly

Step 1. Machine the back rails (D), the front apron (E), and the drawer stretchers (F) to size.

Step 2. Lay out the drawer front (L) outline on the front apron. If you want to use the cut-out as the drawer front, drill two small holes (³⁄₃₂") at the inside corners. Make sure to drill the holes outside your cut lines. Use a scroll saw or a jig saw with a thin blade to cut the two short, vertical lines. Use a coping saw to get one corner of the long cut started, then finish with jig saw. Clean up both surfaces, keeping the reveal between the drawer front and the apron small and consistent.

Step 3. Align the back rails and the front apron with the leg assemblies, and mark for #20 biscuits. Make sure the back rails and the front apron are set in ⅛" from the outside faces of the legs. The top edge of the bottom back rail should be 7" above the bottoms of the legs. Machine for #20 biscuits, and sand the faces of the legs you just machined.

Step 4. Mark the back rail, front aprons, and drawer stretchers for #20 biscuits. The drawer stretchers should be flush with the drawer front cut-out and an equal distance from the ends of the back rail. Machine for biscuits, sand all parts with 120-grit sandpaper, insert #20 biscuits, and glue and clamp the back rail, front apron, and drawer stretchers together.

Step 5. Insert #20 biscuits, and glue and clamp the apron assembly and back rail to the leg assemblies. Immediately wipe up any glue squeeze-out on any outside surfaces. Sand the outside surfaces of the legs with 120-grit sandpaper. Note that all outside surfaces of the table assembly should now be sanded.

C   Building & Attaching the Top

Step 1. Machine the long top edges (G) and the short top edges (H) to correct width and thickness, but keep them long in length. Machine the top center panel (I) to size.

Step 2. Machine a ¼-wide × 7/16"-deep dado in the top edges and the top center panel for a spline.

Step 3. Machine a 1/16" V-groove on the top inside edge of the top edges (see top edge detail).

Step 4. Machine the long top splines (J) and the short top splines (K) to size.

Step 5. Fit the top splines into the top center panel dado, and miter the top edges to fit around the center panel.

Step 6. After cutting all edging to fit, glue and clamp the edging to the top center panel.

Step 7. Sand the tabletop with 120-grit sandpaper, and machine a 3/8" chamfer around the top edges.

Step 8. Attach the desktop fasteners to the aprons and then attach the top to the table assembly.

D   Building the Drawer & Attaching Drawer Slides

Step 1. Machine the drawer front (L) if necessary. Machine the drawer sides (M), the drawer back (N), and the drawer bottom (O) to size.

Step 2. Machine a ¼ × ¼" dado ¼" from the bottom edge on one face of all parts. The drawer front has a blind dado, stopping 5/8" from each end.

Step 3. Mark and machine the drawer parts for #0 biscuits. Note that the sides are held in 7/16" from each end of the drawer front and are flush with the bottom.

Step 4. Insert #0 biscuits, and glue and clamp the drawer box together. After the glue is dry, turn the drawer box over and run a bead of hot-melt glue between the drawer sides, front, and back and the drawer bottom.

Step 5. Attach the drawer slide hardware to the drawer and the table per manufacturer's specifications.

Step 6. Drill the drawer front for a drawer pull.

E   Applying a Finish & Installing Decorative Hardware

Step 1. Finish sand the library table with 180-grit sandpaper, and apply a finish of your choice.

Step 2. After the finish has dried, attach the drawer knob.

Plinth Arc Detail

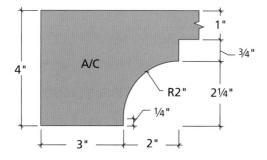

Linen cabinet

Cabinetmaking is among the most highly regarded forms of woodworking, and rightly so: there is little that is simple about making a simple box.

This linen cabinet is two not-so-simple boxes and incorporates a variety of cabinetmaking techniques. The end result is both beautiful, highly functional, and built to last.

Take care that the upper and lower cabinet carcasses are square before attaching the face frames. It's also worthwhile to consider where you will place the finished piece before you decide which way the doors will swing.

Beadboard panels and the simple plinth design give this piece a cottage-style look, but a well-crafted cabinet of this sort can find a place in any home.

A Building the Plinth

Step 1. Machine the plinth front (A), the plinth back (B), and the plinth sides (C) to size. Miter the front and sides to fit.

Step 2. Cut the arc in the plinth front and sides using the pattern provided (see plinth arc detail, below left).

Step 3. Machine the plinth stretchers (D) to size.

Step 4. Mark and machine all the plinth pieces for #20 biscuits per the drawing.

Step 5. Insert #20 biscuits, and glue and clamp the plinth assembly, making sure the miters are tight.

Step 6. Finish sand the outside surface with 180-grit sandpaper.

B Machining the Frame & the Panel Sides & Doors

Step 1. From solid stock, machine to size the lower side frame back stiles (F), the lower side frame front stiles (G), the lower side frame rails (H), the lower door rails (P), the lower door stiles (Q), the upper side frame back stiles (Y), the upper side frame front stiles (Z), the upper side frame top rail (AA), the upper side frame bottom rail (BB), the upper door stiles (II), and the upper door rails (JJ).

Step 2. Using a stile-and-rail router bit (round shown), machine all the stiles and rails on one long edge.

Step 3. Using the opposite profile router bit, machine the ends of your rails.

Step 4. For the upper door stiles and rails only, machine a rabbet for the glass (see cabinet top detail).

Step 5. Machine the lower side frame panels (I), the lower door panel (S), and the upper side frame panels (CC) to size from ¼" beadboard. Sand the panel faces with 180-grit sandpaper.

Step 6. Glue and clamp the side frames (4) and the doors (2) with their panels in place (except the upper door with glass insert).

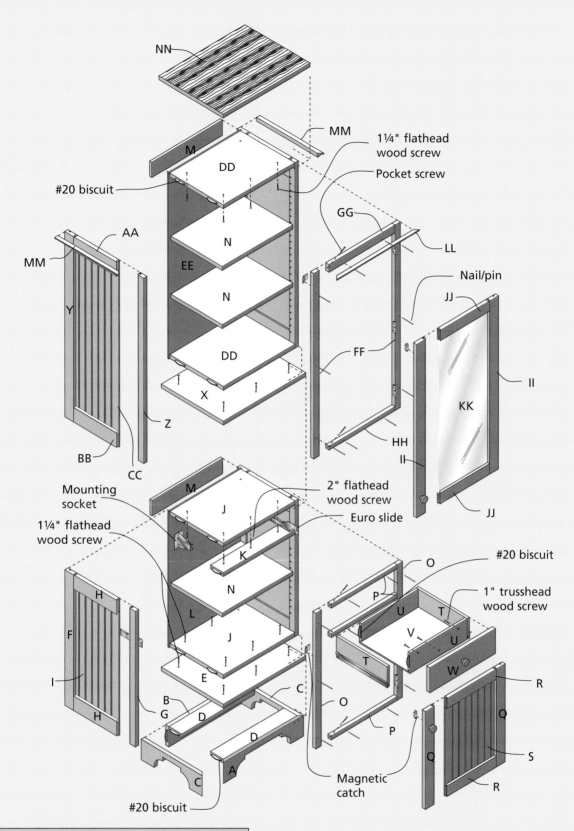

NN

MM

1¼" flathead wood screw

Pocket screw

#20 biscuit

GG

M

DD

LL

AA

MM

N

EE

Nail/pin

JJ

Y

N

FF

II

DD

HH

Z

II

KK

X

BB

JJ

CC

Mounting socket

M

2" flathead wood screw

J

Euro slide

1¼" flathead wood screw

#20 biscuit

O

H

K

P

1" trusshead wood screw

F

N

U

T

L

J

V

U

I

E

W

H

B

O

R

G

D

P

Q

D

Magnetic catch

Q

S

C

A

R

#20 biscuit

Shopping List
Total board feet required: 19
Plywood required: ¼ × 48 × 48"
Beadboard plywood required: ¼ × 48 × 48"
Plywood required: ¾ × 48 × 96"
Veneer tape required: ⅞" × 23'
Glass required: ⅛ × 11⅜ × 30⅛"

Materials List					
Key	Part name	Qty.	Thickness	Width	Length	Material

Key	Part name	Qty.	Thickness	Width	Length	Material
Overall dimensions (20"ww × 15"d × 69"h)						
Plinth (18½"w × 14¼"d × 4"h)						
A	Plinth front	1	¾"	4"	18½"	Solid wood
B	Plinth back	1	¾"	4"	17"	Solid wood
C	Plinth side	2	¾"	4"	14¼"	Solid wood
D	Plinth stretcher	2	¾"	3"	17"	Scrap
Lower cabinet (18"w × 14"d × 26½"h)						
E	Lower horizontal trim panel	1	¾"	14½"	19"	Plywood
F	Lower side frame back stile	2	¾"	2¼"	26½"	Solid wood
G	Lower side frame front stile	2	¾"	1½"	26½"	Solid wood
H	Lower side frame rail	4	¾"	3¹⁄₁₆"	10"	Solid wood
I	Lower side frame panel	2	¼"	10¼"	21⅛"	Beadboard sheet stock
J	Top/bottom	2	¾"	12½"	16½"	Plywood
K	Stretcher	1	¾"	3"	16½"	Plywood
L	Lower back	1	¼"	17"	26½"	Plywood
M	Nailing cleat	2	½"	3"	16½"	Scrap
N	Adjustable shelf	3	¾"	12"	16¼"	Plywood
O	Lower face frame stile	2	¾"	1¼"	26½"	Solid wood
P	Lower face frame rail	3	¾"	¾"	15½"	Solid wood
Lower door (15⅜"w × 19⅛"l)						
Q	Lower door stile	2	¾"	2¼"	19⅛"	Solid wood
R	Lower door rail	2	¾"	2¼"	11⅜"	Solid wood
S	Lower door panel	1	¼"	11⅝"	15⅜"	Beadboard sheet stock
Drawer box (14½"w × 12"l × 4"h)						
T	Drawer box side	2	½"	4"	12"	Solid wood or Baltic birch plywood
U	Drawer box front/back	2	½"	4"	13½"	Solid wood or Baltic birch plywood
V	Drawer bottom	1	¼"	14"	11½"	Plywood
W	Drawer front	1	¾"	4⅞"	15⅜"	Solid wood
Upper cabinet (18"w × 14"d × 36¼"h)						
X	Middle horizontal trim panel	1	¾"	14½"	19"	Plywood
Y	Upper side frame back stile	2	¾"	2¼"	36¼"	Solid wood
Z	Upper side frame front stile	2	¾"	1½"	36¼"	Solid wood
AA	Upper side frame top rail	2	¾"	3¹³⁄₁₆"	10"	Solid wood
BB	Upper side frame bottom rail	2	¾"	3¹⁄₁₆"	10"	Solid wood
CC	Upper side frame panel	2	¼"	10¼"	30⅛"	Beadboard sheet stock
DD	Top/bottom	2	¾"	12½"	16½"	Plywood
EE	Upper back	1	¼"	17"	36¼"	Plywood
FF	Upper face frame stile	2	¾"	1¼"	36¼"	Solid wood
GG	Upper face frame top rail	1	¾"	1½"	15½"	Solid wood
HH	Upper face frame bottom rail	1	¾"	¾"	15½"	Solid wood
Upper door (15⅜"w × 33⅞"l)						
II	Upper door stile	2	¾"	2¼"	33⅞"	Solid wood
JJ	Upper door rail	2	¾"	2¼"	11⅜"	Solid wood
KK	Door panel glass	1	⅛"	11⅝"	30⅛"	Tempered glass
LL	Front molding	1	¾"	¾"	19½"	Solid wood
MM	Side molding	2	¾"	¾"	14¾"	Solid wood
NN	Top horizontal trim panel	1	¾"	15"	20"	Plywood
Hardware						
	Magnetic catch	2				For inset doors
	Glass clip	10				
	Door hinge	5				
	Drawer slide	1 pr.			12"	
	Mounting bracket	1 pr.				
	Door knob	3				
	Shelf pin	12	¼" dia.			
	Joining biscuit					#20
	Pocket screw				1¼"	
	Trusshead wood screw				1"	
	Flathead wood screw				1¼", 2"	

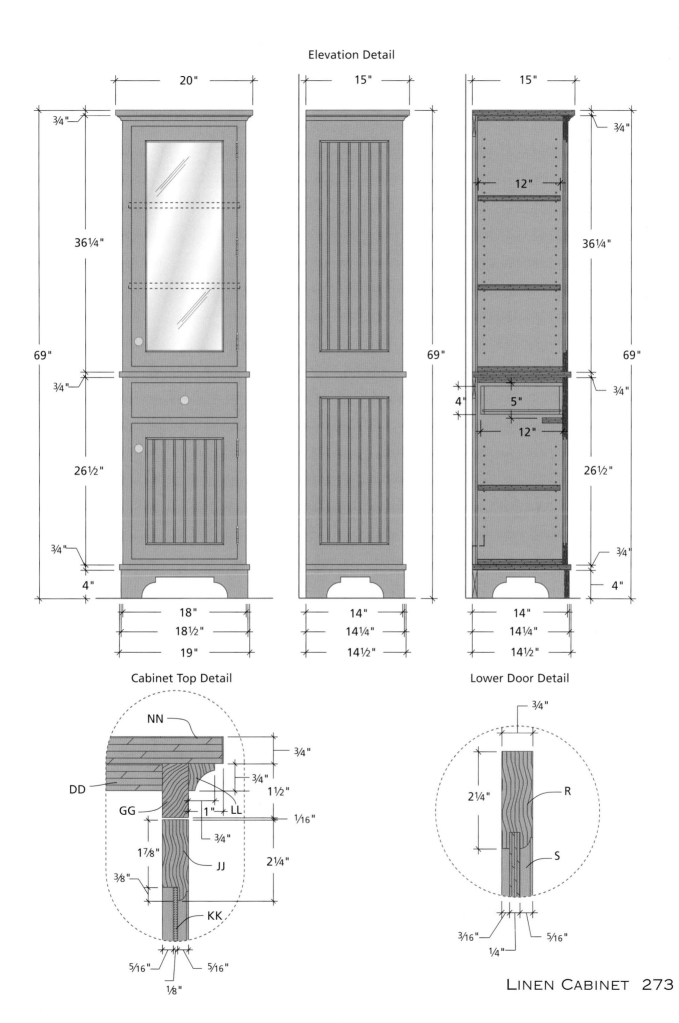

Elevation Detail

20"
15"
15"

¾"
36¼"
69"
¾"
26½"
¾"
4"

12"
36¼"
69"
¾"
4"
5"
12"
26½"
¾"
4"

18"
18½"
19"

14"
14¼"
14½"

14"
14¼"
14½"

Cabinet Top Detail

NN
DD
GG
LL
JJ
KK
¾"
¾"
1½"
1"
1/16"
¾"
1⅞"
2¼"
⅜"
5/16"
5/16"
⅛"

Lower Door Detail

¾"
2¼"
R
S
3/16"
¼"
5/16"

Step 7. After the glue has dried, mark the inside of the side frames for shelf pin holes; 11 holes in the lower sides and 25 holes in the upper sides are good arrangements. Holes should be 1¼" on center, 1" in from the front edge and 1¾" in from the back edge.

Step 8. Along the back edges of the upper and lower back stiles, machine a ¼ × ¼" dado ½" in from the inside back edge for the backs.

C   **Assembling the Upper & Lower Cabinets**

Step 1. Machine the tops (J) and the bottoms (DD), the stretcher (K), and the adjustable shelves (N) from ¾" plywood.

Step 2. Apply veneer tape to the front edges of the adjustable shelves.

Step 3. Mark and machine the tops and bottoms and the upper and lower side frames for #20 biscuits per the drawing. Make sure all the front edges are flush. There should be 5" of space between the top of the lower cabinet and the stretcher.

Step 4. Sand all the interior surfaces with 180-grit sandpaper. You can also pre-finish the interior at this stage. Make sure to avoid getting finish in the biscuit slots.

Step 5. Insert #20 biscuits, and glue and clamp the upper and lower side frame panels to the tops and bottoms, making an upper and lower cabinet. Remember the stretcher in the lower cabinet.

Step 6. Machine the upper back (EE) and the lower back (L) from ¼" plywood. Sand with 180-grit sandpaper.

Step 7. Fit the backs to their respective cabinets by sliding them into the dados and attaching with 1" flathead wood screws. Make sure the cabinets are square while attaching the backs.

Step 8. Machine the nailing cleats (M) from ½" scrap wood.

Step 9. Glue and clamp one nailing cleat to the top of each cabinet. Use hot-melt glue.

D   **Building the Face Frames & the Drawer & Attaching the Doors**

Step 1. Machine the lower face frame stiles (O), the lower face frame rails (P), the upper face frame stiles (FF), the upper face frame top rail (GG), and the upper face frame bottom rail (HH) to size.

Step 2. Dry-fit the face frames and verify that they fit the cabinet properly. All edges should be flush.

Step 3. Glue and clamp the face frame assemblies. Install pocket screws to strengthen the joints.

Step 4. Apply glue to the back faces of the face frames. Nail or pin the face frames to the upper and lower cabinets.

Step 5. Finish sand the exteriors of the cabinets with 180-grit sandpaper.

Step 6. Machine the drawer box sides (T), the drawer box front and back (U), and the drawer bottom (V) to size.

Step 7. On one face of the drawer front, back, and sides, machine a ¼ × ¼" dado ¼" up from the bottom.

Step 8. Align the drawer parts and machine for #20 biscuits per the drawing.

Step 9. Insert #20 biscuits, and glue and clamp the drawer box together. After glue is dry, turn the drawer box over and run a bead of hot-melt glue between the drawer sides, front, and back and the drawer bottom.

Step 10. Attach the drawer slide hardware to the drawer and the lower cabinet per manufacturer's specifications. Slide the drawer box into the cabinet.

Step 11. Machine the drawer front (W) to size. Attach the drawer front to drawer box using double-sided tape or clamps to create consistent ¹⁄₁₆" reveals. Use 1" trusshead wood screws in oversized holes to attach the drawer front to the drawer box.

Step 12. Attach the doors to cabinet using a non-mortising hinge. Make sure all reveals are the same, approximately ¹⁄₁₆". Use three hinges for the top door. The doors can be hinged left or right (right shown).

Step 13. Mount magnetic catches on the doors and the frames per the manufacturer's specifications.

E   Assembling the Cabinet

Step 1. Machine the lower horizontal trim panel (E), the middle horizontal trim panel (X), and the top horizontal trim panel (NN) to size.

Step 2. Apply veneer tape to all 4 edges of each piece.

Step 3. Finish sand 2" in from the outside edge on both faces of each horizontal trim panel with 180-grit sandpaper. Sand all of the top face of the top horizontal trim panel.

Step 4. Attach the lower horizontal trim panel to the plinth, making the panel flush in back with a ¼" overhang at the front and sides. Screw 1¼" flathead wood screws into the stretchers of the plinth per the drawing.

Step 5. Attach the lower cabinet to the lower horizontal trim panel using 1¼" flathead wood screws. The cabinet should be flush in back and have a ½" reveal at the front and sides.

Step 6. Attach the middle horizontal trim panel to the top of the lower cabinet using 1¼" flathead wood screws. The panel should be flush in back and have a ½" overhang at the front and sides.

Step 7. Using 2" flathead wood screws, attach the upper cabinet by screwing through the top of the lower cabinet. The cabinet should be flush in back and have a ½" reveal at the front and sides.

Step 8. Attach the top horizontal trim panel to the upper cabinet with 1¼" flathead wood screws, screwing up into the panel from inside the upper cabinet. The panel should be flush on the back with a 1" overhang at the front and sides.

Step 9. Machine and miter the front molding (LL) and side moldings (MM) per the drawings. Attach the molding with small nails or pins, making sure the miters are tight.

F   Applying a Finish & Installing Decorative Hardware

Step 1. Do any final sanding with 180-grit sandpaper and apply a finish.

Step 2. After the finish has dried, attach door and drawer knobs.

Step 3. For the door panel glass (KK), have a piece of tempered glass cut to size. Use glass clips to attach it to the upper door.

Step 4. Install the adjustable shelves using shelf pins.

Mission bookcase

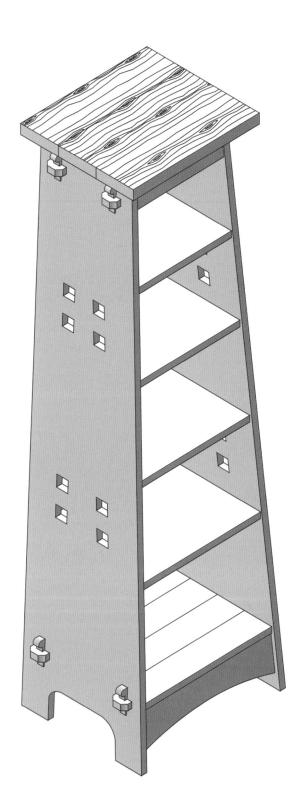

The Mission style of furniture is an excellent one for all woodworkers, but especially for beginners. Mission pieces tend to be substantial, with beautifully accented joinery. But they don't often require highly specialized skills or equipment or piles of intricately machined pieces.

This Mission bookcase is no exception. It is well proportioned and economical in its materials, but it is a useful size for books or for displaying small objects. And it is definitely an attention-getting piece on its own. This design has the additional touch of being easy to disassemble for travel or shipping.

As with all Mission furniture, quartersawn oak is an excellent choice for lumber. Consider using a contrasting species or color of wood for the tenon keys.

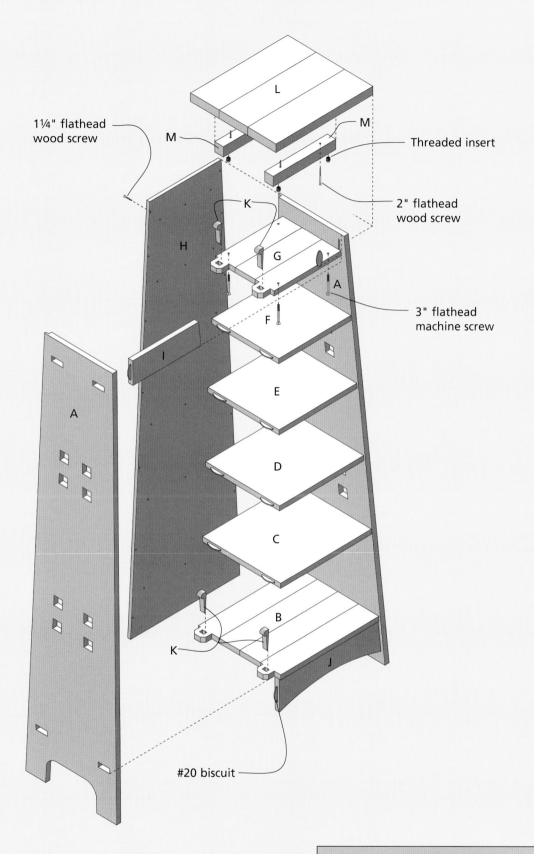

1¼" flathead
wood screw

M

M

Threaded insert

2" flathead
wood screw

K

H

G

A

3" flathead
machine screw

F

I

A

E

D

C

B

K

J

#20 biscuit

Shopping List
Total board feet required: 9
Plywood required: ½ × 24 × 72"
Plywood required: ¾ × 24 × 72"
Veneer tape required: ⅞" × 16'
Dimensional lumber: 2 × 2 × 24"

Materials List					
Key	Part name	Qty.	Thickness	Width	Length	Material
Overall dimensions (19½"w × 16¾"d × 64"h)						
A	Side	2	¾"	16"	62⅞"	Plywood
B	Shelf #1	1	¾"	14½"	20⅞"	Solid wood glue-up
C	Shelf #2	1	¾"	13¾"	16"	Plywood
D	Shelf #3	1	¾"	13"	14⅞"	Plywood
E	Shelf #4	1	¾"	12½"	13¾"	Plywood
F	Shelf #5	1	¾"	11¾"	12¾"	Plywood
G	Shelf #6	1	¾"	10¼"	15⁵⁄₁₆"	Solid wood glue-up
H	Back	1	½"	19"	62¾"	Plywood
I	Top rail	1	¾"	4"	11¹³⁄₁₆"	Solid wood
J	Bottom rail	1	¾"	4½"	17¹³⁄₁₆"	Solid wood
K	Tenon key	8	⅞"	¾"	3"	Solid wood - contrasting species/color
L	Top	1	1¼"	15"	17"	Solid wood glue-up
M	Top blocking	2	1½"	1½"	11"	2 × 2 dimensional lumber
Hardware						
	Joining biscuit					#20
	Veneer tape			13⁄16"		Species to match
	Flathead wood screw				1¼", 2"	
	Threaded brass insert	4	¼"-20			
	Flathead brass machine screw	4	¼"-20		3"	

Tenon Key Detail

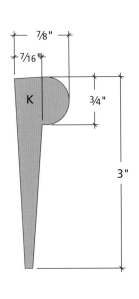

Mortise Detail

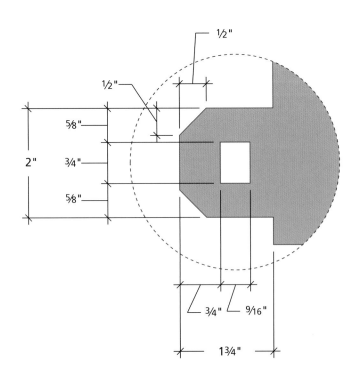

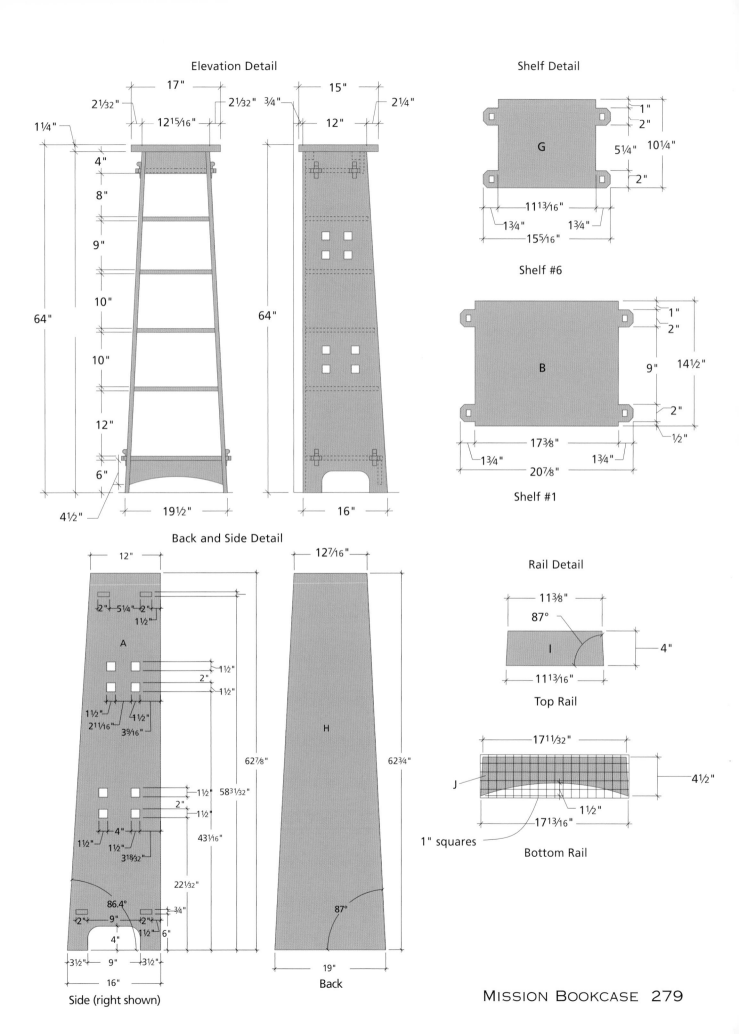

Elevation Detail

17"
2¹⁄₃₂"   2¹⁄₃₂"
12¹⁵⁄₁₆"
1¼"
4"
8"
9"
10"
10"
64"
12"
6"
4½"   19½"

¾"   15"   2¼"
12"
64"
16"

Shelf Detail

G
1"
2"
5¼"   10¼"
2"
11¹³⁄₁₆"
1¾"   1¾"
15⁵⁄₁₆"

Shelf #6

B
1"
2"
9"   14½"
2"
½"
17³⁄₈"
1¾"   1¾"
20⁷⁄₈"

Shelf #1

Back and Side Detail

12"
2" 5¼" 2"
1½"
A
1½"
2"
1½"
1½"
2¹¹⁄₁₆" 1½"
3⁹⁄₁₆"
62⁷⁄₈"
1½" 58³¹⁄₃₂"
2"
1½"
43¹⁄₁₆"
4"
1½"
1½"
3¹⁸⁄₃₂"
22¹⁄₃₂"
86.4°
¾"
2" 9"
1½" 6"
4"
3½" 9" 3½"
16"

Side (right shown)

12⁷⁄₁₆"
H
62¾"
87°
19"

Back

Rail Detail

11³⁄₈"
87°
I
4"
11¹³⁄₁₆"

Top Rail

17¹¹⁄₃₂"
J
4½"
1½"
17¹³⁄₁₆"
1" squares

Bottom Rail

A   Machining the Sides

Step 1. Using the drawing (see back and side detail), machine the sides (A) to size. Note that the front and back cuts will be square, but the top and bottom cuts will be beveled at 3° (the edges should remain parallel).

Step 2. Veneer the front edge of each side using veneer tape.

Step 3. Lay out all the cut-outs on each side. Make sure you lay out for a left and a right, and that the layout is done according to the diagram, on the outside surface.

Step 4. Machine the cut-outs at the bottoms using a jig saw. Veneer the edges using tape.

Step 5. Machine the decorative cut-outs (four in each side). Edges can be finished with veneer tape or veneer with contact adhesive or yellow glue.

Step 6. Machine the mortises for the through tenons at 3°. Make sure you take into account that you have a left and right side.

B   Machining the Shelves

Step 1. Glue up solid stock for two shelves. Machine to rough size. Mortise shelf #1 (B) and shelf #6 (G) per the drawing (see shelf detail); see the tenon-key mortise detail for additional dimensions. The front and back cuts on the shelves are square but the sides are beveled at 3°. The materials list measurements are for the bottom dimensions (the longest). The ends of the tenons can be cut square.

Step 2. Machine shelf #2 (C), shelf #3 (D), shelf #4 (E), and shelf #5 (F) to size. Note that the front and back cuts are square but the sides are beveled at 3°. The materials list measurements are for the bottom dimensions (the longest).

Step 3. Veneer the front edge of each shelf.

C   Machining the Back & the Tenon Keys

Step 1. Cut the back (H) to size using the diagram provided. All cuts are square.

Step 2. Cut the tenon keys (K) to shape using the diagram provided (see tenon key detail). It's a good idea to make extras in case of breakage.

D Dry Fitting & Machining for Biscuits

Step 1. Assemble bookcase starting with the sides, shelf #1, and shelf #6. Use the tenon keys to hold the unit together.

Step 2. Attach the back using 1¼" flathead wood screws drilled into the sides only. Make sure back is flush with the top and bottom of the sides.

Step 3. Starting with shelf #2, mark the shelf locations on the sides (mark from the top of the shelf). Place the shelf inside the cabinet and push up until the shelf fits tightly. Make sure the shelf is level and an equal distance on all sides from the bottom shelf. Mark the shelf and the sides for two #20 biscuits in each edge of the shelf-shelf. Repeat this process for shelf #3, shelf #4, and shelf #5.

Step 4. Machine the top rail (I) and bottom rail (J) to size (see rail detail). Verify that the diagram dimensions are the same as your assembled bookcase and make adjustments as necessary.

Step 5. Cut the arc on the bottom rail using the pattern (see rail detail).

Step 6. Mark the locations of the rails on the sides and mark for one #20 biscuit in the end of each rail.

Step 7. Disassemble and machine the sides, shelves, and rails for #20 biscuits at all locations previously marked. Make sure you are on the correct side of the lines.

Step 8. Glue #20 biscuits into the shelves and rails and dry-fit the entire unit. Mark shelf locations on the back so you can drill pilot holes. Do not disassemble until you have attached the top.

E Machining & Attaching the Top

Step 1. If necessary, glue up solid stock for the top (L), and machine to size.

Step 2. Cut the top blocking (M) to size.

Step 3. Position the top on the assembled bookcase according to the drawings and draw a line representing the outside of the bookcase.

Step 4. Using 2" flathead wood screws, attach the top blocking to the top inside the lines you just drew.

Step 5. Set the top assembly back on the bookcase and check the fit.

Step 6. Drill four ¼" holes through shelf #6 into the top blocking.

Step 7. Install threaded inserts in the top blocking.

Step 8. Test fit by attaching the top to the bookcase using 3" machine screws.

Step 9. Disassemble the bookcase, marking the parts on where necessary to aid in final assembly.

Step 10. Drill pilot holes in the back for securing shelves.

F Finishing & Assembling

Step 1. Finish sand all parts with 180-grit sandpaper. Apply a finish.

Step 2. Assemble the bookcase. You may wish to assemble it without glue so it can be easily disassembled and transported. Attach the top to the bookcase using 3" machine screws.

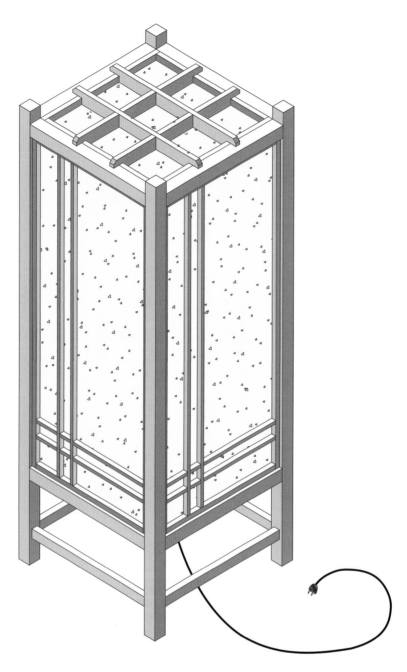

Rice paper lamp

This lamp owes its simple yet elegant design to the Japanese *shoji*. Shoji are doors, windows, and folding screens made of rice paper and wood, the constructon of which is an ancient woodworking art form.

Shoji had a tremendous influence on architects and designers like Frank Lloyd Wright and Charles and Henry Greene, who adapted elements of it to windows, doors, and decorations.

Unlike cheaply manufactured versions of this lamp, this design features strong joinery and solid-wood construction to make a sturdy and functional work of art.

The design for the mullions is a traditional shoji pattern called the double cross. You can find other shoji patterns suitable to this lamp on the Internet and in books—or you can design your own.

The relatively small amont of wood required for this project makes it an ideal candidate for an exotic hardwood.

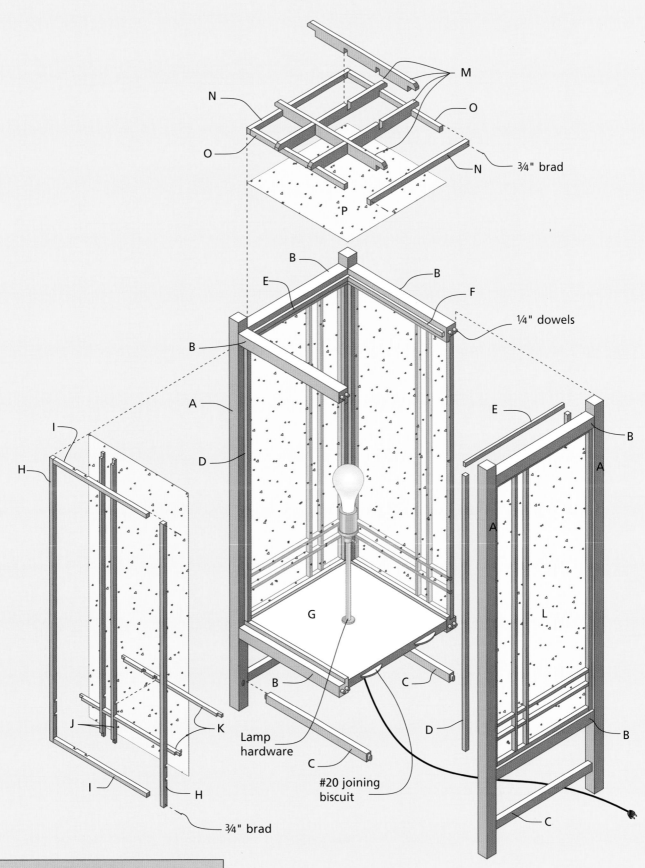

M

N

O

O

N ¾" brad

P

B

E

B

B

F ¼" dowels

A

D

I

H

E

B

A

A

L

G

J

K

C

H

B

Lamp
hardware

C

D

B

#20 joining
biscuit

C

I

H

¾" brad

C

B

Shopping List
Total board feet required: 6
Plywood required: ¾ × 12 × 12"
Rice paper required: 11 × 132"

Materials List						
Key	Part name	Qty.	Thickness	Width	Length	Material
Overall dimensions (13"w × 13"d × 36"h)						
A	Leg	4	1"	1"	36"	Solid wood
B	Top/middle rail	8	1"	1⅜"	11"	Solid wood
C	Bottom rail	4	½"	¾"	11½"	Solid wood
D	Frame blocking	8	⅜"	⅜"	25½"	Solid wood
E	Long top frame blocking	2	¼"	⅜"	11"	Solid wood
F	Short top frame blocking	2	¼"	⅜"	10½"	Solid wood
G	Bottom	1	¾"	11"	11"	Plywood
Frame - 4 required (11"w × 26¼"l × ⅜" thick)						
H	Frame stile	8	⅜"	⅜"	26¼"	Solid wood
I	Frame rail	8	⅜"	⅜"	10¼"	Solid wood
J	Long mullion	8	¼"	⅜"	26¼"	Solid wood
K	Short mullion	8	¼"	⅜"	11"	Solid wood
L	Frame rice paper	4	1/64"	11"	26¼"	Rice paper
Top grid (12"w × 12"l × 1" thick)						
M	Top grid	4	⅜"	1"	12"	Solid wood
N	Long top frame	2	⅜"	½"	11"	Solid wood
O	Short top frame	2	⅜"	½"	10¼"	Solid wood
P	Top rice paper	1	1/64"	11"	11"	Rice paper
Hardware						
	Lamp hardware					
	Cord with switch					
	Dowels			¼" dia.		
	Brads				¾"	
	Joining biscuits					#20

Top Frame End Detail

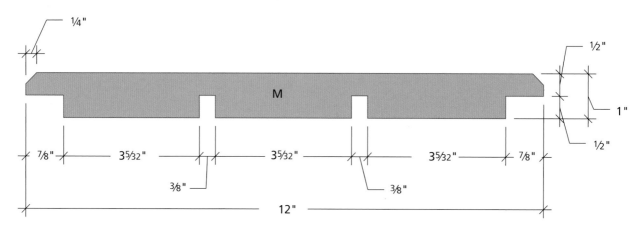

Top and Elevation Detail

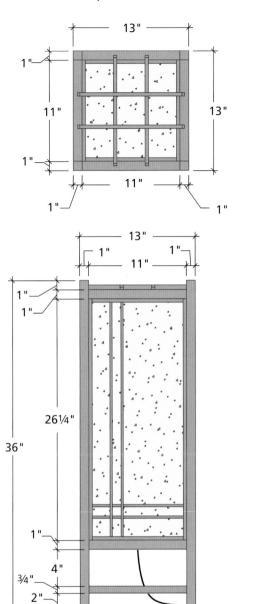

Mullion Layout Detail

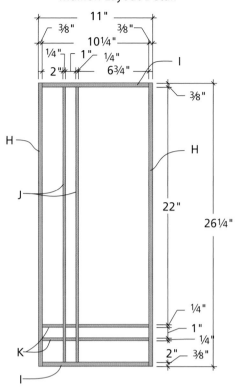

Top Edge Detail

Section Detail

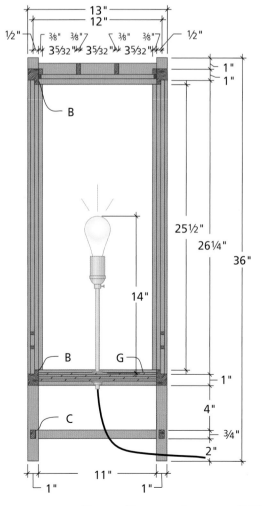

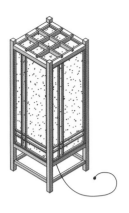

A · Machining the Legs & Assembling the Lamp Base

Step 1. Machine the legs (A), the top and middle rails (B), and the bottom rails (C) to size.

Step 2. Machine a ⅜-wide × ⅝"-deep rabbet on one edge of each top and middle rails (see top edge detail).

Step 3. Mark the legs for the rail locations per the drawing (see top and elevation detail).

Step 4. Mark and drill for ¼" dowels in the top and middle rails and legs. You should be able to get two dowels per joint.

Step 5. Mark and machine the bottom rails and the legs for mortises and tenons per the drawing. The bottom edge of the bottom rails should be 2" above the bottom of the legs. Tenon size should be ¼ wide × ½ high × ¼" long. Drill two adjoining ¼" holes in the legs for each mortise.

Step 6. Dry fit the rails and legs. You will will have two of each type of rail left over.

Step 7. Insert ¼" dowels, and glue and clamp the two leg assemblies together.

Step 8. Cut the bottom (G) from ¾" plywood.

Step 9. Drill a ⅜"-diameter hole in the center of the bottom for your lamp hardware. Verify the fit with the hardware you will be using.

Step 10. Mark and machine the leg assemblies for #20 biscuits. Note that the top of the bottom is ¼" below the top of the middle rail.

Step 11. Glue and clamp the remaining rails, the bottom, and the leg assemblies together.

Step 12. Machine the frame blocking (D), long top frame blocking (E), and short top frame blocking(F) to size.

Step 13. Glue and clamp the frame blocking on the legs between the top and middle rails (see top edge detail). The frame blocking should be flush with the inside edges of the legs.

Step 14. Glue and clamp the top frame blocking so it is ½" below the top edge of the top rails.

Step 15. Finish sand the exterior of the lamp with 120-grit sandpaper.

B · Machining the Frames

Step 1. Machine the frame stiles (H), the frame rails (I), the long mullions (J), and the short mullions (K) to size.

Step 2. Using the pattern provided (see mullion layout detail), mark the locations of the mullions on stiles and rails.

Step 3. Notch the stiles, rails, and ends of the mullions for half lap joints. The notch is ¼" wide and ³⁄₁₆" deep.

Step 4. Using the pattern provided (see mullion layout detail), mark the locations of half lap joints on the mullions.

Step 5. Notch the mullions for half lap joints. Notch is ¼" wide and ³⁄₁₆" deep.

Step 6. Attach the frame rails to the frame stiles using glue and ¾" brads. Check the frame for square.

Step 7. Glue and clamp the mullions to the frame.

Step 8. Finish sand both sides of the frame and the inside edges with 120-grit sandpaper, making sure surfaces are flush.

Step 9. Fit the frames to the lamp base. They should be tight but easy to remove.

C Machining the Top Grid

Step 1. Machine the top grids (M), the long top frames (N), and the short top frames (O) to size.

Step 2. Using the pattern provided (see top frame end detail), mark and machine the notches and chamfers on the top grids.

Step 3. Dry-fit the top grids together, and check for square.

Step 4. Attach the long top frames to the short top frames using glue and ¾" brads. Check for square.

Step 5. Finish sand the inside edges of the top frame and the grid using 120-grit sandpaper.

Step 6. Glue and clamp the top grids to the top frame.

Step 7. Finish sand the bottom surface of top grid using 120-grit sandpaper, making sure surface is flush.

Step 8. Fit the top grid assembly to the lamp base. It should be tight but easy to remove.

D Finishing the Lamp, Installing the Hardware & Attaching the Paper

Step 1. Finish sand the entire project with 180-grit sandpaper.

Step 2. Apply a finish on all surfaces. An oil-based finish is a good choice.

Step 3. Attach the lamp hardware following the manufacturer's recommendations. A compact fluorescent bulb is a good idea because they tend to generate much less heat compared to an incandescent for a similar amount of light.

Step 4. Cut the frame rice papers (L) and the top rice paper (P) to approximate size.

Step 5. Attach the rice paper to the backs of the frames and the top grid using wallpaper-type adhesive. Apply adhesive to the frame, then align and press on the rice paper, working from inside to outside edges. Keep the rice paper as taut as possible.

Step 6. After the adhesive has dried, press fit the frames and top grid into the lamp base.

Step 7. Plug in, turn on, and enjoy.

Rolling file cabinet

Everyone needs a filing cabinet for storing important papers and records, but almost no one wants an ugly sheetmetal filing cabinet.

This filing cabinet is as useful as its steel cousins, but it's just as much a piece of furniture as it is a storage unit. And it has added details like casters on the legs and a wide drawer with solid sides.

Simple cabinet- and drawermaking techniques are all that is required to build this piece. The biscuit joints are not fancy, but they are very strong. Take time to get the carcass square and solid, and the drawer will slide easily and reliably.

The wide top and ample storage makes this cabinet ideal for doing double duty as a printer cart.

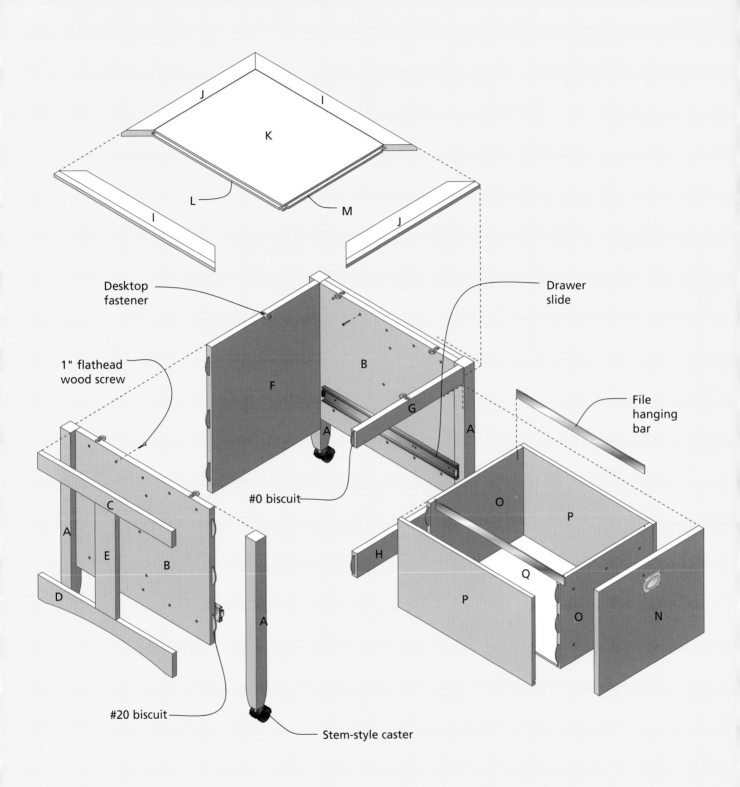

Desktop fastener

Drawer slide

1" flathead wood screw

File hanging bar

#0 biscuit

#20 biscuit

Stem-style caster

Shopping List
Total board feet required: 9
Plywood required: ¼ × 24 × 24" and ¾ × 24 × 96"
Baltic birch plywood required: ½ × 24 × 48"
Veneer tape required: ⅞" × 6'

Materials List

K	Part name	Qty.	Thickness	Width	Length	Material
Overall dimensions (20"w × 24"d × 24"h)						
A	Leg	4	1½"	1½"	21¼"	Solid wood
B	Side panel	2	¾"	20"	17"	Plywood
C	Side top rail	2	⅝"	2"	20"	Solid wood
D	Side bottom rail	2	⅝"	3"	20"	Solid wood
E	Center stile	2	⅝"	3"	13¼"	Solid wood
F	Back panel	1	¾"	16"	18¼"	Plywood
G	Front top rail	1	¾"	2"	16"	Solid wood
H	Front bottom rail	1	¾"	3"	16"	Solid wood
I	Long top edge	2	¾"	2½"	24"	Solid wood
J	Short top edge	2	¾"	2½"	20"	Solid wood
K	Top center panel	1	¾"	19"	15"	Plywood
L	Long top spline	2	¼"	¾"	18"	Solid wood or plywood
M	Short top spline	2	¼"	¾"	14"	Solid wood or plywood
Drawer dimensions (15"w × 20"d × 11"h)						
N	Drawer face	1	¾"	13"	15¾"	Solid wood or plywood w/ veneer edge
O	Drawer front/back	2	½"	11"	14"	Baltic birch plywood
P	Drawer side	2	½"	11"	20"	Baltic birch plywood
Q	Drawer bottom	1	¼"	19½"	14½"	Plywood
Hardware						
	Drawer slides - sidemount, heavy duty	1 pr.		20"		
	Drawer pull - Mission style	1				
	Desktop fasteners	6				
	File hanging bars	2	⅛"	1"		Aluminum or steel flat bar stock
	Casters	4		1⁹⁄₁₆"		
	Joining biscuits					#0 and #20
	Flathead wood screws				1"	
	Trusshead wood screws				1"	

Taper Detail

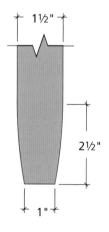

1½"

2½"

1"

Top Edge Detail

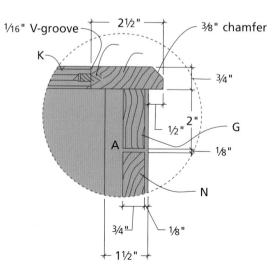

1⁄16" V-groove   2½"   ⅜" chamfer

K

¾"

½"   2"   G

A   ⅛"

N

¾"   ⅛"

1½"

Elevation Detail

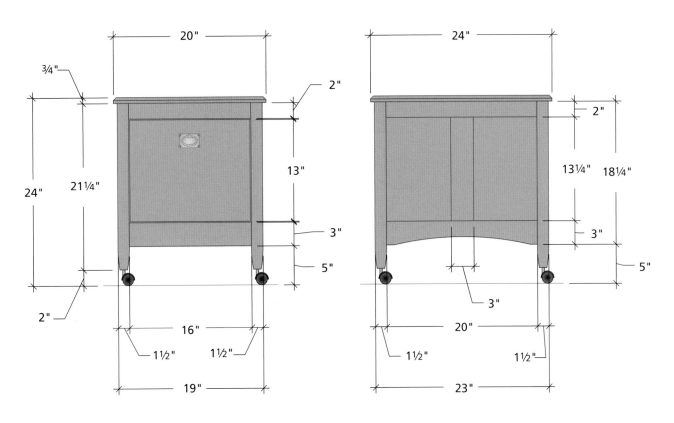

Plan Section

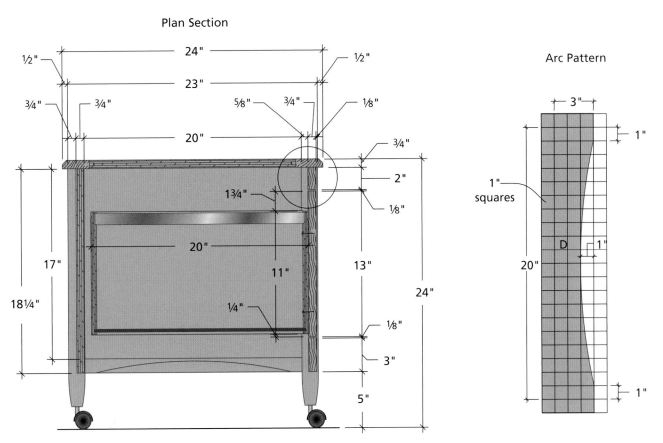

Arc Pattern

A Building the Leg Assemblies

Step 1. Machine the legs (A) to size.

Step 2. Cut the tapers on bottom of the legs per the drawing (see taper detail). Note that the taper is on all four faces.

Step 3. Drill a hole in the bottom of each leg for a stem-type caster per manufacturer's specifications.

Step 4. Cut the side panels (B) to size.

Step 5. Machine the side top rails (C), the side bottom rails (D), and the center stile (E) to size. Note that these parts are ⅝" thick.

Step 6. Cut an arc on bottom of two bottom side bottom rails per the pattern (see arc pattern).

Step 7. Mark and machine the legs and the side panels for #20 biscuits. The side panels are flush with the inside faces and tops of the legs.

Step 8. With 120-grit sandpaper, sand the faces of the legs you just machined for biscuits, and sand the outside surfaces of the side panels.

Step 9. Insert #20 biscuits, and clamp and glue the legs and side panels together.

Step 10. Sand the faces and inside edges of the side top rails, side bottom rails, and center stiles with 120-grit sandpaper.

Step 11. Attach the side top rails to the side panels with glue and 1" flathead wood screws. Countersink the screws slightly and be careful to avoid glue squeeze-out on the side panel.

Step 12. Attach the center stiles in the same manner, making sure they are spaced equally from the legs.

Step 13. Attach the side bottom rails, making sure they are tight against the center stiles.

Step 14. Sand the joints between the rails and stiles with 120-grit sandpaper.

B Assembling the Cabinet

Step 1. Cut the back panel (F) to size.

Step 2. Machine the front top rail (G) and front bottom rail (H) to size.

Step 3. Align the front top rail and front bottom rail with the leg assemblies. Both rails should be set in ⅛" from the outside face of the legs. The top edge of the front bottom rail should be 6" from the bottom of the leg. Mark for biscuits. Use #0 biscuits at the front top rail and #20 biscuits at the front bottom rail.

Step 4. Align the back panel with the leg assemblies. The top of the back panel should be flush with the tops of the legs, and the inside face of the back should be flush with the inside face of the legs. Mark for #20 biscuits.

Step 5. Sand the surfaces of the legs you will be joining to with 120-grit sandpaper. Also sand the outside surfaces of the back panel and front rails.

Step 6. Insert biscuits, and glue and clamp the back panel and front rails to the leg assemblies. Immediately wipe up any glue squeeze-out on the outside surfaces. Sand the outside surfaces of the legs.

C   Building & Attaching the Top

Step 1. Machine the long top edge (I) and the short top edge (J) to correct width and thickness but keep long in length. Cut the top center panel (K) to size.

Step 2. Machine a ¼-wide × 7⁄16"-deep dado in the top edges and the top center panel for a spline.

Step 3. Machine a 1⁄16" V-groove on the top inside edge of the top edges (see top edge detail).

Step 4. Machine the long top splines (L) and the short top splines (M) to size.

Step 5. Place the splines into the top center panel, and miter the top edges to fit around the center panel.

Step 6. After cutting all edges to fit, glue and clamp the edges to the top center panel.

Step 7. Sand the tabletop and machine a ⅜" chamfer at the top edge.

Step 8. Attach the desktop fasteners to the top rails and panels, and then attach the top to the cabinet assembly. It should be centered on the cabinet assembly with a ½" overhang.

D   Building the Drawer & Attaching Drawer Slides

Step 1. Machine the drawer face (N) to size.

Step 2. Machine the drawer front/back (O), the drawer sides (P), and the drawer bottom (Q) to size.

Step 3. Machine the drawer front and back for the hanging-file rails. Machine a ⅛-wide × 1 1⁄16"-deep stopped dado so that the centerline of the hanging rails are exactly 12¼" apart (correct spacing for letter-size hanging files).

Step 4. Machine a ¼ × ¼" dado in the drawer front, back, and sides, 1/4" from the bottom.

Step 5. Align the drawer parts and machine for #20 biscuits.

Step 6. Insert #20 biscuits, and glue and clamp the drawer box together.

After the glue is dry, turn the drawer box over and run a bead of hot-melt glue between the drawer sides, front, and back and the drawer bottom.

Step 7. Attach the drawer slide hardware to the drawer and the cabinet per the manufacturer's specifications.

Step 8. Attach the drawer face to the drawer box using double-sided tape or clamps to create consistent 1/8" reveals. The drawer box sits 1/4" above the bottom of drawer face and is spaced equally from side to side. Use 1" trusshead wood screws in oversized holes to attach the drawer face to the drawer box.

Step 9. Drill for a drawer pull.

E   Applying a Finish & Installing Decorative Hardware

Step 1. Finish sand the filing cabinet with 180-grit sandpaper and apply a finish.

Step 2. After the finish has dried, attach the drawer pull. Attach the casters to legs.

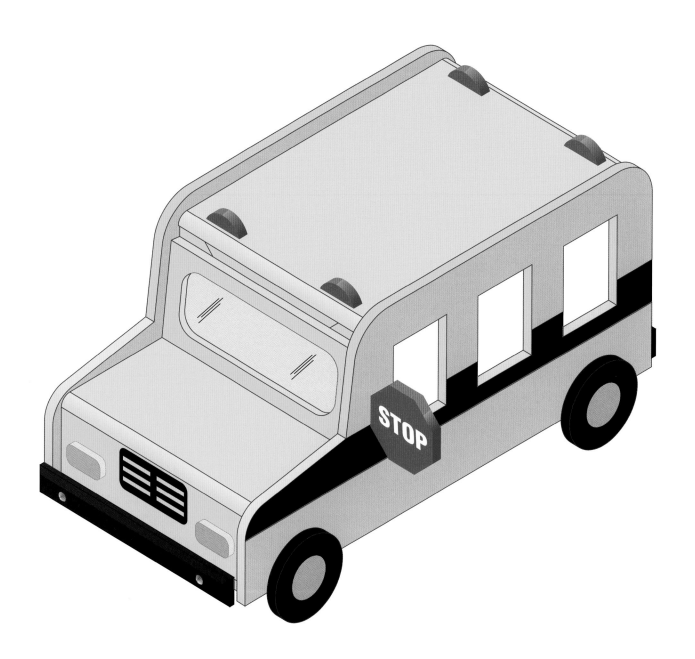

School bus toy box

Carpenters and woodworkers have been building wooden toys and dollhouses forever, and this toy box is a worthy part of that tradition.

It not only provides ample storage, but the front serves as a bench, and the windows have retainers for pictures.

The toy box is designed with strong joinery and heavy-duty lumber and hardware to take whatever kids dish out without getting bent out of shape.

The suggested paint scheme looks great (be sure to use a heavy-duty, kid-safe paint), but you could also come up with a scheme to match the decor of a bedroom or play area.

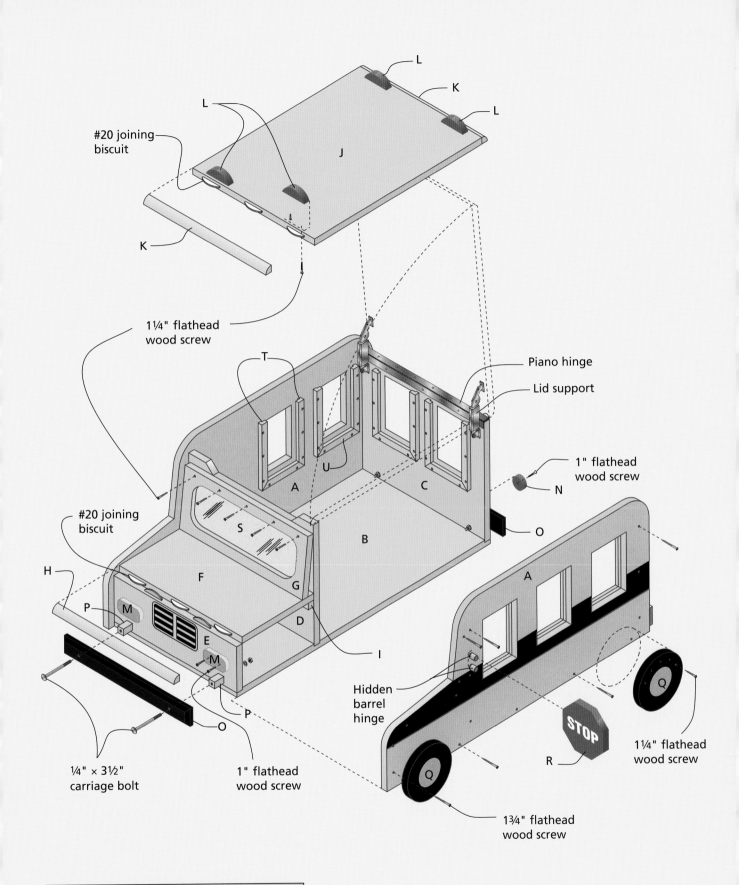

#20 joining biscuit

L

K

L

L

J

#20 joining biscuit

K

1¼" flathead wood screw

T

Piano hinge

Lid support

U

A

C

1" flathead wood screw

N

#20 joining biscuit

B

O

H

S

F

A

P

M

G

E

D

M

I

P

Hidden barrel hinge

O

Q

¼" × 3½" carriage bolt

1" flathead wood screw

R

STOP

1¼" flathead wood screw

Q

1¾" flathead wood screw

Shopping List
Total board feet required: 3
MDO or plywood required: ¾ × 48 × 96"
Plexiglass: ¼ × 5⅜ × 15"

Materials List

Key	Part name	Qty.	Thickness	Width	Length	Material
\multicolumn{7}{l}{Overall dimensions (19½"w X 38½"l X 19"h or 41½"h with lid open)}						
A	Bus side	2	¾"	16"	36"	Plywood or MDO
B	Bottom	1	¾"	16½"	34½"	Plywood or MDO
C	Back	1	¾"	16½"	13⅝"	Plywood or MDO
D	Interior divider	1	¾"	16½"	13¾"	Plywood or MDO
E	Front	1	¾"	16½"	5¼"	Plywood or MDO
F	Bench seat	1	¾"	16½"	9¾"	Plywood or MDO
G	Bench back	1	¾"	16½"	6⅞"	Plywood or MDO
H	Bench edge	1	¾"	¾"	16½"	Solid wood
I	Bench blocking	1	¾"	¾"	16½"	Solid wood
J	Lid	1	¾"	16 1/4"	22¾"	Plywood or MDO
K	Lid edge	2	¾"	¾"	16¼"	Solid wood
L	Lid light	4	¾"	1"	3"	Solid wood
M	Headlight	2	½"	1½"	3"	Solid wood
N	Tail light	4	½"	1½" dia.		Solid wood
O	Bumper	2	¾"	2"	17"	Solid wood
P	Bumper support	4	¾"	¾"	1¼"	Solid wood
Q	Wheel	4	¾"	6" dia.		Plywood or MDO
R	Stop sign	1	¾"	6" dia.		Plywood or MDO
S	Window	1	¼"	5⅜"	15"	Plexiglass
T	Long picture retainer	14	½"	¾"	7½"	Solid wood
U	Short picture retainer	7	½"	¾"	5¾"	Solid wood
\multicolumn{7}{l}{Hardware}						
	Lid support	2				
	Lid hinge	1			48"	Single wrap piano hinge
	Stop sign hinge	2				Hidden barrel
	Flathead wood screw					½", 1", 1¼", 1¾"
	Joining biscuits					#20
	Carriage bolts	4	¼"		3½"	With nuts & washers

Picture Retainer Detail

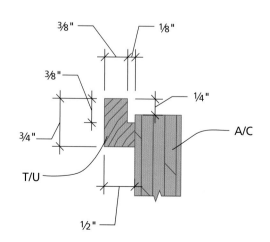

Bumper Detail

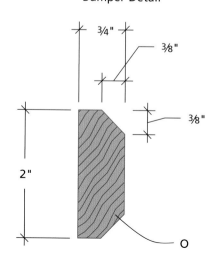

Elevation Detail

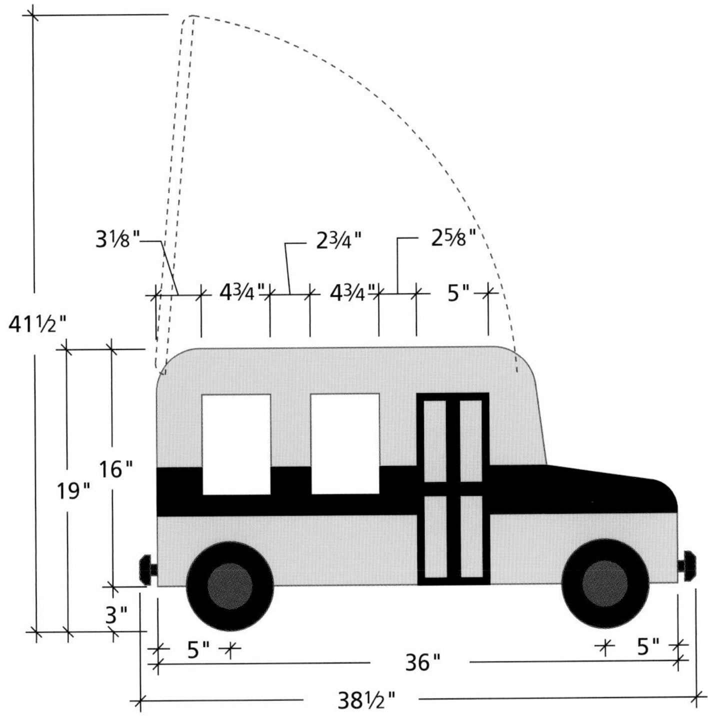
3⅛"
2¾"
2⅝"
4¾"
4¾"
5"
41½"
19"
16"
3"
5"
36"
5"
38½"

Passenger Side

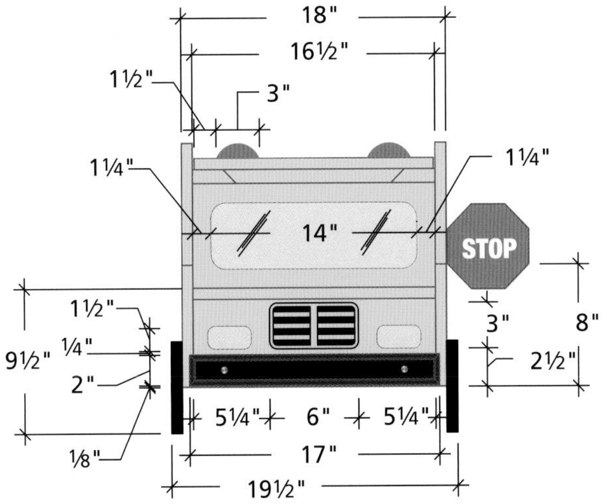
18"
16½"
1½"
3"
1¼"
1¼"
14"
STOP
1½"
¼"
9½"
2"
3"
8"
2½"
5¼"
6"
5¼"
⅛"
17"
19½"

Front

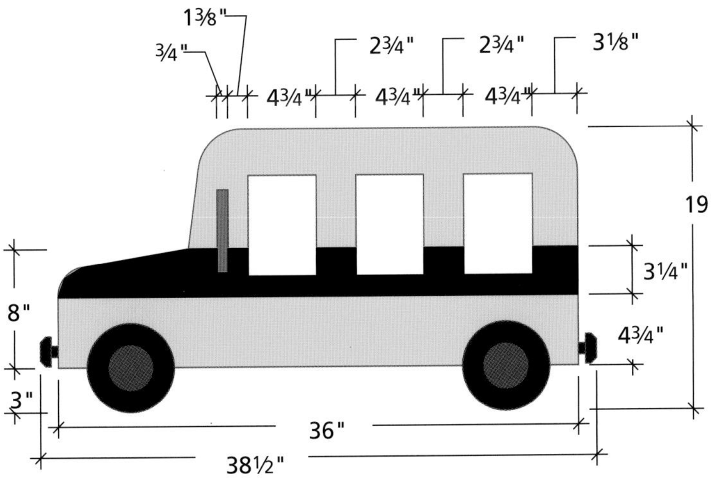
1⅜"
¾"
2¾"
2¾"
3⅛"
4¾"
4¾"
4¾"
19"
3¼"
8"
4¾"
3"
36"
38½"

Driver's Side

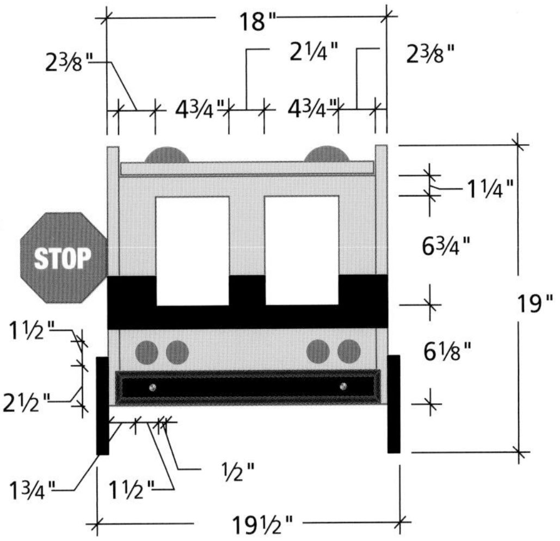
18"
2⅜"
2¼"
2⅜"
4¾"
4¾"
1¼"
6¾"
STOP
19"
1½"
6⅛"
2½"
1¾"
1½"
½"
19½"

Back

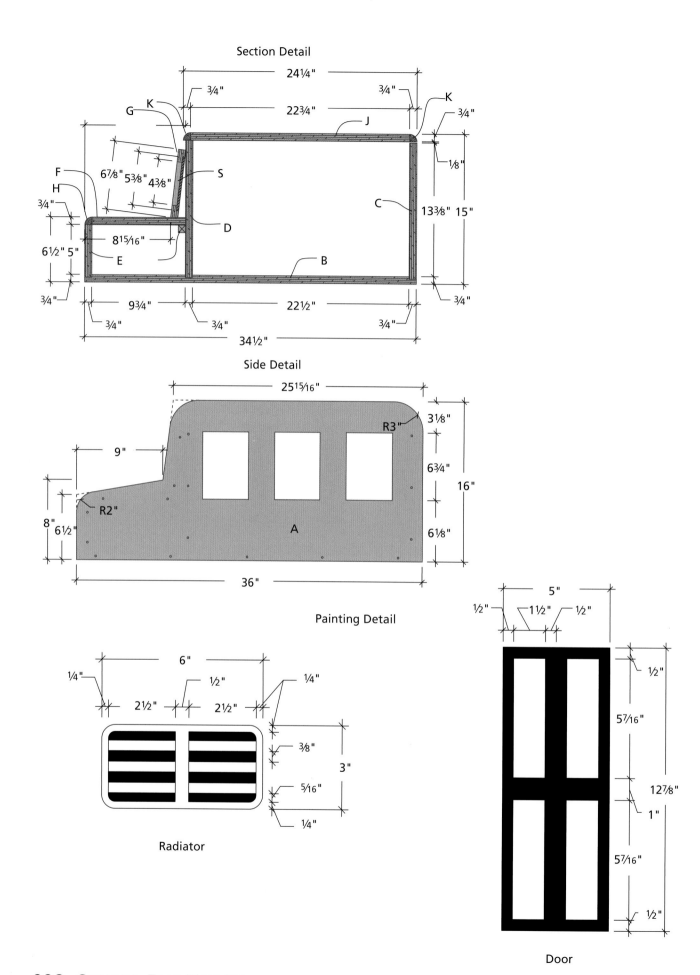

Section Detail

Side Detail

Painting Detail

Radiator

Door

A   Assembling the Sides & Back

Step 1. Machine the bus sides (A) to size.

Step 2. Lay out the pattern for the bus sides (see side detail) on one blank. Layout all three windows on this blank.

Step 3. Stack the two blanks, with the pattern on top. Use a couple of screws inside of the cut line to keep blanks from moving.

Step 4. Machine the outside profile of the bus side.

Step 5. Cut out the windows. Only cut out the two rear windows on both bus sides. The forward-most window is only on the right bus side. Drill holes in the corner of each window opening and use a jig saw to cut out the window. Make the cuts as straight as possible. Separate blanks from each other and cut out the final window on the right bus side.

Step 6. Machine the back (C) to size.

Step 7. Lay out the window locations (see elevation detail).

Step 8. Drill holes in a corner of each window opening, and use a jig saw to cut out the window. Make cuts as straight as possible.

Step 9. Machine the long picture retainers (T) and the short picture retainers (U) to size, leaving long in length for miters.

Step 10. Machine a ¾-wide × ⅛"-deep rabbet in each piece (see picture retainer detail).

Step 11. Miter and fit around the window openings. They should overlap the opening by ¼". Attach to sides and back with 1" flathead wood screws.

B   Building the Toy Box Carcass

Step 1. Machine the bottom (B), the interior divider (D), the front (E), and the bench seat (F) to size.

Step 2. Machine a finger slot at the top of interior divider. Slot is 12½" wide and 1" deep.

Step 3. Machine the bench back (G) to size. The bottom edge is beveled at 7°.

Step 4. Lay out the window opening in the bench back. Mark a 1¼" border with 1"-radius corners.

Step 5. Drill a hole in the window opening and cut out with jig saw.

Step 6. Machine a ½ × ¼" rabbet on the back side of the window opening.

Step 7. Cut the window (S) to size from ¼" plexiglass. Cut a 1" radius at each corner.

Step 8. Attach the window to the bench back using ½" flathead wood screws.

Step 9. Mark and machine the bench seat and bench back for #20 biscuits. The front of the bench back is 8³⁄₁₆" from the front edge of the bench seat.

Step 10. Mark and machine the bottom for ¾ × ¼" rabbets and dados (see section detail).

Step 11. Drill pilot holes in the bottom for attaching the front, back, and interior divider.

Step 12. Machine the bench edge (H) and the bench blocking (I) to size.

Step 13. Mark and machine the front, the bench seat, and the bench edge for #20 biscuits.

Step 14. Insert #20 biscuits, and glue and clamp the bench edge to the front and bench seat.

Step 15. Attach the bench blocking to the interior divider with 1¼" flathead wood screws. The bottom of the blocking is 4½" above the bottom of the interior divider.

Step 16. Glue and screw the front and bench seat assembly, interior divider, and back to the bottom using 1¼" flathead wood screws. Screw the bench seat to the bench blocking using 1¼" flathead wood screws.

Step 17. Using #20 biscuits and 1¼" flathead wood screws, attach the bench back to the bench seat and interior divider.

Step 18. Machine a ¾" radius on the bench edge.

C Building the Lid

Step 1. Machine the lid (J) to size.

Step 2. Machine the lid edges (K) to size.

Step 3. Mark and machine the lid and the lid edges for #20 biscuits.

Step 4. Insert #20 biscuits, and glue and clamp the lid edges to the lid.

Step 5. Machine a ¾" radius in the lid edges.

Step 6. Finish sand the lid with 120-grit sandpaper.

Step 7. Cut the lid lights (L) to size. Cut an arc with a jig or band saw.

Step 8. Locate and mark the lid light locations on the lid. The lights are 1½" in from the sides and 1" in from the front and back.

Step 9. Drill pilot holes and attach the lights to the lid using 1¼" flathead wood screws.

D Building & Installing Adornments

Step 1. Machine the headlights (M) to size. Cut a ½" radius on each corner of each headlight.

Step 2. Attach the headlights to the front, 1" in from the side and 2½" up from the bottom, using 1" flathead wood screws.

Step 3. Machine the tail lights (N) to size (a 1½" diameter circle).

Step 4. Attach the tail lights to the back, 1½" in from the side and 2½" up from the bottom, with ½" between each pair, using 1″ flathead wood screws.

Step 5. Machine the bumpers (O) and bumper supports (P) to size.

Step 6. Machine a ⅜ × ⅜" chamfer on all four edges of each bumper.

Step 7. Drill ¼" holes through the center of each bumper support.

Step 8. Drill two ¼" holes in each bumper, 2⅜" from each end and centered top to bottom.

Step 9. Clamp the bumpers onto the front and back of the carcass. The bumper should be ⅛" above the bottom and centered from side to side.

Step 10. Drill ¼" holes through the bumper into the front and back. Attach the bumpers and bumper supports to the carcass using 3½" carriage bolts.

E   Attaching the Sides, Lid, Wheels & Stop Sign

Step 1. Align one bus side with the carcass and mark for pilot holes. The sides are flush with the bottom and overhang the front and back by ¾". Mark the locations of the vertical divider and bench seat and back.

Step 2. Stack the bus sides and drill pilot holes (see side detail) in both sides.

Step 3. Attach the bus sides to the carcass using 1¼" flathead wood screws. Make sure the front, back, and interior divider are at 90° to the bottom.

Step 4. Fill all screw holes with wood putty and sand with 120-grit sandpaper.

Step 5. Attach the piano hinge to the carcass and lid following the manufacturer's instructions.

Step 6. Attach the lid support hardware to the back and lid following manufacturer's instructions.

Step 7. Cut the wheels (Q) and stop sign (R) to size.

Step 8. Lay out an octagon on the stop sign, and cut to shape with a jig saw.

Step 9. Mark the stop-sign location on the right side of the bus. The stop sign is 8" above the bottom and centered on the vertical divider.

Step 10. Follow manufacturer's specifications and drill for two hidden barrel-type hinges.

Step 11. Attach the wheels to the bus sides using 1¼" flathead wood screws. The center of the wheel is 5" from each end and aligned with the bottom of the carcass.

F   Painting the Toy Box

Step 1. Finish sand all surfaces with 120-grit sandpaper. Fill any voids on exposed edges with wood putty. Ease all exposed edges to aid in paint retention.

Step 2. The following paint scheme works well for the bus:

• Paint the stripes, radiator, door, tires, and bumpers black. (See step 3.)

• Paint the headlights, door glass, and wheel centers silver.

• Paint the stop sign, lid lights and tail lights red.

• Paint the bus exterior and interior yellow.

Step 3. See paint detail for door and radiator paint patterns. Paint on black first then cover with tape and paint contrasting colors.

Step 4. Make sure lid is operating properly, and fill with toys.

INDEX

CONTRIBUTORS

BINKY'S WOODWORKING
WWW.BINKYSWOODWORKING.COM

DEWALT
WWW.DEWALT.COM
800-433-9258

GEORGIA-PACIFIC
800-BUILD-GP
WWW.GP.COM

ROCKLER WOODWORKING SUPERSTORES
WWW.ROCKLER.COM

SEARS
800-349-4358
WWW.SEARS.COM

SHOPSMITH, INC.
800-543-7586
WWW.SHOPSMITH.COM

WOODCRAFT SUPPLY CORP.
800-535-4482
WWW.WOODCRAFT.COM